Designer Drafting
for the Entertainment World

Designer Drafting for the Entertainment World

Theatre
Motion Pictures
Television
Trade Shows
Amusement Park Scenery
Computer-Drafted Scenery
Virtual Scenery

Patricia Woodbridge

Focal Press

Amsterdam   Boston   Heidelberg   London   New York   Oxford   Paris   San Diego
San Francisco   Singapore   Sydney   Tokyo

Focal Press is an imprint of Elsevier.

 This book is printed on acid-free paper.

Library of Congress Cataloging-in-Publication Data
Woodbridge, Patricia, 1946-
    Designer drafting for the entertainment world / Patricia Woodbridge.
        p.   cm.
    Includes bibliographical references and index.
    ISBN 0-240-80424-4 (pbk : alk. paper)
    1.   Mechanical drawing. 2. Theaters-Stage-setting and scenery. I. Title.

    T357.W56   2000
    792'.025-dc21   00-037595

British Library Cataloguing-in-Publication Data
A catalogue record for this book is available from the British Library.

The publisher offers special discounts on bulk orders of this book.
For information, please contact:
Manager of Special Sales
Elsevier Science
200 Wheeler Road
Burlington, MA 01803
Tel: 781-313-4700
Fax: 781-313-4802

For information on all Focal Press publications available, contact our World Wide Web homepage at http://www.focalpress.com

10 9 8 7 6 5 4 3
Printed in the United States of America

Dedication
This book is dedicated to my grandmother
Dr. Helen McFarland Woodbridge and to my teacher
Oliver Smith. It was made possible with the financial
generosity of The Lucia Chase Foundation.

Contents

Introduction

When I started my fourteen years of teaching drafting at New York University Tisch School of the Arts, I was unable to find a good scenic drafting textbook to assign to my students. The comprehensive drafting books were for engineering or architecture students, and after a couple of relevant chapters they started discussing trade specifics such as milling jacks, piping symbols, or wall insulation. The few books or chapters of books specific to scenic drafting were primarily written by educators who had limited experience working professionally. In my research I discovered that a group called United States Institute for Theatre Technology had published a set of standard scenic drafting conventions to be used for educational purposes. These standards showed such things as line weight conventions or how to draw the plan of a window. There was only one problem: most of the standards were not what I encountered when I worked on or off Broadway, or when I worked as an art director on Hollywood feature films or for the major television studios.

This book is a reference book for other teachers of scenic drafting, for students of scenic drafting, and for beginning scenic designers and art directors. The book evolved from the work I collected for my classroom as I continued to work as a professional designer and draftsperson, and the work I collected after I left Tisch and continued to work professionally. The principles of drafting are explained with simple drawings from the world of scenery. It also contains many examples of more complex draftings from some of the finest scenic designers working professionally. Since the examples of drafting are taken from a wide variety of different scenic applications, it indirectly gives the young designer a survey of scenic career possibilities. Although the book is not a software manual, there are many examples of computer drafting and rendering.

The basics of orthographic projection remain universal, but there is a big difference between architecture and scenic design. Unlike most architectural design, scenic design can be sculptural, fantastical, or abstract. It can recreate the architectural detailing of specific periods and geographical places. It can be drawn with perspective built into the design, or it can be drawn to show the effects of aging with sags, irregularities, and the buildup of layers of materials. Drafting such designs encourages creative rather than formulaic approaches.

The architectural world, dominated by large firms, rapidly codified its drafting conventions. Scenic design, however, remained the province of the freelance artist who tends to use those scenic drafting conventions that suit his or her particular style of design and the scenic genre in which he or she is working. The freelance nature of designing and assisting encourages the development of personal styles. The typical young designers or draftspersons in the professional scenic design world learn the basics of drafting in a design classroom, but most of their knowledge of scenic drafting conventions is gained over a period of years as they work under and with other experienced people. My first experience of professional scenic drafting was in the theatrical studio of the esteemed designer, Ming Cho Lee, who had as a young assistant designer himself worked in the studio of Joe Mielziner.

While all drafting is a language of graphic communication, scenic drafting remains very much a living language that keeps mutating. I have seen scenic drafting conventions slowly change over a period of years as they adapted to changes in our design sensibility and construction techniques. For example, elevations with revolved sections placed directly on top of the elevation were adequate for the mostly flat sceneries with painted details that were characteristic of design in the 1950s and early 1960s. When heavily molded scenery came into vogue, this method of drawing was confusing, and so the section was removed to the side of the elevation. In the last few years, many architects on the West Coast started working in the Hollywood film studios, bringing with them architectural conventions of layout and referencing. As people crossed over between coasts and between theatre and film, these architectural conventions started to be used in theatrical drafting.

The many styles of scenic drafting make it difficult to choose which to teach. From the many scenic drafting conventions that I encountered working professionally, I have chosen for this book to illustrate as drafting principles those that seem the clearest and most prevalent methods of description. Over many years of teaching, I have determined that these conventions form a clear method for students to organize and communicate graphic information.

Many young people enter scenic design from an art or liberal arts rather than a technical background. These students undertake the large commitment of time and attention required in learning the technical aspects of their craft, but it is also important that they continue to visualize the goal towards which they strive. For this reason the many beautiful design examples in the book are not only there as information but also to inspire the young student of scenic design. In my teaching, I stressed that scenic drafting is not just a translation by a technician at the end of the design process but an integral part of the design process. To this end, I developed a series of sequentially more complex drafting problems, each of which was also a design assignment.

In making this book, I discovered that the reproduction of large pencil drawings in the smaller size required for publication posed a problem. Attempts to maintain the light lines of a drawing in photographic reproduction produced a gray background that made all the information difficult to decipher. Photostatic reproduction produced a white background but lost all the light pencil tones. Since this book is primarily a learning tool, I felt that it was extremely important for students to be able to study and cull information from the graphics. Most of the drafting examples in the book were therefore copied in ink to maintain line clarity in a reduced size. This was a difficult decision for me to make for the ink copies lost the "hand" of the individual artist/draftsperson. In examples of scenic renderings or "drawn" draftings such as those of Ming Cho Lee, which by their nature could not be traced, the reproductions were done photographically.

Today, all graduate theatre programs face the emerging world of digital scenic and lighting design. Some departments are refusing to teach computer drafting, rendering, and modeling skills, as they believe these tools hamper artistic development. Other schools are emphasizing computer training with little foundation in hand sketching, drafting, and model construction. An increasingly large part of the entertainment industry is having difficulty finding talented scenic designers who posses high-level computer skills, while at the same time, many graduate students are have difficulty finding employment. Lacking trained scenic designers, the emerging field of virtual scenery is using graduates from architecture and engineering schools.

The digital revolution has increased the technical demands on scenic designers and draftspersons, and our training needs to reflect that demand. If we do not teach the new computer skills increasingly required by our industry, we may not give our students the opportunity to achieve their professional potential but relegate them to a career on the fringes. CAD (Computer Assisted Drafting) software, however, is primitive and does not yet have the flexibility needed by scenic designers. If we emphasize CAD too early in the training process, we risk condemning our students to careers as "CAD monkeys," placed in front of machines and endlessly inputting the work of others. Several years ago, many architecture schools, excited by the new technology, emphasized computer drafting at the expense of hand drafting. Later they found that they had trained a generation of students who didn't know how to design and had to revise their curriculum.

I feel strongly that the beginning student will be a better designer/draftsperson if he or she first learns to draft with a simple pencil before using a complex machine. In my teaching, I stressed that drafting is a specialized form of drawing. It contains all the elements of drawing: layout, shape, proportion, contour, mass, and detail. The student first learns eye-hand coordination by freehand sketching. The process of learning to draw evolves into learning to draft by sketch-drafting, then drafting in scale using only broad measurements and minimal or no tools. The broad soft line or multiline contour that hardens as a designer clarifies his or her vision is the way a young designer learns to see, just as it is the way that an experienced designer finds his or her image on the paper. The young draftsperson learns to gradually tighten the drawing and finally "hard draft" the image. Computer drafting forces the drawn line immediately from point-to-point rather than allowing the draftsperson to find the line. By jumping immediately to the final product, computer drafting does not allow the young designer/draftsperson to slowly discover an image and to evolve a personal way of seeing. It is my belief that for scenic designers, three years of technical training are now needed at the graduate level. A full foundation year of scenic pencil drafting and perspective sketching needs to be taught along with computer graphic programs, followed by a year of scenic CAD, and a final year of computer modeling and texturing.

Many people made this book possible. First and foremost, the late, great Oliver Smith who, early on, believed in this project enough to get me a much-needed grant from the Lucia Chase Foundation. Lloyd Burlingame and New York University Tisch School of the Arts sponsored the grant. I had hoped to fulfill Oliver's wishes and include draftings from his epochal design for Agnes DeMille's ballet Fall River Legend. Unfortunately, since the dance is often revived, Oliver's estate felt they could not give me permission to reproduce the drawings. I am greatly indebted to all the fine designers who allowed their work to be included. I am grateful as well as to the television production companies, motion picture companies, and to the many people along the way who gave work, made suggestions, and who helped me in the long process of getting copyright approvals.

Many years ago, Marion Kolsby's gift of several weeks of her time jump-started this project. Jennifer Houston did the splendid, meticulous ink tracings. Katherine Spencer and Joseph Tenga shared with me their expertise in CAD. I want to especially thank Tony Walton and Patricia MacKay who, over the years, gave me the encouragement to complete this project. Karl Ruling, my technical editor, was instrumental in the organization of the book and the accuracy of the technical information. The fine art photographer Anthony F. Holmes did the digital photography, and Elizabeth Popiel assisted me in organizing and retouching the digital illustrations. This book, with its many illustrations, was expensive to produce, and it would not have been published without the belief of Marie Lee, Acquisitions Editor for Focal Press, that it would be a success. Jennifer Plumley, Assistant Editor, and Maura Kelly, Senior Production Editor, guided me through the bookmaking process at Focal Press with great care and professionalism. Special thanks to Rita Rosenkranz of Rita Rosenkranz Literary Agency. Most of all I want to thank my husband, the writer Robert Dunn, who helped me edit the early draft of the manuscript. Without his assistance and encouragement, I would not have been able to write this book.

Part I

Principles and Conventions of Scenic Drafting

1

Drafting Tools

Drafting Tables

A professional drafting surface should be a minimum of 38 inches by 60 inches. This allows you to roll out a standard 36-inch roll of paper.

You can make a drafting board by placing a cut sheet of plywood on top of a table, covering it with vinyl board cover, and giving it an angle with some books or a board. For comfortable, long-term drafting, you need a drafting table with legs or a pedestal base and with a mechanism to adjust the height and angle of the board. The more expensive tables are sturdier and have a greater range of board angles. The most expensive tables have a motorized adjustment mechanism.

The height and angle of your drafting board is important as drafting for many hours each day can cause repetitive stress injuries. If you find you are having back or shoulder problems, you need to be able to change the angle of your board. Some professional draftspeople feel that only an almost vertical board combined with a drafting machine prevents shoulder and back problems.

Drafting Surfaces

Hard plastic or wooden drafting tabletops need to be softened by covering them with a sheet of vinyl board cover. This covering allows for greater flexibility in pencil pressure and helps to prevent pencil tips from breaking. Attach the vinyl cover by running a strip of double stick tape along the top edge of the board. Use a metal straight edge and mat knife to trim the vinyl to the edge of the board. Overnight, gravity will flatten the vinyl and hold it in place.

Cleaning Your Vinyl Drafting Surface
Eventually graphite will smudge your vinyl drafting surface and you will need to clean it. For an extremely dirty board rub with Ajax or Comet cleanser on a sponge and a minimum amount of water to loosen the graphite. Then use clear water rinses until all the cleanser is gone. Dry the vinyl with paper towels. For small touch-up cleanings, you can purchase a board cleaner or rubber cement thinner. These cleaners are highly toxic, but they remove grease as well as dirt and evaporate instantly. Be careful of using household cleansers to clean the vinyl as some of them leave a greasy film residue that your drafting tape won't stick to.

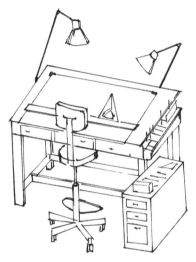

Figure 1.1 A drafting setup using a parallel ruler.

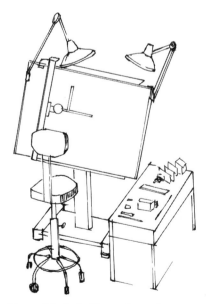

Figure 1.2 A drafting setup using a drafting machine.

Drawing Protectors

If you find you need to draft sheets taller than the height of your table and need to protect the bottom of the sheets from being creased or smudged, you can buy a metal tube called a drawing protector that mounts flush to the bottom of your drafting board. The portion of your sheet that extends over your table will curl up inside the tube.

Drafting Chairs

If you draft for many hours at a stretch, you want a sturdy comfortable chair with a back and footrest. The height of the chair needs to adjust so that you are in the most comfortable relationship with your drafting table, able to reach the top of your sheet of paper without getting up. All drafting chairs adjust in height; the best also let you adjust the backrest height and the depth of the backrest.

Lighting

To avoid shadows you need a light on either side of your table. Architect lamps have mounting brackets that attach to your board and spring balanced arms that allow you to position the light at the best angle. The best lamps are a combination of incandescent and fluorescent, which used together approximate daylight and are easiest on your eyes.

T-Square

The earliest and simplest drafting instrument with which to draw horizontal and vertical lines is the T-square. The T-square is relatively inexpensive to buy, travels easily, and can be used on any table with a straight side. In a pinch, you could construct one yourself that would be adequate for simple drafting.

The T-square is a long thin piece of wood called the blade attached at a 90-degree angle to a short piece of wood known as the head. The head rides up and down the metal edge of a table or board. A manufactured T-square has a comfortably shaped head, and the blade has thin plastic edges, which allow you to see slightly underneath. When buying a manufactured T-square you want to make certain that the head is strongly attached at exactly 90 degrees and that the blade is straight. To test the edge of the blade draw a sharp line along the entire length of the blade and then turn the T-square over and draw the line again, along the same edge. The two lines should coincide. If you are right-handed, the head rides along the left edge of your drafting table, allowing you to draw horizontal lines along the top edge of the blade. (See Figure 1.3.) Left-handers ride the head along the right side of the table edges and reverse hands, in the following directions.

To draw a horizontal line, you use your left hand to press the head firmly against the table edge. Then slide your hand onto the blade, holding it steady while using your right hand to draw the pencil line along its upper edge from left to right. The motion of drawing a vertical or angled line involves physical dexterity and takes some getting used to. You position the blade at a convenient height, slightly below where you wish to draw the line. You then slide a plastic triangle along the foot to the position where you want the line. Use your left hand to

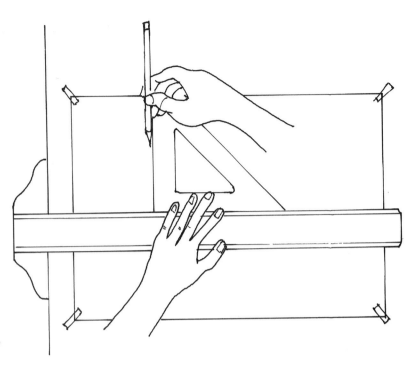

Figure 1.3 Drawing a vertical line with a T-square (right-handed draftsperson).

check that the head is firmly against the side edge of your table, and then twisting your body slightly toward the triangle, you gently slide the palm of your left hand along the blade until the fingers of your left hand can hold both the T-square and the triangle in position. You then use your right hand to draw a vertical or angled line upward. This sounds more complicated than it is.

While a T-square is fine for small sheets of paper, the long blade required for large sheets is awkward to use and slows down the drafting process.

Parallel Rules

Professional draftspeople use a parallel rule, triangles, and a scale ruler, or they use a drafting machine. The parallel rule is a plastic or metal and plastic straight edge that moves up and down on a set of thin cables mounted on the sides of a drawing board. (See Figure 1.1.) The guide cables cross inside the rule allowing it to maintain a horizontal position as it is moves up and down. A small clamp in the upper-left-hand corner allows the angle of the rule to adjust. Tightening or loosening the wire around the mounting screws at the front of the board adjusts the tightness of the cable.

You want a parallel rule with clear plastic rather then metal edges as the transparent edge helps you position the rule exactly on a horizontal line. While some parallels have their entire base touching the paper, you want to minimize the possibility of smudging lines by getting a parallel rule that moves on small rollers. You can get parallel rulers that ride on either plastic or metal rollers. Metal rollers are better since plastic ones tend to pick up adhesive particles, which can collect graphite and cause streaks. If you find your drawings have vertical streaks, you need to loosen the guide wires, turn the parallel over, and clean your rollers with liquid board cleaner and a cue tip. Mayline is a good manufacturer of parallel rulers.

The Adjustable Triangle

If you draft with a parallel rule, a clear plastic adjustable triangle is your primary instrument for drafting any straight lines that are not horizontal. This versatile tool combines a protractor with an adjustable angle. The adjustable triangle is designed so that you line up one outside edge of the triangle on either side of your vertical or horizontal axis line. After you set a specific degree with the protractor, you complete the angle by drawing a line against the other outside edge of the triangle. You never draw inside the triangle.

A 10- or 12-inch adjustable triangle is your basic tool. Many draftspeople find it helpful to also have a smaller, 6-inch adjustable triangle for small-scale plans and elevations. If you need to clean your adjustable triangle, Pledge is a good cleaner; other cleaning solvents may remove the printing on the protector.

Using the Adjustable Triangle

To learn to use the adjustable triangle draw vertical and horizontal axis lines that divide your page into 90-degree quadrants. Place the adjustable triangle in its closed position on your parallel in the upper-left-hand quadrant as illustrated in Figure 1.4. Note that the hypotenuse of the triangle divides the quadrant into two 45-degree angles. Loosen the knob and slowly open the triangle, reading the protractor. You will see that in this position you can draw any angle from 45 degrees to 90 degrees up to 45 degrees to the left side of the vertical axis line.

Lock the protractor gauge at 20/70 degrees. Drop the adjustable triangle, making sure that the outside right edge still goes through the intersection of your vertical and horizontal axis lines. You will see that you are able to draw a 20-degree angle to the right of the vertical axis in the lower quadrant. In other words, a single protractor setting creates the same angle in the opposing quadrant. (See Figure 1.5.)

With the protractor locked at 20 degrees, rotate your adjustable triangle into the top right quadrant. (See Figure 1.6.) With the upper outside edge going through the intersection of the vertical and horizontal axis

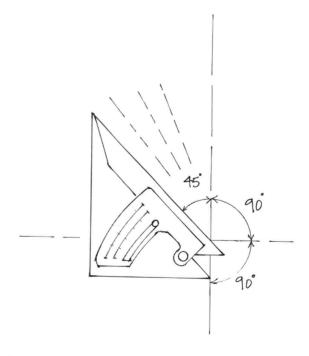

Figure 1.4 A vertical and horizontal axis line divides space into 90-degree quadrants.

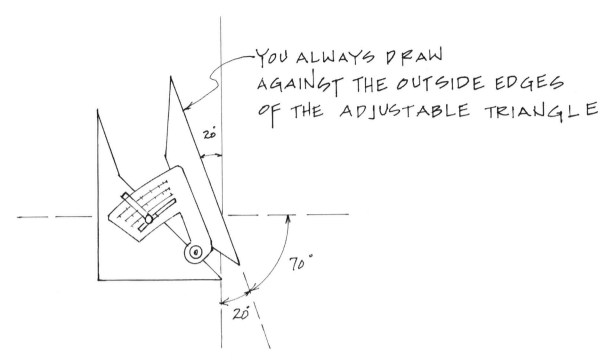

YOU ALWAYS DRAW
AGAINST THE OUTSIDE EDGES
OF THE ADJUSTABLE TRIANGLE

20°

70°

20°

Figure 1.5 A single protractor setting creates the same angle in the opposing quadrant.

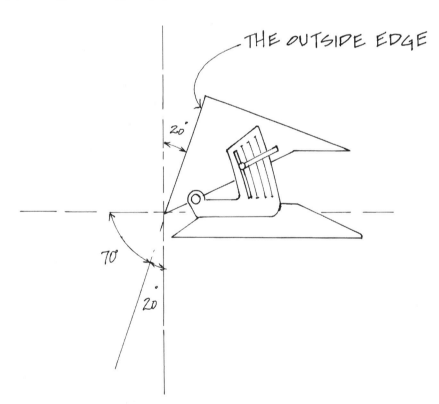

THE OUTSIDE EDGE

20°

70°

20°

Figure 1.6 Rotating the adjustable triangle into the next quadrant allows you to draw a symmetrical angle.

lines, you will have a 20-degree angle off the right side of your vertical axis line. In other words, by rotating your adjustable angle to the other side of the axis line, you can draw a symmetrical angle. Since we often draw symmetrical objects, this is an extremely convenient function.

Rotate your adjustable triangle so that it is in the position shown in Figure 1.7. When you unlock the protractor and open it, you can draw any angle in the lower-right quadrant up to 45 degrees. By sliding your

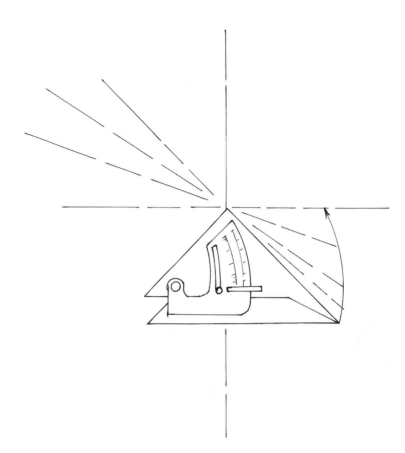

Figure 1.7 Rotating your triangle to draw the remaining angles in the upper-left quadrant.

adjustable triangle into the upper-left quadrant, you can draw opposing angles.

Positioning your adjustable triangle around the center point of the quadrants allows you to draw all 360 angles. If you are confused about how to place your adjustable triangle when drafting a specific angle, first lightly draw the quadrants.

Additional Triangles

For drawing very long vertical lines, you will find it an advantage to have a 30/60-degree triangle that is about 18 inches long. For coding angled walls, you will find it helpful to have a small 3- or 4-inch 45-degree triangle that can ride on top of your adjustable angle.

Drafting Machines

Drafting machines combine the parallel rule, scale ruler, and adjustable angle in one instrument. These machines attach to drafting tables and come in right-handed or left-handed models (see Figure 1.2). They all have two plastic strips marked with scales, which attach to an adjustable protractor head. You can jump the protractor head to 15-degree increments, or move it more slowly in one-degree stops in between. The drafting machine scales come in 12-inch or 18-inch lengths. The rulers detach from the head so you can insert different scales or scale combinations: 1/8, 1/4, 1/2, 1 inch to the foot; 3/8, 3/4, 1 1/2, 3 inch to the foot; and various metric or engineer's scales.

The better drafting machines are tracked. In these machines, the head attaches to a solid bar, which glides along a top-mounted track. The most expensive machines now have a digital readout and magnetic levitation to allow instant response to your movement. Avoid the less expensive drafting machines, which have a free-floating elbow. Their joints tend to loosen, causing them to drift off square, and you will find that lines that should be parallel are not. Mutah is a good manufacturer of drafting machines.

There are also drafting lights, which attach to and travel with the moving arm of the drafting machine to insure that the area where you are drawing has maximum light.

The advantage of using a drafting machine is that, since it combines many drafting tools in one place, it speeds up the drafting process. Also, since the tools are attached to the board, it allows you to position the board in a vertical position without them sliding. Over long periods of time, the vertical board position is much easier on your back and shoulders. The disadvantage of the drafting machine is that the good ones are extremely expensive. Since you may find yourself working in situations without a drafting machine, you should know how to use a parallel rule.

Bow Compasses

A **large bow compass** is used for drawing circles with a radius of 1 inch or larger. The large bow compass has a center wheel that, when turned, widens or narrows the legs of the compass. (See Figure 1.8.) Most compasses come with a removable needlepoint that gives you the option of removing the lead and turning the compass into a divider by inserting metal points. The long, plain side of the point is turned down when you are using the instrument as a divider, and the thin short point is turned down when you are drawing circles.

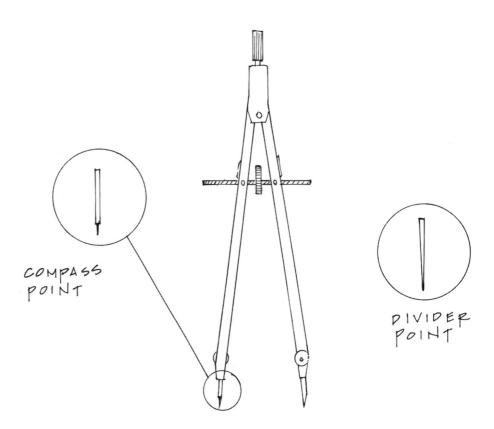

COMPASS POINT

DIVIDER POINT

Figure 1.8 A large bow compass.

9

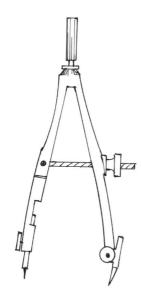

Figure 1.9 A small bow compass.

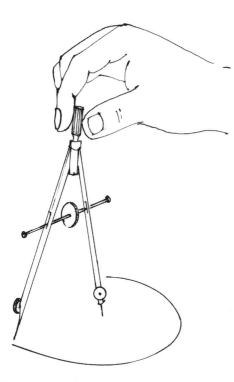

Figure 1.10 To use a bow compass twirl the knob between your fingers.

The quick-acting bows that can be adjusted by simply opening and closing the compass legs rather than turning the wheel should be avoided as they can too easily loose a set width. To quickly open or close a normal bow compass, roll the center wheel against your table until the legs approximate the size you want, and then fine-tune the distance by moving the wheel with your finger.

A **small bow compass** (Figure 1.9) has a side wheel to adjust the width between the legs. It is used for circles with radii of less than 1 inch.

Using a Bow Compass

You can sharpen the short leads in a compass by rubbing one edge gently on a sandpaper block creating one flat elliptical side. If you draw a circle with a large bow compass, the flat side should face out, but it should face in for small bow compass circles.

The other method of sharpening a compass lead is to remove it from the compass, place it in a lead holder, sharpen it on a mechanical lead pointer, and replace it in the compass.

To draw a circle with the compass you turn the center wheel until the legs of the compass are the correct radius and then, holding the top knob between your thumb and forefinger with a slight forward angle to the lead leg, you complete the circle with one twirling motion (Figure 1.10). Because this motion does not allow you to press down, in order to have the line of your circle the same weight as your other lines, you usually need a slightly softer lead.

If you are making several arcs or circles from a single point, to avoid punching a large hole in your drafting paper, tape a small piece of thin cardboard under your drafting paper at the center point.

Beam Compass

There are extension arms that fit on some bow compasses to enable you to increase somewhat the length of the legs, but if you want to draw very large arcs or circles, you will need a beam compass. A beam compass consists of a lead point holder and a needlepoint holder that roll along a long, thin, square rod. (See Figure 1.11.) After you adjust the holders to the correct radius, you tighten them in place. Then, grasp the needlepoint holder and hold its end on the center point of your circle as you use your other hand to rotate the lead holder. (See Figure 1.12.)

Dividers

Dividers have a flexible center pivot with two sharp-pointed ends. (See Figure 1.8.) They are used to transfer measurements and to divide a line in any number of parts. Geometrically dividing a line into parts is explained in Chapter 4, "Geometrical Construction." You can also use your dividers to divide a line into equal parts by trial and error. You do this by first estimating the distance of each part, then stepping off each part by "walking" the dividers along the line. You observe what remains over or under the length of the line and adjust the dividers until you find the correct spacing.

It is best to get another bow compass and turn it into bow dividers by inserting the divider points. You can then adjust the width of the legs by turning the center or side wheels. If you use splay dividers without a center wheel, it is very easy to accidentally change the leg width.

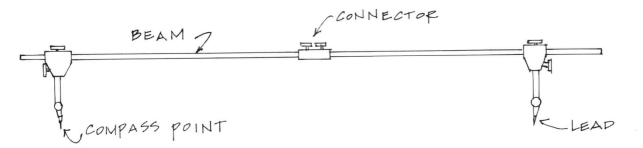

Figure 1.11 **The parts of a beam compass.**

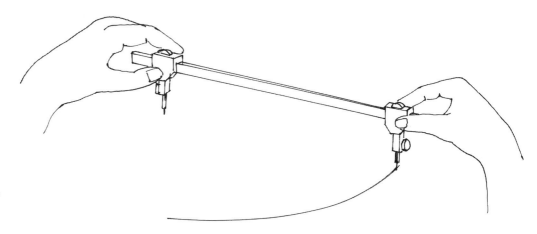

Figure 1.12 **Use two hands to draw with the beam compass.**

A **proportional divider** is used to quickly enlarge or reduce drafting drawings. (See Figure 1.13.) A sliding locking wheel between two sets of pointed legs can be set to a variety of proportions. For example, you can adjust the wheel so that 1/4 inch between the short legs equals 1/2 inch between the long legs.

A **spacing divider** allows you to quickly divide a line into any number of equal parts. (See Figure 1.14.) This expensive tool has a series of prongs (as many as eleven) that open or close the same amount by interlocking pivots.

French or Irregular Curves

You need a set of French or irregular curves to draw curved lines that are not arcs of a circle. From a set of curves, choose the clear plastic template whose curve or portion of curve most closely aligns with a light, freehand drawing of the curve. It may take several different portions of different templates to hand draw a single curve. To guarantee a smooth transition when using several templates to draw a single curve, start and stop your pencil line just shy of where the edge of the template splays away from the line you are tracing.

To draw symmetrical curves you will want to use the same portion of a single template. To mark the area of the template that you want to duplicate, rub the template with a hard pencil eraser and mark the points with light pencil lines before flipping it over.

Adjustable Curves

Long irregular curves can be drawn with an adjustable curve. There are several different varieties of adjustable curves: flexible rubber rods with

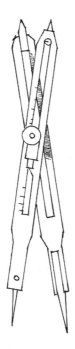

Figure 1.13 **Proportional dividers.**

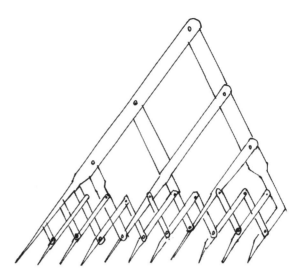

Figure 1.14 Spacing dividers.

Figure 1.15 It often takes several positions of a plastic curve to draw an irregular curve.

edges that bend to the required shape, and adjustable curves with movable spines and attachable weights to help hold the spine to the desired shape.

The quickest easiest adjustable curves to use are flexible rods composed of a series of thin inter-locking clear plastic tubes. Acu Arc is one brand name. As you form a curve, the tubes slide against each other and are held together by friction. The flat side edge of the curve is the one for drawing with a pencil. The side with a bead is for drawing with ink. They also make this adjustable curve with a ruled edge.

A List of Scenic Drafting Equipment

Basic Equipment
Parallel Rule
Adjustable Triangle, 12-inch
30/60 Degree Triangle, 18-inch

or

Drafting Machine (right- or left-handed)

Drafting Surface or Table

Vinyl Board Cover (Attach the vinyl cover to your board with a strip of thin double-stick tape across the top edge of your board. If possible, place books on top of the cover and let it flatten overnight before trimming the edges. Slowly trim the edges of the cover to the size of the board using a long metal straight edge and a matte knife.)

Drafting Chair

Architect's Scale Ruler, 12-inch

Two Drafting Lights (Ideally, both or at least one should be a combination incandescent and fluorescent lamp.)

Bow Dividers, 6-inch

Large Bow Compass, 6-inch

Small Bow Compass

Beam Compass

Sandpaper Block

Set of French Curves (clear, not colored plastic)

Sketching Pencils

Drafting Pencils
  and/or

Leadholders and Leads, or Mechanical Pencils and Leads (H, 2H, and HB leads to start with)

Electric Pencil Sharpener

Electric Eraser

Eraser Strips for electric eraser

Pink Pearl Eraser

Erasing Shield (with row of small circles)

Dry-Cleaning Pad or Dry-Cleaning Powder

Drafting Brush

Drafting Tape Dispenser

Drafting Tape or 1/2-inch Masking Tape or Drafting Dots

Template—Various sizes of small circles

Template—Various sized shapes, such as hexagonal, triangular, and square

Template—Master ellipse template

Template—1/4-inch furniture

Template—Large circles

Additional Equipment

Adjustable Triangle, 4-inch

45-Degree Triangle, 4-inch

Pocket Scale Ruler

Opera Scale Ruler

Metric Scale Ruler

Engineer's Scale Ruler

Proportional Dividers

Spacing Dividers

Adjustable Curve

Electric Lead Pointer

Dimensional Calculator

Templates of other ellipses in various sizes

Template—1/4-inch American Standard Plumbing Fixtures

Template—Interior design, kitchen, bathroom, bedroom

Template—Arrows

Template—Structural Cross-Sections
Template—Interior design, tables and chairs
Template—Office furniture
Template Holder (organizes templates and holds them vertically)
Builder's Calculator
Tube-Drafting Carrier
Stamp—"For Estimate Only"
Stamp—"Not to Scale"
Stamp—"Revised"
Ink Pad

Traveling Kit Extras

Exacto Knife and #11 Blades
Mat Knife and Blades
Self-Healing Plastic Cutting Board
Magnifying Glass
Scotch Tape Dispenser and Tape
Scotch Double-Stick Tape Gun and Tape
Glue Sticks
Rubber Cement Pick-Up
Rubber-Backed 12-inch Metal Ruler
Liquid Paper—Multifluid
Parallel Rule Replacement Cable
Parallel Rule Hardware Kit
Plyers
Needle-Nosed Plyers
Assorted size/type nails
Hammer
Awl
Small Clamps
Coping Saw and Blades
Phillips Head Screrwdriver
Screwdriver
3-Hook Punch

2

Pencils, Paper, and Reproduction

Sketch Tissue Paper or Tracing Paper

Inexpensive tissue paper with a high level of transparency comes on yellow or white-toned rolls and is useful for sketching and rough layouts. Convenient sizes are 12-inch and 24-inch wide rolls. More expensive are pads of heavyweight trace. Convenient sizes are 8 1/2 inches by 11 inches, and 19 inches by 24 inches.

Drafting Paper

Drafting papers are semitransparent papers on which drawings are made in ink, pencil, or marker for the purpose of reproduction. They come in different degrees of transparency. Some are more suitable for markers and some erase more easily then others. Vellum papers are very transparent but age makes them brittle and yellow. Papers made of good quality rag are less transparent than vellum but are durable and long-lasting. Common brands of drafting paper are Clearprint and Charprint.

The standard drafting sheet sizes for scenic work is 24 inches by 36 inches, although 30 inches by 42 inches is sometimes used on large feature films. Boxed precut sheets, although more expensive than rolls, are usually purchased on large projects to save time in trimming paper to size. Rolled paper comes up to 42 inches wide. A limited length of larger-sized rolled paper is often needed for studio and theatre ground plans, which usually demand a larger sheet size than the others in their set.

One side of the tracing paper is better to draft on than the other. This is indicated by the watermark letters, which should be right side up.

The draftsperson needs to remember that tracing papers are porous and that graphite particles from pencil lines go through the paper. To completely erase a line, it is necessary to turn the paper over and erase the back as well as the front.

Humidity affects tracing paper. If you leave paper on your drafting table overnight, do not leave your parallel ruler or anything else on top of it, as temperature changes may surround it with wrinkles the next morning.

Polyester Films and Coated Sheets

Polyester film for drafting is available in standard-sized sheets and rolls and will accept ink or lead drawing. Although more expensive then tracing paper, it is extremely transparent, long-lasting, and unaffected by humidity. Erasures on film are not made with rubber but with vinyl erasers especially formulated to erase either ink or graphite.

Even though drafting film is made with a matte surface, it tends to have a slickness to it that causes pencil leads to slide. This slickness can increase the draftsperson's speed but makes control difficult. Film is therefore a poor surface for a beginning draftsperson who is learning to control his or her line, or for drawing a setting with elaborate detail. Film is excellent for ink drawing, and certain films such as Denril allow ink lines to be erased with erasers made to erase ink on film.

Film/Paper combination drafting sheets are now being manufactured that try to combine the best qualities of both—durability and stability. Dura-Lene is one brand.

Leads, Holders, and Pencils

- **Leads** are harder or softer, the degree being indicated by "H" for hard or "B" for soft. A 9H lead will be extremely hard; an HB lead will be middle range; and a 6B lead will be extremely soft. The same lead number will vary in hardness with different brands and will be affected by changes in the weather. Different hand pressure of the same lead will result in a different weight line, so hardness and softness are a personal choice.

  Hard leads maintain their points longer, make thinner, more exact lines, and lines that are lighter. Hard leads are good for initial, light layout of measurements and for precise drawing. Hard points need to be used carefully as they can tear the paper.

  Soft leads give darker, wider lines. Soft leads are good for rough, soft, initial sketches, for large-scale details, and for lettering. The loose graphite in soft leads can smudge and dirty a sheet and require clean hands and clean drafting tools.

- **Wooden pencils** with lead cores are the drawing tools of choice for many scenic draftspeople. Variations in pressure with a single-weight pencil can create thin and light or thick and heavy lines. The diameter of the lead in wood pencils gets larger as the pencil gets softer, so the soft leads are better for soft, rough layouts. Berol, Turquoise, and Mars are common pencil brands made just for drafting. Many people like to draft with regular Mongol #3 pencils with attached erasers on their end. Three pencils with soft dark leads made for sketching and roughs are Draughting pencils, Mirado Black Warriors, and Tombow, a Japanese brand.

- **Nonprint blue pencils** are used to mark originals and will not print when the original is copied.

- **Lead holders** hold a single-weight lead strip. All weights of lead strips are the same diameter, and variations in hand pressure cause only a moderate variation in line quality. Draftspeople usually use several weights of lead, identifying the hardness by different colored lead holders. Berol and Mars are two common brands of drafting leads. Drawing on plastic film rather than paper requires you to use a plastic-based lead formulated for strength and to resist smears.

- **Mechanical pencils** hold around ten very thin leads at a time, and clicking the tip advances a lead. Mechanical pencils are best for exact, mechanical drafting. Their advantage is that the leads do not have to be sharpened, and they maintain a consistent line weight. Their disadvantage is that to change line weight or thickness you must change pencils.

The choice of drawing tool like the choice of lead is a matter of individual comfort and preference. Many draftspeople vary their choice of drawing tools for the type of drawing they are doing. They might use a soft pencil for roughs, a lead holder with a 2H lead for a 1/2-inch-scale elevation, and a Mongol B pencil for full-size detailing. The final drawing of a complex 1/4-inch-scale ground plan might be initially laid out with a 4H lead, drawn with a 2H lead, and the section outline emphasized with an HB lead.

Sharpeners

Serious draftspeople need electrical rather than mechanical sharpeners as mechanically sharpening takes too long.

- **Electric pencil sharpeners** sharpen pencils.
- **Electric lead pointers** sharpen lead holder leads. The best brand is the Pierce Power Pointer, which has a replaceable cutter.

Erasing

- **Erasers** are either handheld or strips that go into erasing machines. Both hand and erasing-machine erasers come in different degrees of abrasion for different purposes and different surfaces.

   Pink Pearl is the basic hand pencil eraser with mild abrasion. ParaWhite is a very soft hand eraser with mild abrasion. A double-end vinyl eraser has one end for erasing ink and one end for erasing pencil from drafting film or vellum. Koh-i-noor Rapidograph is formulated to remove ink from tracing paper and polyester films.
- **Erasing machines** are either electric or cordless and battery-operated. Electric machines are more durable than battery but are heavier and the cord can get in the way. Bruning is a good brand. The electric cord can be placed over the back of the drafting table with the machine above the drawing when not in use, or you can screw a large hook in the front edge of your drafting board and hang your erasing machine on it.

   Cordless machines have a recharging stand. The lighter, cordless erasing machines are easier to lift for long periods but have thin plastic housing that can crack. Pierce is a good brand of cordless machine. All erasing machines accept eraser strips of different formulations for ink or paper drawing, for paper or plastic sheets, and for soft or hard pencil lines.
- **Eraser shields** are thin metal shields with various slots to permit accurate erasures of small, precise areas. The shield with a row of equally spaced small holes is good for making equally spaced dashed lines from a single line.
- **Dry-cleaning powder** is eraser powder that, sprinkled onto a drafted sheet, picks up pencil lead dust. The particles act like small ball bearings beneath a parallel, helping it to glide over paper without smudging.
- **Dry-cleaning pads** (affectionately known as scum-bags) are soft mesh bags with powder inside. The particles tend to be somewhat larger than the powder. The bag itself can be rubbed over an area of a drawing to lighten the entire area. Both pads and powder have to be used with care as too much powdering can erase an image.

Storage

Film or vellum originals should never be folded but always stored flat or rolled. While blueprints can be folded for temporary storage, for long-term storage they should also be stored flat or rolled.

- **Flat files** of wood or metal are made to store drawings by laying them flat in drawers with easy accessibility.
- **Binder clamps** are used to clamp the short edges of a flat stack of drawings together. To remove a drawing you must loosen the wing knobs. You can purchase individual clamps in different sizes, or a system of vertical files or pivoting racks that hold multiple clamp sets. You can also build print clamps with two strips of thin wood and two thin bolts.
- **Tube storage** is used to store inactive originals or blueprints. Tube file systems are sold that allow many rolls to be stored in a single, stackable, end-labeled rectangular box.
- **Cardboard portfolios** allow long-term storage of flat drawings.

Transporting Drafting Drawings

It is best to transport originals and blueprints rolled around a cardboard tube and placed inside a plastic tube. To avoid ripping edges, never tape a roll of drawings to itself; instead, roll a piece of paper around the drawings and tape it.

Draftspeople can purchase a variety of sizes and styles of plastic tubes with tops, and some with shoulder straps, that can be used to carry rolled drafting. It is a good habit to always include your name and phone number on or in the roll so you have a chance of getting your drafting back if it is mislaid. Federal Express and Express Mail sell tube-shipping containers.

Folding Blueprints

Blueprints can be folded for temporary storage or mailing. The best method of folding them is so that the title block is on the front lower-right corner. The method is illustrated in Figure 2.1.

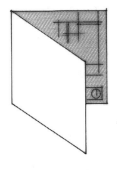

FOLD IN TWO
PRINT INSIDE

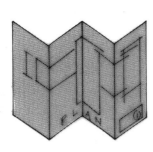

FOLD SIDES BACK
INTO QUARTERS
BRINGING PRINT TO OUTSIDE

½'S

⅓'S

FOLD INTO TWO OR THREE
DEPENDING ON SIZE

Figure 2.1 How to fold a blueprint.

Printing Drafting

Drafting print paper comes in rolls or in boxed precut sheets the same sizes as drafting paper. Blueprinting is essentially a photographic reproduction process in which transparent drafting paper covered with dark lines acts as a negative. After a sheet of drafting paper is laid over the print paper, it is exposed to light and then fixed in a chemical bath or vapors. Print paper is chemically coated to make it light-sensitive, and it must be carefully stored away from light or its yellow-gray color will gradually turn blue-gray and the paper will be useless.

When people say "blueprinting" they usually mean Diazo printing. Most current drafting reproduction is done by either a Diazo-moist or a Diazo-dry printing process. In Diazo printing you lay the original tracing onto a chemically treated sheet of paper and then expose it to light. Diazo printing can print blue, black, brown, or red lines on an off-white background, depending on the chemicals on the print paper.

Diazo-moist printing fixes the print by dampening one side of it with a developing solution, and Diazo-dry printing fixes the print by exposing it to ammonia vapors. The moist method smells less than the dry method.

When buying or renting a printing machine consider the following:

- The better the filter systems of the dry machine, the less the ammonia smell. The moist method smells less than the dry method of printing.
- You probably want a machine that accepts at least 42-inch-wide paper.
- The speed of the machine is controlled by the number of lamps. (There are also print papers with faster speeds.)
- Rented machines charge a monthly fee plus an hourly fee for printing (not running) time. It is best to purchase print paper from the same company from which you rent the machine.

Sepia Prints

A sepia print is printed in the same manner as a Diazo print but on a specially coated, very transparent, oily paper that allows it to function as an original. Prints can be made from a sepia print, and lines can be added or removed from a sepia print before reprinting. The print reproduction from a sepia is less clear than one made from the original.

Sepia paper has a matte side and an oily side. When you make a print on sepia paper, you want the empty matte side on top so you can draw on it without the oily residue, and the print on the oily underside of the paper. This means that when you print your original on sepia, you print the original upside down so that it will be right side up when you turn the sepia paper over to draw on it.

Changes are made on a sepia print by using a clear liquid sepia eradicator, which dissolves the printed lines. As the dissolved dye colors the liquid, light Kleenex tissue dabs are needed to soak it up. Additions can be made to sepia prints with ink or pencil. Some sepia papers allow you to make changes by erasing.

Sepia prints allow a designer to give someone a sheet that can be printed while keeping possession of the original. They also allow changes to be quickly made without changing or retracing the original.

Sepia prints can be used to speed up the drafting process When drawing repeating images with additions, the draftsperson can makes prints of the repeating area and add the changes to multiple sepia prints, each of which can then be printed. For example, the stage house and permanent setting of a multiset musical can be printed on sepia prints, and then the additions can be added for each shift in plot. Another example would be in drawing the director's plan and the technical plan of a stage set. To avoid drafting the ground plan twice, the draftsperson could draw the ground plan and the stage house and run a sepia print. Furniture could be added to the paper original, and dimensions and technical notes could be added onto the sepia print.

Photocopy Printing

Photocopy prints are positive prints of black lines on top of a lighter background. In the process of photocopy printing, a camera projects the original onto a selenium-coated, electrostatically charged plate. A negatively charged plastic powder is spread across the plate and sticks only to the positively charged areas of the image. A positive charge holds the powder to the paper, and heat is used to bake the image onto the surface of the paper.

Because photography is involved in photocopy printing, it is possible to enlarge or reduce the original image, and thus photocopy printing has become an important drafting tool. Most large art departments have or have close access to a photocopy machine, which is often leased as part of the production equipment. The best photocopy machine for the scenic designer is one that prints as large as 11 by 17 inches and goes from 50% to 200% in increments of 1% as this allows maximum control of resizing.

Xerography is a completely dry process that will reproduce any copy. It is possible to print onto thin colored or metallic papers or onto clear acetate sheets. You can also photocopy onto clear, adhesive-backed film, which allows you to "copy" onto your drafting.

You can attach smaller photocopied acetate sheets onto a larger sheet with clear tape and then print the layered imagery. This is especially useful in situations such as a soap opera, where the studio remains the same and the individual sets often change.

The disadvantage of photocopy reproduction is that in order to reproduce a drawing with dark lines against a clean white background, you sacrifice the lightweight pencil lines.

Giant Photocopy Machines

Some large-volume blueprint companies and some copy companies like Kinko's have giant photocopy machines that print up to 36 inches wide by any manageable length. These machines can print on plain paper, clear acetate, or erasable vellum. Printing on 24-by-36-inch vellum or clear acetate allows you to make another clear original from an original. It allows you to:

1. Make another original from which to blueprint.
2. Take an old or damaged drafting and make a new, clean original.
3. Cut and paste pieces of sheets of drafting onto a 24-by-36-inch sheet and copy it onto a single vellum sheet.
4. Make a composite original from acetate overlays.
5. Mask out large sections of a drafting and make a new original.

The development of erasable photocopying on vellum allows you to make changes easily on an original without the liquid mess of Sepia eradicator.

Photostats

The Photostat printing process is essentially a specialized camera, and, like a camera, it allows any degree of enlargement or reduction. It is more expensive than photocopy printing but gives a better quality print. The original may be either transparent or opaque. You can get a Photostat print on matte or gloss paper, or on clear acetate. Because it uses a camera, Photostatting is a two-step process. First, a negative of white lines on a black background is made. Then a positive print of black lines on a white background is made from the negative.

Photostats onto heavy-duty clear acetate are especially useful for large-scale film, theatre, and studio plans that will be stored and printed many times.

Fax

Many draftsmen and art departments are finding that they need to buy or rent a fax machine for rapid transmission of information, including drafting. In fax transmission a document scanner uses reflected light, converted into electrical signals, that vary in accordance with print density. A modem then modulates the electronic signal to a form used for standard telephone transmission. The quality of the scan is affected by the number of resolutions of the scanner, so to reproduce a drawn image you want the highest setting.

In fax reception, a processor receives the transmitted signal, returns it to the original document form, and sends it to a printer. Most fax machines use a thermal printer, which supplies current that is modulated by information to individual resistors, in contact with chemically treated paper. The heat generated by the transistors turns the paper black.

Most types of thermal fax machine printers use a roll of chemically treated heat-sensitive paper that is 8 1/2 inches wide and up to 164 feet long. Machines can be purchased with an automatic paper cutter, which can be set to cut rolls every 11 inches so you don't have to hand cut them. High-end fax machines use an ink jet printer with replaceable cartridges. These plain paper faxes have the advantage of printing on any 8 1/2 by 11 sheet of paper, and unlike thermal faxes, the image won't fade away.

The quality of a faxed image is affected by the quality of the receiving as well as of the transmitting fax machines. As this transmission often results in an extreme amount of distortion, it is very important that the draftsperson use written dimensions to indicate sizes, as scaling off the faxed image will be inaccurate. In addition, before faxing any pencil drawing, first photocopy it darkly to insure the clearest possible fax image.

When transmitting by fax, it is best to use an 8 1/2-by-11-inch format so that both single and roll paper fax machines can receive it. Match lines (see Chapter 9, "Dimensioning") allow the designer to send sheets so they can be reassembled upon reception. If you divide a large sheet horizontally and vertically into many small pieces to be coded for reassembly the process is called tiling. Figure 2.2 illustrates a system of tiling.

Accuracy of Reproduction

It is important for the designer/draftsperson to be aware that all printing methods to a greater or lesser degree stretch the imagery and are less accurate then the original. Only dimensioning guarantees precise accuracy.

Tracking Copies

If you will be giving copies of drawings and revised drawings to many people, it's a good idea to set up a distribution log so you have a record of who got which sheets on what date.

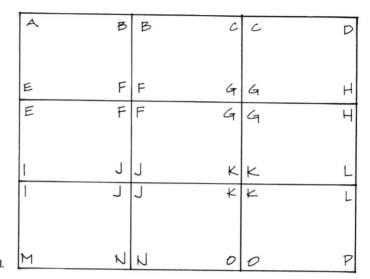

Figure 2.2 Coding a large sheet for fax transmittal.

Copies	Name	Sht. #	Print Type	Drawing	Date
1	Director	1, 2	Blue Line	Dir. Plan, Section	1/3/99
5	Shop	1, 2, 2A	Sepia	Dir. Plan, Tech Plan, Cross-Sect.	1/3/99
2	Ltg. Dsr.	1, 2, 2A	Blue Line	Dir. Plan, Tech Plan, Cross-Sect.	1/3/99
5	Shop	3, 4, 5	Sepia	Elevations	1/5/99
5	Shop	6, 7	Sepia	Wall Details, FPL Details	1/5/99
1	Director	1 Rev., 2 Rev.	Blue Line	Rev. Dir. Plan, Rev. Cross-Sect.	1/8/99
1	Ltg. Dsr.	1 Rev., 2 Rev.	Blue Line	Rev. Dir. Plan, Rev. Cross-Sect.	1/9/99

3

Lines

Process

Scenic drafting is first about designing. The object itself must be designed, then its details and particulars must be designed, then after the clearest method of explaining it is chosen, its layout must be designed on the sheet. Only then is the draftsperson able to construct a tight, measured drawing. Some extremely experienced designers are able to do most of the designing in their heads and jump to the final drawing. Most draftspeople, however, follow a process of first using soft, sketch lines to draw the object. This sketching is done in scale using the normal views to explain the object, but it is still "loose" with an emphasis on the draftsperson choosing the best shapes, proportions, and details. Such drawing uses large critical measurements—for example, the overall size of the object or the given width of an opening—but the lines of the drawing are still somewhat rough and not entirely measured. Only after the design and layout are satisfactory, which may take any number of tracing overlays during which the image gradually tightens, does the draftsperson switch to the hard line and the exact measurements of the final drawing.

Sketch Drafting

Many experienced designers and draft people can draw freehand orthographic views that are surprisingly accurate as to scale. A good exercise for beginning drafting students is to draw an object such as a ground plan using a scale ruler but none of the other drafting tools. A second exercise is to take an object such as a toy automobile and reproduce it in orthographic layout at any size other than the original using all the drafting tools except the scale ruler. An example of such a drawing can be seen in George Tsypin's drawing of a horse (Figure 7.6) in Chapter 7, "Orthographic Projection."

Soft and Hard Drafting

It is important for the student of scenic drafting to understand that drafting can be loose, tight, or anywhere in between. I used to tell my students that I wanted them to be able to "set the rheostat." In other words, the draftsperson needs to choose the degree of accuracy needed for the job at hand. An extremely tight, accurate, measured, and completely dimensioned drafting may be required for the final ground plan that is sent to the shop for building, but it would be a waste of time and intimidating to a director who is choosing a plan for moving his actors in space and doesn't want to feel locked into anything.

The Scenic Drafted Pencil Line

In architectural or engineering drafting, line weights tend to remain constant. There are three standard line weights: thick, for cutting planes (the contours of sections) and for short break lines; medium, for visible outlines and hidden outlines; and thin, for section lines (crosshatch), center lines, extension lines, dimension lines, long break lines, and alternate position and repeat lines.

Scenic drafting often tends to be much freer and more like drawing. Many scenic draftspeople feel that variations in pencil weight can clarify their image. By changing the pressure of his or her hand, the draftsperson gives a line a beginning, middle, and end. (See Figure 3.1.) This increase at the beginning and end of the line means that the corners of objects are darkened, pulling the eye of the viewer to the informative area of the picture and allowing him or her to more easily and quickly "read" the drawing. (See Figure 3.2.) In addition to directing the eye of the viewer, changes in line weight can suggest foreground, middle ground, or background on a flat view much as they can do in sketching.

The style of pencil line work is the mark of each individual draftsperson. In reproducing most of the drafting in this book by tracing them in ink, I lost the individual line. This was not a decision I made easily or lightly, or without extensive testing of methods of reproducing the pencil lines of large draftings at the reduced size needed for book illustrations. In the end, I decided it was more important for the student to see clearly the information on each sheet than to maintain the hand of the draftsperson.

Often in Scenic Drafting the Primary Lines of the Shape of an Object Are Darker than Those that Are Less Important

While the darkest weight line is reserved for the cutting plane (contour of a section), a convention used by many scenic draftspersons is to draw

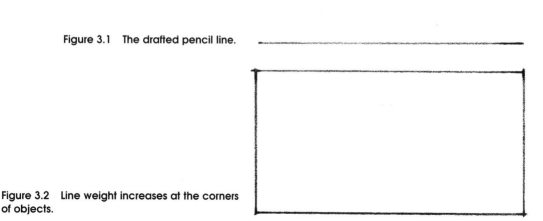

Figure 3.1   The drafted pencil line.

Figure 3.2   Line weight increases at the corners of objects.

the profile of an object with a darker weight line than the lines of secondary information. This change in emphasis allows the viewer to "read" the lines of the drawing in the order of their importance. For example, on an elevation, the overall outline of a flat and the hole in it, the edge of the window reveal, are drawn with a heavier line than the lines of the molding on that flat. The line at the edge of a molding is drawn at a heavier weight then the individual lines that compose the molding. (See Figure 3.3.)

The Centerline

A centerline indicates the center of an object. This center may be the center of a symmetrical shape, the center of an object such as a pilaster, or the center of a room or a stage. The graphic symbol for a centerline is always a long dash followed by a very short dash (so short that it is almost a dot), followed by a long dash, and so on. (See Figure 3.4.)

Centerlines Are Often Emphasized with the Letters "CL"

Often the end of the centerline has an interlocked "CL" to give it additional importance. (See Figure 3.5.)

Figure 3.3 The primary lines of the shape of an object are darker than those that are less important.

Figure 3.4 The centerline.

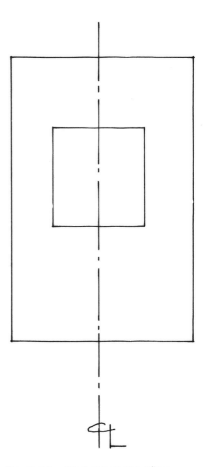

Figure 3.5 Centerlines are often emphasized with the letters CL.

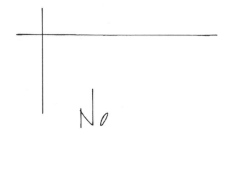

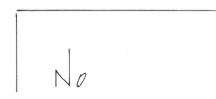

Figure 3.6   Lines at the corners of objects slightly overlap.

Lines at the Corners of Objects Must Just Slightly Overlap

In the top example in Figure 3.6, the lines at the corner overlap too much. The eye of the viewer follows their extension and then has to pull back to the object. In the bottom example in Figure 3.6, the lines do not touch. The viewer has to imagine them meeting before he or she can read the object. Figure 3.2 shows the very slightly overlapped meeting of lines at corners.

Hidden Lines

Hidden lines indicate the position of objects behind, above, or underneath another object. A hidden line is drawn as a series of equal sized dashes, with the spaces between the dashes smaller than the lines. (See Figure 3.7.)

Hidden Line Dashes Must Meet at the Corners of Objects

To clearly define the shape of objects it is important that the dashes meet at an object's corners. (See Figure 3.8.)

Hidden Lines Must Jump Primary Lines

The dash of a hidden line must break before hitting a primary line. If hidden lines are drawn across primary lines, they confuse the shape of the objects. (See Figure 3.9.)

If Two Hidden Lines Cross, the Nearest One Is Primary

The dash line of a hidden line that is further away must not cross through the dash line of a hidden line that is above it. The classic example of this principle is illustrated by three playing cards piled on top of each other. The top card is drawn with a solid edge and the next card is drawn with a hidden line to show where it lies underneath the top card. The closest card in the stack is also drawn with hidden lines, but its lines "jump" over and do not cross the hidden lines of the second card in the pile. (See Figure 3.10.)

Figure 3.7   Hidden line.

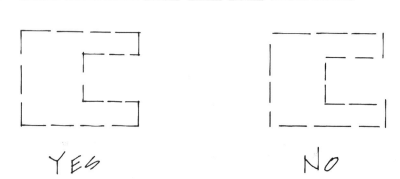

Figure 3.8   Hidden line dashes must touch at the corners of objects.

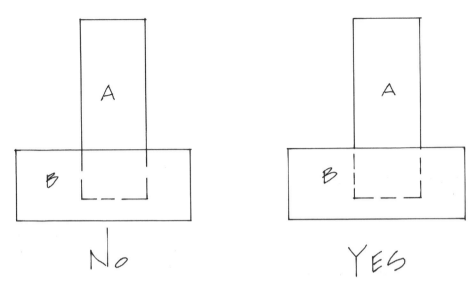

Figure 3.9 Hidden lines must jump primary lines.

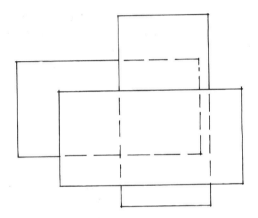

Figure 3.10 If two hidden lines cross, the nearest one is primary.

If we were to draw the elevation of a wall, the surface might have projections such as moldings. In drawing the object as a flat surface, we compress several layers of depth and draw the wall and moldings with solid lines. We would do the same thing if we were to draw the plan of a deck with a stair unit on it. The edges of the deck, the risers, and handrail of the stairs would be drawn with solid lines.

Say we wanted to show several layers of pipes hanging above the deck. If the pipes were at different heights, the draftsperson might choose to compress them into one plane in the drawing and indicate their perimeter with a dashed line. If, above the pipes, the design had a large circular light box, the draftsperson might draw this with another dash line, "jumping" the dashes over the dashes of the pipes. If, under the deck, there were an actor's tunnel leading to a deck hole, then the draftsperson would indicate that it was below rather than above the deck by using an alternative hidden line.

In organizing a drawing, the draftsperson chooses which levels of depth to compress and draw as a flattened two-dimensional image. To indicate the primary spatial planes, she can draw them with solid lines. She uses hidden lines and alternative hidden lines to show other layers of depth either above or below the primary level. To indicate that one hidden depth layer is further away, she can "jump" its dashes over the dashed lines that indicate the place that is closer to the primary plane. With attention to the placement of the dashes of hidden lines, complicated layering situations such as the ground plan of a musical can be clearly explained.

Hidden Lines Are Used to Indicate Scenery Movement

To show an object that moves, draw its primary position as a solid line and the extreme position of its move as a hidden line. (See Figure 3.11.) Use hidden line dashes to indicate the edge of its path of movement.

Alternative Hidden Line

The alternative hidden line is drawn with a long dash followed by three short dashes, followed by a long dash, and so on. (See Figure 3.12.) If a

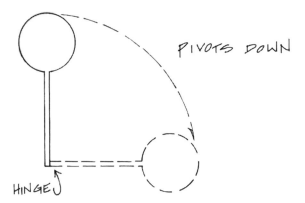

Figure 3.11   Hidden lines are used to indicate scenery movement.

Figure 3.12   Alternative hidden line.

hidden line is used to indicate one level of hidden information, the alternative line can be used to indicate another level. For example, in drawing a ground plan with three stories, you can show the first floor as a solid line, the second level as a hidden line, and the third level as an alternative hidden line.

In Figure 3.13, the facia of the platform is hidden underneath its surface and drawn as a hidden line. The alternative hidden line is used to indicate a lighting fixture hanging above the platform. The use of an alternative hidden line is especially valuable when drawing complex ground plans.

Match Lines

If you wish to draw a single view of an object that is too big to fit on a single sheet of paper, you can break it into parts and show where they would join together by drawing a match line. (See Figure 3.14.) This is an alternative line, made up of a long dash followed by three short dashes and so on. The ends of the lines are coded with a bubble divided in half with each side given a matching letter of the alphabet.

The reader of the drafting aligns the match lines on two sheets of drafting, essentially creating a single large sheet. Smaller-scale drawings usually show less detail than the same object in a larger scale. Match lines are very important as they allow a draftsperson to combine

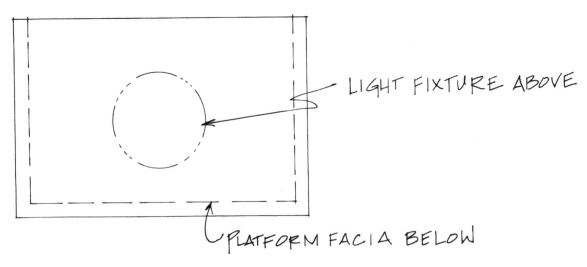

Figure 3.13   Use of an alternative hidden line.

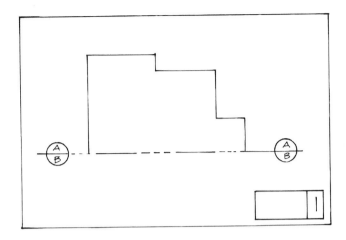

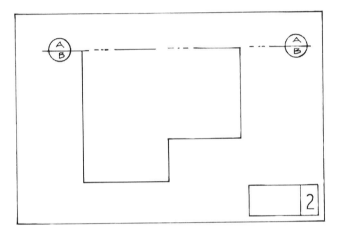

Figure 3.14   Match lines.

sheets to draw large objects in large scales without sacrificing details. For example, by using match lines the draftsperson can combine several sheets in a long full-size section through a wall that shows the depth relationships of a cornice, chair rail, wainscot, paneling, and baseboard. Match lines can be used to tile drafting sheets in any direction. If a draftsperson wished to draft a very large object in a large scale, such as the plan of a theater and its auditorium, he or she might use match lines to tile the sheets. Figure 2.2 in Chapter 2, "Pencils, Paper, and Reproduction," is an illustration of coding tiled sheets for fax transmission; this procedure can also be applied to coding match lines of multiple sheets of drafting.

4

Geometrical Construction

Practical Plane Geometry

Many shapes that we construct in drafting are based on plane geometry. A familiarity with geometrical construction allows the draftsperson to apply the principles to specific problems. The following are the most frequently used constructions.

To Bisect a Given Straight Line

Draw a straight line AB. Using your compass, with a radius greater than half the length of the line from the ends of the line, points A and B, draw two arcs on either side of the given line. Draw a line through the intersection of these arcs, from point D to E. The line you have drawn will be perpendicular to your original line and will divide it in half at the midpoint C. (See Figure 4.1.)

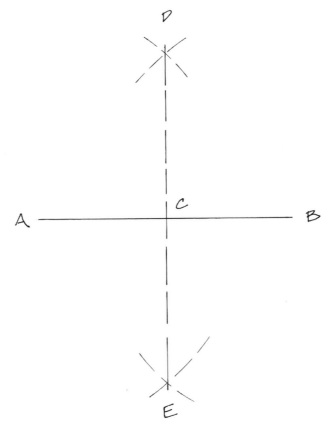

Figure 4.1 To bisect a given straight line.

To Bisect a Given Angle

Draw an angle A, B, C. Use B as the center and any convenient radius to draw the arc DE. Use points on the angle at D and E as the centers to draw two arcs that intersect at F. The line drawn from F to B will bisect the angle. (See Figure 4.2.)

To Divide a Given Straight Line into Any Number of Equal Parts

The following construction is used often in scenic design and drafting. For example, it can be used to divide a certain given height into equal stair risers, or to divide a wall into an equal number of panels.

Draw a line AB that you wish to divide into a certain number of equal parts. (In Figure 4.3, we are dividing the line into seven equal divisions.) From either end of the line, draw a second line, AC, at any length and making any angle to the original line. Using your dividers or ruler, space off equal divisions along the line from A to C, numbering them 1, 2, 3, 4, and so on. Join division 7 and G with a straight line. Lock your adjustable triangle to the angle of the line from 7 to G. Now draw parallel lines from each point on AC. These parallel lines will intersect AB in seven equal divisions.

To Find the Center of a Given Circle

Given a circle of any size, draw two chords AB and CD. Bisect each chord with a perpendicular line. The intersection of the two perpendiculars is the center of the circle. (See Figure 4.4.)

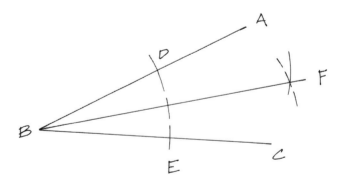

Figure 4.2   To bisect a given angle.

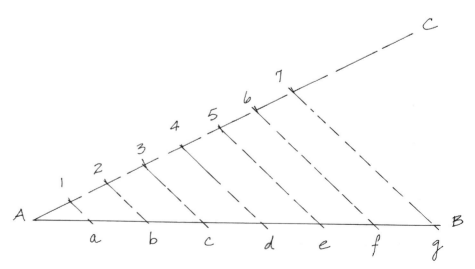

Figure 4.3   To divide a given straight line into any number of equal parts.

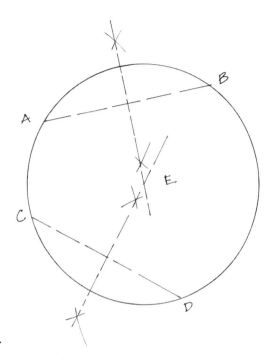

Figure 4.4   To find the center of a circle.

To Inscribe a Square in a Given Circle

Given a circle of any size, draw two diameters AB and CD at right angles to each other. Draw the lines AC, CB, BD, and DA at the points of intersection along the circumference of the circle, and they will form the sides of a square. (See Figure 4.5.)

To Inscribe a Regular Hexagon in a Circle

Given a circle of any size draw its diameter ACB. From the points A and B with dividers set equal to the radius of the circle, draw arcs intersecting the circle, points 1, 2, 3, and 4. Join these points with straight lines and they will form the sides of the hexagon. (See Figure 4.6.)

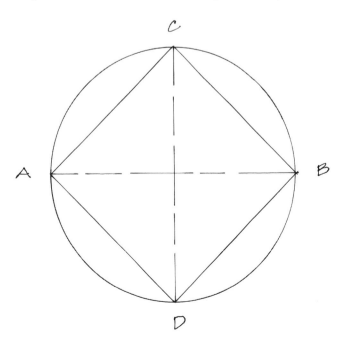

Figure 4.5   To inscribe a square in a given circle.

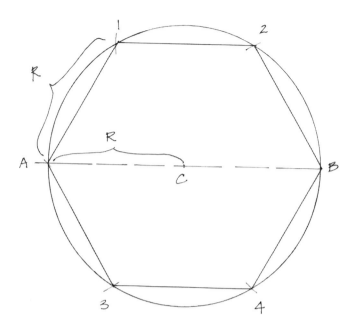

Figure 4.6   To inscribe a regular hexagon in a circle.

To Inscribe a Regular Pentagon in a Given Circle

Given a circle of any size, draw two diameters AB and CD at right angles to each other. Bisect one of the radii as shown with line FG at point E. With E as the center and EC as the radius, draw an arc cutting line AB at H. Then with C as the center and CH as the radius, draw another arc intersecting the circumference of the circle at I. The straight line IC is one side of the pentagon. Using your dividers, mark the remaining sides. (See Figure 4.7.)

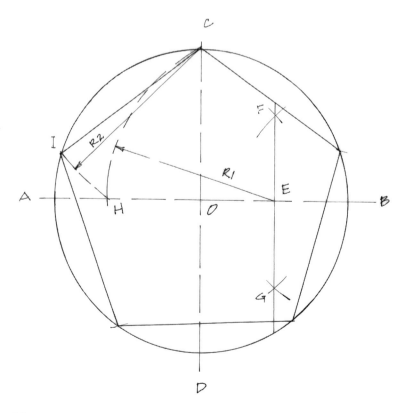

Figure 4.7   To inscribe a regular pentagon in a given circle.

To Inscribe a Regular Octagon in a Given Circle

Given a circle of any size, draw the two diameters AE and CG at right angles to each other. Bisect one of the four equal arcs as shown with H bisecting arc AG. Draw the diameter HOD. Bisect another of the equal arcs as shown in Figure 4.8, with B bisecting arc AC. Draw the diameter BOF. Straight lines connecting the points on the circumference A, B, C, D, E, and F will form the sides of the octagon.

To Draw a Circle Tangent to a Line at a Given Point

Given line AB, construct a perpendicular line at the point of tangency. The radius of any tangent circle will be along the perpendicular. (See Figure 4.9.)

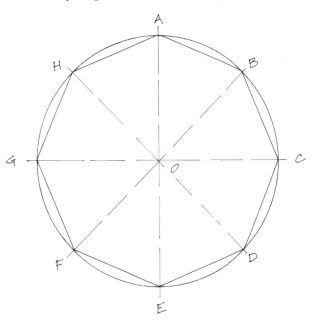

Figure 4.8   To inscribe a regular octagon in a given circle.

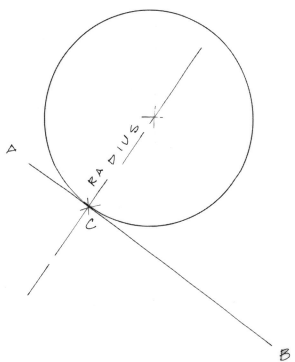

Figure 4.9   To draw a circle tangent to a line at a given point.

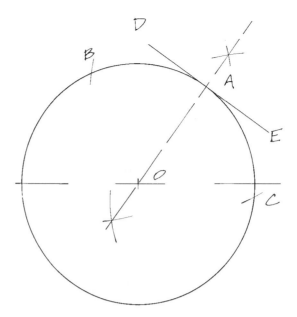

Figure 4.10   To draw a tangent to a circle through a given point on the circle.

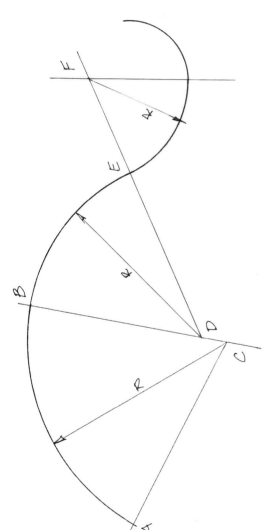

Figure 4.11   To draw a series of tangent arcs forming a curve.

To Draw a Tangent to a Circle through a Given Point on the Circle

Given point A on the circle, draw a radius from the center of the circle through the point, line 0A. A perpendicular to this line at point A will be the tangent. (See Figure 4.10.)

To Draw a Series of Tangent Arcs Forming a Curve

Understanding the nature of the construction in Figure 4.11 allows the draftsperson to easily draw graceful curves that can be accurately reproduced from specific radii.

Lightly freehand the desired curve. By trial and error, locate the center point C and radius CA that most closely create the beginning of the curve. Draw a line from the point where the compass arc deviates from the curve, point B. Draw the straight line BC. The center points of any tangent arc to point B will fall on this line. By trial and error, locate the center point D and radius DE that most closely conform to the next arc. Draw the straight line DE. The center point, F, of an opposing curve will fall on the extension of line DE.

To Draw a Tangent Arc in a Right Angle

Use the center of a given right angle, ABC, to draw an arc at any convenient radius, R1. The arc intersects the right angle at points D and E. With these points as centers, use the same radius to draw two arcs that will intersect at point F, which is the center of the tangent arc. (See Figure 4.12.)

To Draw a Tangent Arc to Two Lines at an Acute or Obtuse Angle

Given the angle ABC, draw an arc, R1, at any convenient distance. Use the points of the intersection of the arc with the sides of the angle, points

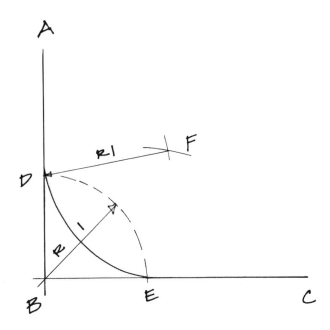

Figure 4.12   To draw a tangent arc in a right angle.

D and E, as the centers to draw two arcs of any size with equal radii, R2. Draw lines parallel to the sides of the original angle at the distance R2, which will intersect at F, the center. Perpendiculars from F to each side of the angle will locate the points of tangency, 1 and 2, and R3 will be the radius. (See Figures 4.13 and 4.14.)

To Find a Straight Line Equal to the Circumference of a Given Arc

Figure 4.15 provides an approximate distance that is useful for most practical purposes. The exact distance can be found by a trigonometric equation.

Find the center of a given arc AB and draw the radius CA. At point A, draw a perpendicular line. Draw the chord BA and extend it to

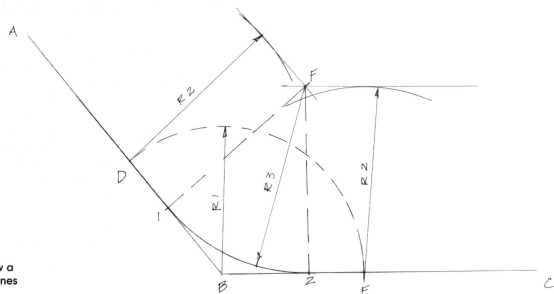

Figure 4.13   To draw a tangent arc to two lines at an obtuse angle.

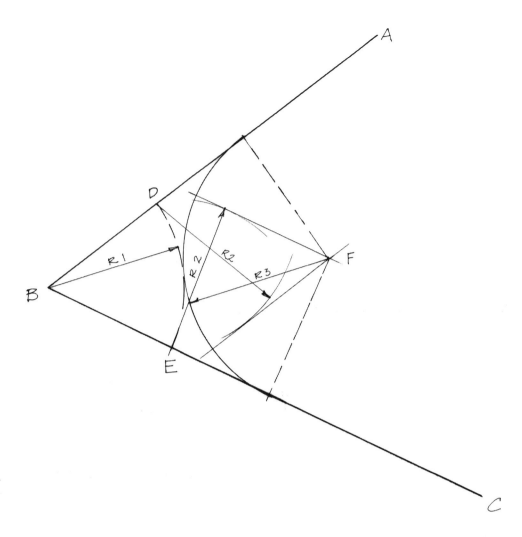

Figure 4.14 To draw a tangent arc to two lines at an acute angle.

point D so that one-half AB equals AD. With D as the center and the radius DB, draw the arc BE cutting AE at E. Line AE is very nearly equal to arc AB.

To Draw a True Ellipse with Given Diameters

Construct the long diameter AB, or the major axis of the ellipse, and the short diameter CD, or the minor axis of the ellipse, so that they intersect at right angles to each other at the center of the ellipse, point O. With O as the center and OD as the radius, draw a circle. Then, with O as the center and OA as the radius, draw another circle.

The establishment of one ellipse point is shown in the upper right-hand quadrant of Figure 4.16. Draw a diagonal line OX at any angle through both circles. Where the line intersects the large circle, point X, drop a vertical line. Where the line intersects the smaller circle, point Y, draw a horizontal line. The point where the horizontal and vertical lines intersect, point Z, is one point on the ellipse.

The completed ellipse is drawn by establishing a series of points on its circumference. After you have located a series of points, fit a French curve to the points to draw the edge of the ellipse.

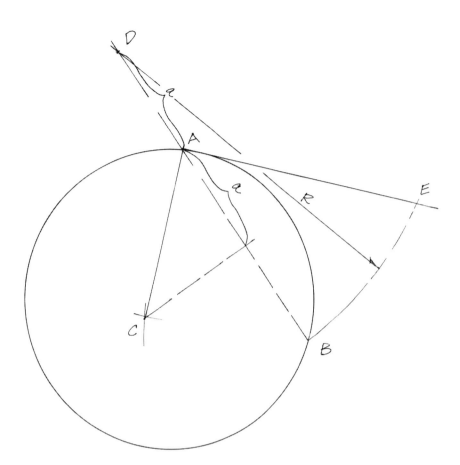

Figure 4.15   To find a straight line equal to the circumference of a given arc.

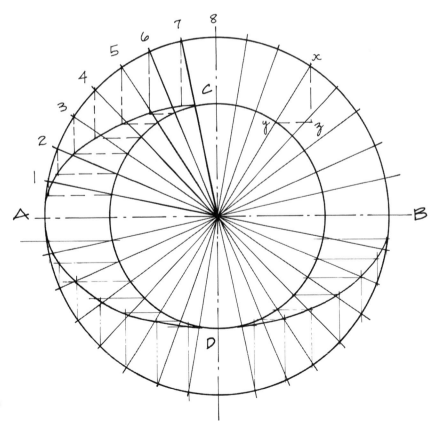

Figure 4.16   To draw a true ellipse with given diameters.

5

Scale

Draftspersons often use a photocopy machine to enlarge or reduce images by percentage increments. Rather then reducing a drawing to a specific scale, they may reduce a drawing to a convenient size to fit on a fax machine. They may work internationally and need to quickly translate a drafting from American Standard Measurement to metric scale. For these reasons, among others, it is essential for the modern designer/draftsperson not merely to use common scales but also to understand the nature of scale.

As it would be impractical to draft large items in their full size, a smaller increment of measurement is often chosen to represent a larger distance. (Or, on a small object, a larger length is chosen to represent a smaller distance.) It is important to understand that as long as the relationship between the longer and shorter measurements remains constant, *any* length can become the basic module for a scale. There are thus an infinite number of possible scales.

Once a scale is established, all measurements between the actual size and the reduced or enlarged representational size remain in proportional relationship: If one-half the actual size equals the scale size, then one-quarter of the actual size equals one-half the scale size, and so on. Graphically, this principle can be illustrated by drawing a line of any length on a piece of paper and calling it a foot. Half of the line would be 6 inches. One quarter of the line would then be 3 inches, and so on. You could say that the same line represented a meter, a 100 centimeters. If so, one-half the length of the line would then equal 50 centimeters, and one-quarter of the length of the line would equal 25 centimeters.

Ancient Greek and Roman Scale

In the Greek and Roman architectural orders, the basic measuring unit was called a module (from the Latin word *modus*, meaning a measure). The module was equal to one-half of the diameter of a column and was subdivided into 30 equal parts.

The primary unit of measurement for ancient Greek and Roman scale was thus based on an architectural element common to all their buildings rather then on a specific measurement. By scaling in this manner, once they determined the most elegant of architectural proportions for a single building, they could duplicate the proportions in all their buildings.

Graphic Scale as Opposed to Numeric Scale

In the illustration of a Grecian Corinthian column in Figure 5.1, at the bottom of the left side, there is a graphic scale showing a length that

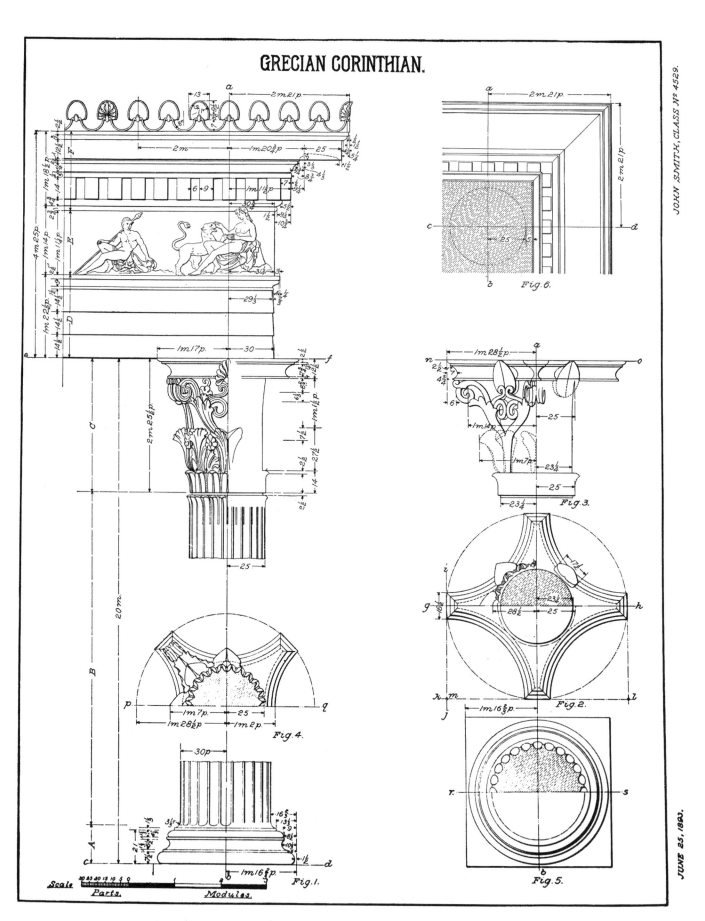

GRECIAN CORINTHIAN.

Figure 5.1   Greek architectural order with a graphic scale. The above plate is reprinted from "Advanced Architectural Drawing," *The Elements of Architectural Drawing and Design, Vol. II.* The Colliery Engineer Co. Scranton, PA, 1899, p. 9. Prepared for Students of The International Correspondence Schools.

represents a module. This module sets the scale for measuring the drawing. It is subdivided into 30 parts for finer measurements. You can consider a graphic scale a small ruler that can be used to measure any part of the drafting.

Although the contemporary draftsperson draws in American Standard Measurement or metric numerical scales, it is often valuable for him or her to include a graphic scale along with and sometimes instead of the numerical scale.

As a drafting is enlarged or reduced by mechanical or electronic means, a graphic scale adjusts along with the drawing, but the numerical or written scale stays the same. However, a graphic scale can only give you an approximate measurement; it won't be as exact as a written measurement.

As a scale can be based on any unit of length, it can be based on lengths of common metric scales. You can thus use a graphic scale to help you quickly (but only approximately) adjust a drafting from American Standard Measurement to metric or from metric to American Standard Measurement scale.

The Proportional Relationship of Scale

Figure 5.2 is a visual illustration of how the size of a picture, or its scale, may change while the proportions of the drawing remain constant. This geometric principle is illustrated in the following manner: Draw a rectangle around any image. Draw a diagonal line through that rectangle. Intersect the horizontal and vertical lines at any point along the diagonal and the resulting rectangle will be in the same proportion as the original rectangle.

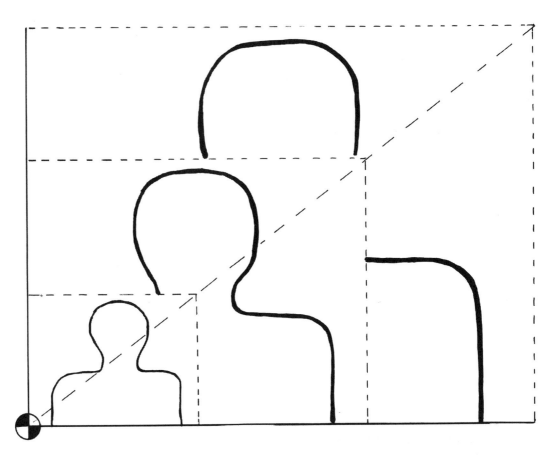

Figure 5.2 The proportional relationship of scale.

43

The Geometrical Calculation of Scale

This geometric principle is used when you have any rectangular image, one side of which you plan to enlarge or reduce to a specific length, and you need to find out the change in the length of the other side.

To find the exact size of any enlargement or reduction, enclose any shape in a rectangle. Draw and extend a diagonal line through the rectangle. Draw a vertical line at the desired height of the rectangle, or a horizontal line at the desired width of the rectangle, until it intersects the diagonal. The remaining side will also intersect the diagonal at the same point where its length can be measured. (See Figure 5.3.)

The Mathematical Calculation of Scale

You can calculate this proportional relationship between mathematically by using the formulae in Figure 5.4.

The Proportional Scale Wheel

To use a photocopy or Photostat machine to change the size of a drawing, you need to set the percentage of enlargement or reduction. A simple circular plastic tool called a proportional scale wheel allows you to quickly calculate the percentage change in size (Figure 5.5). You operate

Figure 5.3   The geometric calculation of scale.

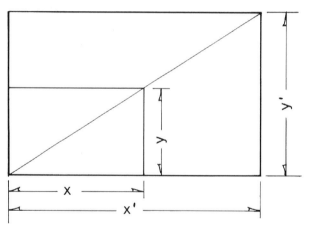

FORMULAE

$$\frac{x}{y} = \frac{x'}{y'}$$

EXAMPLE

LET x' = 3 AND y' = 9   MAKE y = 15

$$\frac{x}{15} = \frac{3}{9}$$

$$9x = 3 \cdot 15$$
$$9x = 45$$
$$x = 5$$

Figure 5.4   Mathematical calculation of scale.

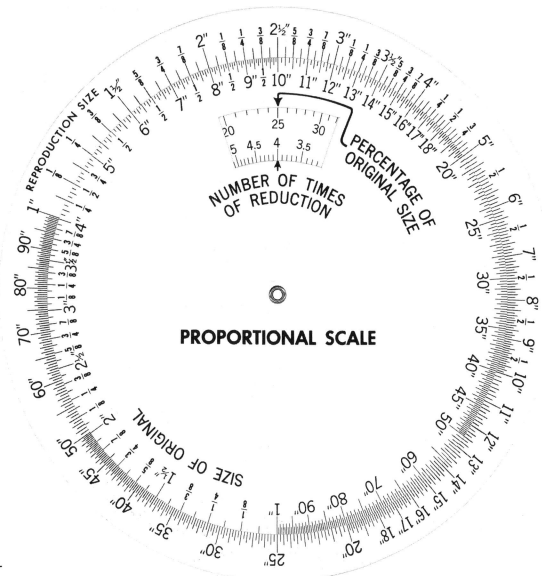

Figure 5.5 The proportional scale wheel.

it by finding the existing numerical size of one side of your drawing on the inner wheel. You then revolve the wheel until this measurement lines up with the measurement you want it to become, locating the number on the outer perimeter of the plastic circle. When the two numbers are aligned, the percentage of the enlargement or reduction appears in a small square toward the center of the plastic circle.

Example: We have a drawing with one side measuring 8 inches. We want to reduce it to 2 inches. By revolving the number 8 on the inner wheel until it lines up with the number 2 on the perimeter of the circle, as in Figure 5.5, we see in the small square the percentage reduction of 25%.

Determining the Scale of a Photographic Image

Sometimes a draftsperson needs to treat a photograph as if it were an elevation. He or she may wish, for example, to scenically recreate a particular architectural structure. In order to do this, the draftsperson will first need to determine the approximate scale of the photograph.

To determine the scale of the photograph, the draftsperson/designer must either know the exact measurement of one item in the picture, or guess the approximate measurement of a common object in the picture. An exact measurement might be found by measuring the height of a door on the wall that was later photographed. An approximate measurement might be the assumption that a door in the photograph was about 7 feet tall, or that a person near the wall was about 6 feet tall. The length of the known measurement is subdivided until a foot increment is established. This length is essentially a graphic scale, which can be used to measure the entire surface.

In Figure 5.6a, for example, we want to estimate the size of the tree in the picture. In Figure 5.6b, we assume that the figure of a man standing near the tree is 6 feet tall, then we draw a line equal to his height that we divide into six equal parts, each part representing one foot. Since the tree is an organic shape, we use the length representing a foot to overlay a grid of foot increments. The height of the tree measures approximately 11 feet and 3 inches tall.

American Standard Measurement

In the United States and some English-speaking countries, the basic unit of measurement is a foot, based on the length of an average-sized man's foot. The foot is subdivided into 12 equal units called inches, each approximately the size of the last joint of the middle finger of a man of average size. A yard, which is 3 feet, was primarily used for measuring cloth and is the approximate distance between fist and shoulder with the arm extended. A bolt of cloth could thus be held in one hand and yard lengths rapidly pulled out and counted. American Standard measurements are difficult to work with mathematically since they are based on a division of 12 rather then 10, but they are easy to estimate since they are based on the size of the human body. Some designers have

Figure 5.6a Determining the approximate scale of an object.

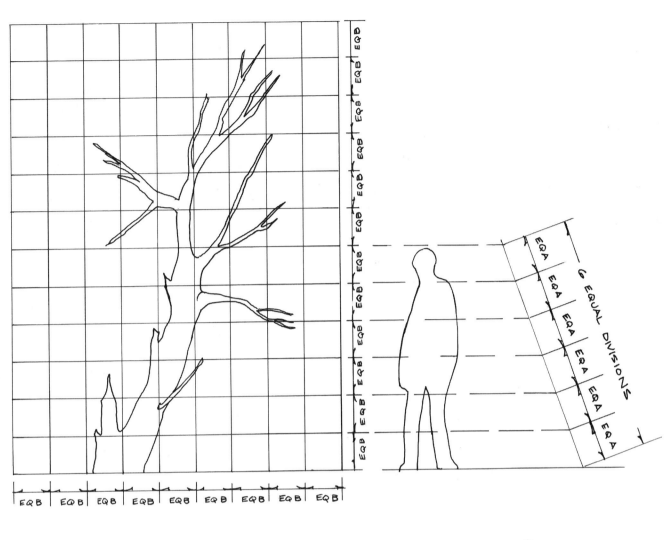

SCALE GRID

GRAPHIC SCALE

EACH UNIT IS APPROXIMATELY ONE FOOT LONG

Figure 5.6b Determining the approximate scale of an object.

developed a 3-foot stride, which they use to pace the length of a room to get a quick (but inexact) measurement.

Commonly Used American Standard Scenic Scales

The commonly used American Standard scenic scales are simple divisions of a foot or of an inch: 1 inch, 1/2 inch, 1/4 inch, or 1/8 inch representing a foot; or, for closer views, 1 1/2, 3, or 6 inches representing a foot.

Figure 5.7 shows part of an American Standard ruler and the divisions within an inch that are commonly used as scales. Using a common ruler to measure in different scales will help the beginning draftsperson understand the principles of scale. Since a scale ruler may not always be available, it is also useful for all draftspeople/designers to be able to use a common ruler to measure a scaled drawing.

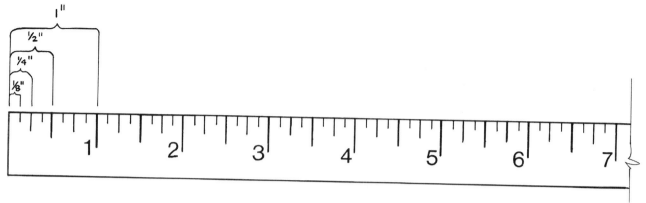

Figure 5.7 Commonly used American Standard scenic scales.

The Larger the Image, the Greater Detail Required

The scale that is chosen for a specific drawing determines the amount of detail needed to describe an object. As the image of a drawing enlarges, greater specificity of detail is required. Designers use smaller scales for initial designing so they can concentrate on shape rather than detail. As a design develops, ever-larger scales are chosen to describe smaller areas of the object in greater detail.

Scenic Scale Conventions

There are certain scales that are commonly used for specific types of scenic drafting:

Full Size		1:1 Ratio
12″	=	1′–0″
6″	=	6″
3″	=	3″

A full-size (1:1) drawing shows the actual size of an object. Because it is usually a large, drawn image, it is used to draw specific details such as baseboard or cornice moldings, structural connections or joints, or complete small objects such as period door hardware. A full size detail allows the builder to easily modify the construction by drawing on top of a blueprint. Most film detailing on the West Coast is done full size, without dimensioning but with stock molding shapes specified. Most film detailing and much theatrical detailing on the East Coast is done full size, with the sizes of lumber dimensioned and the stock moldings specified.

6″=1′-0″		1:2 Ratio One-Half Size
6″	=	1′–0″
3″	=	6″
1 1/2″	=	3″
3/4″	=	1 1/2″
1/2″	=	1″
1/4″	=	1/2″
1/8″	=	1/4″
1/16″	=	1/8″

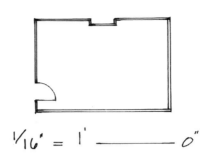

1/16" = 1' —————— 0"

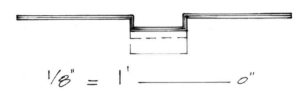

1/8" = 1' —————— 0"

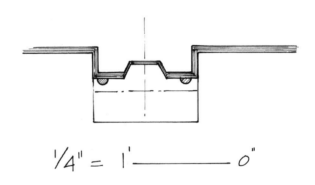

1/4" = 1' —————— 0"

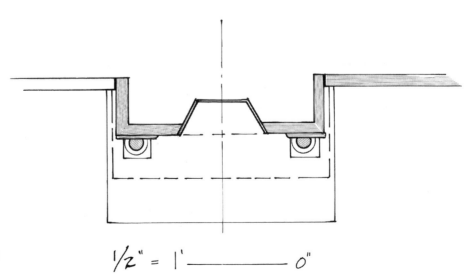

Figure 5.8a   Larger scales require and show greater detail.

1/2" = 1' —————— 0"

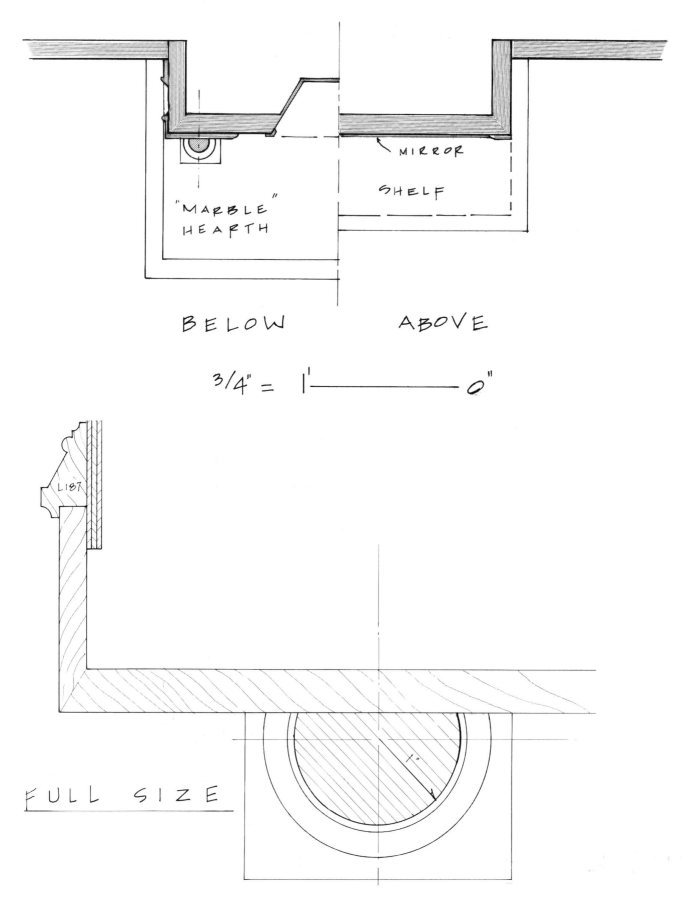

"MARBLE" HEARTH

MIRROR

SHELF

BELOW   ABOVE

3/4" = 1'————————0"

L187

FULL SIZE

1"

Figures 5.8b and 5.8c   Larger scales require and show greater detail.

A 6-inches-to-the-foot or one-half-size drafting is rarely used to draw large-size details. A full-size drawing, even with match lines or removed sections with break lines, is easier for a builder or technical director to comprehend and, if necessary, adjust.

3″=1′-0″		1:4 Ratio	One-Quarter Size
3″	=	1′–0″	
1 1/2″	=	6″	
3/4″	=	3″	
1/2″	=	2″	
1/4″	=	1″	
1/8″	=	1/2″	
1/16″	=	1/4″	

A one-quarter-size scale is rarely used. It might used for a very large piece of detailing that needs to be seen as a complete shape, such as a curved Victorian bracket. However, not drawing the bracket full size would require the builder or scenic artist to proportionally enlarge it before building. This scale is favored by on-site builders, as 1/4 inch on a tape measure equals 1 inch on the drafting drawing.

1 1/2″=1′-0″		1:8 Ratio
1 1/2″	=	1′-0″
3/4″	=	6″
1/2″	=	4″
1/4″	=	2″
1/8″	=	1″
1/16″	=	1/2″

The 1:8 ratio/1 1/2″ scale is occasionally used for medium-size drawings of complex scenic elements that you wish to show in their entirety, such as a window or a fireplace. On-site builders favor this scale, as 1/8 inch on their tape measure equals 1 inch on the drafting.

1″=1′-0″		1:12 Ratio
1″	=	1′-0″
1/2″	=	6″
1/4″	=	3″
1/8″	=	1 1/2″
1/16″	=	3/4″

The 1:12 ratio/1″ scale is also used for medium-size drawings of complex scenic elements, such as a window or a fireplace.

3/4″=1′-0″		1:16 Ratio
3/4″	=	1′-0″
1/2″	=	8″
1/4″	=	4″
1/8″	=	2″
1/16″	=	1″

The 1:16 ratio/3/4″ scale is a good choice of scale for detailed wall elevations that need to be larger then the 1:12/1/2″ scale. In

film drafting, this scale is commonly used to draw larger-sized elevations of doors, windows, and other scenic pieces. On-site builders who do not want to deal with a scale ruler prefer this scale for elevations and ground plans as each 1/16 inch on a tape measure equals 1 inch.

1/2"=1'-0"		1:24 Ratio
1/2"	=	1'-0"
1/4"	=	6"
1/8"	=	3"
1/16"	=	1 1/2"

The 1:24 ratio/1/2" scale is the scale most often used in theatrical drafting as it is large enough to clearly indicate detail without having to be totally specific about it. In theatrical drafting, the master ground plan, the cross-section, and the wall elevations are commonly drawn in this scale.

1/4"=1'-0"		1:48 Ratio
1/4"	=	1'-0"
1/8"	=	6"
1/16"	=	3"
1/32"	=	1 1/2"

The 1:48 ratio/1/4" scale is often used for preliminary drafting, as its small size allows the designer to avoid details and concentrate on the overall design.

Plans and elevations for film drafting are commonly done in 1/4-inch scale rather than 1/2-inch scale. In a studio situation the plan is drawn in 1/4-inch scale and completely dimensioned so the carpenters can draw it out on the studio floor. Elevations are then drawn in 1/4-inch scale with height dimensions but with no width dimensions, as these are taken off the floor layout in the studio. If scenery is being built in a shop and then installed at a location, it is common to dimension widths on both the plan and the elevations.

Plans and elevations for television scenery, which is usually fairly simple, on both the East and West Coast are usually drafted in 1/4 inch. Often the plan is drawn and labeled in 1/4-inch scale with the walls elevated above the plan in 1/2-inch scale.

1/8"=1'-0"	1:96 Ratio

This scale is most often used to give a simple plan overview. The layout of multiple sets in a studio is commonly drawn in 1/8-inch scale. It is also often used to draw multiple-shift plots for a musical. Some designers like to draw preliminary elevations in this scale, as it allows them to eliminate detail and concentrate on the big picture.

1/16"=1"-0"	1:192 Ratio

This scale might be chosen to draw the plan of a large location, such as several city blocks.

Geometrical Principles of Numerical Scale

The principle that geometric scale is a proportional continuum and that common numerical scales are certain specific points on that continuum is shown in Figure 5.9.

The Architectural Scale Ruler

Although a regular ruler can be used to draw or read a scaled drawing, the lengths of the common numerical scales are laid out on an architect's scale ruler in a form that is more exact and easier to read.

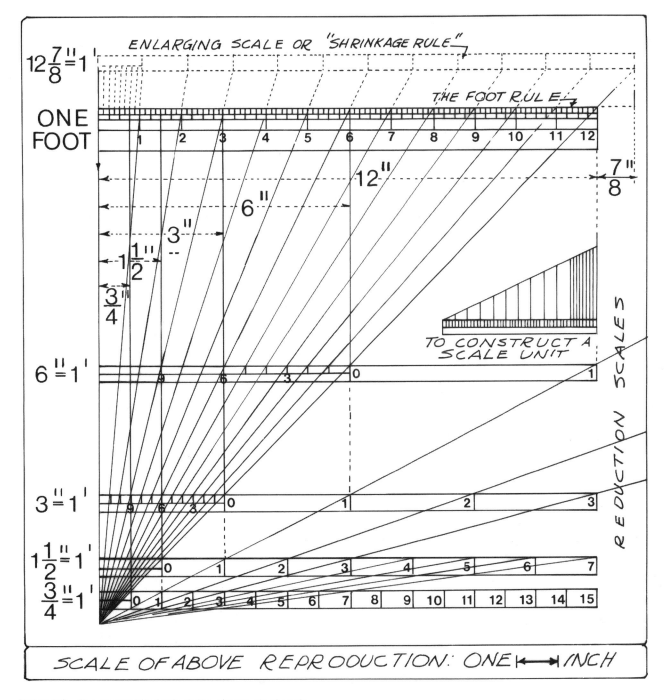

Figure 5.9 The geometrical principles of numerical scale.

Architectural scales are shaped as a three-sided triangle or a two-sided bevel. See Figure 5.10. The draftsperson chooses the one which he or she feels more comfortable using.

Each scale ruler has two scales laid out on either end of each side. A scale that is twice the size of a smaller scale is laid out on the same side but reads in the opposite direction. For example, the 1/4-inch scale reads from right to left, and the 1/8-inch scale reads from left to right on the same side. This is confusing at first, but on closer inspection, you will note that the numerical values of the smaller scale are always written above and are in a smaller font than those of the larger. In addition to the lines and numerals representing feet, each scale on the ruler has a foot increment behind the zero mark that is subdivided into smaller divisions, which represent inches. On the larger scales, numerals are written at the 3-, 6-, and 9-inch divisions, and there are 1/2-inch marks between the inches for fine measurement. On the smaller scales of the ruler, the inch markings are progressively simplified and the fractional divisions are eliminated.

Using the Architectural Scale Ruler

To draw a measured line or to measure the distance of a line you will have to measure the feet first and then the inches. Marks representing feet will be ahead of the numeral 0 on the ruler while marks representing inches will be behind it. You will need to slide your ruler until the relationship between the feet and the inches is correctly aligned.

Several distances are laid out in Figure 5.10 so that you can see how a specific length of feet and inches is measured along the edge of a scale ruler.

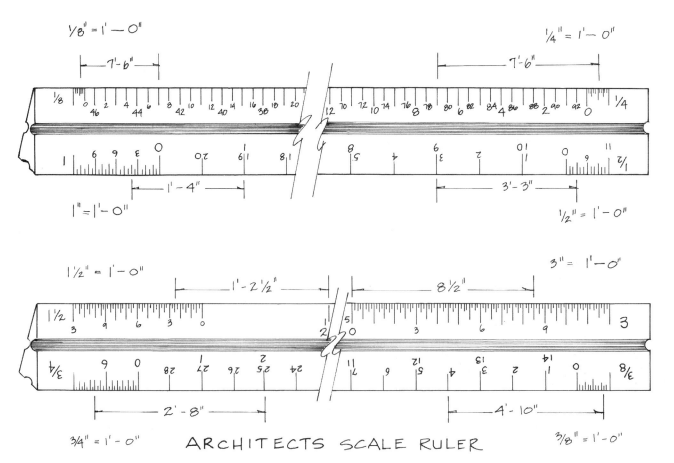

Figure 5.10 The architectural scale ruler.

Specialty Scale Rulers

The opera scale ruler is exactly like a regular scale ruler except it is 36 inches long. It is very useful for measuring long distances on a drafting without having to keep moving the scale and adding lengths together.

They also make short scale rulers about 4 inches long that easily fit into a bag or your pocket.

Proportional Dividers

Proportional dividers enable the draftsperson to quickly transfer measurements from one scale to another. There is an adjustable fulcrum with which you can set the ratio.

For example, to enlarge from 1/4-inch scale to 1/2-inch scale, as in Figure 5.11, you adjust the fulcrum of the dividers so that the shorter side opens a quarter of an inch and the longer opens a half inch.

Metric Measurement

Metric measurement is the International Standard of Measurement. Metric measurement is used throughout the world; the United States is the only country that is not metric. England is using the metric system more and more. As scenic designers are increasingly working with or in other countries, it is important that draftspeople understand the metric system and can use a metric scale ruler.

The basic unit of the metric system is the meter, an abstract length measured as one ten-millionth of the distance from the earth's equator to its pole. The meter, like the American foot, is subdivided, but it is divided into 10 rather then 12 equal parts, which makes it easy to work with mathematically.

Divisions of the Metric Scale

1 meter (m) =	10 decimeters (dm) =	100 centimeters (cm) =	1000 millimeters (mm)
1 decimeter (dm) =	10 centimeters (cm) =	100 millimeters (mm)	
1 centimeter (cm) =	10 millimeters (mm)		

It is difficult for a designer trained in feet and inches to visualize metric distances just as it is difficult for a designer trained in metric to visualize in feet and inches. The designer/draftsperson drawing in the unfamiliar language will find it helpful to purchase a tape measure with American Standard divisions on one side of the tape and metric divisions on the other. You can also purchase a computer that converts between American Standard and metric. While this can help in direct translation, what poses a greater difficulty are the numerous agreed upon sizes of common objects. For example, we have decided that a standard, modern, American interior door will be 6 feet 8 inches tall, and we visualize the rise of a step in inches.

The Figure 5.12 illustrates the visual relationship between inches and centimeters.

Figure 5.11 Proportional dividers.

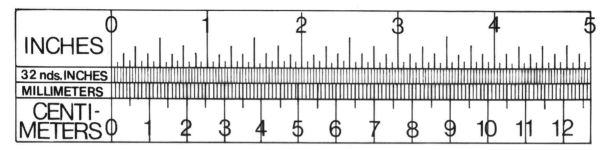

Figure 5.12   Comparing an American Standard and metric ruler.

Metric to American Standard Conversion

Unit	Abbreviation	Length in Meters	Approx. U.S. Equivalent
millimeter	mm	0.00010	0.039 inch
centimeter	cm	0.01	0.39 inch
decimeter	dm	0.1	3.94 inches
meter	m	1	39.37 inches (1.1 yards)
decameter	dm	10	32.81 feet
hectometer	hm	100	109.36 yards
kilometer	km	1000	0.62 miles

American Standard to Metric Conversion

1/16 inch	=	1.5875 mm
1/8 inch	=	3.175 mm
1/4 inch	=	6.35 mm
1/2 inch	=	9.70 mm
1 inch	=	25.4 mm or 2.54 cm
1 foot	=	304.8 mm or 30.48 cm
1 yard	=	914.4 mm or 91.44 cm
1 mile	=	160.93 dm

American Standard/Metric Calculators

There are several good electronic calculators that convert between American Standard and metric. Most construction calculators include metric calculations and conversion.

Metric Scales

Since the metric system is based on mathematical units of 10 rather than 12, it has many more convenient scales than does the American Standard system of measurement. Metric scales are especially valuable when dealing with very small-scaled units such as those needed for engineering precision, or very large-scaled units such as those used for making maps.

The scales of 1:1 (full size) and 1:2 (half size) are easily recognized by both metric and American Standard draftspeople. Figure 5.13 shows a visual relationship between several other commonly used scenic metric scales, as well as their relationship to American Standard scenic scales. For this illustration the American man, shown in the 1/4" and 1/2" scale, is drawn at 6 feet, and the metric man is drawn at 1 meter and 80 centimeters.

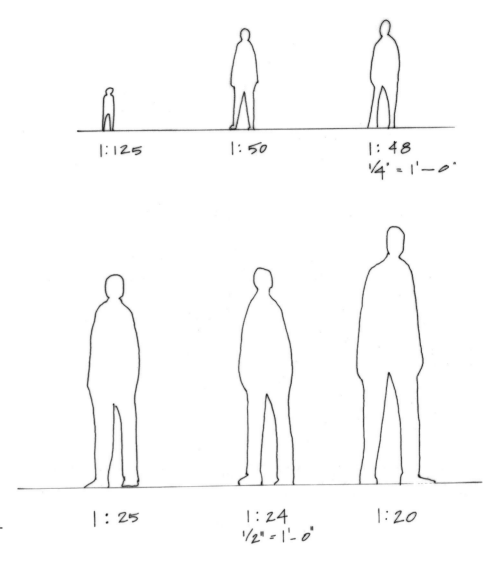

Figure 5.13 The relationship of metric and American Standard scales.

The metric scale of 1:50 is the scale of choice for small scenic drawings. It is slightly smaller than the 1:48 of the American Standard 1/4″=1′. The metric scale of 1:25 is slightly smaller than the 1:24 of American Standard 1/2″=1′. However, the metric scale of 1:20 is the scale of choice for most final metric scenic elevations.

Since there are many possible metric-drafting scales, when purchasing a metric scale ruler, be certain it has the scales that you want. (See Figures 5.14a and 5.14b.) As a single scale ruler has a limited number of scales, you may need to purchase more than one ruler. The metric scale ruler works like the American Standard scale ruler, but its primary measurements are in meters and centimeters (1:8 m means 1 meter and 8 centimeters).

The engineer's scale ruler is a scale ruler that attempts to alleviate the problems of drafting very large or very small distances using American Standard scales. An engineer's scale ruler is a good instrument to use if you are drafting the ground plan of a film location for a very large area, such as several city blocks, or several acres of land. In the engineer's scale, each inch is divided into 10 rather than 12 units (Figure 5.15). Units of 1 inch on the scale are divided into 10, 20, 30, 40, 50, or 60 equal parts. You decide that 1″ equals 10 feet or 100 feet, or whatever length is a convenient size for your drawing.

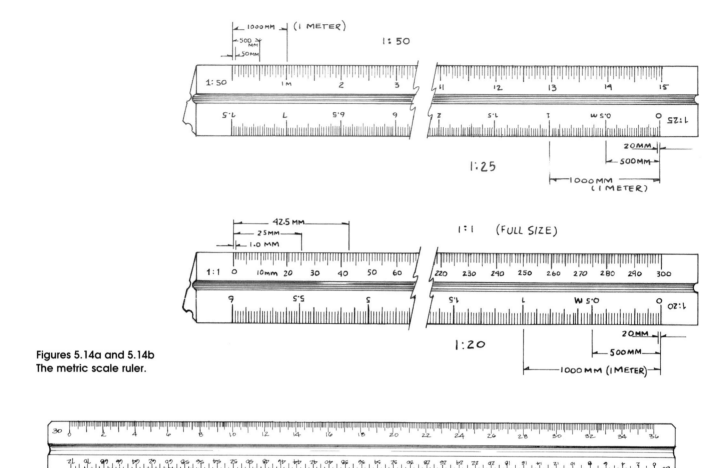

Figures 5.14a and 5.14b
The metric scale ruler.

Figure 5.15   The engineer's scale ruler.

6

Lettering

The Basic Block Lettering Style

The quality of the lettering on a sheet of drafting is the first indication of the level of the draftsperson's professionalism.

Lettering should be clear and easy to read without confusing stylistic embellishments. Single stroke vertical block lettering of uniform height, proportion, spacing, and line weight has become the basic lettering style for scenic drafting. (See Figure 6.1.) This is also the style of hand-lettering that is used by architects. The letters are roughly the same size as each other and are square, except for the W and M, which are slightly wider than the other letters.

Students should first concentrate on the basic block lettering style. Only when they have mastered it, should they attempt stylistic variations.

Guidelines

To have attractive lettering it is essential that you first draw guidelines. You should draw guidelines not only for all words on your sheet of drafting but also for all the numerals of your dimensions. The purpose of guidelines is to keep similar lettering the same height and to keep all lettering horizontal on a sheet. The top and bottom lines of guidelines are used to guide horizontal top and bottom strokes.

Some draftspeople prefer to draw light guidelines with a very hard lead, such as a 4H, while others are able to get both light and dark lines

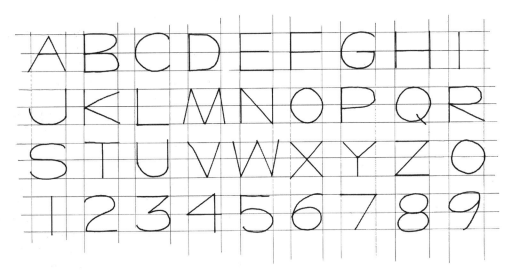

Figure 6.1 Vertical block lettering alphabet.

"DRAFTING FOR ENGINEERS" BY SVENSEN

"REGARDLESS OF HOW SKILLFULLY THE LINE WORK OF A DRAWING MAY HAVE BEEN EXECUTED, ITS APPEARANCE AND USEFULNESS ARE PRACTICALLY RUINED BY POOR LETTERING. ON THE OTHER HAND WELL FORMED LETTERS AND FIGURES WILL GREATLY IMPROVE THE APPEARANCE OF ANY DRAWING EVEN THOUGH THE LINE WORK BE POOR; HOWEVER THIS IS NO EXCUSE FOR POOR WORK. THE PRIMARY PURPOSE OF LETTERS AND FIGURES IS TO GIVE INFORMATION AS TO SIZE LOCATION, ACCURACY, MATERIAL, KINDS OF FINISH, METHODS OF ASSEMBLING, NUMBER REQUIRED, VARIOUS NOTES, AND TITLES."

Figure 6.2 Vertical block lettering example.

LETTERING BY BONNIE BRINKLEY

from a single pencil. Guidelines should be dark enough so that you can just see them, but so light that they barely print or don't print at all.

When lettering several rows of words, always leave blank rows between lettered rows.

Size of Lettering

Adjust the height of your letters to the scale of your drafting. Drafting in a small scale should have smaller-sized lettering than drafting in a larger scale, otherwise the image will overpower the words. A 3/16-inch-high guideline is a good height for a 1/2-inch scale drafting.

The labeling of views such "Courthouse Plan" or "Section A-A" can be larger than less important information such as dimension numerals or notes.

All similar types of information should be the same size: all dimension numerals the same size; all notes the same size; and so on.

You may find it helpful to make a series of measured marks on a strip of strong paper to transfer guideline measurements to a sheet of drafting. Eventually you will be able to draw accurately spaced guidelines by eye.

Lettering Guides

Although most professional scenic draftspeople find lettering guides more trouble than they are worth, several types are sold to draw guidelines. These instruments can help the beginning draftsperson train his or her eye to space guidelines accurately. All of them are small plastic triangles with a series of measured holes at regular intervals. (Many draftspeople do not take the time to switch to a small triangle when lettering, using their large adjustable triangle to draw verticals instead.) The Ames Lettering Guide has a small plastic triangle that can be revolved to adjust the height of the guidelines. A sharp, hard lead point or pencil is placed in the holes and the guide slid along a parallel rule. The pencil is then placed in the next hole to draw the next line.

Technique of Lettering

Some draftspeople do both drafting and lettering with a single, usually 2H, lead or pencil. Others prefer to letter with a softer pencil such as an HB. If you use different lead weights, keep each weight in a different colored lead holder to avoid confusion.

Sharpen your lead or pencil to a fine point. (If your lead tends to break off, it may help to dull the tip slightly on a piece of scratch paper.)

Rest your wrists on the table and hold the pencil securely but freely between your fingers. Hold your pencil firmly but do not tense your fingers, as this will result in awkward lines.

There are only three types of strokes in lettering: vertical, horizontal, and circular. You want to increase the pressure of the lead slightly at the beginning and end of each stroke to give your line character, but your primary aim is a single, loose but secure stroke that results in a clean, unwavering line.

Practice lettering by first concentrating on the three types of strokes, horizontal, vertical, and curved, then by lettering the alphabet, and finally by practice in copying text. If you are having difficulty with the strokes, you may find it helpful to place a sheet of tracing paper over the lettering example in Figure 6.2 or another letter example that you admire, and trace the letters.

All the vertical strokes in lettering should be perpendicular. Many draftspeople use a small (about 3-inch) triangle to draw vertical strokes. They slide the triangle along the parallel and push it out of the way when drawing curved or horizontal strokes.

General Rules for Lettering

Keep all verticals perpendicular to the guidelines. Make certain that the top and bottom horizontal strokes of the letters are drawn along the guidelines or at the same exact angle to the guidelines. See Figure 6.3 for an example of poor lettering of verticals.

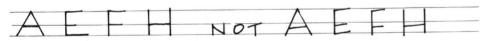

Figure 6.3   Poor lettering verticals.

Figure 6.4   Make the O, C, G, Q, and D fat, filling the whole space.

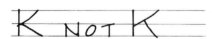

Figure 6.5   Keep the horizontal crossbar of the A, E, F, and H midway between the guideline or slightly above the midpoint.

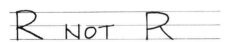

Figure 6.6   Take the arm of the K all the way into the vertical of the K.

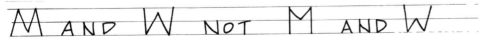

Figure 6.7   Take a lobe of the stem into the vertical of the R.

Figure 6.8   Make the centers of the M and the W touch the guideline.

Figure 6.9 Leave a wedge in the center of the B.

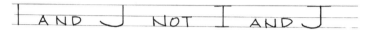

Figure 6.10 Do not put serifs at the top of I or J.

A NOT A   W NOT I/\I

Figure 6.11 Don't leave gaps between the strokes of letters, as it makes them hard to read.

DON'T CROSS STROKES

Figure 6.12 Don't cross the strokes of individual letters, as it makes them hard to read.

Left-Handers

Left-handers must develop their own system of strokes. They may prefer to draw horizontal strokes from right to left and to draw from the bottom up: the base curve of the B, for example, before the top curve so as not to hide the one from the other.

Fractions

Use a slant rather than a horizontal line between fractions. The total height of a fraction should be slightly larger than that of a single numeral. (See Figure 6.13.)

The Oval Lettering Style

There are many stylistic variations of basic block lettering that add interest without confusion. Whichever style you choose, you must be consistent in its application. One common variation of basic block lettering is the oval style, in which all vertical lines remain vertical, all horizontal lines remain horizontal, but the round letters C, D, G, O, and Q are drawn as slightly slanted ovals and the curved lobes of B, P, and R are slanted in the same manner. (See Figure 6.14.)

The Slanted Horizontals Lettering Style

Another common variation is to slant all the horizontals except for Z, which looks odd when it is slanted. (See Figure 6.15.)

Figure 6.13 Lettering fractions.

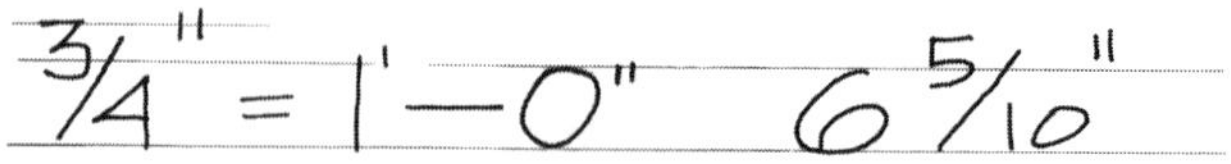

$3/4'' = 1'-0''$ $6 \, 5/10''$

Figure 6.14 The oval style of lettering.

IN ORDER TO DO ARCHITECTURAL WORK,
CLEAR, WELL PROPORTIONED LETTERING
IS AN ABSOLUTE ESSENTIAL.

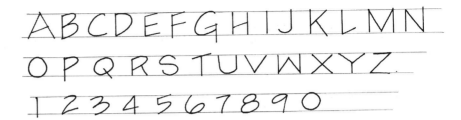

Figure 6.15 Lettering with slanted horizontals.

The Lettering Style of Ovals with Slanted Horizontals

It is possible to combine the oval style with slanted horizontals as in Figure 6.16.

Spacing of Letters

The spacing of individual letters within words is a matter of visual not mechanical balance. (See Figure 6.17.) In this example you can see that the letter A can tuck close to the letters P and C. The letter S can nudge towards P and the letter G can move slightly towards N. In short, attractive lettering is an artistic endeavor. There are no hard and fast rules for spacing, as the draftsperson must adjust the space between letters depending on the shape of the letters.

For purposes of spacing and practicing lettering, it helps to group the letters of the alphabet into the following:

Circular: B-C-D-G-O-P-Q-R-S;
Regular: E-H-I-M-N-U;
and Irregular: A-F-J-K-L-P-R-T-V-W-X-Y-Z.

Letters can also be grouped by:

Normal: C-D-G-H-O-Q-R-U-V-X-Z;
Narrow: B-E-F-I-J-L-P-S-T;
and Wide: A-M-N-W.

Figure 6.16 Oval lettering with slanted horizontals.

Figure 6.17 Optical versus mechanical spacing.

Figure 6.18 The gaps between irregular-shaped letters can be avoided by fitting them closer together according to their shape.

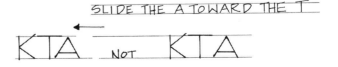

Figure 6.19 Circular and irregular letters should be closer together to compensate for their fat shapes.

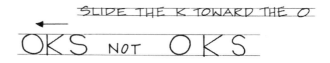

Figures 6.20a and 6.20b Compressing a wide letter to make it fit into a space whose size requires a narrow or normal letter causes it to appear blacker than the rest of the letters, and stretching a narrow letter into the space of a wide one makes it appear lighter than the rest of the letters. These seemingly darker or lighter letters distract the reader.

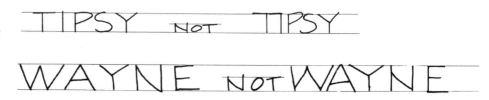

Figure 6.21 Stretching a narrow letter into the space of a wide one makes it appear lighter than the rest of the letters. These seemingly darker or lighter letters distract the reader.

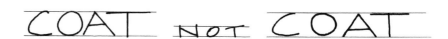

Spacing Between Words

A good rule of thumb for spacing between words is to:

- Keep the space of a single fat O between each word.
- Keep the space of two or three fat Os between sentences.

Layout

When you initially organize the layout of your sheet of drafting, you need to allow spaces for lettering the titles below the view. Lettering, however, is usually the last thing to be added to a sheet.

The position of notes are important. If written information refers to specific parts of the drafting, it should be located nearby and leaders used to point out the specific place to which the note refers. If there is a string of notes with leaders, they should all line up vertically.

If a note is general rather than specific, it can be located to help achieve a visually balanced sheet. Careful location of lettering can offset a lopsided sheet arrangement. Some draftspeople like to box in their general notes for emphasis and clarity.

Keep all of your written information in tight blocks and don't indent it.

Title Blocks

A title block belongs in the lower-right corner of each drafting. A simple title block is a small, about 2-inch-by-4-inch rectangle. (See Figure 6.22.) On expensive productions these blocks may be elaborately designed and extend across the base of the drawing or down the right-hand edge of the drawing.

Critical to all title blocks is the following:

- Number   The sheet number and, if needed, the set identification number belong in the lower-right corner of the block. This allows someone to quickly locate a particular sheet in a stack by flipping through them.

- Drawing Title

  The drawing title is a simple verbal description or name for the drafting. It should be in a large font and easy to locate. Usually it is the first line of the block.

- Scale

  The scale of the drafting should be noted on each title block. If you have used several different scales on a single sheet, you should note each scale beneath its view and in the scale position on the block mark "as noted."

- Production

  The name of the show belongs on each title block.

- Designer

  The name of the designer of the production belongs on each title block.

- Production People and Their Titles

  It is usual for the title block to include the name of the director. Often it includes the producing company and/or the producers. For a film, it may include the production manager and art director. In theatre, it may include the lighting designer and the general manager.

- Design Office Phone and/or Address

  If there are many independent contractors involved in the construction, it helps to include the mailing address and phone of the design office.

- Drawing Date

  On each title block include the date the sheet was turned into the shop. This avoids confusion about when the shop received the information.

- Revision Dates

  In or near the title block you should date the time that a revised drawing is given to the shop. It is also helpful to note a brief description of the revision next to the revised date.

The following are also often included on a title block:

- Draftsperson's Initials

  A small section of the box may be designed for the draftsperson's initials. If there are several draftspeople and the shop has a question about a drawing, the shop then knows which draftsperson to contact.

- Disclaimer

  Disclaimers are notes that help absolve the designer of legal responsibility. A simple disclaimer can say:

  Check Critical Site Measurements

  More complex disclaimers might appear as the following:

  These drawings represent visual concepts and construction suggestions only.

  The designer and his or her employees are unqualified to determine the structural appropriateness of this design and will not assume responsibility for improper engineering, construction, or handling.

  All materials, finishes, and construction must comply with the most stringent fire and safety codes as applicable.

  Written dimensions on drawings shall have authority over scaled dimensions.

  Contractors and manufacturers shall verify and be responsible for all dimensions and conditions on the job and shall inform this office of all variations from drawings prior to performing the work.

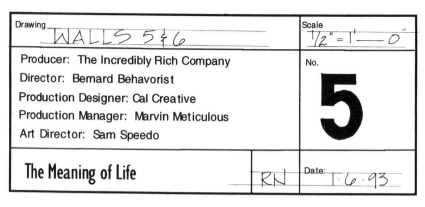

Figure 6.22 A simple title block using reproduction film.

Templates

There are many kinds of thin plastic templates with shapes that can be quickly traced. Among these are:

- Circle templates — Templates of different sizes of circles.

- Ellipses — Templates of different sizes and shapes of ellipses.

- Lettering — 3/4" Pickett Modern Bold Vertical (thin Helvetica). 3/8" Berol R 135 (fat Helvetica).

- Flow process symbols — Arrows, squares, and triangles.

- Theatrical lighting — Plan and sections of lighting instruments in 1/4- and 1/2-inch scale.

- House furniture and office furniture — Plans of modern furniture in 1/4- and 1/2-inch scale. Pickett is a good brand.

- Lavatory planning — Plans and sections of bathroom fixtures. Pickett has a good template.

  The American Standard Plumbing Fixtures template includes a helpful 1/4-inch tile layout.

- Structural steel — A template showing sections of common sizes of steel angles and I-beams in 1-inch scale. Pickett has a good template.

Self-Made Templates

If you find that you are repeatedly using graphic imagery, consider making your own tracing templates to speed up the drafting process. Copy or draw the imagery onto thin paper or clear plastic. Although you can't place these templates on top of your drafting sheets, you can slide them underneath and trace over them. For an individual image that you will use repeatedly, you might want to make a template that can be quickly laid on top of your paper. You can make such a template by copying the imagery onto thin cardboard or medium weight plastic and then use an Exacto knife to cut out a traceable shape.

For example, if you often draft plans with period furniture, you can find 1/4-inch scaled plan drawings in early editions of *Architectural Graphic Standards.* Another example would be the pages in a full-size molding catalogue. If you photocopy them onto separate sheets, you will find it easy to slip them under your drafting. If you photocopy them onto clear acetate, you can flip the molding profile in either direction.

Stamps

Rubber stamps to be used with an ink block can be ordered with any information on them. When using stamps remember that ink, unlike pencil, cannot be removed from a drafting. Common ink stamps are: "Revised," "For Estimate Only," and "Preliminary." Stamps are particularly useful for quickly marking sets of blueprints without affecting the original.

Revisions

For small revisions, some people use a "Revised" stamp such as the one pictured in Figure 6.23. The arrow is stamped pointing to the specific place on a drafting where a revision has occurred. The date of the revision is marked in pencil, inside or just next to the stamp.

If a drawing is likely to have many revisions, a good method of notation is to use a "Revised" stamp and printed reproduction film that includes a small box where you list each revision and the date it was revised, as in Figure 6.24.

Adhesive-Backed Reproduction Film for Xeroxing or Laser-Printing

Reproduction film is an 8 1/2-inch-by-11-inch sheet of translucent film attached to a sticky, opaque back sheet. By photocopying or laser-printing images or words onto reproduction film, a draftsperson can attach pictures or lettering to an original drafting.

Figure 6.23   Revision stamp.

REVISED	
DATE	DESCRIPTION

Figure 6.24   A box designed for noting multiple revisions.

There are several different kinds of adhesive-backed reproduction film. It comes in clear or slightly opaque film, and also in a hard plastic or a soft, flexible plastic meant to take pencil lines.

Productions with many sheets of drafting save time by designing a title block that can be duplicated on reproduction film. Usually the title block is designed in a computer illustration program. Title blocks often include a logo or small piece of clip art. Most of the examples of professional drafting in this book use reproduction film to make title blocks.

To avoid pulling up the edges of your title block with your horizontal rule and to make it easier to write and erase on it, reverse print the image and paste it on the underside rather than the front of your drafting paper.

Reproduction film can be purchased at art stores under many names, including Raven Repro Film, Ad Heer Adhesive Film, and Laser Printable Adhesive Backed Reproduction Film.

Photocopied Vellum Title Edge Strips

A long, elaborate title edge strip can be added to the edge of a vellum original by finding a giant photocopy machine that will duplicate the original strip onto vellum. The edge strips are sliced and attached to each sheet of drafting with matte clear tape.

7

Orthographic Projection

Principles of Orthographic Drawing

The basis of drafting is orthographic or straight-line projection. It allows us to take a three-dimensional idea and express it on a two-dimensional sheet of paper as a measurable drawing. Orthographic projection thus enables a builder to construct an object from a drawing.

The easiest way to visualize orthographic projection is to imagine a glass box containing an object such as a model of a car. Now imagine beams of light from the point of each corner of the object rising straight up and burning small holes in the sides of the glass box. If you then connected the holes with lines as you would do in a follow-the-dot drawing, you would have on each of the glass sides—front, rear, top, bottom, right, and left—a simple flattened view of the object in its true, measurable size and shape with no perspective distortion. It is very important to remember that in orthographic projection the line of sight, or the direction of the point of view, is always taken perpendicular to a plane of projection that sits between the viewer and the object(s) being viewed.

In the theoretical exercise in Figure 7.1, we constructed a flattened, measurable drawing on all sides of a glass box, but the glass box itself remained a three-dimensional shape. In order to transfer the entire box onto a flat sheet of paper we would need to hinge some of the edges of the box and clip some of the others to flatten it out.

You could find several different ways of hinging, cutting, and laying out the six sides of the box. In a similar manner, there are several ways to lay out an orthographic projection on a sheet of paper. To avoid confusion, in the United States we have agreed on a standard layout of the view positions. This layout has the front view in the center, the top view above, the bottom view below, the right side view to its right, the left side view to its left, and the rear view to the left of the left side view. This standard layout is shown in Figure 7.2.

Characteristics of Orthographic Layout

Several characteristics of this orthographic layout are important:

1. In an orthographic drawing of an object, the three spatial dimensions of height, width, and depth remain constant and are the same in all the views.
2. In the standard layout, the position of all width measurements, those for the top, front, and bottom views are in a line, above or below each

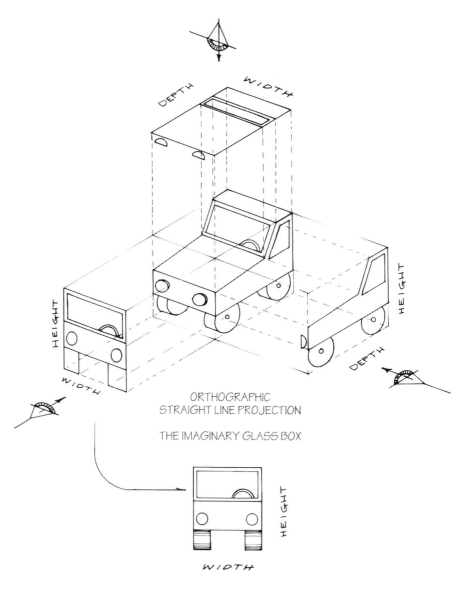

ORTHOGRAPHIC
STRAIGHT LINE PROJECTION

THE IMAGINARY GLASS BOX

ORTHOGRAPHIC LAYOUT

Figure 7.1   The imaginary glass box.

other. This means that any width measurement can be quickly transferred between views by drawing vertical lines.

3. In a similar manner, the position of all height measurements, those for the front, right side, left side, and rear views, are in a line to the right or left of each other. This means that any height measurement can be quickly transferred between views by drawing horizontal lines.

4. While depth measurements remain the same for the top, bottom, right, and left side views, they are not in a line. There are several ways of transferring depth measurements.

Transferring Depth Measurements

When transferring depth measurements between the nonaligned views, you must be careful to take your measurements from the same spatial position. This means that you need to choose an imaginary or real line that will be in the same position in either view and measure widths

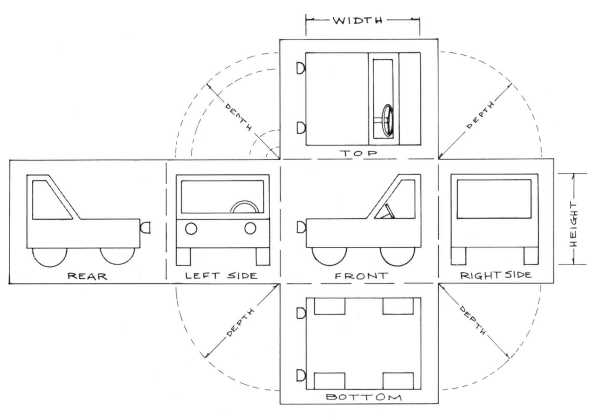

Figure 7.2   Unfolding the imaginary glass box. (This layout is the United States standard layout for view positions.)

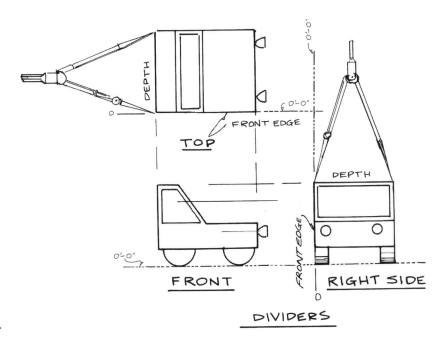

Figure 7.3a   Transferring depth measurements.

from this point. Often the centerline of the object or the nearest edge of an object is chosen to measure from.

There are three methods to transfer depth measurements in non-aligned views. You should learn to use all the methods, as each is most useful for a specific drafting situation.

1. You can use dividers to transfer depth measurements between views. This method is very useful for quick, orthographic sketching

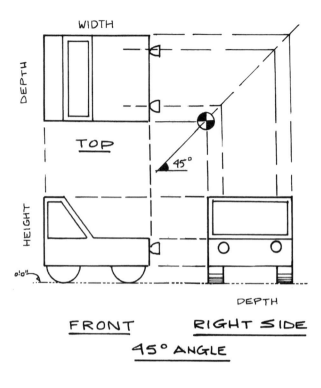

FRONT   RIGHT SIDE

45° ANGLE

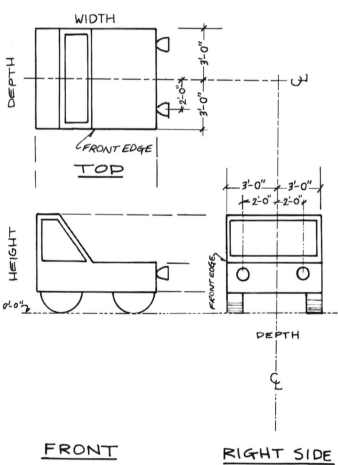

FRONT   RIGHT SIDE

MEASUREMENT

Figures 7.3b and 7.3c   Transferring depth measurements.

when you are working out a shape in three dimensions but are not yet concerned with its measurements. (See Figure 7.3a.)

2. You can use a 45-degree angle to project points between views. Extend the front edge line of the top or bottom view and the front edge of the side view until they intersect. At the point of intersection, draw a 45-degree angle. Any point on the object, if extended to the 45-degree angle, can now be projected to the other view. This method is most useful for working out a sculptural shape such as a scenic train or automobile. (See Figure 7.3b.)

3. You can use a scale ruler to measure a specific depth on one view, and then measure the same depth on the other view. This method is best to draft a final, exact view. (See Figure 7.3c.)

The Drafted Orthographic Layout

When we draft the orthographic layout of an object, we don't draw the edges of the theoretical glass box but separate each view of the object from its adjacent view. Between views, we allow a visually pleasing distance, leaving enough room to add measurements and title views. The draftsperson and the reader of the drafting keep in mind that the flat views are actually "hinged": if they were to meet and join they would create a three-dimensional shape. (See Figure 7.4.)

Often, an orthographic layout contains several repetitive or unneeded views, which are eliminated from the drafting. This is especially true in scenery where we are rarely concerned with the bottom or back of an object.

Figures 7.5 and 7.6 contain two lovely examples of orthographic layout by beginning drafting students at New York University, Tisch

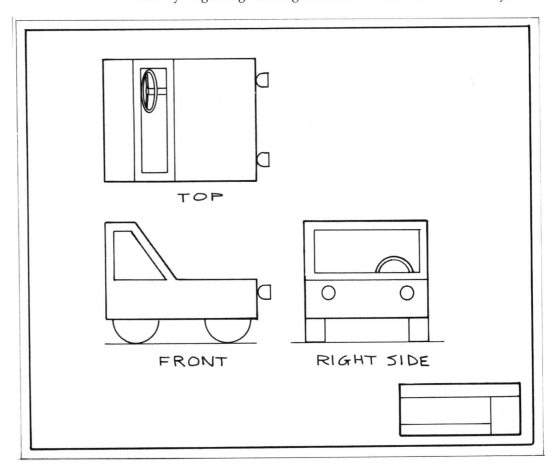

Figure 7.4 Drafted orthographic layout.

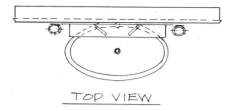

TOP VIEW

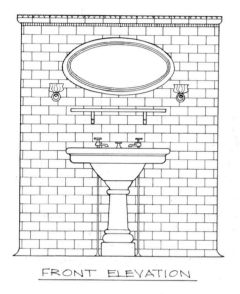

FRONT ELEVATION

RIGHT SIDE

ORTHOGRAPHIC PROJECTIONS	
SCALE: NONE	DWG: M. LOPEZ
DATE: 10·28·86	

Figure 7.5 Orthographic projection of a wall unit and sink by Miguel Lopez, New York University Tisch School of the Arts. Used by permission.

School of the Arts. The drawing of the horse by George Tsypin is particularly interesting as he chose the difficult problem of laying out an organic, sculptural shape on a flat surface.

Orientation of Viewer

It is important to understand that the position of the viewer to the side of the theoretical glass box remains fixed. The line of sight is always perpendicular to the planes of projection. Inside the "glass box," the object can be turned or angled in any direction. See Figure 7.7. *Any* side of the object can become the front elevation. When you are drawing a car, for example, the front of the car may not necessarily be the best choice for the front elevation. You will find that the car lays out better on your sheet when you put the side of the car in the front view position, lining it up with the top view of the car. With this choice, the two longest and most complicated views are adjacent. Since all the orthographic views of an object are fixed, once you choose the front view position of the object the other views are set.

Usually an object is positioned so the front view contains the most informative surface. In scenery, the clearest example of this is the elevation of a wall, which is almost always placed in the front view.

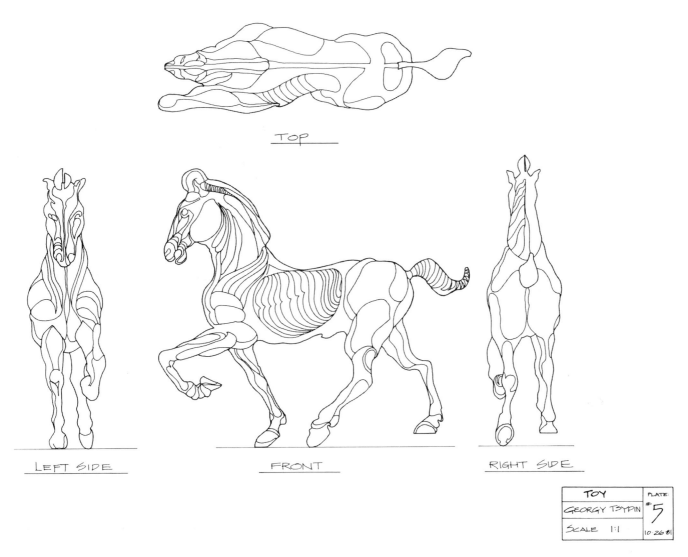

TOP

LEFT SIDE

FRONT

RIGHT SIDE

TOY	PLATE:
GEORGY TSYPIN	#5
SCALE 1:1	10·26·81

Figure 7.6   Orthographic projection of a horse by George Tsypin, New York University TISCH School of the Arts. Used by permission.

Alternate View Position

There is an exception to the standard layout that is often done in drafting scenery. To clarify the drawing of a wide, flat object such as a large platform or a ceiling, the theoretical glass box may be hinged so that the right side view is located directly beside the top view. This layout gives a clear visual relationship between a platform and its height or a ceiling and its angle. (See Figure 7.8.)

Auxiliary Views

In an orthographic projection only the lines on the object that are parallel or perpendicular to the plane of projection appear at their true and therefore measurable length. All other angled lines are distorted, appearing shorter than they really are.

Occasionally a surface of an object is angled so it is not perpendicular to the viewer in one or more of the normal views. In the normal

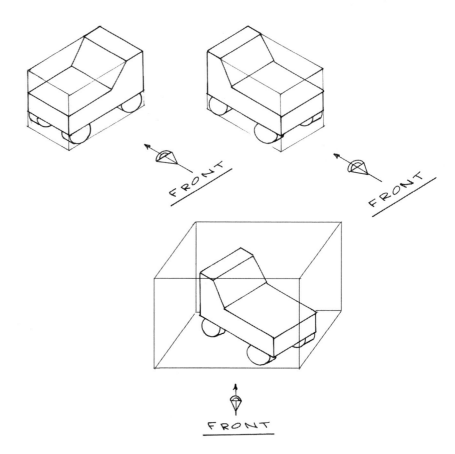

Figure 7.7   Orientation of viewer.

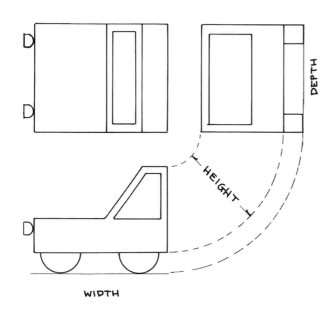

ALTERNATE VIEW POSITION

Figure 7.8   Alternate position.

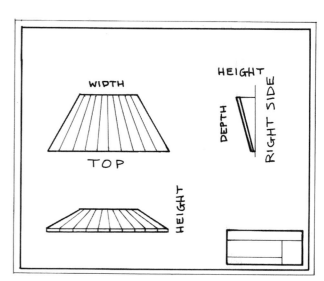

RAKED PLATFORM

SHOWING ALTERNATE VIEW
POSITION

views, this surface is not seen in its true size and shape, and several or all of its edges are angled to the viewer and therefore not measurable. To draft the true size and shape of this surface an auxiliary view must be developed. This view is also called a true view. (See Figure 7.9.)

There is a mechanical method for separately rotating the line of each edge of an inclined surface and reconstructing a true view. However, constructing a true view from an edge line relates directly to orthographic projection and gives the draftsperson more flexibility when designing.

Inclined Planes

An object with an inclined plane has an angled surface. This plane is oriented within the theoretical glass box such that at least one of its side edges is parallel to the plane of projection and perpendicular to the line of sight. This side edge is seen in its true length. This allows us to construct the true view of the plane directly off the edge view.

An example of a simple inclined plane would be a raked square deck on a proscenium stage with the deck measuring 2 inches in height along its front and 12 inches in height along its back. We could see the true length of the front and back edges of the deck in both the top view and the front view. Though the depth of the deck is distorted in the top view, its true length is seen as the top edge of the side view. (See Figure 7.10.)

Skewed Planes

An object with a skewed plane also has an angled surface. It is oriented within the theoretical glass box so that none of its side edges are parallel to the plane of projection or perpendicular to the line of sight. If you

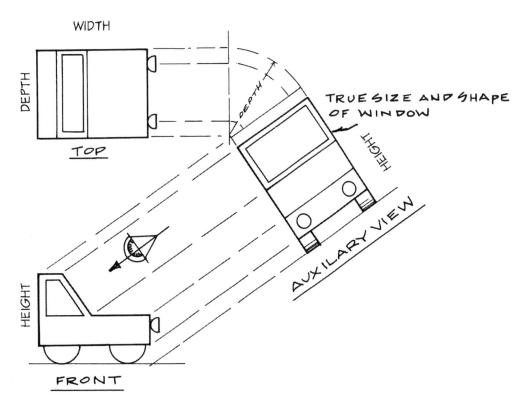

Figure 7.9 Auxiliary view.

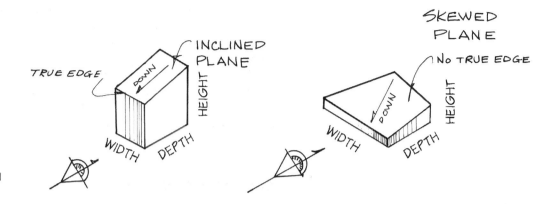

Figure 7.10 Inclined and skewed planes.

took the raked deck we described earlier and rotated it very slightly within the glass box, say about 10 degrees, its angled surface would be a skewed plane. The edges of the skewed plane are never seen in their true and measurable length.

To draw the true shape of a skewed plane you must construct a theoretical line through a view of the object. This theoretical line must be parallel to the plane of projection and perpendicular to the viewer. The position of the perpendicular lines are then drawn from the corner points of the object to the theoretical line, and the distance from the corner to the theoretical line is measured. The true view of the skewed surface can then be constructed in another position on the page by drawing the theoretical line and transferring the measurements to the corner points.

Figures 7.11 to 7.14 show how to develop true views of inclined planes. They show how a simple inclined plane progresses to a skewed plane.

In Figure 7.11, the true length of the inclined plane is seen as the top edge in the front view. To develop the true view of the surface, construct perpendicular lines at both ends of the true edge line. Draw a line parallel to the edge line between the perpendiculars. This line will be one long side edge of our true view. The width of the inclined plane is seen in its true length in both the top view and the left side view. From either view, by measuring or using dividers, transfer the width measurements to the true view and complete the sides of the parallelogram.

In Figure 7.12, the true length of the inclined surface is seen as the top edge in the front view. To develop the true view of the surface, construct perpendicular lines at both ends of the true edge line. Draw a line parallel to the edge line between the perpendiculars. This line will be one long side edge of our true view. Width measurements of the inclined plane are seen in their true length in both the top view and the left side view. Since the short sides of the inclined plane are not the same length, we need to measure the widths at both the top and bottom edges, A and B, and transfer the lengths to the true view.

In the example of an inclined plane in Figure 7.13, no edge is seen in its true length in the front view. However, the top edge of the front view is the true length of the inclined plane. The true widths of the short sides of the surface can be seen in both the top and the side edge views. To establish their angle to the side edges, we need to locate the points of their corners perpendicular to a common line.

To develop the true view of the surface, construct perpendicular lines from the top and bottom of the true edge line. In the plan view, draw a line, P, perpendicular to the line of view and at any convenient location,

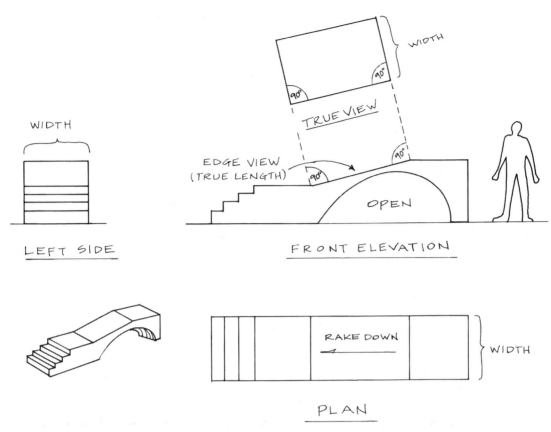

WIDTH

LEFT SIDE

TRUE VIEW

EDGE VIEW
(TRUE LENGTH)

90°

OPEN

FRONT ELEVATION

RAKE DOWN

WIDTH

PLAN

Figure 7.11 The true view of an inclined plane with parallel and perpendicular edges.

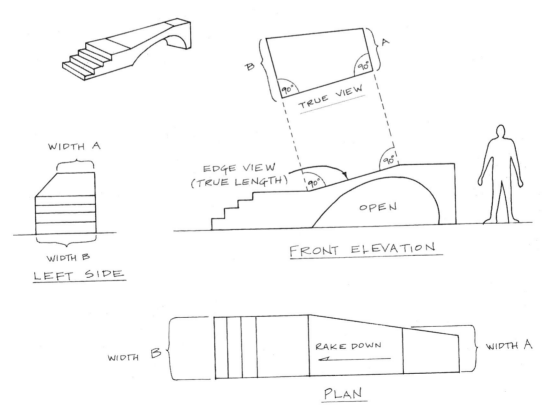

WIDTH A

WIDTH B
LEFT SIDE

B

TRUE VIEW

90°

A

EDGE VIEW
(TRUE LENGTH)

90°

90°

OPEN

FRONT ELEVATION

WIDTH B

RAKE DOWN

WIDTH A

PLAN

Figure 7.12 The true view of an inclined plane with two parallel edges and one edge not perpendicular to the viewer.

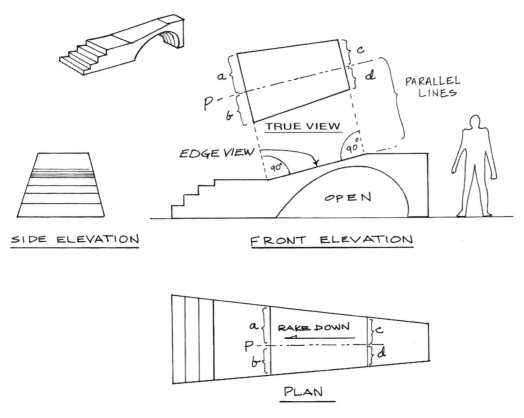

Figure 7.13   True view of an inclined plane with two parallel edges and two edges not perpendicular to the viewer.

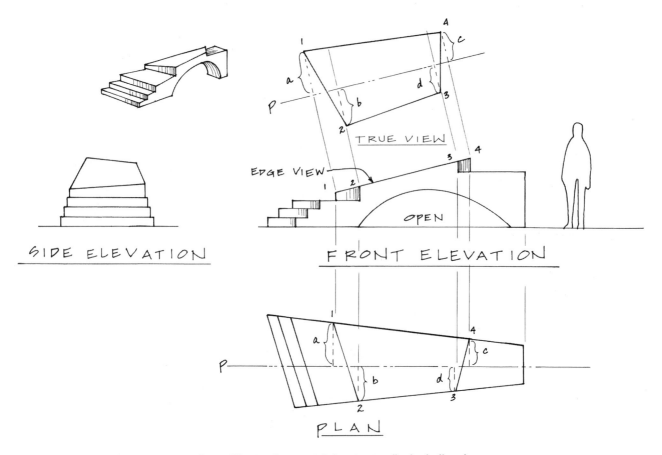

Figure 7.14   True view of a skewed plane with no edges parallel or perpendicular to the viewer.

usually down the middle of the surface plane of the object. At the location of the auxiliary view, draw a line parallel to the edge line through the lines drawn perpendicular to the edge line. Mark this line P as well.

On the plan, measure the widths from line P to each corner, a, b, c, d, and transfer these measurements to the true view. Connect the points, completing the true view.

To develop the true view of an inclined surface we first establish a theoretical line, P-P, parallel to the plane of projection and perpendicular to the line of sight. We then locate the positions of the corners of the plane by measuring them from P-P.

In Figure 7.14, none of the sides of the inclined planes are parallel or perpendicular to the others. However, in the top edge of the front view you see the true length of the inclined plane. As in all orthographic projection, widths are seen in both the plan and side elevation.

To develop the true view of the surface, in the plan view draw a line, P, perpendicular to the line of view and at any convenient location, usually down the middle of the surface. Take each corner point, 1, 2, 3, and 4, on the plan and project them up to the edge line in the front elevation. Draw perpendicular lines from each of these points on the edge line. At the location of the auxiliary view, draw a line parallel to the edge line across these perpendiculars. Mark this line P as well. Measure the widths perpendicularly from line P on the plan, and mark as lines a, b, c, and d. Transfer these widths to the true view by measuring their lengths perpendicularly from P. Connect the corner points to draw the true view.

When drafting scenery we usually describe an object by drawing the elevation of its most informative side, and then describing the depth of the object with a vertical and horizontal cut through the object. The horizontal cut view is called a plan of the object, and the vertical cut view is called a section. When designing scenery with inclined planes such as raked decks or angled ceilings, we often first work out the plan and section and only then the elevations. The top edge of the sectional cut view is often a true edge line, which can be used to construct a true view of the angled surface.

Sections can be cut through an inclined surface at any angle. A section is a true edge line only if it is a cut perpendicular to the plane of the incline; it shows the true length of the surface if it extends from the lowest to the highest point of the inclined plane.

In Figure 7.15, an angled ceiling piece is an inclined plane. Its front and rear edge lines are parallel to the front and rear views of the picture planes. The edge lines of the ceiling are perpendicular to the line of sight and are therefore seen in their true and measurable lengths. To draw the true size and shape of the ceiling, first establish the edge view of the plane, in this case a section, which shows the true length of the ceiling.

On either the front or the plan view, draw a theoretical line, P, perpendicular to the plane of the elevation. From P, measure the widths to the corner points, a, b, c, and d. Draw a line parallel to the edge line crossing the perpendiculars. Mark this line P as well. Transfer the width measurements from the plan or front elevation to the true view and connect the corner points to draw the true view.

Note that any point on the true view, such as a center medallion, could be projected horizontally from the front elevation to the edge line of the section and then perpendicularly to the true view. Any widths, such as the width of a medallion, could be measured perpendicularly from P in the front view and transferred to the true view.

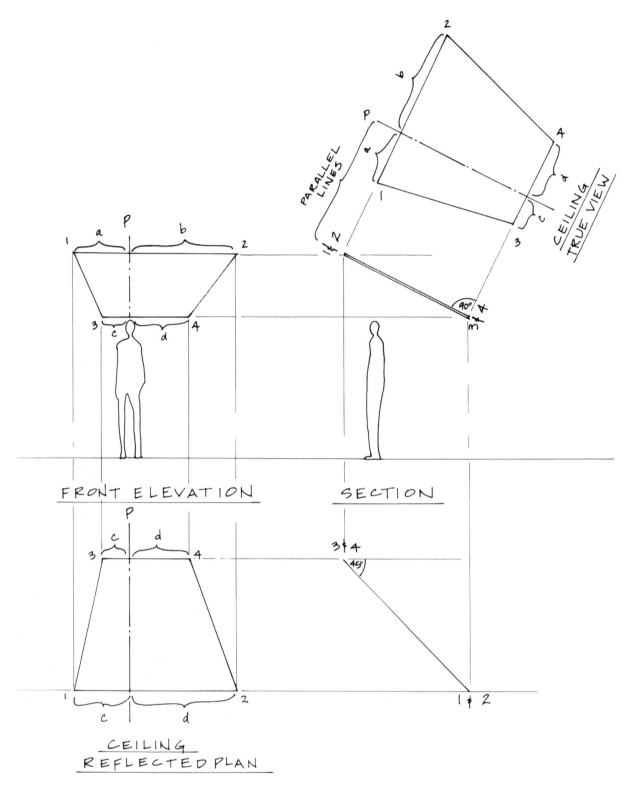

Figure 7.15 True view of an inclined ceiling.

In the example of a skewed plan in Figure 7.16, the deck surface is angled to all the normal views and no edge of the deck is seen in its true length. A section through the deck, parallel to the rake line, creates a true edge line from which to construct the true view.

On the top view, draw the section cutting line, P, perpendicular to the risers and parallel to the rake. Draw a floor line parallel to P and con-

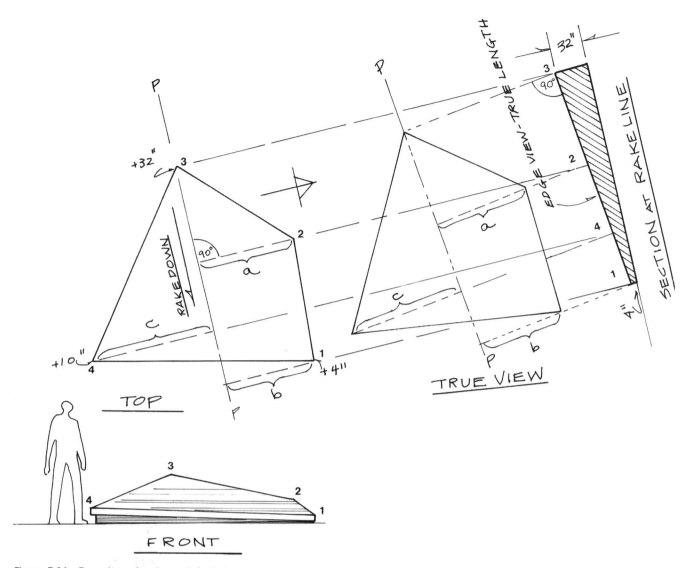

Figure 7.16   True view of a skewed deck top.

struct the section of the platform, transferring the heights from the front view.

Draw lines perpendicular to P from each corner point on the platform until they intersect the top edge line of the section. These points are marked 1, 2, 3, and 4. From the edge, line project these points perpendicularly to the auxiliary view position.

Draw another line P parallel to the top edge line of the section. Locate the corners of the true view by transferring the widths from the top view to the true view, measuring from each corner perpendicularly to P. Connect the corner points to draw the true view.

In Figure 7.17, the top plane of the bridge is a skewed plane. In neither the front, side, or plan view is this plane seen in its true size and shape, and no true edge line of the plane is seen in any of the normal views. To determine the true view of the plane we must first construct its edge view. We can then treat it like any inclined plane and project the true view from the edge view. One way to construct the edge view is to use the top edge of a section taken through the object perpendicular to one of the normal views.

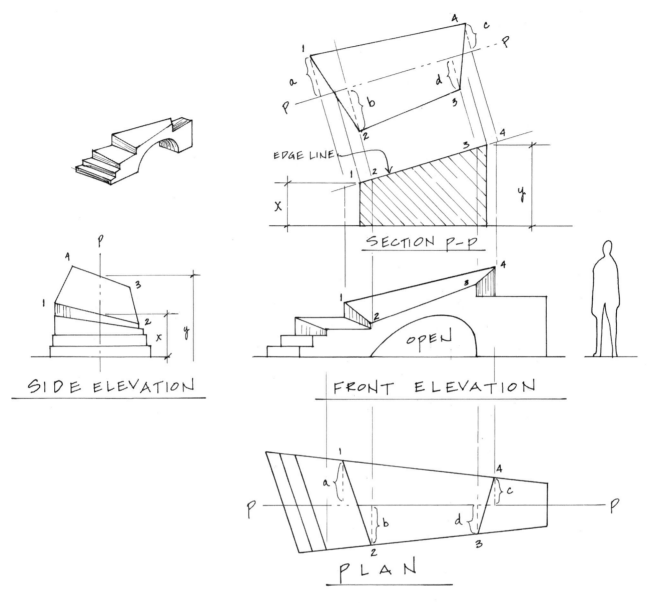

Figure 7.17 True view of a skewed plane developed from a section.

Developed Views

A curved object that needs to be seen in its true size and shape is drawn as a developed view or flattened view. It is as though the object were sliced and unrolled on a flat plane the way you would need to lay it out to build a model. (See Figure 7.18.)

Figure 7.19 shows the developed view of a circular stairway. To construct this developed view transfer the distances of the curved sides in the top view to their flattened length in a side view. To mark key points on a curve you can use a thin strip of paper, carefully bending it to the shape and then flattening it, or you can calculate geometrically. See Figure 4.15. In our example, all of the exterior step edges would be the same length, so you would want to check these distances and make any necessary adjustments.

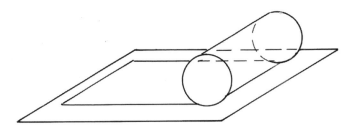

DEVELOPMENT OF A CYLINDER
ROLLED OUT ON A PLANE

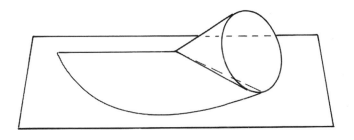

Figure 7.18   Developed views.

DEVELOPMENT OF A CONE
ROLLED OUT ON A PLANE

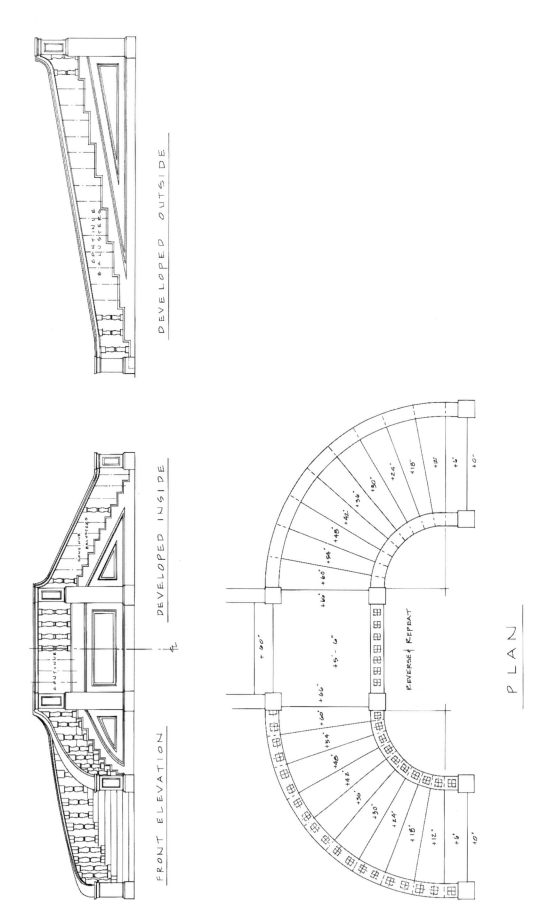

Figure 7.19 Developed view of a curved staircase.

8

The Section

Description of a Section

A section is a cut through an object that exposes its interior. It often presents an object in a clearer, more quickly comprehensible way then does an exterior view with dashed lines to indicate hidden parts. (See Figure 8.1.) A section can also be used to show the internal construction of an object.

The easiest way to visualize a section is to imagine a serrated knife slicing through the object much as you would slide through a loaf of bread. The knife cuts in a straight line, revealing the interior cut plane scored by serrations. (See Figure 8.2.) The viewer always observes the plane of the cut section perpendicularly, thus seeing a profile of the true size and shape of the object. The beginning draftsperson may find it helpful to explore the nature of sections by modeling objects in soft clay and cutting through them with a knife.

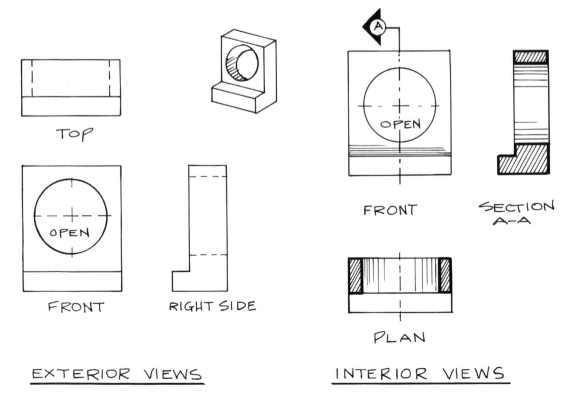

Figure 8.1 The imaginary cut through the object.

87

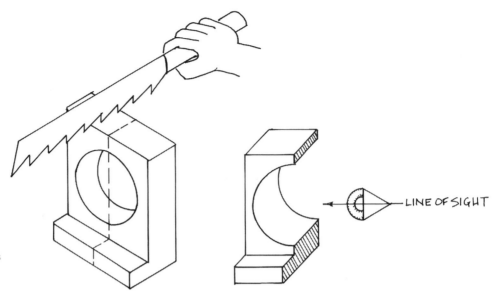

LINE OF SIGHT

Figure 8.2 The clarity of sections as opposed to hidden lines in a plan and section.

A cut through an object can also indicate what is revealed beyond the cut plane. In Figure 8.2 the inside curve of the hole is revealed beyond the edge of the serrated plane.

Vertical and Horizontal Elevation Cuts

Although a section may be cut through an object in any direction, there are two cuts through an elevation that are most common. A vertical cut through the object looking perpendicular to the cutting plane is called a **Section**. A horizontal cut through an object looking down and perpendicular to the cutting plane is called a **Plan**.

In the example of a scenic wall in Figure 8.3, the section is cut vertically through the most informative area of the wall, the paneling of the door. Here we see the height and thickness of the wall, the door reveal, the casing, and the door panels. The plan is a horizontal cut through the paneling of the door. Here we see the length and thickness of the wall, the door reveal, the door casing, and the panel.

Graphic Symbol to Indicate the Cutting Line

The path of the cutting line is indicated on the plan or elevation with a line drawn as a dash followed by two dots followed by a dash and so on. Although there are several graphic methods of indicating sectional cuts, the following is the most common. (See Figure 8.4.)

For sectional views that show just the profile of the cut area, a circle is attached at the top and, on long objects, also at the bottom of the cutting line. Inside the circle are the letters and sometimes numbers that identify the section. (Coding sections is covered in Chapter 14, "Multisheet Sets and Coding.")

For sectional views that show distant elevations in addition to the profile of the cut area, the circle is contained within a shaded triangle that points in the direction of the point of view. The circle is not drawn directly at the end of the cutting line but attached to it by a short, perpendicular line.

Indicating a Vertical Cutting Path

If the path of the vertical cut is straight and obvious, you can start it and, if necessary, end it, but you do not need to draw it completely. In Figure 8.5, the sectional symbol is indicated and its path begun at the top and bottom of the elevation, but the middle of the path has been

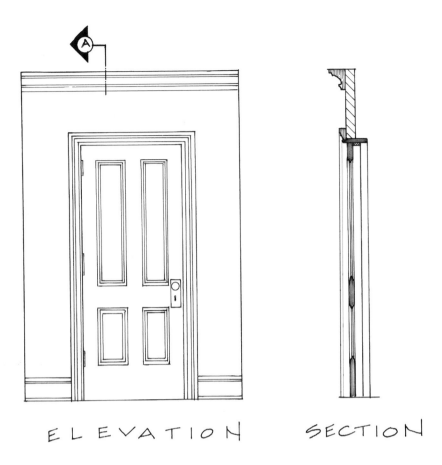

E L E V A T I O N   SECTION

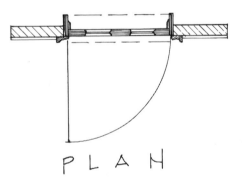

P L A N

Figure 8.3   Elevation, plan, and section of a wall with a door.

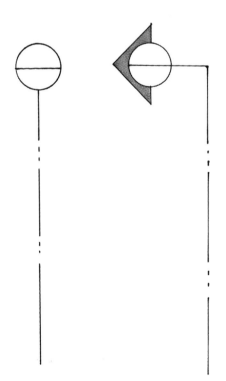

Figure 8.4   The section symbol.

eliminated. Thus, the cutting lines do not distract from the lines of the elevation. The section symbol has been placed outside of the dimensions under the view, allowing the dimensions to remain near the object to which they refer.

On short objects, many draftspeople show only the top section symbol. On cuts through long elevations, you need to draw the section symbol at both ends of the cutting path.

Indicating the Horizontal Cutting Path

The primary horizontal cut through an elevation is known and labeled as a **Plan**. It is assumed that this cut is taken through the most informative

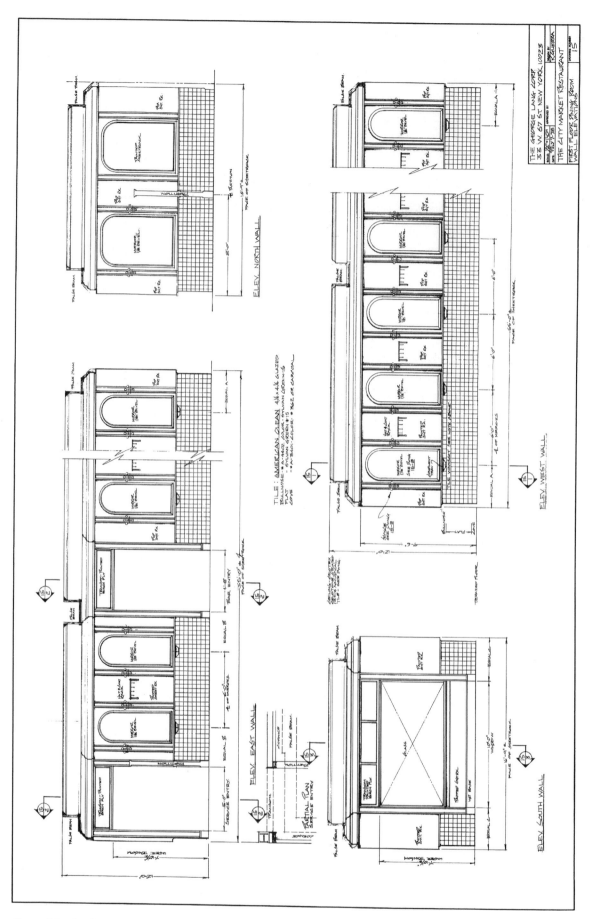

Figure 8.5 Drafting showing the position of section symbols on elevation restaurant. Design and drafting by Robert Guerra for The City Market Restaurant, George Lang Corporation. Used by permission.

place on the elevation. If the location of the horizontal cut is obvious, it is common not to indicate the cutting path.

However, if the location of the cut is not obvious, you must indicate and label the cutting path. If you need several cuts to describe an object, you must label each of them, and if the path of your cut jogs you need to indicate its entire path.

Location of Elevation Plan and Section

The **Section** is a vertical cut through an elevation and is usually placed to the right of the elevation between or replacing the side view. If several vertical sections are necessary they may all be placed to the right of the elevation, or one may be to the right and others on a separate sheet.

The **Plan** is always located directly below its elevation, replacing the bottom view position in an orthographic layout. Unlike a bottom view, however, the plan is flipped so the rear edge of the plan is the edge closest to the elevation. This makes a plan view easy to read as we can read the view from the front of the object to its back.

Occasionally a horizontal cut is made through an elevation looking up, perhaps, to see a ceiling or the top of an arch. In such a circumstance, the cutting line is drawn below the surface in question, and the arrows of the section symbol point upward, indicating the surface above. The view is then placed above the elevation. (See Figure 8.6.)

Offset Section

A cut through an object that jogs perpendicularly and then continues in the same direction as before is known as an offset section. Such an internal jog can be made without changing the size or silhouette of the object. An offset section allows the draftsperson to show, in a single section, informative areas that are not in a straight line on the elevation. When drawing an offset section it is important to draw the entire path of the cutting line so the reader understands what you are "sectioning."

The cutting line for an offset section is the same as that for any other section: a dash followed by two dots, followed by a dash, and so on. For clarity, it is important to connect the dashes at the exact corner where a bend occurs. (See Figure 8.7.)

Figure 8.8 shows a vertical section through the center of a fireplace unit and an offset plan section. The offset plan allows us, in a single view, to see the depth relationships at two critical levels.

Graphic Technique for Drafting a Section

The exterior edge of a section is always drafted with the darkest weight line that the draftsperson uses. There are various techniques for indicating the inside mass of a section, depending on the scale of the drawing and the amount of internal detail required.

Interior Crosshatch Technique

The most common way to indicate the inside mass of a section is to fill the inside of the dark contour line with 60-degree angled lightweight lines.

In a medium-scale drawing such as 1/2 inch to the foot, the section is considered a single mass containing no lines other than the crosshatches. In this scale, the crosshatch lines would be about 1/16 inch apart from each other. In larger scales, the lines would be further apart.

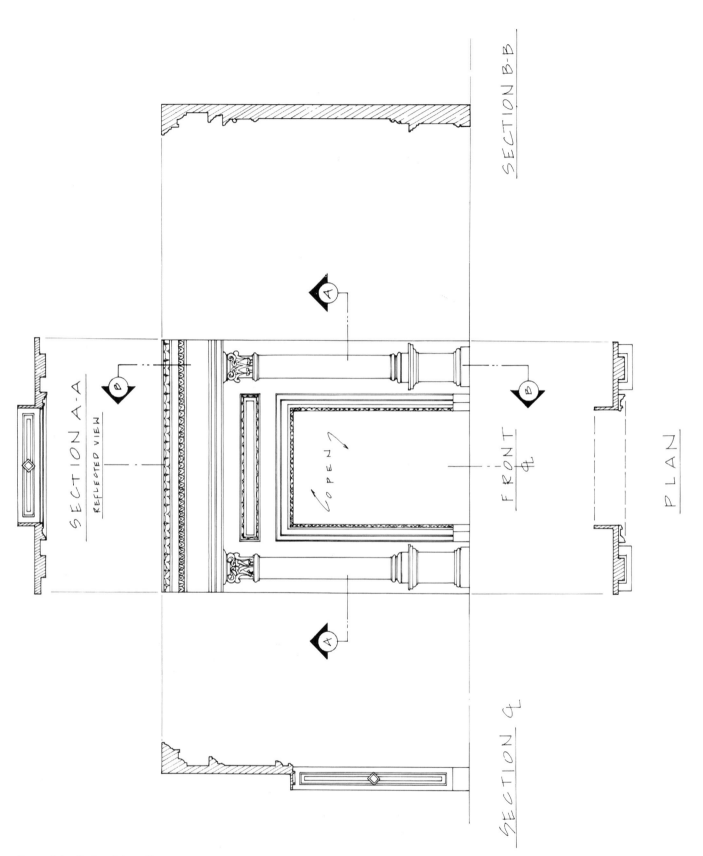

Figure 8.6 Horizontal section looking up.

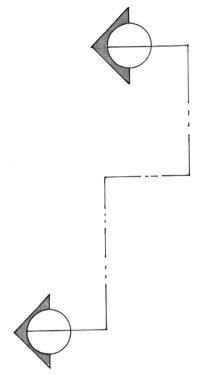

Figure 8.7   The path of the cutting line in an offset section.

In scenic drafting as opposed to architectural or engineering drafting, we are primarily concerned with the external surface of things. The crosshatch indicates not an empty section but the shape of an object whose internal construction and materials are left up to the construction foreman or builder.

Figure 8.9 shows the elevation, plan, and section of an entranceway. Since the mass of the section is large, the crosshatched lines have faded out towards the center so as not to overpower the picture. Note how clearly the section explains the shape of the arch and how it also is able to show us the inside of the archway beyond the sectioned door.

Techniques for Omitting the Inside Fill of a Section

At times you will find that the crosshatched lines defining the inside mass of the section have been omitted. This is often done for large-scale detailed drawings, but it is sometimes done for smaller scale, elevation sections. (See Figure 8.10.)

If you use this style, it is important that the exterior edge line of the section be dark enough to differentiate it from the normal elevation lines. Sometimes the section edge line is emphasized by adding several lightweight lines on the inside edge of the section line.

Technique of Shading the Interior Mass of a Section

For small mass sections, including the plan view of both theatrical and film flats, the common technique for indicating a section is a dark edge line surrounding a lightly shaded interior mass (Figure 8.11). The inside tone is often made of straight, lightweight lines drawn closely together. Sometimes the inside of the section is shaded with the edge of a soft pencil. With this technique, it is best to turn the drafting paper over and shade on its backside to avoid future smudging.

The interior mass of the section may also be shaded with a medium-value magic marker such as a #4 Pentel. If changes need to be made, you cannot erase these lines and will be forced to redraft the sheet. (See Figure 8.12.) A nice technique to emphasize the edge line of a large-scale detail is to draw it with a soft lead and then rub along the inside edge with a paper stump. This creates a soft edge tone, shading from dark to light.

Techniques for Drawing Large-Scale Detail Sections

A full-size detail section shows the actual size, shape, and often the construction of an object through an important and typical part of an elevation. Many scenic details are composed of a series of moldings and pieces of wood that are layered together to make a larger shape. These pieces that compose the whole should be drawn as separate, darkly outlined sections. Another technique for indicating the mass of a section is to use a soft pencil to lightly indicate the architectural material of which the element is to be constructed. In Figure 8.13 a soft, freehand pencil line indicates the wood grain on a full-size molding detail. Note that the angle of the grain in each piece of molding is different from the next to differentiate the separate pieces of wood.

In order to detail construction, a scenic draftsperson must have knowledge of stock sizes of lumber and materials, of the "thickness" of materials, and of scenic construction techniques. If the scenic designer does not have such knowledge, it is better to draw the edge line of the overall shape, identify only stock molding choices, and leave the method of construction up to the carpenter. The practice of full-size detailing is discussed in Chapter 15, "Period Shapes and Scenic Details."

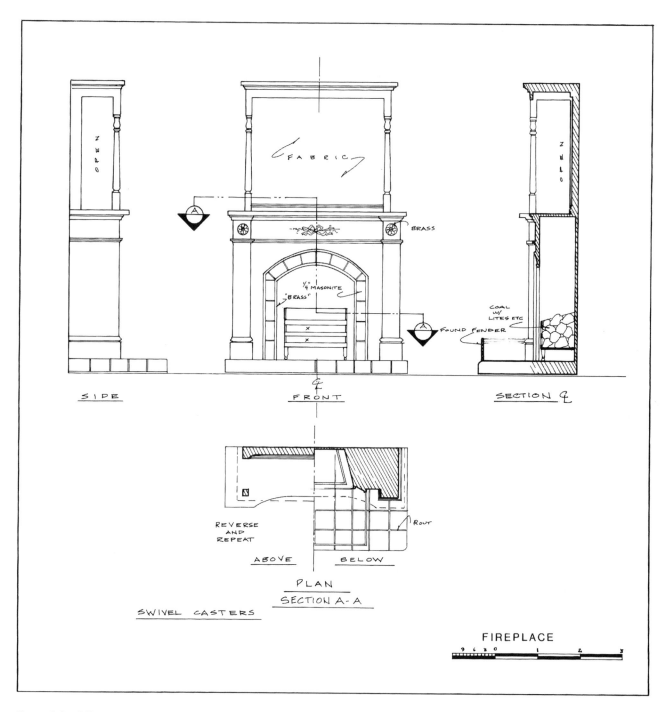

Figure 8.8   Offset plan/section of a fireplace.

Architectural Symbols

When drawing sections the scenic draftsperson should know that every material has its own architectural fill symbol to indicate marble, wood, glass, steel, brass, and so on. A complete pictorial list can be found in *Architectural Graphic Standards,* the best and most basic architectural reference book. Figure 8.14 illustrates those symbols most commonly used by the scenic designer.

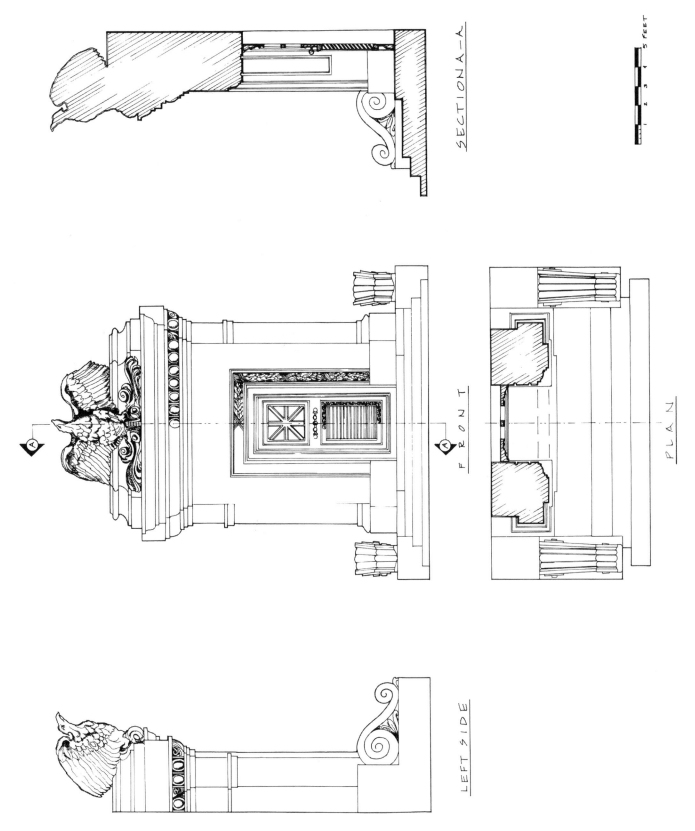

SECTION—A

5 FEET

FRONT

PLAN

LEFT SIDE

Figure 8.9 Crosshatch to indicate the interior mass of a section.

95

Revolved Section

A revolved section is cut through an elevation, revolved 90 degrees to the elevation, and drawn directly on top of it. In Figure 8.15, since the object is symmetrical, a single view with a revolved section can show the front elevation and section, and another single view can show the top elevation and plan.

When most scenery was painted and built parts were minimal, it was common theatrical practice to draw revolved sections directly onto the front elevation of flats. This practice is rare today as most detail is built and the lines of a revolved section interrupt the lines of the elevation. (See Figure 8.16.)

Revolved sections are still often used by the scenic draftsperson in large-scale detailing. A characteristic or important portion of an elevation is drawn at a larger scale, usually full size, with revolved vertical or horizontal sections showing molding shapes and construction specifics.

Figure 8.17 was drawn by Speed Hopkins, detailing a Victorian Archway for the 1982 feature film *A Little Sex*, designed by Stephen Hendrickson. It shows a removed section taken through the upper side casing, a vertical revolved section drawn on the header of the arch, a horizontal revolved section drawn on the side center of the casing, and a revolved vertical section drawn on the plinth block at the bottom of the casing.

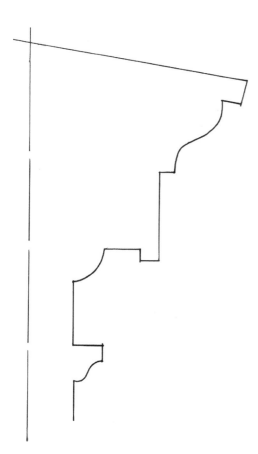

Figure 8.10   The section defined by only a dark edge line.

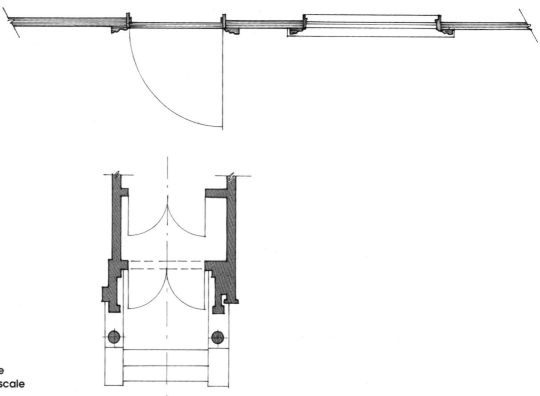

Figure 8.11   Shading the interior mass of a small-scale plan.

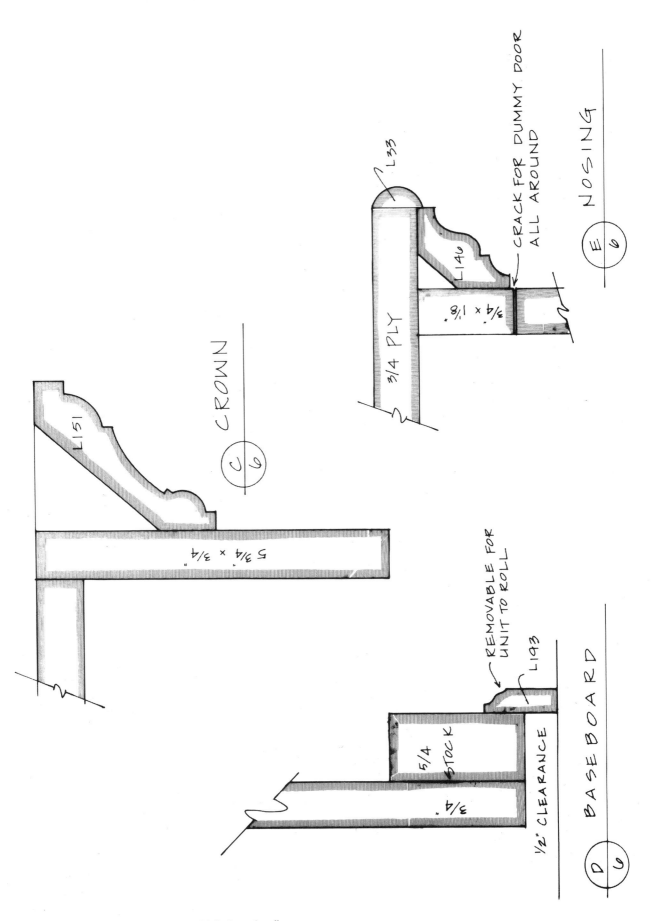

CROWN

L151

5 3/4" × 3/4"

$\overset{C}{\underline{6}}$

3/4 PLY

L33

L146

CRACK FOR DUMMY DOOR
ALL AROUND

3/4" × 1 1/8"

$\overset{E}{\underline{6}}$ NOSING

REMOVABLE FOR
UNIT TO ROLL

L193

5/4
STOCK

3/4"

1/2" CLEARANCE

$\overset{D}{\underline{6}}$ BASEBOARD

Figure 8.12 Full-size detail with shaded interior edge line.

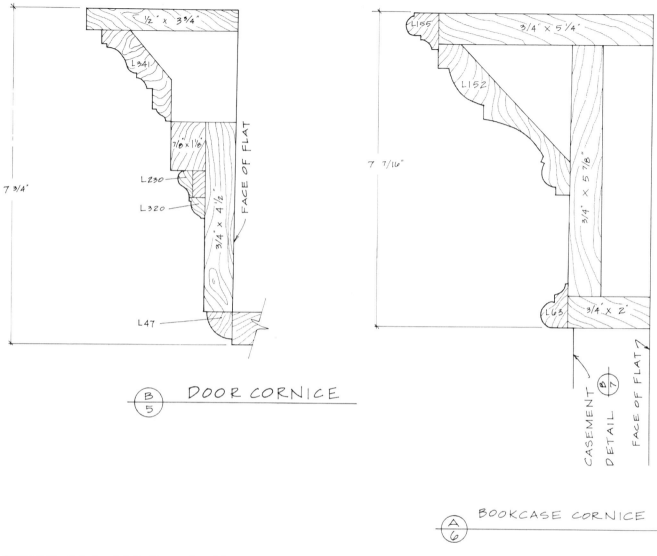

Figure 8.13   Full-size detail with wood graining.

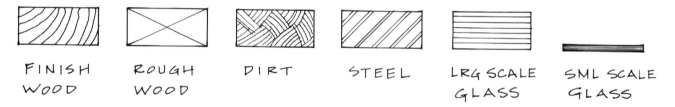

Figure 8.14   Common scenic architectural material symbols.

Broken-Out Sections

A broken-out section is used to simultaneously show many layers of a single object. Each layer is drawn as though a piece has been ripped off, revealing what is underneath. A curved freehand line indicates the edge of the peel line. The example of a broken-out section in Figure 8.18 shows a floor designed to be lit from below. Three overlapping layers are shown on a single view: the frame layer, a layer of colored Plexiglas, and a top surface of painted boards with gaps between them.

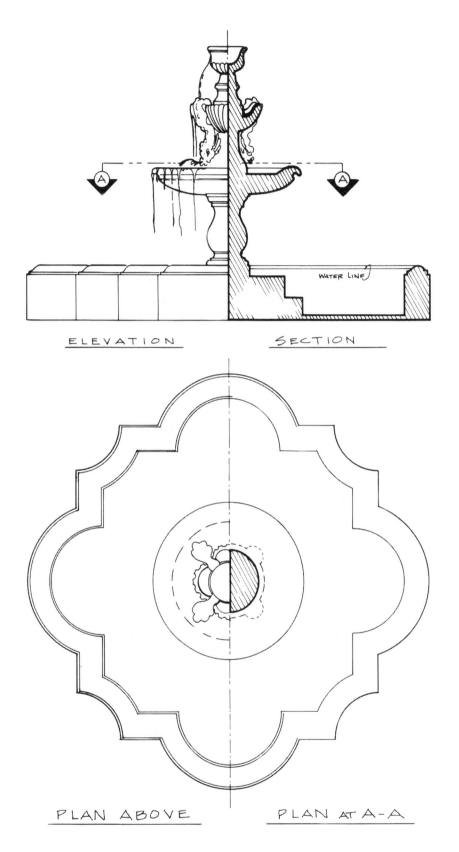

ELEVATION   SECTION

WATER LINE

PLAN ABOVE   PLAN AT A-A

FOUNTAIN

SCALE

Figure 8.15　A revolved section on
a front elevation.

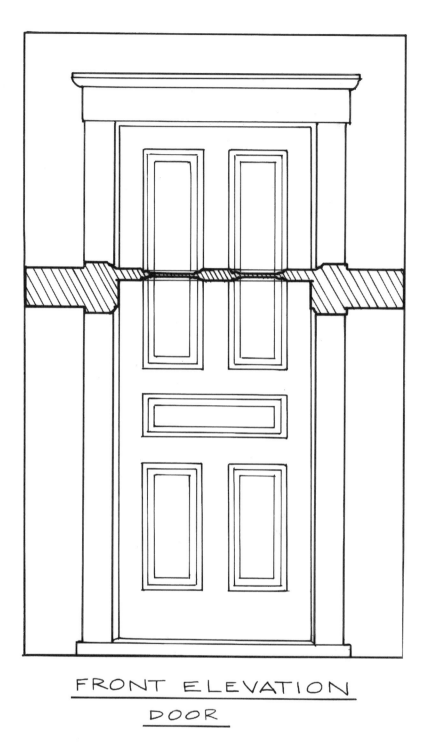

FRONT ELEVATION

DOOR

Figure 8.16 Revolved section on the elevation of a scenery flat.

Ground Plan

A **Ground Plan** is a horizontal cut through an entire set. Ground plans often eliminate details and show shapes in simple, schematic ways that allow them to be easily read. The cutting plane of a ground plan is not taken at floor level but through the most informative area of the set. A ground plan is an offset section, and the cutting plane can move up or down to show those heights of most concern. Generally, these heights are about shoulder level for an actor on the first floor.

Heights on a ground plan, such as stairs or window seats, are labeled with the numeral preceded by a plus. Levels below the floor line are

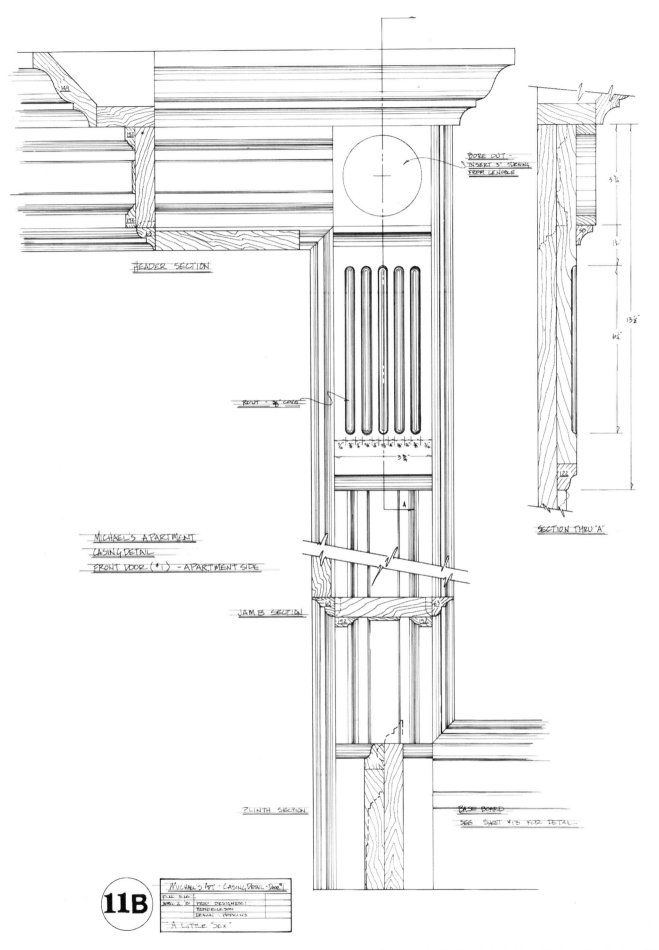

HEADER SECTION

BORE OUT — INSERT 3" TURNING FROM LENOBLE

ROUT · ⅜" COVE

MICHAEL'S APARTMENT
CASING DETAIL
FRONT DOOR (#1) — APARTMENT SIDE

JAMB SECTION

PLINTH SECTION

SECTION THRU "A"

BASE BOARD
SEE SHEET #13 FOR DETAIL

11B

MICHAEL'S APT · CASING DETAIL · DOOR #1		
FULL SIZE	PROD DESIGNER:	
APRIL 2, '81	HENDRICKSON	
	DRAWN : HOPKINS	
"A LITTLE SEX"		

Figure 8.17   Examples of revolved full-size sections. Drafting of Michael's Apartment—Casing Detail—Door #1, from the feature film *A Little Sex*. Production designed by Stephen Hendrickson; drafting by Speed Hopkins. Designs courtesy of MTM Enterprises, Inc.

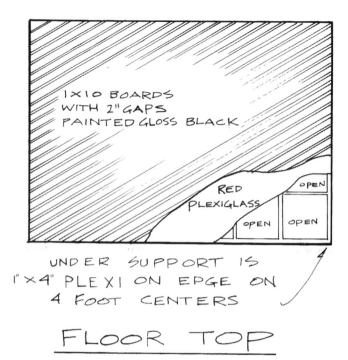

Figure 8.18   Broken-out section.

indicated by a numeral preceded by a minus. Structures above the level of the section, such as overhead platforms or arches, are indicated with hidden lines (a series of dashes). The heights of overhead structures are preceded by a plus sign (indicating height). They may be noted as "clear." For example, "Overhead Pipe +10′–3″ clear" means that this is the minimum clearance beneath the pipes. Structures under the floor or deck can be indicated with a secondary hidden line (dash-dot-dot-dash, and so on).

There are specialized ground plans that show particular types of information. And there are complex, multiset ground plans that indicate the position of sets within a theatrical or studio space. Although there are specific types of ground plans, in simple situations several types of plan can be combined. For example, a Theatrical Ground Plan may combine the Director's Plan, the Floor and Deck Plan, and the Technical Plan in a single drawing.

The **Theatre Ground Plan** labels, positions, and dimensions the set, masking, and lighting positions into the theatrical space.

The **Technical Plan** is a ground plan of the set, which dimensions the widths and lengths of the set in the theatrical space, codes each view, labels each part, and may include technical specifics for construction.

The **Director's Plan** is a simple ground plan for the director. It shows and labels furniture and important props such as telephones. It does not have view identification numbers or construction specifics.

The **Master Plan** is a complex theatrical ground plan for a multiset show. On a single sheet it shows the permanent scenery, masking, and lighting positions in the theatrical space, as well as the storage positions (dashed-line profile) and playing positions (solid-line profile) for each piece of scenery in each shift position.

Shift Plots are individual ground plans that show a single phase of a multiset show in a theatrical space. Shift plots are used to show the director each specific scenic setup and to indicate the positions of scenery before and after each scenic shift. The playing positions of scenery and furniture are drawn in solid lines; the storage position of oncoming sets is drawn with dashed lines, and the movement of the scenery on and off the stage is indicated with dashed lines and arrows.

A **Floor Plan** is a plan through the entire set taken just above the floor levels that indicates the treatments of floor surfaces such as parquet or carpet pattern, linoleum, or tile layout. The floor plan indicates door saddles or other items on the floor.

A **Deck Plan** shows the construction of a deck. Dashed lines can indicate the position of structural support members, facings, clear passageways underneath, and so on. In a theatrical show with winched scenery, the deck plan indicates the tracks for the scenery guides.

A **Reflected Ceiling Plan** is the elevation of a ceiling drawn as though a large mirror were placed on the stage or studio floor directly below the ceiling.

The **Studio Plan** is the ground plan of a television or film studio that shows and dimensions the sets into the space.

Cross-Sections

A **Cross-Section** is a vertical cut through an *entire* set, looking beyond to see what is in the distance. It is assumed that the cutting path of a cross-section is taken through the centerline of a set. If the position of the cutting plane is not taken at the centerline but at another place, it should be clarified by indicating its cutting path on the *plan* of the set. At the end of the cutting path is a circle with an arrow that points, to indicate the point of view, towards an elevation or elevations seen beyond the cut plane. Inside the circle are the letters and sometimes numbers that identify the section.

The commercial in Figures 8.19a and 8.19b was designed by Stephen Hendrickson and drafted by Dan Davis. Since the set is simple and symmetrical, a longitudinal and a latitudinal cross-section are all that are needed to explain all the elevations. It would have been possible to label and draw each wall as a separate view, but for this simple structure, it is faster to draft and easier to read cross-sections.

A **Theatrical Cross-Section** is always taken through the centerline of the stage, looking towards the most informative side of the scenery. In complex situations, it may be necessary to draw two cross-sections that look at both sides of the stage.

The theatrical cross-section is used to check vertical audience sight lines, to show the height of scenery in relationship to lighting pipes and instruments, and to set the trim positions of any hanging or flying pieces of scenery.

Cross-Sections of Multi-Roomed Sets

One method of laying out a film interior with many rooms is to treat the whole dwelling as a single object and cut a series of cross-sections through the entire set. The cross-sections are taken along each wall of the ground plan. Latitudinal and longitudinal directions are kept clear by coding them with identifying numbers in one direction and with letters in the other. On the elevation of each cross-section, intersecting walls appear as sections and are identified with their codes.

This method of organizing the views of an interior setting is better as a pictorial rather than a construction drawing. It is good for small-scale, preliminary drafting as it gives a sense of the total shape of the space for the designer and the director, not unlike a camera dollying through the

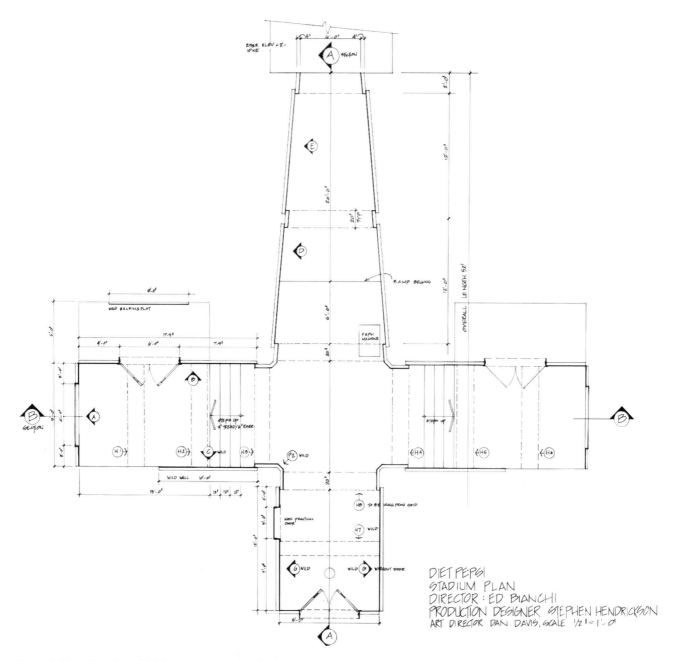

Figure 8.19a Plan for a Diet Pepsi commercial. Designed by Stephen Hendrickson. Drafted by Dan Davis. Used by permission.

rooms of the house. If design time is limited and the room details are simple and repetitive, this method also eliminates the need to elevate every wall. However, this is a confusing system of layout for the draftsperson and builder. If the interior contains many unusual architectural elements and each wall needs to be elevated, one has to jump from view to view to see all the walls of a single room.

Removed Sections—Trees, Built Animals, and Complex Shapes

While a section can look beyond the cutting line to see distant elevations, it can also show only the cut profile of the shape without the distant view.

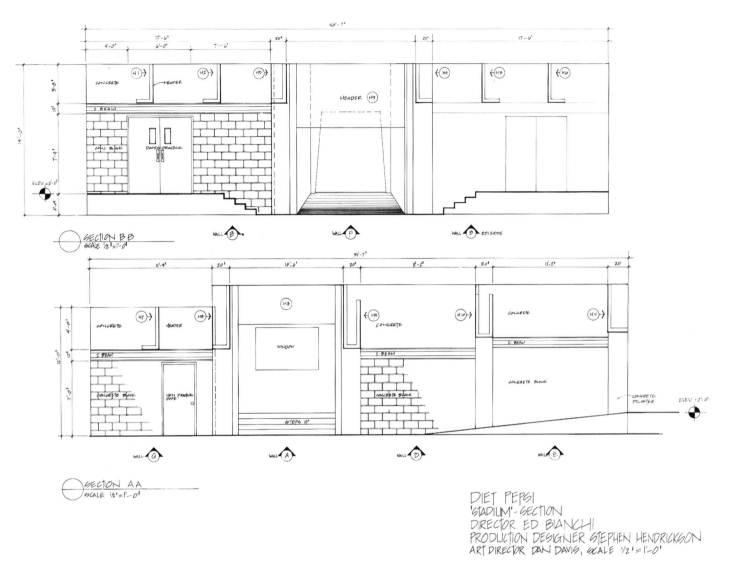

Figure 8.19b   Cross-section for a Diet Pepsi commercial. Designed by Stephen Hendrickson. Drafted by Dan Davis. Used by permission.

In such a case, the end of the cutting line is marked with a coded circle without an arrow pointing in the direction of the point of view.

Complex objects may require multiple plan sections and vertical sections to explain their shapes. This is especially true of organic shapes such as rocks, mountains, or built animals, which have no geometric point of reference. Drafting them requires that a series of sections be taken at measured intervals. These multiple sections are known as **removed sections** as they are usually removed from the elevation or plan and drawn in any convenient location on the same page or on a separate sheet. It is important that each removed section is clearly coded with its cutting path indicated on the elevation or plan. (See Figure 8.20.)

The illustrations in Figures 8.21a to 8.21d were drafted by John Berger for *The Rocketeer*, a 1991 film designed by Jim Bissell. This set was a cafe shaped like a bulldog on the outside. Drawing this organic shape required elevations, cross-sections, and removed sections.

The "Bulldog Cafe," a restaurant designed in the shape of a dog, was a very large and hollow organic shape. Drawing such an object required many cross-sections in addition to exterior elevations. The set was "sliced" at regular intervals vertically and horizontally. Not all the sheets for this

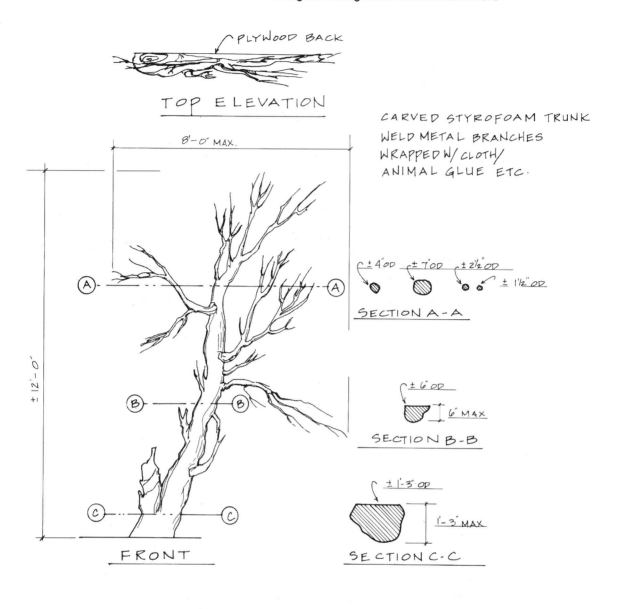

PLYWOOD BACK

TOP ELEVATION

CARVED STYROFOAM TRUNK
WELD METAL BRANCHES
WRAPPED W/ CLOTH/
ANIMAL GLUE ETC.

8'-0" MAX.

± 12'-0"

A — A

± 4" OD ± 7" OD ± 2½" OD

± 1½" OD

SECTION A-A

B — B

± 6" OD

6" MAX

SECTION B-B

C — C

± 1'-3" OD

1'-3" MAX

SECTION C-C

FRONT

TREE

Figure 8.20   Removed sections of an organic shape.

set are shown. However, you can see what was required to describe the object by the many labeled cutting lines on the plan and cross-section.

- The ground plan, drafted in 1/2-inch-to-the-foot scale, shows important width dimensions.
- Exterior elevations are labeled A, B, C, D.
- A major cross-section, E, cuts through the width of the structure, looking toward the inside front entrance of the cafe. It is located to cut through the center of a curved banquette seat. Another major cross-section, H, looks towards the inside rear exit to the cafe. It is located to show a straight banquette seat.
- Two major cross-sections, F and G, cut through the length of the structure on its "longintudinal" centerline looking in opposite directions.
- Additional cross-sections, J through W, cut through the structures length at two-foot intervals.

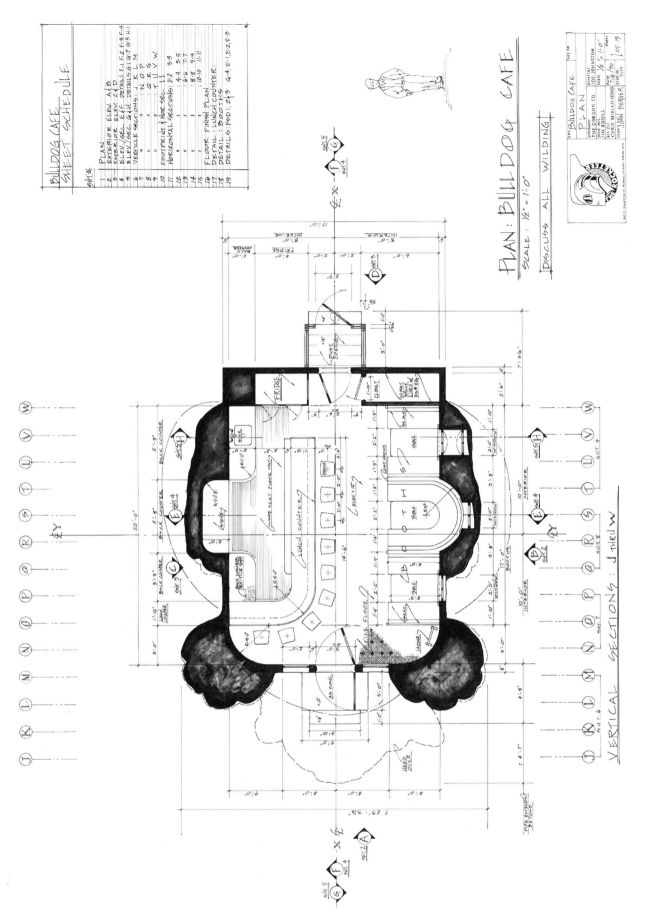

Figure 8.21a   Sheet 1. Groundplan. Draftings of "The Bulldog Cafe" from Walt Disney Pictures' feature film *The Rocketeer*. Directed by Joe Johnston. Production design by Jim Bissell. Drafting by John Berger. Used by permission from Disney Enterprises, Inc.

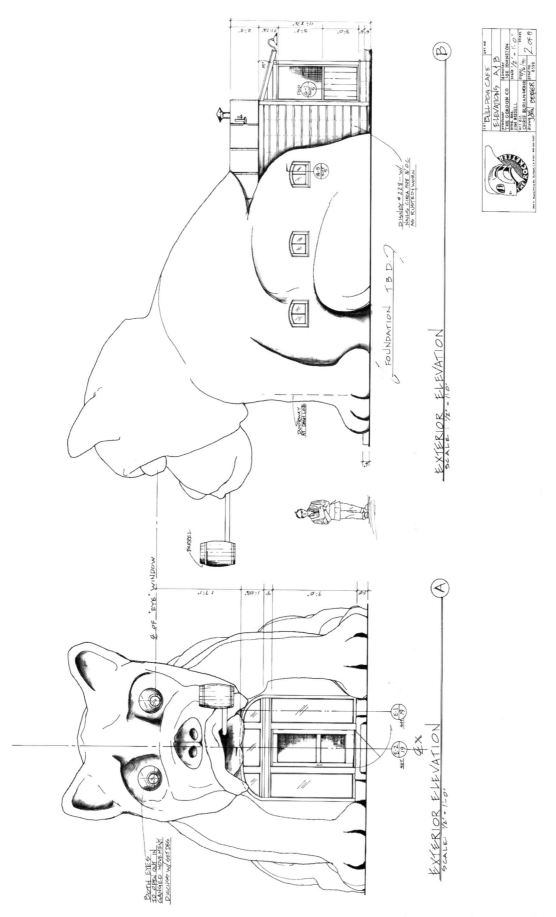

Figure 8.21b Sheet 2 shows two of the exterior elevations, A and B. Draftings of "The Bulldog Cafe" from Walt Disney Pictures' feature film *The Rocketeer*. Directed by Joe Johnston. Production design by Jim Bissell. Drafting by John Berger. Used by permission from Disney Enterprises, Inc.

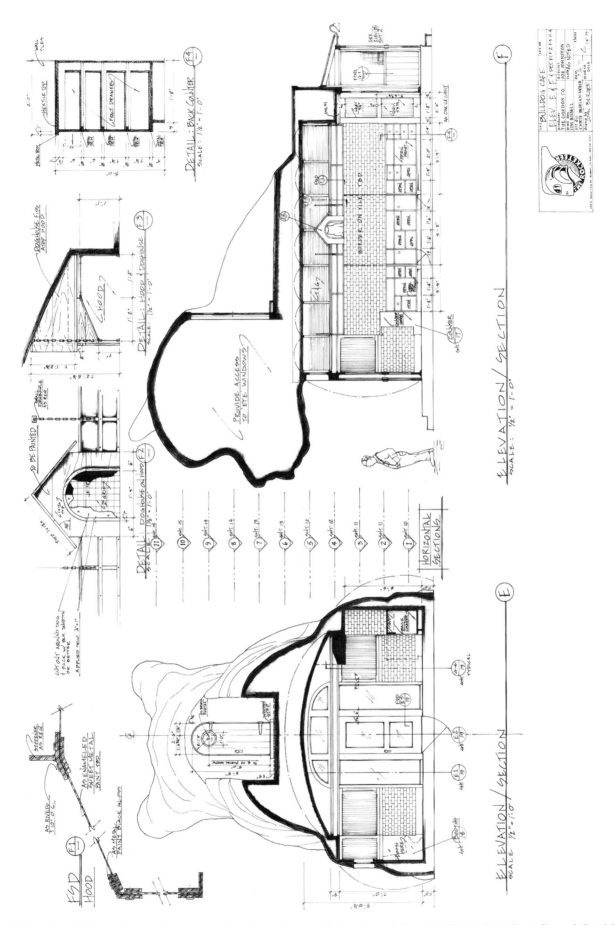

Figure 8.21c   Sheet 4 shows two major cross-sections, E and F: one is taken through the object's length and one through its width. On these full views, horizontal sections are indicated at two-foot intervals and coded as 1 through 11. Draftings of "The Bulldog Cafe" from Walt Disney Pictures' feature film *The Rocketeer*. Directed by Joe Johnston. Production design by Jim Bissell. Drafting by John Berger. Used by permission from Disney Enterprises, Inc.

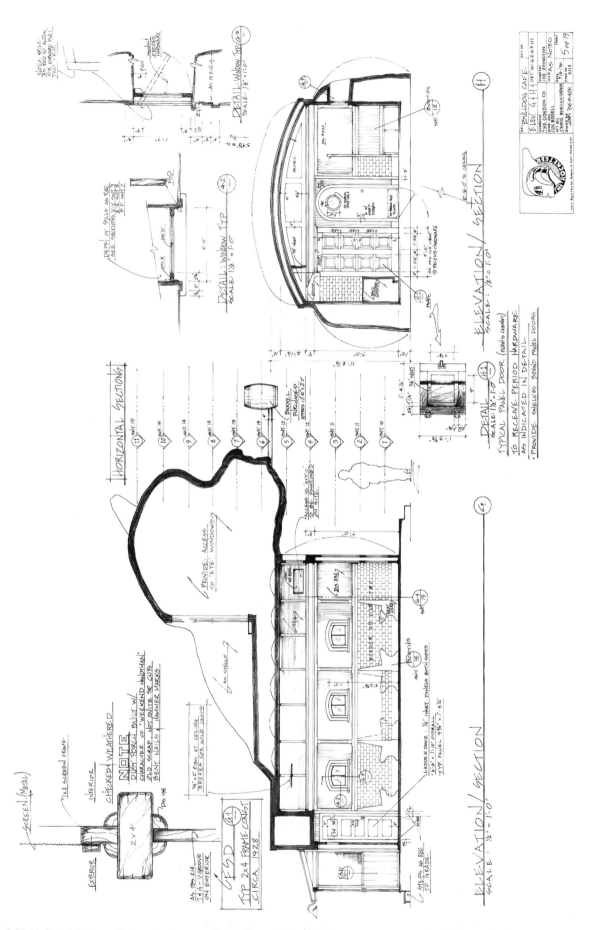

Figure 8.21d   Sheet 5 shows the major cross-sections, G and H, looking in the opposite direction. Draftings of "The Bulldog Cafe" from Walt Disney Pictures' feature film *The Rocketeer*. Directed by Joe Johnston. Production design by Jim Bissell. Drafting by John Berger. Used by permission from Disney Enterprises, Inc.

Large Convex Sculptural Shapes—Caves and Mountains

When drafting a large convex organic shape such as a mountain, or a large concave organic shape such as a cave, or a series of organic shapes on a surface such as ice floes on the ocean, the best method is to enclose the total shape in a three dimensional grid so that any point on the object has a height, width, and depth position that relates to all other points. Each line of the grid can become a cutting plane for a drawn section; the section can become support structure of the built object. The grid drawn on the floor of the studio or theatre positions the set into the performance space.

Starting in the left-hand corner, the plan of the object is measured at regular intervals, with X coordinates in one direction and Y coordinates in the other. Heights (Z coordinates) are drawn at the same measured intervals but in plus numbers. In Figure 8.22, the coordinates are drawn at four-foot intervals.

Figures 8.23 and 8.24 illustrate how such a system is used to define a large organic shape. The draftings were done by Patricia Woodbridge and are of a cave designed by Wolf Kroeger for the 1992 feature film *The Last of the Mohicans*. A Styrofoam model of the cave was built in 1-inch scale on a surface gridded at 4-inch intervals for the X and Y coordinates. The model was sliced along the coordinates both vertically and horizontally. The cross-sections were traced on gridded paper and then hard-drafted with coordinates.

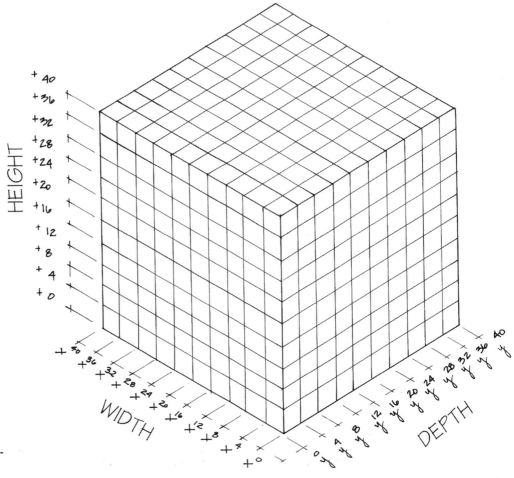

Figure 8.22 X, Y, and Z coordinates defining a space.

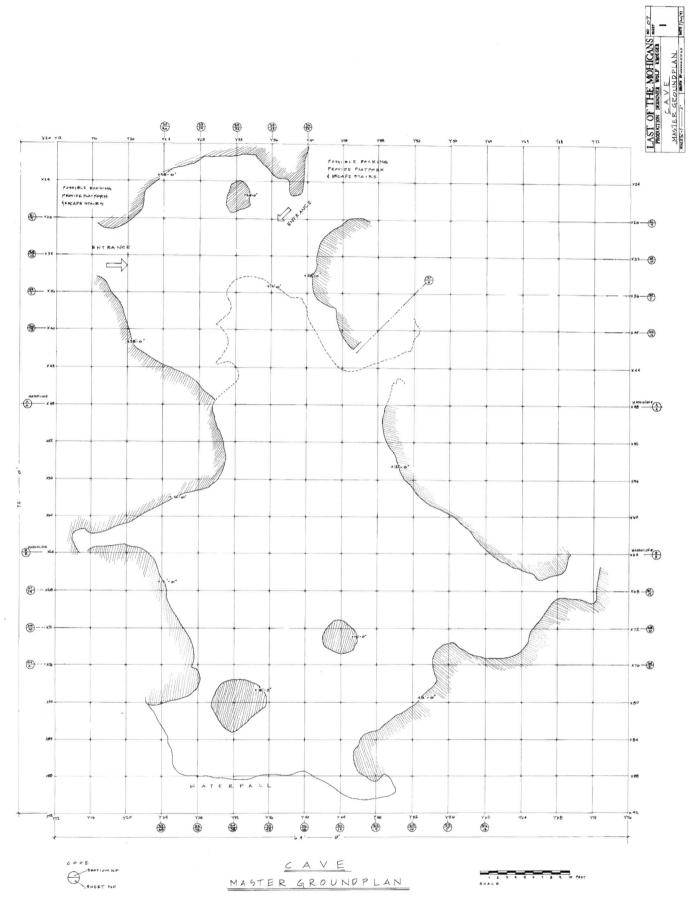

Figure 8.23   Ground plan of a cave showing the XY coordinates and numbered section, from the feature film *The Last of the Mohicans*. Directed by Michael Mann. Production design by Wolf Kroeger. Drafting by Patricia Woodbridge. Designs courtesy of Twentieth Century Fox.

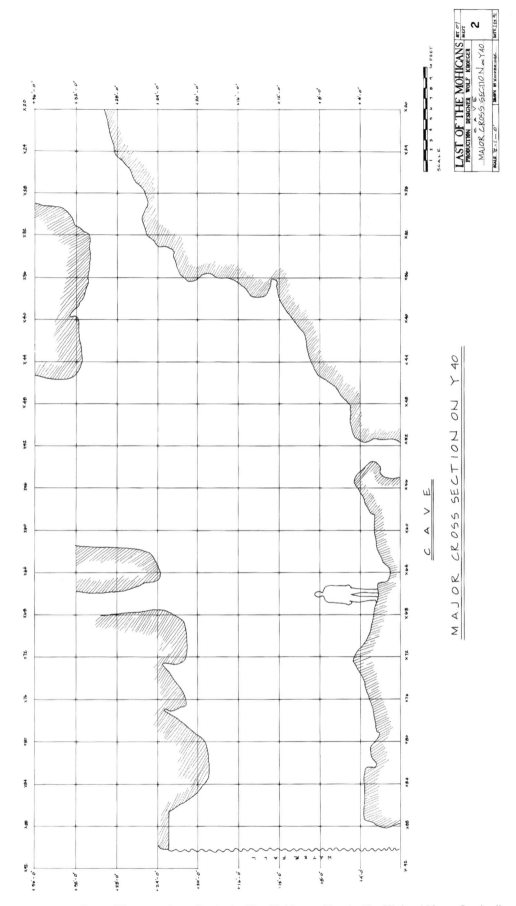

Figure 8.24 One of many cross-sections of the cave from *The Last of the Mohicans.* Directed by Michael Mann. Production Design by Wolf Kroeger. Drafting by Patricia Woodbridge. Designs courtesy of Twentieth Century Fox.

9

Dimensioning

Defining Dimensioning

A dimension gives the distance between two points. It consists of a numerical value of the actual rather than the scaled distance. Dimension lines indicate the direction of the measurement, and arrowheads, slashes, or dots indicate the beginning and end of the dimension. Extension lines refer the dimension to specific points on the object, while allowing the dimensions to be placed in a convenient location, away from those points. (See Figure 9.1.)

Notes are also considered part of dimensioning. Notes may be either specific or general. General notes that refer to the whole object may be placed on the page in any visually balanced location. Sometimes they are boxed or underlined for emphasis. Leaders are angled or curved lines that refer a note to a specific part of the drawing.

Amount of Dimensioning

A low quality scenic shop or an inexperienced carpenter will try to build directly off the designer's drafting. They therefore require extremely clear, precise, and complete dimensioning to prevent them from making errors.

A good scenic shop takes the scenic designer's drafting and does a series of working or construction draftings that are given to the carpenters who

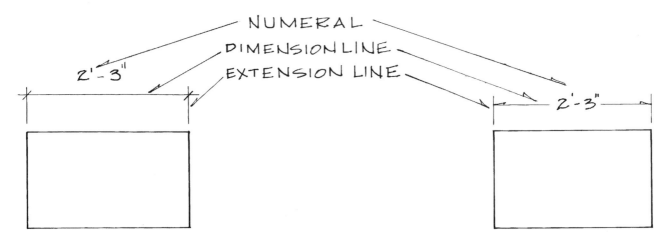

Figure 9.1 Extension and dimension lines and numerals.

build the scenery. These draftings show how the scenery is to be built and are completely dimensioned by the shop. In some shops, these very exact draftings are done in ink or on a computer. There is thus an important step between the designer's drafting and the construction of a piece of scenery. An act of translation occurs by someone who is both technically and artistically skilled.

Some designers prefer to have only minimal or no dimensioning of theatrical sets on their scaled drawings as they feel it is the responsibility of the scenic shop to make the set work. Increasingly, however, as draftspeople work in both film and theatre, it is becoming common practice to completely dimension theatrical scenery just as is done for film and television.

Film carpenters, to save time, usually build directly from designers' drafting. These are unionized, highly skilled builders who essentially do the working drawings in their heads. It is the film draftsperson's responsibility to completely dimension his or her drafting so as not to require carpenters to take the time to scale off a drawing.

Numerals in Dimensioning

In order to avoid confusion and mistakes it is important for the scenic draftsperson to make information easy to comprehend. Unless it is important to the design or construction, you should try to design so that your dimensions work out to simple numbers. On very large distances, this means your dimensions will work out to an even number of feet—240 feet instead of 241 feet. On large distances this means using half or quarter foot increments—20 feet 6 inches instead of 20 feet 5 inches, or 9 feet 3 inches instead of 9 feet 2 inches. On smaller distances, this means making your dimensions work out to inches rather than fractions. Although you may be able to design larger shapes with simple numbers, when you are drafting full-size molding details, a small measured increment such as 1/16 of an inch may be important to the proportion of the overall shape. With a long distance, complex dimensions, such as 17 feet 3 1/4 inches act as a red flag to the builder and suggests that tolerances are critical. For example, it may mean that if the scenery extends beyond the numerical distance it will run into an obstruction.

Dimensioning measured spaces on actual locations should be as exact as possible. The scenery within the space is usually designed allowing for tolerance and can therefore be simply dimensioned.

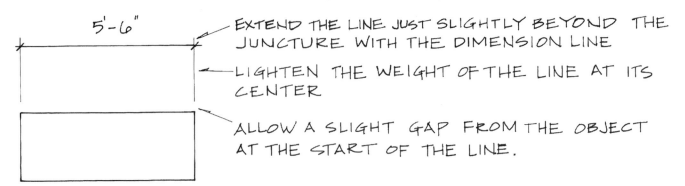

Figure 9.2 Characteristics of the extension line.

116

Extension Lines

Extension lines extend any point on the object, thus allowing the draftsperson to place the dimension line away from the object in an adjacent but empty area of the drafting. In scenic drafting, it is common not to draw the extension lines through the object being dimensioned but to start them a slight distance away (about 1/16 of an inch). The extension line should extend slightly (about 1/16 of an inch) beyond the point of contact with the dimension line. If it extends too much beyond, it leads the viewer's eye off and makes the information difficult to read.

Extension lines are thin, lightweight lines. They are less important and therefore lighter than the lines of the elevation. If you are using lead lines it is helpful to increase the pressure of your lead at the start of the line, lighten it in the middle, and increase it again at its juncture with the dimension line. In this way, you help lead the eye of the viewer to the important points of information.

Whenever possible you should use your extension lines to place your dimensions outside an object. If you must dimension on top of an elevation, try to locate the dimensions so that they do not confuse the lines of the elevation. If, for clarity, you must draw an extension line across the edge of an elevation, keep the extension line light as it crosses the elevation and darken it thereafter.

If possible, dimension lines should not be crossed by extension lines or by other dimension lines. Extension lines can and often do cross each other and, if needed, they can stop and start again, "jumping" across a dimension line or other information. (See Figure 9.3.)

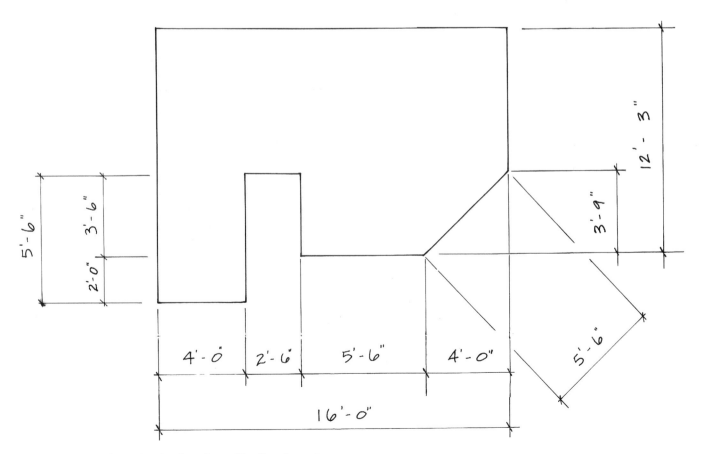

Figure 9.3   Crossing extension lines to position the dimensions.

A common error of the beginning draftsperson is to crowd the dimension lines and numerals too close to the object. Extension lines should be located so as to place the dimensions close enough to visually refer to the object but far enough away so as not to impinge upon and thus confuse the object being dimensioned.

Dimension Lines

There are several stylistic variations for drawing dimension lines and their numerals. Once a style is chosen, however, it must be consistently applied.

A dimension line is a thin, solid line indicating the direction of a measurement between two points. The dimension line can end in an arrowhead, a slash, or a dot.

Formerly, theatrical dimension lines always ended in an arrowhead and were broken in the middle to provide a small space for the insertion of the dimension numeral. Arrowheads are drawn with a loose, free-hand movement of the fingers. They should be neat, small, of the same size, and should touch but should not extend beyond the extension lines. (See Figure 9.4.)

In film, and increasingly in theatrical drafting, the dimension line is drawn in the architectural convention of ending in a dot or a short 30-degree slash. (See Figure 9.5.) In measuring a site, it is clearest to write the dimensional numeral on top of the dimension line.

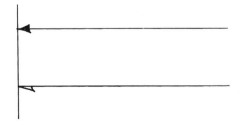

Figure 9.4   Dimension line arrowheads.

Placing the Dimension Numeral

The dimension line may be broken at its center and the numeral inserted, or the dimension line can be unbroken with the numeral placed just above the line. (See Figure 9.6.) If you are positioning the dimension numerals outside the extension lines, to avoid confusion it is important that the numeral is always above the dimension line.

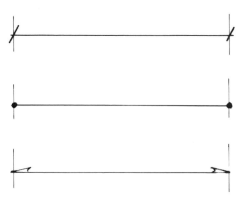

Figure 9.5   Ending the dimension line.

Position of the Numeral to the Reader

If you are insetting the numeral, you may choose to have all the numerals face the reader and be read from the bottom of the page. This makes them easier to read, but the numerals that dimension height will take up more space. (See Figure 9.7.) In a string of height dimensions that face the reader, it is often necessary to stagger the numerals rather than place each of them at the center of the dimension line.

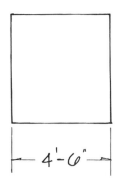

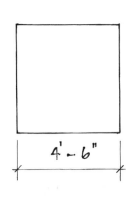

Figure 9.6   Placement of the dimension numeral.

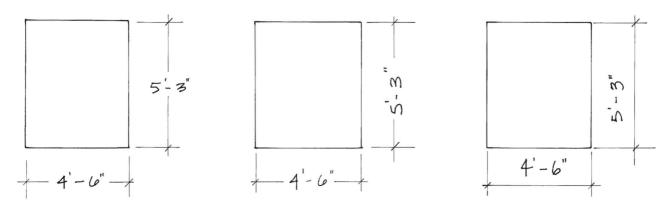

Figure 9.7 Position of the numeral to the reader.

If you choose to place your numerals beside the dimension line, they will be read from the bottom and the right side of the page as in Figure 9.8.

Leaders

Leaders are short lines that extend from a note to the specific part on the object that the note refers to. It is also possible to have a single note with several leaders pointing away from it to several parts of the object.

Leader lines can end in arrowheads or they can end in a small dot. Their lines can be curved, straight, or angled. If you choose to use curved leaders, the curve should be a single, simple, unobtrusive curve. (See Figure 9.9.)

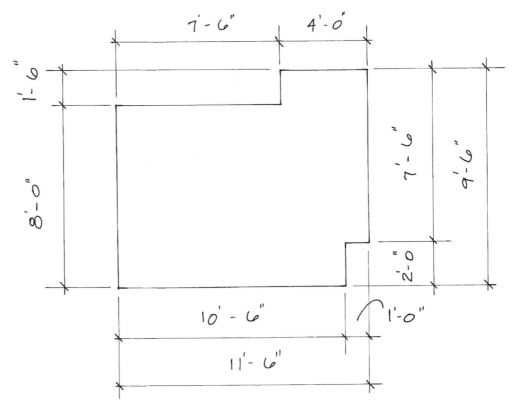

Figure 9.8 Placement of external dimension numerals.

Figure 9.9   Types of leader lines.

Leaders start from the beginning or the end of a note, never from its middle. If needed, they can cross the lines of the image to point within it. A few draftspeople erase a channel through the image for the leader, but this is not commonly done.

If you have a series of notes with leaders on one side of a drafting, you should line up the notes vertically.

Dimensioning Tight Spaces

When dimensioning tight spaces you can place the dimension inside the extension lines and draw short dimension lines just on the outside. For very tight spaces, you can place the numeral outside the space and refer to it with a leader. (See Figure 9.10.)

Dimensioning Arcs and Circles

An arc or a circle is dimensioned by its radius. The radius is drawn as a single, straight line beginning at the center of the circle and ending with an arrowhead or dot touching the edge of the circumference. If the size of the circle allows, the dimension numeral of the length of the radius is inset in the radius line or drawn just above the radius line. The numeral is preceded or followed by an R, as in R=3'-0", or 5" R. (See Figure 9.11.)

If space is tight, the numeral can be moved outside the circumference line and a leader drawn connecting to the radius line. Small circles are often dimensioned as diameters with OD, meaning outside diameter, or ID, meaning the inside diameter of an object such as a tube. (See Figure 9.11.)

Dimensioning Angles

The dimension line for a large angle is an arc from the center point of the angle. Where the arc touches the angle's sides it ends in an arrow-

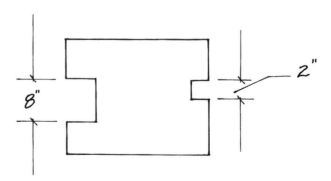

Figure 9.10   Tight space dimensions.

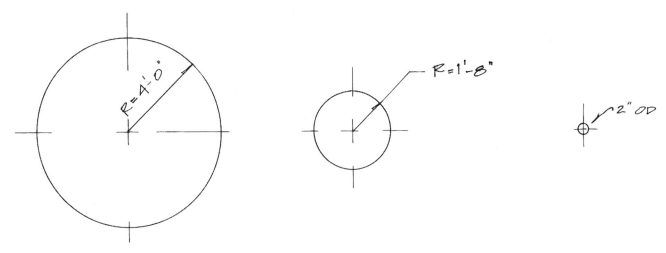

Figure 9.11   Dimensioning arcs and circles.

head or small dot or slash. A small space is erased at its center for the insertion of the angle expressed in degrees. (See Figure 9.12.)

If space is tight, short sections of an arc ending in arrowheads, dots, or slashes may be drawn outside and touching the angle sides. The degree of the angle is drawn inside the arc. This is similar to a small space dimension. If space is very tight, the degree of the angle may be positioned outside the angle and a leader may point within. (See Figure 9.12.)

Another convention for dimensioning angles is to draw a small, external, floating angle mirroring the angle that is being dimensioned (Figure 9.13). The degree numeral is drawn inside the small angle. This method allows flexibility in placing the dimension outside of the view, where it will not confuse the drawing.

Order of Dimensioning

Smaller dimensions should be drawn closer to the object than larger dimensions, and a series of dimensions should always end in an overall dimension that gives the total length of the object. (See Figure 9.14.)

Most objects can be drawn with three lines of dimensions: minor dimensions, secondary dimensions, and a major dimension on the outside. Although minor dimensions may float, it is best not to float secondary dimensions but to relate them in a string of sequential measurements.

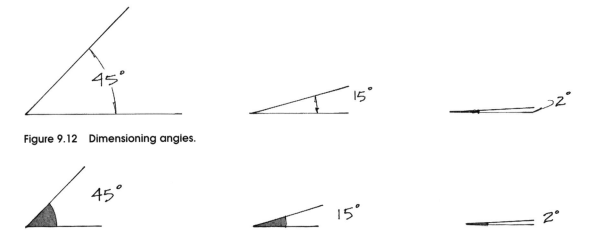

Figure 9.12   Dimensioning angles.

Figure 9.13   Alternative method of dimensioning angles.

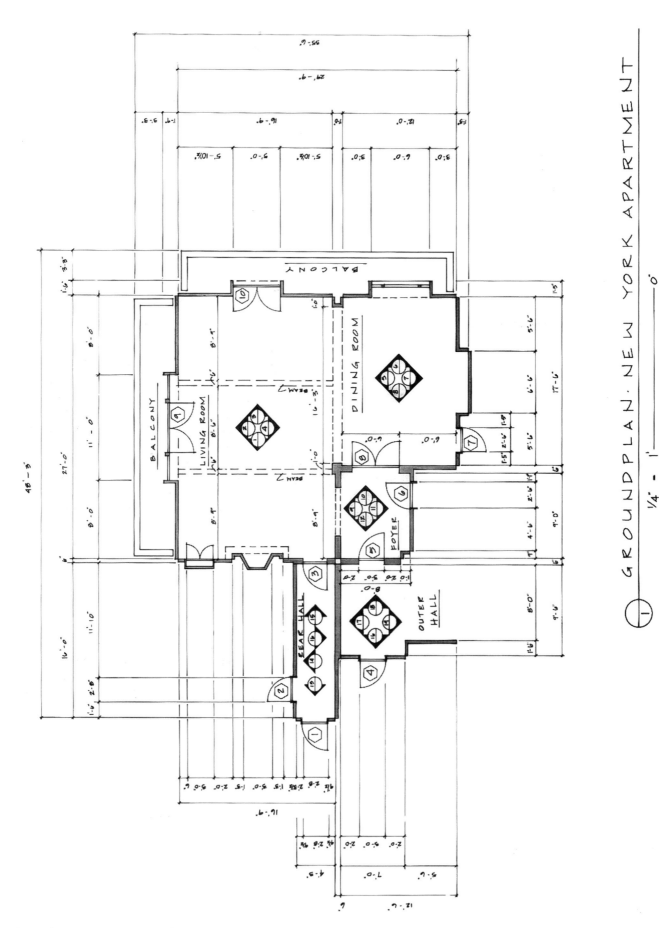

Figure 9.14 Order of dimensioning.

When drafting a scenic flat, the second string of dimensions (drawn just within the overall dimensions) dimension the openings in the flat, such as those for doors and windows. These openings are always dimensioned to the finished opening.

Base or 0'-0" Lines for Dimensioning

The principle dimensions of height, width, and depth, also known as the x, y, z coordinates, are all taken from common reference lines known as 0'-0" lines. The vertical 0'-0" line is also referred to as a base line. It is extremely important that all the dimensions in adjacent planes of a projection be taken from the same 0'-0" line.

In simple scenic drafting, we often assume these reference lines to be the surfaces we commonly dimension from. For example, for height dimensions we usually dimension to the top of the studio or stage floor. For depth dimensions, we usually dimension to the top of the surface that covers the scenery flat. The 0'-0" line for width dimension is often assumed to be a side edge of the object. (See Figure 9.15.)

For depth dimensions, the most common reference line is assumed to be the face of the covering of the flat. When drafting details, which often consist of many separate pieces of molding on different sheets of paper, it is especially important to note the position of the common 0'-0" line that relates all the pieces, and to dimension and draw everything from this same depth reference line.

For more advanced drafting it is important to understand that the 0'-0" reference-line positions of height, width, and depth are always theoretical constructs. As such, they can be placed at any convenient spatial location as long as their location is clearly noted and as long as they are the same location for adjacent views. (See Figures 9.16a and 9.16b.)

Examples of Vertical 0'-0" Lines

A common scenic occurrence is the covering of the stage or studio floor with a platform. The clearest method of height dimensioning is often not to the floor, but to the top of the platform. To make the top of the platform the 0'-0" line, note on the drafting, "All dimensions taken from the 0'-0" line—platform top."

A more complex drafting situation might be one in which a platform is sitting on top of a raked deck with some flats and steps on top of the platform. In drafting the rake, the 0'-0" line would be the stage floor. In drafting the flats and the steps, it makes more sense to make the 0'-0" line the top of the platform. Again, it just has to be clearly noted.

Another example of establishing an arbitrary vertical 0'-0" line would be drafting something that hangs in the air, such as a series of angling, interlocking heating ducts. Rather than taking all height dimensions from the floor, it makes more sense to establish an arbitrary 0'-0" line at the topmost point of the ducts and dimension vertically down from this point. The 0'-0" line can be noted on the drawing as being a set height from the floor, or it could be noted that the exact height of the ducts would be set by the designer at installation.

Establishing the Center Line as the 0'-0" Line for Width Measurements

If a scenic object is an organic shape such as a sculpted animal, width measurements are often best dimensioned from either side of a centerline rather than to an edge line.

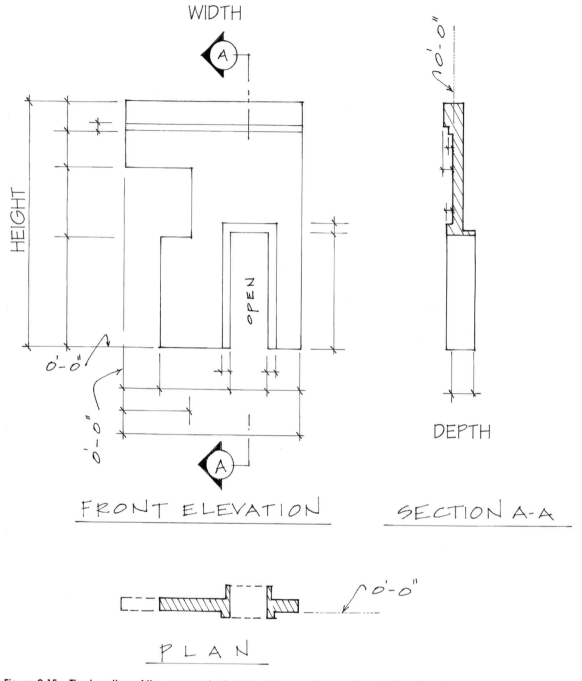

WIDTH

HEIGHT

OPEN

0'-0"

0'-0"

FRONT ELEVATION

0'-0"

DEPTH

SECTION A-A

0'-0"

PLAN

Figure 9.15 The location of the assumed principle reference lines on the drafting of a simple scenic flat.

Examples of 0'-0" Coordinates
on a Master Ground Plan

On the master ground plan of a proscenium set, the width 0'-0" line is always assumed to be the centerline, a point midway between the edges of the proscenium. This point is often marked on the stage floor, sometimes with a small brass circle. However, the 0'-0" line for all depth dimensions must be set by the draftsperson and noted as such on the drawing. Because a set may tour into different theatres, where the distance from the back of the proscenium to the first available line set varies, it is important that the depth 0'-0" line be set by a piece of the

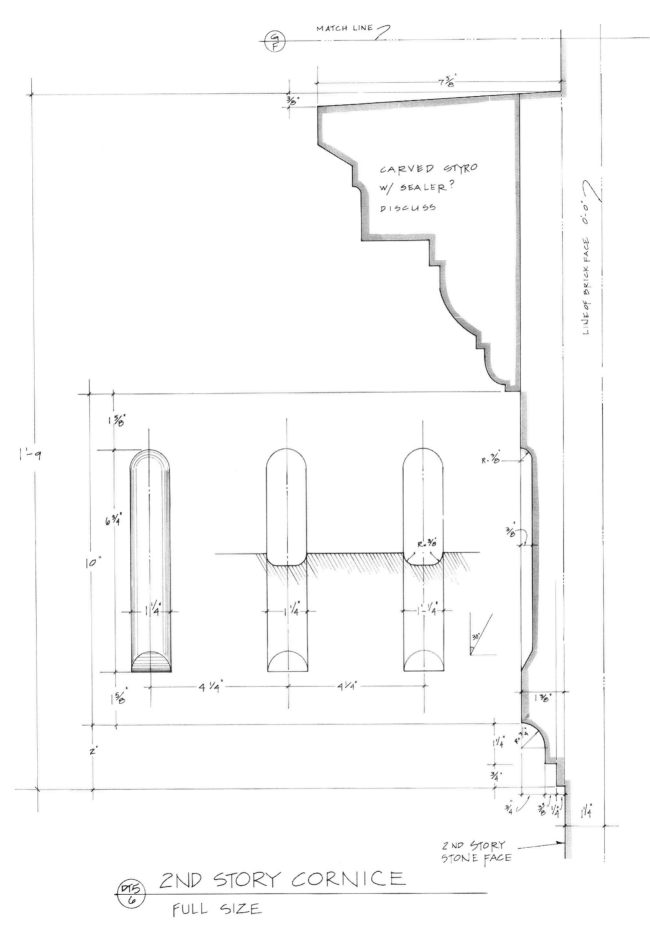

Figure 9.16a Noting the 0'-0" line for the depths of molding details.

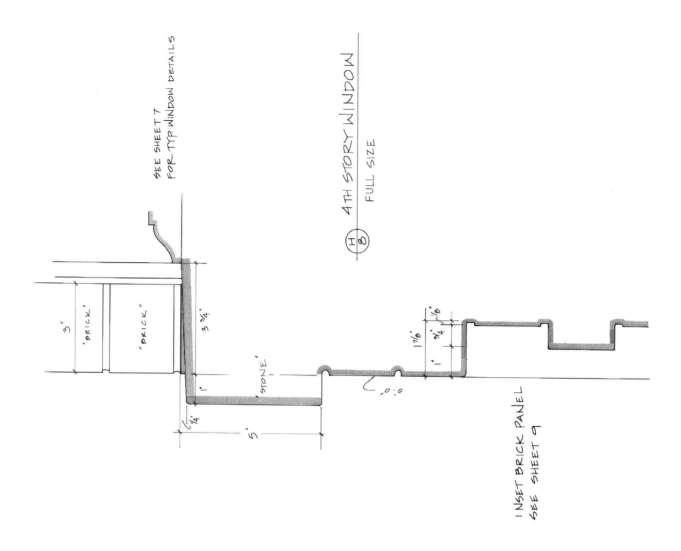

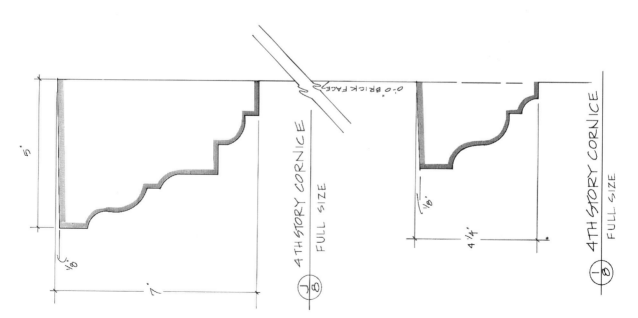

Figure 9.16b   Noting the 0'-0" line for the depths of molding details.

scenery, not by a part of the stage such as the back edge of the proscenium wall. If the 0'-0" line is a piece of scenery such as the show portal, the positions of all the scenery can remain constant while the distance from the proscenium to that show portal may vary.

In a theatrical space other than a proscenium, it may be necessary to set two arbitrary perpendicular 0'-0" width and depth lines from which to dimension. For example, in an arena stage, you may establish two centerlines that cross at the midpoint of the acting space.

While studio sets are usually dimensioned to the sidewalls, if the walls are skewed, it may be necessary to snap two perpendicular coordinates in a corner of the room. All the sets in the studio can then be dimensioned to these lines.

Establishing Arbitrary 0'-0" Lines

Occasionally there is no obvious physical reference point from which to establish a 0'-0" line. For example, in building scenery on a location such as the edge of a hill, there may be no established plane that is an obvious base 0'-0" line for the vertical dimensions. Using a surveyor's transit, a particular height can be established as a base line from which all other heights are measured and dimensioned. Such an arbitrary base line is called a datum. (See Figure 9.17.)

An arbitrary set of 0'-0" coordinates may be established in any view to facilitate dimensioning. In Figure 9.18, drafted by Jeff McDonald for Jeremy Conway's design for the NBC TV Barcelona news studio, multiple center points for complex ellipses were dimensioned to theoretical vertical and horizontal 0'-0" lines. All the radii of the ellipses were dimensioned numerically from the center points to these outside reference lines.

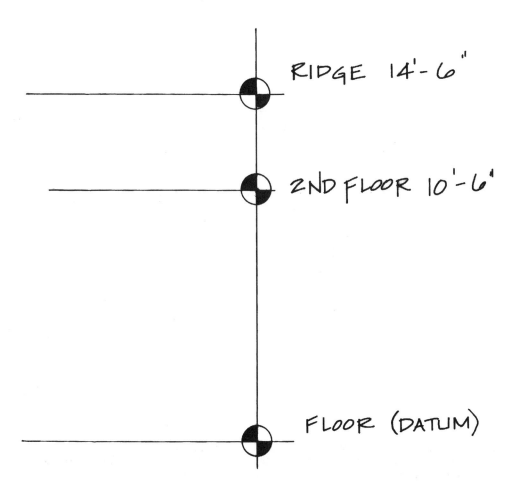

Figure 9.17 Establishing a datum.

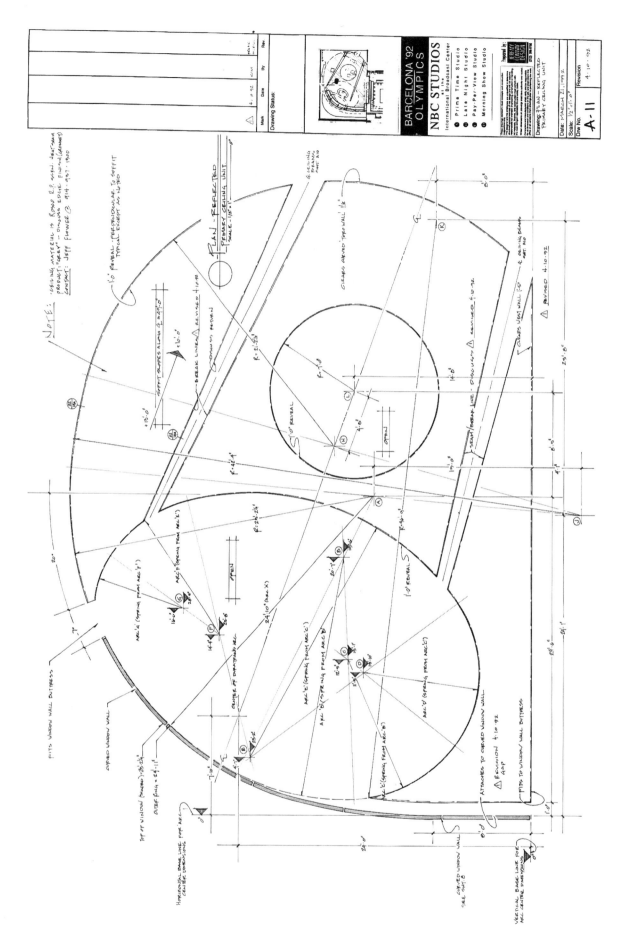

Figure 9.18 Dimensioning multiple center points to theoretical coordinates. Sheet A11—the reflected primary ceiling unit. Drafting of "The Prime Time Studio," NBC Television Studios, for the 1992 Barcelona Olympics. Designed by Jeremy Conway. Art direction by Kim Jennings. Drafted by Jeff McDonald. Courtesy of NBC Television.

Each radius center was thus fixed in relationship to the others, and a complicated drawing was made simpler and more easily comprehensible.

Selection of Dimensions

Measurements reflect the underlying organization of the structure being drawn. It is important to take the time to consider which are the important dimensions of an object and which are less important and belong on an auxiliary detail sheet. Dimensions should not be duplicated unnecessarily, and superfluous dimensions should not be included. In other words, if on a small-scale elevation you indicate the overall size of a molding shape, and if on another sheet or view you draw a detail of that molding, you should not include the internal dimensions of the molding parts on the smaller-scale drafting.

Your dimensioning should also consider the process of building the scenery in order to the give the builder the information he or she will need in a clear manner and in the order needed. The greater your knowledge of scenery construction, the more clearly you will be able to dimension.

Placement of Dimensions

Dimensions should be placed in a logical, orderly arrangement. They should be easy to read and in positions where they can be easily found. In general, height and width dimensions are best drawn on the elevation rather than the section, and depth dimensions are clearest when drawn on a section rather than on a plan. When drawing scenery, however, there is no set rule of placement, and the draftsperson will have to consider the clearest organization and placement of dimensions for each scenic object. (See Figure 9.19.)

Dimensioning Directly on Top of an Elevation

While it is usually best to pull your dimensions to the side of a view so as not to confuse the image, there are occasions when the clearest method of dimensioning is to dimension directly on top of an elevation, as shown in the lovely drafting by Dan Davis in Figure 9.20.

Dimensioning the Scenery Flat

A scenic flat is typically drawn in a quarter-inch- or half-inch-to-the-foot scale elevation. Major sizes, such as the heights and widths of doors and windows, the overall size of the cornice and baseboard, the location of a picture rail, and the height and width spacing of a wainscot, are included in the smaller-scale drawing. Areas of details are coded to refer to larger-scale drawings on which they will be completely dimensioned. (See Chapter 14, "Multisheet Sets and Coding.") The measured dimensions of midsize details, such as the width of door stiles and rails, are sometimes drawn on the smaller-scale drafting, but are better redrawn in a slightly larger scale next to their full-size details.

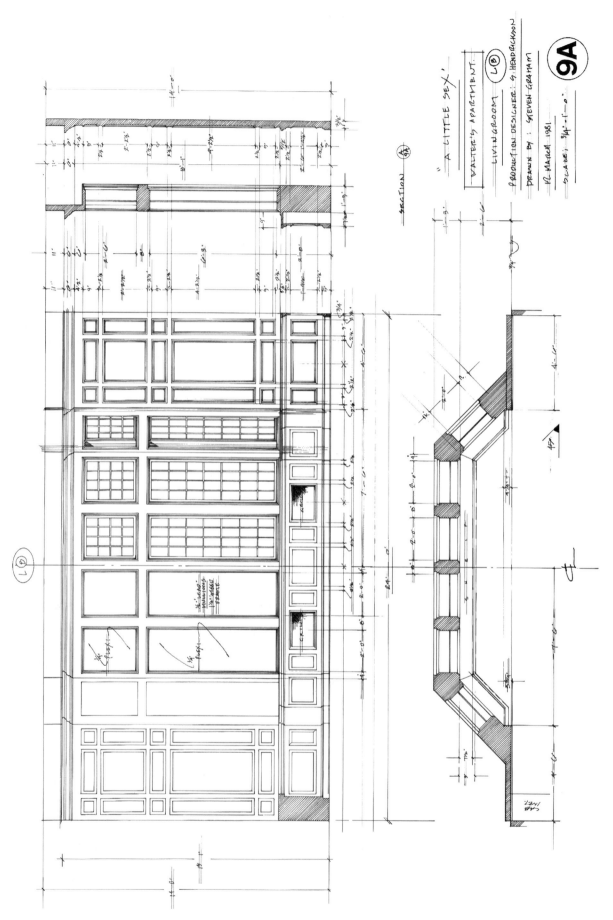

Figure 9.19 A clearly organized page of dimensions. Drafting of "Walter's Apartment Living Room" for the feature film *A Little Sex*. 1982. Directed by Bruce Paltrow. Production designed by Stephen Hendrickson. Drafting by Steve Graham. Designs courtesy of MTM Enterprises, Inc.

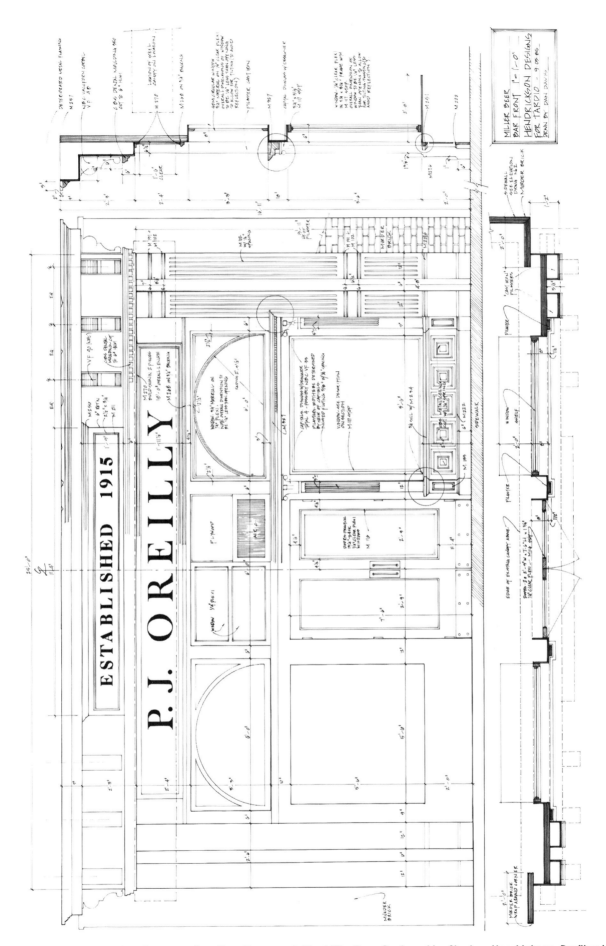

Figure 9.20 Dimensioning directly on an elevation. Commercial for Miller Beer. Designed by Stephen Hendrickson. Drafting by Dan Davis. Used by permission.

Relief Dimensioning

The depth dimensions of an object usually appear on a side view or vertical section. However, in circumstances with multiple projections from the same surface, it makes more sense to dimension depths on a front view or elevation rather than on multiple side views or sections. This is known as relief dimensioning. (See Figure 9.21.)

In relief dimensioning the surface plane of each projection is marked with the numeral of the depth measurement preceded by a plus sign. The position of the base or 0'-0" line from which all these heights are taken must be clearly noted or indicated on a single section so that the builder knows the starting point for all the measurements.

Dimensioning Irregular Geometric Shapes

There are two ways of dimensioning irregular geometric shapes. The most common method used by the scenic draftsperson is to locate and

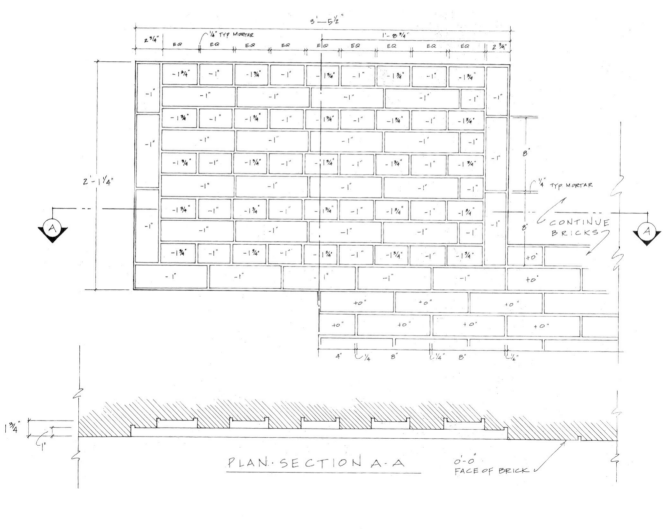

Figure 9.21   Relief dimensioning.

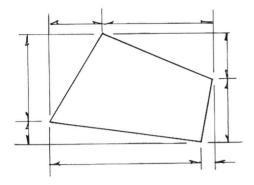

Figure 9.22 Dimensioning an irregular parallelogram from point to point.

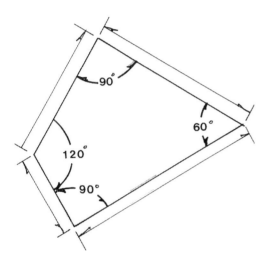

Figure 9.23 Dimensioning an irregular parallelogram with true lines and angles.

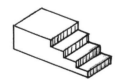

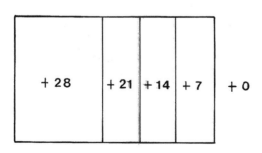

Figure 9.24 Dimensioning stairs and platforms.

dimension to the points that create the shape. Essentially, this method boxes in the object and dimensions the box. All the dimensions are taken parallel and perpendicular to the viewer. (See Figure 9.22.)

The second method, more common in a technical shop than for scenic drafting, is to dimension the true length of each line. With such a method, you must also dimension each angle of the shape. (See Figure 9.23.)

Height Dimensions on a Ground Plan

On a ground plan, all heights, including stair treads and platforms, are treated as relief dimensions from a single base line, usually the floor of the theatre. Their heights are dimensioned as numerals preceded by a plus sign. The height of individual treads is usually dimensioned in inches rather than feet and inches. Platforms are usually dimensioned in feet and inches preceded by a plus sign. (See Figure 9.24.) Drawing diagonals through the corners of platforms is no longer a common convention as it makes the information confusing.

The plus numeral indicating the height of overhead objects such as archways or cantilevered platforms is often followed by the word "clear," meaning that along the underside of that structure that height will have clear passage.

Dimensioning Inclined Platforms

On an inclined platform, the rake line is a line from the lowest to the highest point on the platform. The rake line runs perpendicularly to a series of theoretical lines, each parallel to the floor. Another way to think of this is that a series of parallel support stringers runs perpendicularly to the rake line.

When drafting an inclined platform, the rake line is indicated as a line with an arrow at its end and a note indicating "ramp down" or "rake down." (See Figure 9.25.) The slant of the rake is called the pitch, the plan distance along the rake line is called the run, and the total height is called the rise.

A rake may be dimensioned as the rise in each foot of travel along the run, usually expressed in inches. For example, rake 1"/1'-0" means that the platform rises one inch for each foot of travel. In 10 feet, therefore, this platform would have risen 10 inches.

Rakes may also be expressed as a ratio, as in 1:12 rise. Or they may be expressed as a pitch, as in 1-inch Pitch, meaning it rises 1 inch for every 12. Pitch is commonly used for expressing the angle of roof structures. While a rake may be dimensioned as an angle, it is better to calculate and dimension it as a pitch, ratio, or rise per foot of travel, as this allows mathematical calculation of the height at any point.

It may be necessary to determine the height at a specific point on a rake to calculate the number of stair rises necessary to hit that point. This may be calculated geometrically by taking a section along the rake line and projecting the point across from the plan to see its height on the section. It is more exact, however, to calculate the height mathematically.

If your rake is expressed as a rise per foot of travel, you can multiply the length of the run in feet by the rise per foot. For example, for a rake at 1/2"/1'-0" rise, a 6'-3" run would rise 3 1/8".

If your rake is expressed in a ratio, you can divide the run by the rise per inch. For example, assume that you have a 1:10 rise and your point

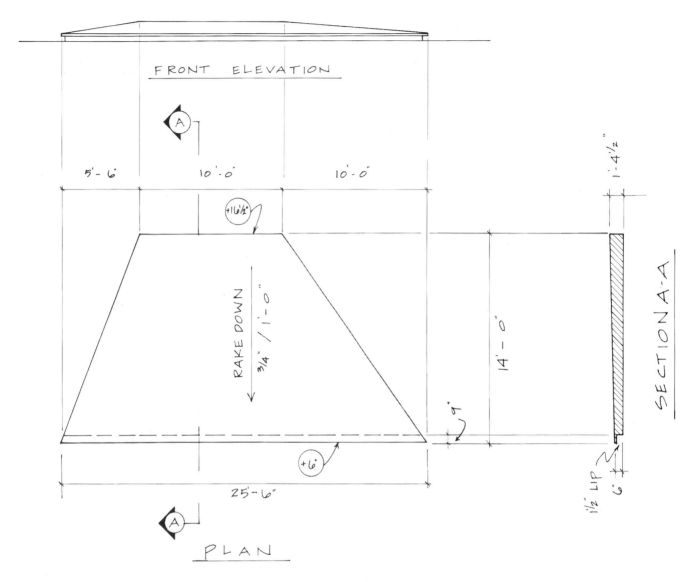

FRONT ELEVATION

A

5'-6"   10'-0"   10'-0"

+16½"

RAKE DOWN
¾" / 1'-0"

14'-0"

9"

+6"

25'-6"

1'-4½"

SECTION A-A

1½" LIP

6"

PLAN

Figure 9.25   Dimensioning a simple rake.

is located 8 feet 2 inches along the run. The rise at that point would be 98 inches divided by 10", or 9 7/8 inches.

As three heights determine the angle of any plane, the rake of any platform can be set by dimensioning the height of any three points. These heights can be indicated on the ground plan as dimensions with leaders indicating the line or point on the rake to which they refer. These three heights and the position of the rake line are enough to dimension a small inclined surface.

A skewed raked platform is one where the line of the rake is not perpendicular to the front edge of the platform. In such a situation, the clearest method of dimensioning is to indicate the rake line, note the direction down, and then dash in the lines of a series of theoretical parallel stringers at regular intervals, perpendicular to the line of the rake. Each of these dashed lines will be the same height at all points along the line. This contour method of dimensioning an inclined surface, especially for a large platform, gives an idea of the height of the rake at most points and can be used to determine the height at any other point. (See Figure 9.26.)

To Determine the Rake
Line of an Inclined Surface

Sometimes an inclined platform is designed and the position of the rake line then needs to be determined. The incline may have been designed in plan form as a shape with several set heights attached to it, or it may have been designed in model form that needs to be drafted.

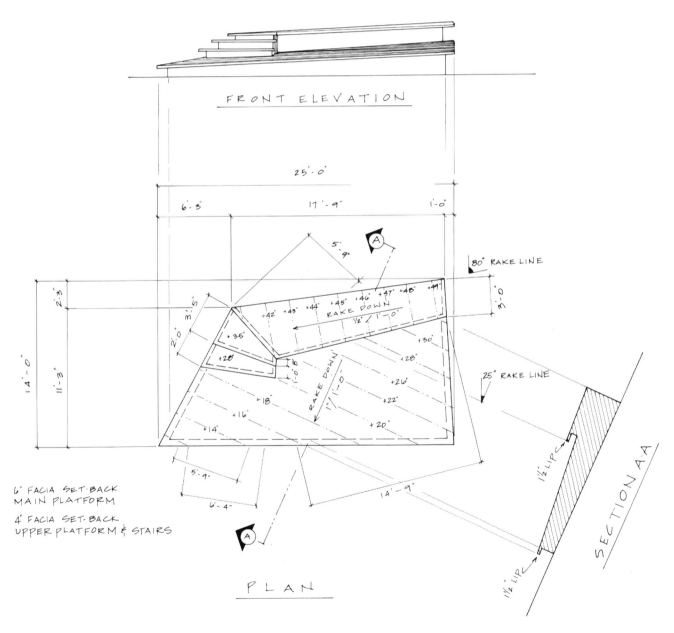

Figure 9.26   Dimensioning a complex rake with structures.

The following method can be used to determine the rake line of any inclined plane and to determine the height at any point on that incline. Familiarity with this procedure will give the scenic draftsperson an understanding of the nature of inclined structures and the ability to manipulate between the mathematical and the physical structure.

1. To determine the rake line of an inclined surface, first establish or measure the heights at three points. It is best to pick points that are approximately the highest and lowest, then a point midway between them. You can establish these points theoretically, marking the heights as points on your plan, or you can measure three points from a model of the incline and transfer the measurements to the same positions on a plan.

2. On your plan, draw a straight line between the highest and lowest of the three points. Divide the length of this line into a series of equal spaces so that one of the divisions is numerically the same as the mid-point height. Call this line X. (See Figure 9.27.)

   For example, assume that the highest point on your rake is 32 inches, the lowest point is 4 inches, and the midpoint is 10 inches. You have a height change between the low and high point of 32 inches minus 4, or a total of 28 inches. These 28 inches can be nicely divided into 14 equal spaces. Each division will now represent a 2-inch rise.

   Write the height of each point along line X.

3. Draw a line from the midpoint height you first measured or determined through the same height point on line X. Call this line Y. Any point along line Y will be the same height.

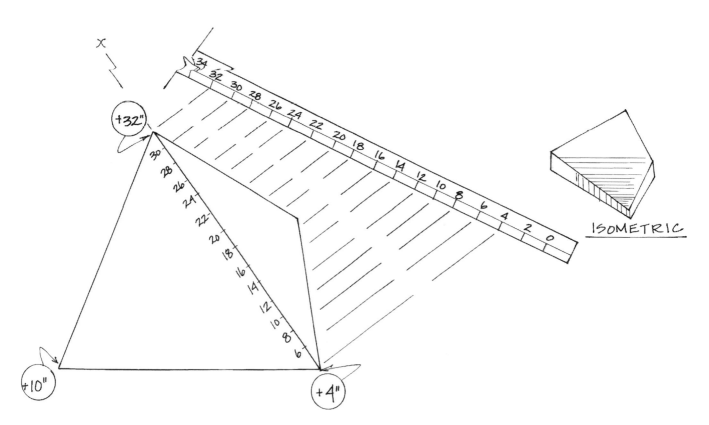

Figure 9.27 Dividing a line between the highest and lowest point on the rake.

In Figure 9.28, you would draw a line Y from the 10-inch midpoint height through the 10-inch point on line X. All points along line Y would measure 10 inches in height. This line could represent a 10-inch-high stringer supporting the platform, with its top parallel to the floor.

4. Draw lines parallel to line Y through each of the other heights on line X. All points along each of these lines will be the same height.

In the final drafting of an inclined or skewed platform (a platform whose edges are not perpendicular to the viewer), you draw a series of dashed (hidden) parallel lines with heights at 2 inches, 4 inches, 6 inches, and so on. A line drawn perpendicular to the parallel lines will be the rake line for that incline. (See Figure 9.29.)

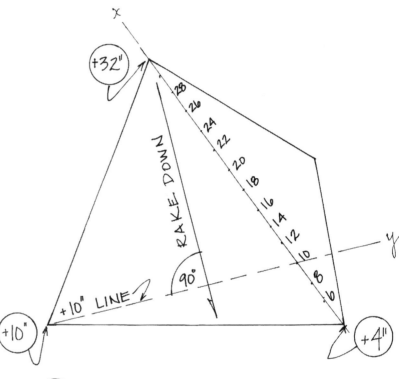

Figure 9.28   Drawing the stringer line at the medium height point on the rake.

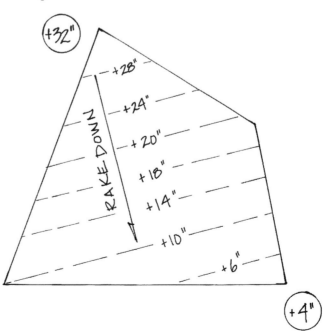

Figure 9.29   Locating the heights of the perpendiculars along the rake line.

Use of "Typical" in Dimensioning

If it is obvious in a drafting that there are many repeating units that are clearly the same size (such as the width of repeating wainscot molding), you do not have to dimension each part over and over but can note the word "typical" or "typ" after one or several dimensions. (See Figure 9.30.)

Use of "EQ" in Dimensioning

If a length of scenery is divided into repeating units, such as the space between the stiles of a wainscot panel, or glass window panes between muntins, it is acceptable practice to dimension the panel spaces as "EQ," meaning equal. (See Figure 9.30.) This means that the builder

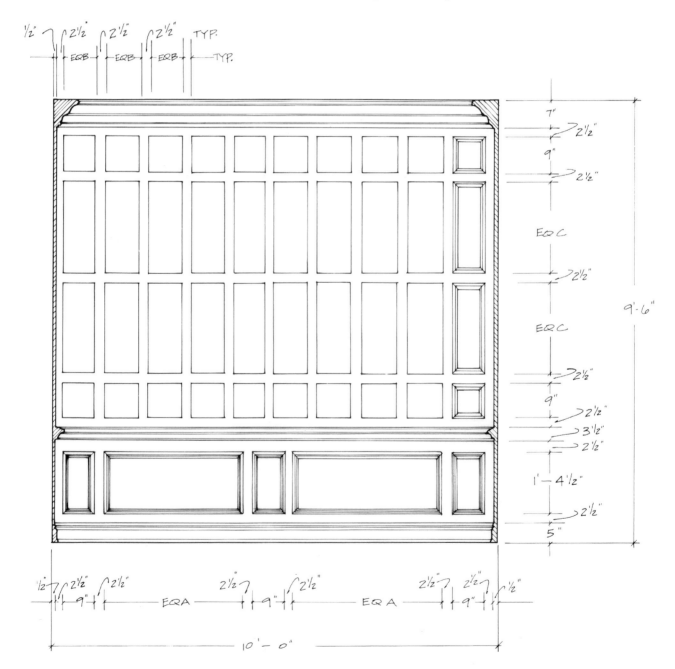

Figure 9.30   Use of "EQ" in dimensioning. Use of "Typical" in dimensioning.

should take the total distance minus the repeating pieces of lumber and divide it into equal spaces. As stock lumber varies slightly in size, this is often a more accurate method of dimensioning than using numerals.

Dimensioning Center to Center on Repeating Units

On repeating units such as columns, pipes, beams, or posts, the best method to dimension between the units is to their centerlines. The widths of the units can be a secondary dimension. This guarantees that even if there is a variation in the size of the units, they will be evenly spaced. The drafting convention is to draw a centerline lightly drawn through each unit, extend it as though it were an extension line, and mark the end of the line with a small "cl." You then draw the dimension lines between the centerlines. (See Figure 9.31.)

If you are drafting many objects that are close together and evenly spaced, such as stair balusters, you can draw each centerline and mark the repeating dimension to each center. An example would be 6" o.c., meaning that the centerlines of all the units are to be spaced with their centers 6 inches apart.

Omitting One Dimension

When dimensioning an object, you must always include its overall dimension. However, in the series of secondary dimensions that add up to the total, it is acceptable and sometimes wise to omit one dimension that is not critical to the look or the construction of an object. This omission says to

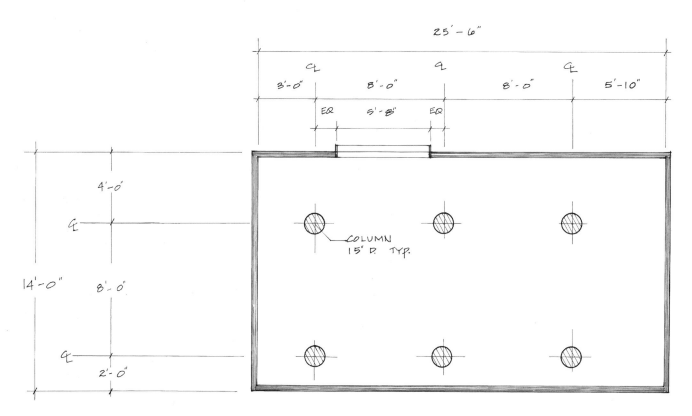

Figure 9.31 Dimensioning to centers.

the builder that, if necessary, he or she can adjust any small inaccurate construction measurement into that space. (See Figure 9.32.)

Plus or Minus Dimensioning

There are times, especially in film location designing, when it is impossible to have an exact measurement of something, but it is important to at least have a relatively accurate measurement. In these cases a small plus or minus is written just before the numeral, indicating that the measurement is close but not firm and should, if necessary, be verified. In Figure 9.33, the arches are sunk into sand and their height is noted as a plus or minus dimension.

Structural Dimensioning

When dimensioning scenery that is structural rather than ornamental, it is often clearest to dimension to the center or side of a structural member. (See Figure 9.34.) For example, if you are building a curved metal truss wrapped with a thin sheet of Plexiglas, the major dimension should be to the outside of the metal framing member. You should note to where you are dimensioning, as in Figure 9.34, which is dimensioned to the "rim joists" not the platform facia. Figure 9.35 shows the structure of the platform.

Dimensioning Break Lines

A long object with an uninformative section may be drawn by removing that section between a series of break lines. Break lines are drawn as two parallel lines with a clear space between them. The parallel lines are drawn with a break symbol, as shown in Figure 9.36. When dimensioning a view with a break in it, give the measurement of the unbroken distance and use a small jog in the dimension line to indicate that the dimension line has been shortened.

Contour Dimensioning

Contour lines enable us to draft and dimension undulating surfaces such as earth, snow, sand dunes, ices floes, or rounded anthropomorphic shapes. The dashed lines of contours on a plan indicate the connection of points of equal height. On a landscape, if extended far enough, every contour line will become a closed loop. On maps, these elevations are taken from the common reference line of sea level, but for scenic replication, a theoretical 0'-0" level plane may be established at any convenient point. Usually this is the floor of the stage or studio, or the top of a built platform.

Contour intervals are the vertical distance between horizontal planes passing through successive contours. On a topographic map, these distances may be as much as 10 feet apart, but the intervals in scenery are usually calculated in smaller amounts, even in inches. If the surface is to be constructed of carved Styrofoam, for example, it helps the builder to have the contour intervals agree with the thickness of the Styrofoam slabs.

On any one drawing, the contour interval should not change. In other words, if you determine that each contour interval is 6 inches, that

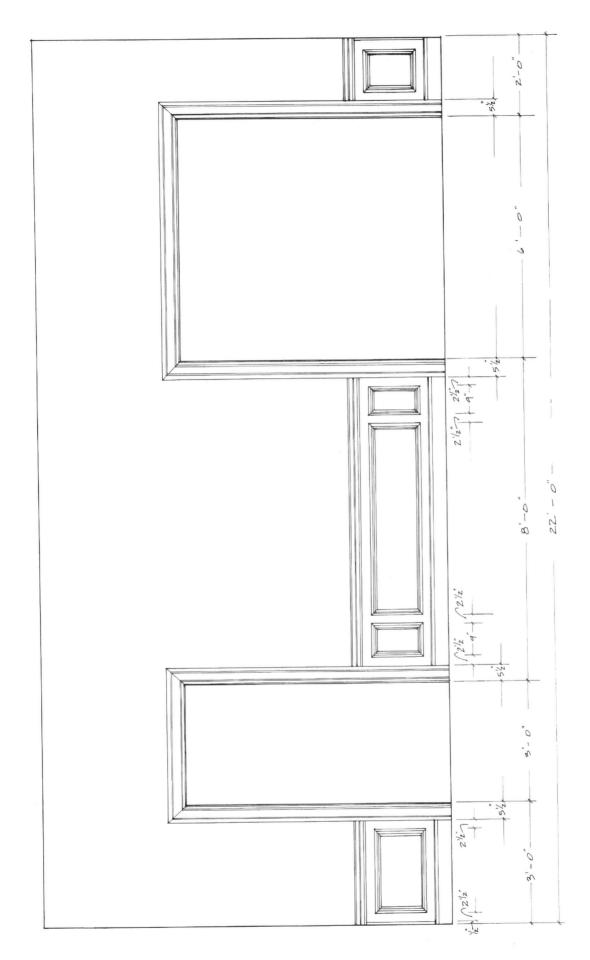

Figure 9.32 Omitting one dimension.

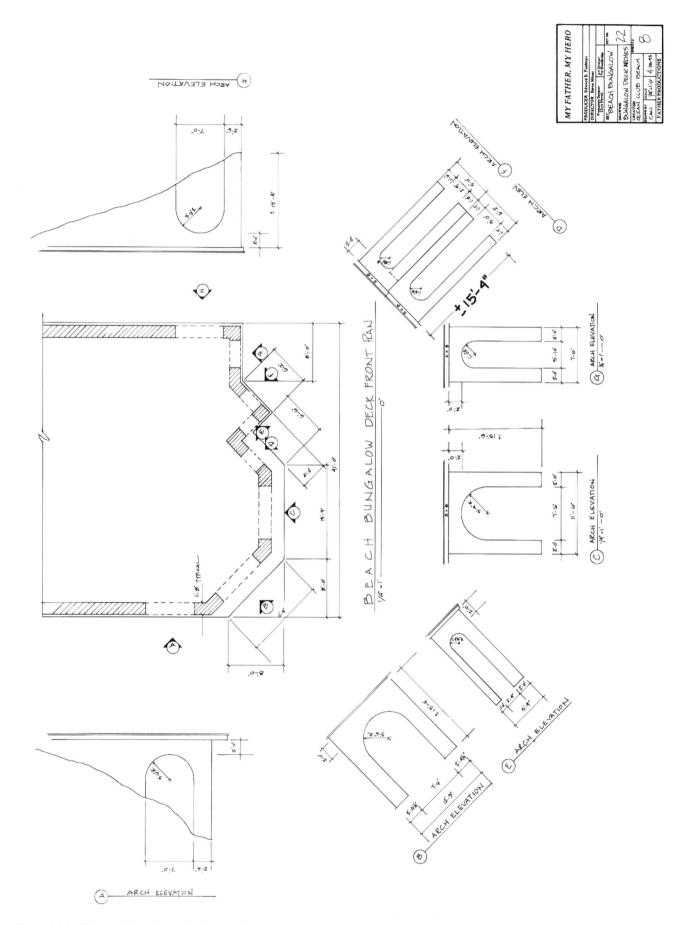

Figure 9.33 Plus or minus dimensioning. Drafting of "Beach Bungalow" from Touchstone Pictures' feature film *My Father, The Hero*. 1994. Directed by Steve Minor. Designed and drafted by Christopher Nowak. Used by permission from Disney Enterprises, Inc.

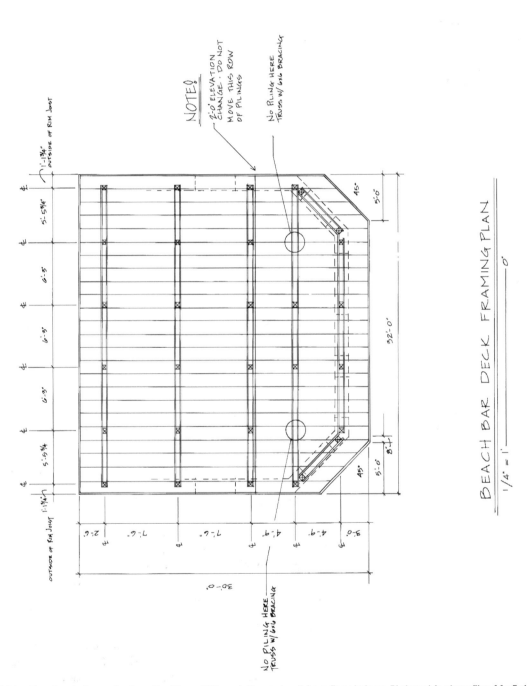

Figure 9.34   Structural dimensioning. Drafting of "Beach Bungalow" from Touchstone Pictures' feature film *My Father, The Hero*. 1994. Directed by Steve Minor. Designed and drafted by Christopher Nowak. Used by permission from Disney Enterprises, Inc.

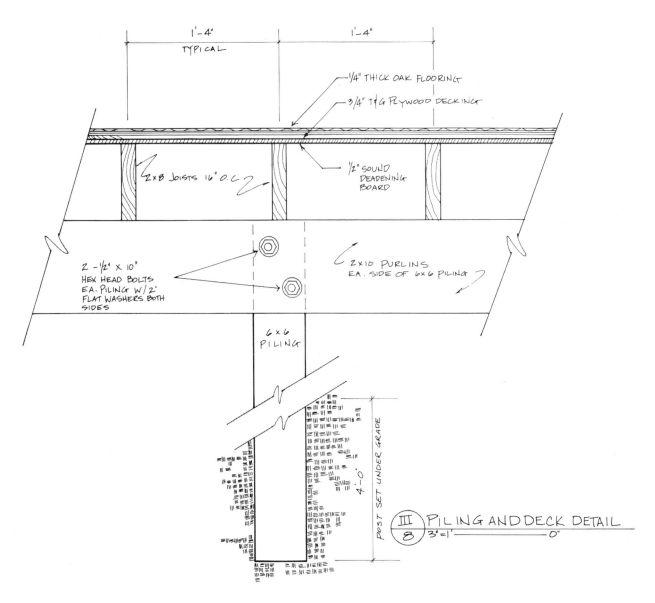

Figure 9.35 Piling and deck detail. Drafting of "Beach Bungalow" from Touchstone Pictures' feature film *My Father, The Hero.* 1994. Directed by Steve Minor. Designed and drafted by Christopher Nowak. Used by permission from Disney Enterprises, Inc.

depth should remain consistent. Contour lines are drafted as thin, dashed lines. A numeral indicating the height along the contour is inset in the contour line. (See Figure 9.37.)

With practice, a designer can read a contour drafting and obtain a sense of the surface. If successive contours are evenly spaced, it means the ground slopes uniformly; closely spaced contours indicate steep changes in level; contours that are far apart indicate a gentle slope.

Cross-sections can easily be developed from contour plans and elevations by plotting and connecting the points. (For a discussion of sculptural shapes, see "Large Convex Sculptural Shapes—Caves and Mountains" in Chapter 8, "The Section.")

Although we are most familiar with contouring in the plan view, contours can also be used to dimension the depths of elevations. Scenic shapes such as animals or the side of a mountain may be drafted as a relief, with contour depths from any convenient base or 0'-0" line. For a small, three-dimensional, anthropomorphic shape such as a cow, a clear

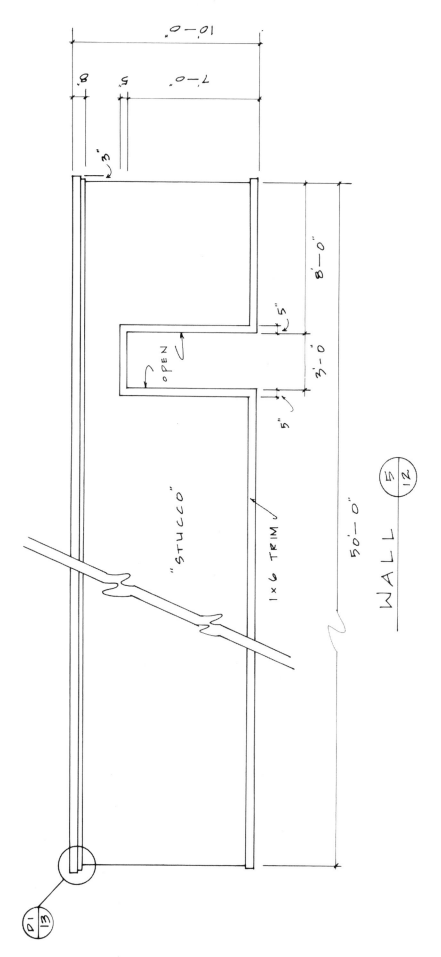

Figure 9.36 Dimensioning break lines.

145

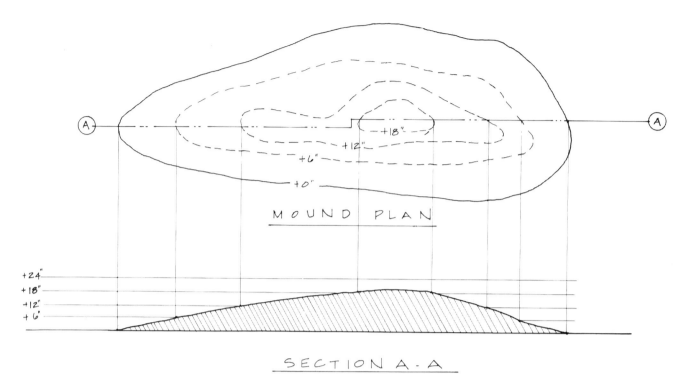

Figure 9.37 Contour dimensioning.

way to draw the front view is to locate the 0'-0" line along the center-line of the animal with contours indicating the depths from that line. The edges of each contour can then be dropped vertically, and their depths measured from the same 0'-0" line on the plan.

To Determine Contour Dimensions from a Model

Sometimes the scenic draftsperson will build a soft, carved shape on a model and then need to draft it. The following is a procedure to use to establish the contours of such a surface. Use of this method will give the student an understanding of the nature of contours.

1. Trace the exterior edge of your sculpted shape onto paper. This will be your plan. Grid the plan at a convenient interval such as 1 foot in scale.
2. Take a hard but porous surface such as a piece of chipboard or presswood and draw the same scaled grid on it. Tack your sculpted shape onto the gridded surface so that it matches the location to the grid on your plan.
3. Label the lines of both grids with matching marks. Use letters for the horizontals and numerals for the verticals.
4. Hammer or push long, thin nails or pins into the board at the end of each grid line Tie thread to each nail and string lines above the sculp-ture along the lines of the grid.
5. Use a thin rod or long nail to measure the height of the sculpture at each thread juncture in the following manner: Slowly push your rod into the sculpture until you feel it touch the wood base. Mark the surface point of the rod with a small dot from a fine-tipped water-

146

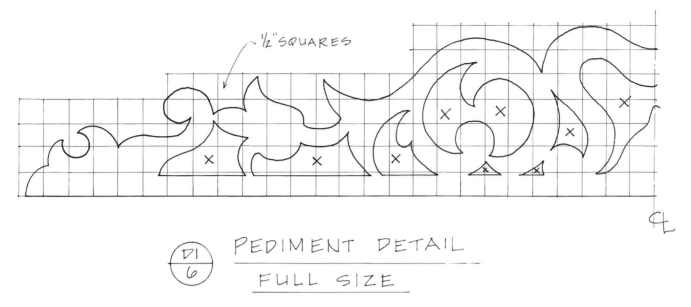

Figure 9.38   Gridding irregular shapes.

soluble marker. Carefully remove the rod and measure the depth using a finely graded ruler. Record each measurement on the corresponding juncture on the grid of your plan.

6. When the depth of all the junctures have been determined, use light lines to connect similar numerical depths on the plan. Now refine these contours on your drawing by studying the sculpted shape and adjusting and curving the lines.

Dimensioning Irregular Shapes

A complex, irregular shape is best dimensioned by overlaying the scaled drawing with a lightweight line of repeating squares at set dimensioned intervals of a convenient distance. This creates a scaled grid that can be duplicated full-size in the shop. (See Figure 9.38.)

Dimensional Calculators

It is a huge help in dimensioning to have a dimensional calculator. The best professional calculator is the Construction Master III-Trig Plus. This calculator can work as a standard math calculator with memory and percent, and it also works with dimensions and translates into metric. It can calculate square and rectangular areas, the circumference of circles, pitch, trig problems, brick courses, and much more.

Clouding a Dimension to Indicate It Has Been Revised

A cloud around a dimension indicates that it has been changed from the last time the drawing was printed. (See Figure 9.39.) It is best to draw the cloud on the backside of the drafting so that, if needed, you can easily erase it.

Figure 9.39   Clouding a dimension to indicate it has been revised.

10

Surveying and Sight Lines

Surveying is used to map existing site conditions on a plan or to position sets on a location site. The following are tools for measuring that are used by art directors and scenic designers to measure objects or sites.

25-Foot Steel Tape Measure

This is a basic tape measure. (See Figure 10.1.) Pushing the lever on the face of the tape measure automatically locks the tape. You need to be able to extend and hold the tape vertically to measure heights of ceilings and other structures above your reach. If you don't have an assistant, you will also want to be able to hold the tape horizontally and parallel to the floor to take a horizontal measurement without the tape buckling. (See Figure 10.2.) The best choice for a tape measure is one that is at least three-quarters of an inch wide and can be extended a reasonable length without buckling. The width of the metal cartridge in which the tape is stored should measure exactly three inches. This allows you to measure more accurately between two points. Rather then bending the tape at the measuring end, you can place the edge of the metal cartridge

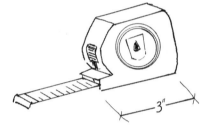

Figure 10.1   25-foot steel tape measure.

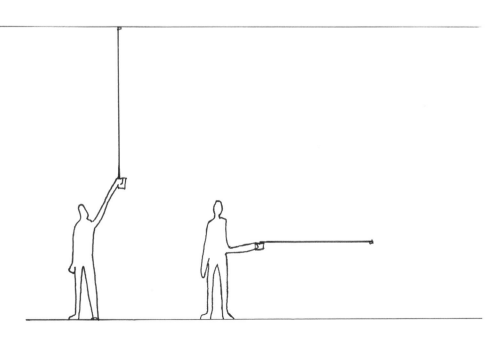

Figure 10.2   Measuring by extending the steel tape measure.

against the surface and add the sum of 3 inches to the measurement on the tape. Stanley is a good brand.

Wooden Folding Ruler

This wooden ruler has swiveling metal joints that allow it to fold up. (See Figure 10.3.) Folding rulers usually extend to 6 feet, although shorter models are available. The end of the ruler has a thin, 6-inch long metal extension that slides out and is accurately calibrated to 1/16 of an inch. This ruler is good for exact measuring inside small tight spaces such as the widths of drawers.

100-Foot Steel Tape Measure

This tape is thin and flexible, but it is metal, allowing you to measure long distances with accuracy. (See Figure 10.4.) To rewind the tape flip up and turn the hand crank on the side of the cartridge. These tapes have a small hook at their end that should be flexible. This flexibility enables the tape to give accurate results whether the end is pressed, hand-held, or nailed. Lufkin is a good brand.

Fiberglass 200-Foot Measuring Tape

To measure a large site such as an exterior landscape you need a 200-foot tape measure. (See Figure 10.5.) These tapes come with a handle, which makes them convenient to carry, and a hand crank that is used to coil up the tape. The tape is usually made of fiberglass, which is flexible and more rigid than cloth and which allows the tape to be easily cleaned. Because of its flexibility, the fiberglass measuring tape stretches slightly and is less accurate than a steel tape. Lufkin is a good brand.

Measuring Wheel

The measuring wheel has a vertical pole handle that is held while rolling the wheel. (See Figure 10.6.) The wheel is attached to an odometer with large numerals that measure the distance traveled. The odometer is manually reset to zero before measuring. While the measuring wheel won't give you tight, point-to-point measurements, it is a good tool for a person working alone to measure a long distance and important sequential points along that distance. For example, it might be used to measure the length of house along a city block, and it would have the added advantage of doing so without disturbing any pedestrians.

Plumb Bob and Mason's Line

Mason's line is a strong string that doesn't stretch. A roll of it can be useful for any site work where you need to locate a temporary line. A plumb bob is a heavy metal weight with a point. The plumb bob is attached to mason's line and held or taped to an overhead point. When the bob stops moving you can measure to the point. For example, to locate the plan position of a lighting fixture in the ceiling, hang a plumb bob from its center and measure from the walls to that point.

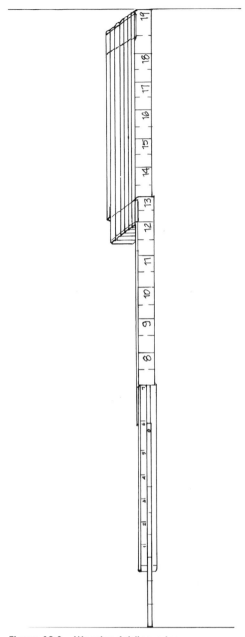

Figure 10.3   Wooden folding ruler.

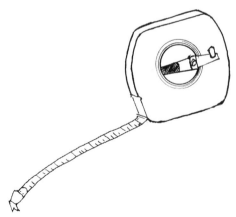

Figure 10.4   100-foot steel tape measure.

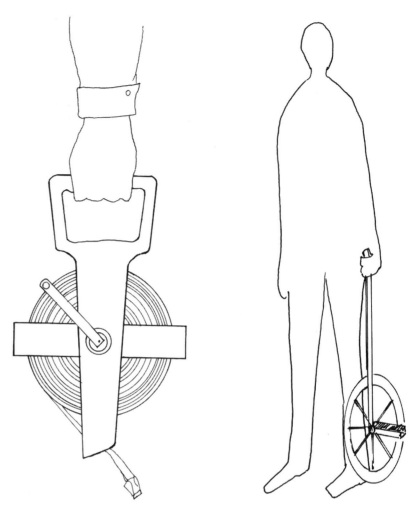

Figure 10.5   200-foot fiberglass tape measure.   Figure 10.6   Measuring wheel.

String Level and Mason's Line

A small level (with a bubble that allows you to locate a true horizontal line) is designed to slide along a length of string, preferably a mason's line. The art director can measure an uneven surface, such as the drainage curve of a road surface, by stretching and leveling the string while measuring sequential depths to plot the curve.

Electronic Measuring Instruments

These electronic devices called "range finders" measure from 3 to 250 feet by emitting a laser or sonar beam that bounces off the surface at which you have aimed. Range finders are good for quickly estimating the size and height of a room. However, because a projection from a wall can distort a measurement, they are not entirely accurate. The more expensive instruments emit a small beam of light that indicates the object being measured.

Arranging to Measure the Site

The theatrical draftsperson often needs to measure the performance space. Even if you receive a ground plan and cross-section, it is good practice to check the measurements for accuracy and to check for any changes that have occurred since it was measured. In a Broadway situation it is common for the producer to arrange to pay the house carpenter to open the theater to be measured. The house carpenter can arrange to get a ladder and can operate the fly system if necessary. For film and many other types of designing, it is often necessary to measure interior and exterior sites that will have scenic elements added to them, or built in or on them. The location manager arranges for access to a location. It is a good idea to try and determine in advance if you need to arrange for specialized equipment, such as a specific type of ladder, to help you measure.

Sketching and Planning before Measuring

Before measuring a location, take the time to study the space and make a simple, proportionally accurate sketch. Gridded paper that comes in pads helps to sketch in scale. The grids come with a square-inch divided into 4 x 4, 8 x 8, or 10 x 10 divisions.

The 4 x 4 and 8 x 8 grids help in laying out 1/8", 1/4", 1/2", 1" or full-scale drawings. The 10 x 10 grid is good for an engineer's scale. For small sketches, an 8 1/2-by-11-inch clipboard provides a good hard sketching surface. For larger locations, you can attach a gridded pad of 17" by 22" to a board or piece of thick chipboard on four sides using large metal clips. For very complicated sites, you may want to set up a board on a surface in the center of the location.

While correct overall proportions are important for any sketch, they are critical in surveying a site plan. Measure or pace off the overall length and width of a room and lightly draw the outlines on your sketch before measuring along a wall. If you are sketching an object, first measure its total length and width and sketch them in scale. To pace a distance means to measure it by the stride of your walk. To determine your pace, measure the average distance you cover with a continuous stride and adjust the length of your stride to a simple length such as three feet. Pacing can give you a quick initial estimated measurement when you lack a tape or do not wish to disturb others with a measuring tape, but it is very inaccurate.

Many art directors visually estimate each length and sketch an entire location before measuring and dimensioning. A few art directors measure and use the grid to sketch in scale as they dimension. Some people find it helpful to sketch in pencil and then plug in the dimensions and extension lines with a fine-tipped felt pen. Many experienced surveyors do all their drawing and dimensioning with a thin ink line for accuracy.

Figure 10.7 is an example of a site survey of several ornate windows in an exterior New York City location. A piece of 4 x 4 gridded paper was used to sketch in roughly 1-inch to 1-foot scale the elevation, plan, and section of the windows for duplication on a built set. The drawing was done with a Mongol #3 pencil, which has an eraser. The dimensions were done with a thin-tipped pen. Scaled sketching of architectural elevations and details is not only required for film work but is also the way a young designer/draftsperson learns period architectural detailing and proportion.

Profile Gauge

The profile gauge is used to copy small shapes such as baseboard moldings. The gauge is composed of many short, thin, sliding rods, or plastic

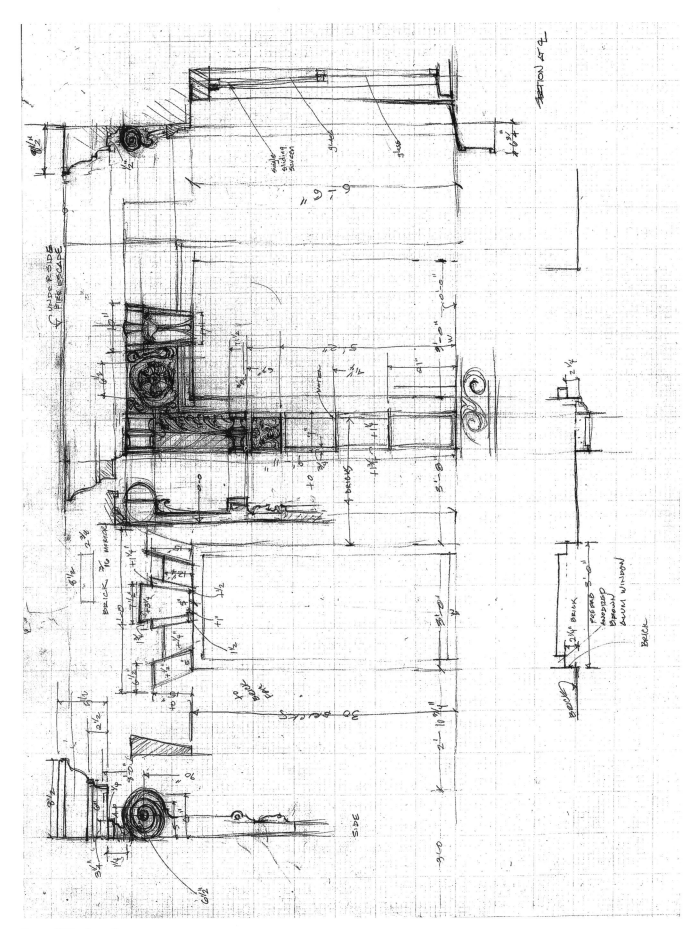

Figure 10.7   Location survey.

153

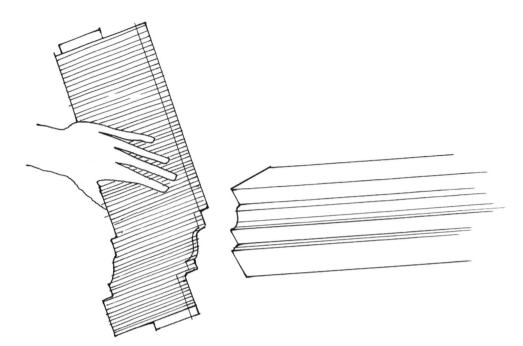

Figure 10.8   Holding a profile gauge against a shape.

strips that slide through a central core When you press the edge of the gauge against an object, the rods conform to its shape. The shape can then be traced on paper. A profile gauge was used to capture details such as the window casing in Figure 10.7.

Detail Rubbings

To quickly copy an embossed detail, treat it like a gravestone rubbing. Tape a piece of thin paper over it, then press down and rub the surface with charcoal or conte crayon. In surveying the details in Figure 10.7 a rubbing was made of the embossed band under the windowsill.

General Procedure for Measuring a Site

It is ideal to have three people to measure a site. One holds the "smart" end of the tape with the numbers, one the "dumb" end of the tape measure, and a third dimensions and sketches. Often, however, there are only two people, with the smart-end person also writing in the dimensions. Occasionally you are by yourself. The general procedure for measuring is to measure the larger distances first and then plug in the shorter distances and finally the details. If you are measuring a series of small distances it is important to measure the overall distance. (See Figure 10.9.) If you make an error or forget a measurement, the critical total will still be accurate and will often allow you to find your error. A dimensional calculator is a great help to check that the smaller lengths add up to the total.

Base Line versus Direct Measurement.

If you are measuring many short distances it is often easier and more accurate to extend your tape the total length of the distance and take sequential measurements rather then a series of direct measurements that will add up to a total distance. Figure 10.10 shows a method of differentiating base line from direct measurements on a sketch.

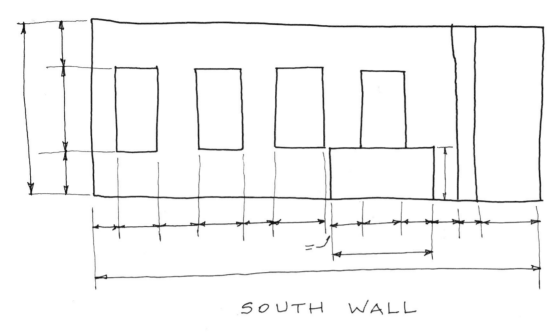

SOUTH WALL

Figure 10.9 Always measure the total length as well as the divisions of that length.

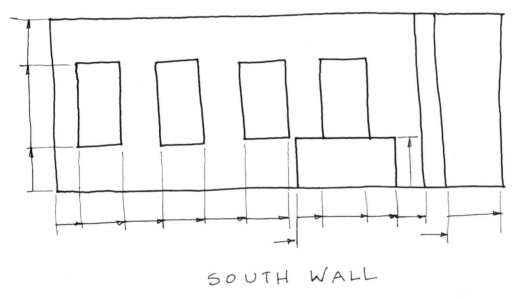

SOUTH WALL

Figure 10.10 Noting base line measurements.

Always mark each location survey you have done with the site address. On large films where several people are making location sketches it is a good idea to organize all the surveys in a single book or drawer.

Photographic Site Reference

When measuring a site the art director usually takes reference photographs. Unlike location photographs that show general camera angles, the art director needs coverage of each elevation as well as close-ups of details. When photographing a long elevation such as the front of a building or street, the art director walks along the street and takes a series of frontal, slightly overlapping shots, each shot approximately the same distance from the surface being photographed. In the art department the prints are matched and joined by clear tape on their back side. The set name is marked on the tab of a legal-sized manila folder with the location address on its front. A paper cutter or exacto knife is used to trim off the tabs of additional manila folders that are taped by their base inside the first folder, creating pages in a book. The photographed elevations and details of each location are taped to the pages of the book. If one of the elevations extends beyond the edges of a page, it is lightly scored on its rear side and folded. The photographs should be laid out in a coherent journey through the location.

If you don't have time to measure a lot of small details such as moldings, you can get a fairly clear idea of their size and shape by holding a tape measure next to or across them and taking a close-up photograph for later reference. With practice you can hold the metal measuring tape at the correct position while simultaneously taking the photograph.

In the art department, keep track of your negatives in a negative box, labeling them by location, address, and date so they will be easily found if you need additional prints.

Cameras

In general, the art director wants a fast, autofocus camera with an electronic flash and a powerful zoom lens for close-ups of details. People who use eyeglasses can purchase a camera that allows visual correction in the camera rather than with eyeglasses. The Kodak Advantix Camera, which has what is called an "Advanced Photo System," is particularly good for production designers and art directors. This camera requires its own special film and processing system, but it allows, in a single roll of film, the choice of three print formats: Classic, HDTV, or Panoramic. Prints are returned in a neat, cardstock folder organized for archiving. In addition to the prints you receive a 4-by-6-inch color proof showing small numbered images of each print. The film cassette containing processed negatives is attached to the folder.

When you are photographing a tall building, the higher the shot the more the perspective will be distorted. You can rent specialty cameras that compensate for the vertical distortion and shoot a direct elevation of a tall building.

Story Pole

A story or range pole (Figure 10.11) can be rented from an architectural supply store to be held against a surface such as a building that is being photographed. These fiberglass poles are a series of nested extendible lengths, dimensioned with large numerals that can be read from a distance. You can make your own story pole by measuring and marking a long stick of wood. The dimensions on the story pole allow the art director to scale a photograph. (See Figure 5.6b.)

Triangulation

Any triangle has three sides that result in a fixed shape. Many difficult spaces can be measured by dividing them into triangles and laying them out on paper with a compass.

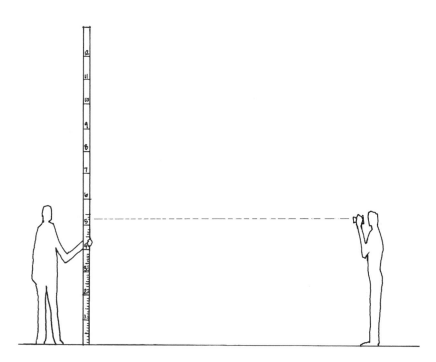

Figure 10.11 Person holding a story pole.

Figure 10.12 shows a room that is not square. Measuring the diagonal of the room creates two triangles and can transcribe the parallelogram.

Using a 45-Degree Triangle to Estimate Heights

In a 45-degree triangle two of the sides are equal in length. If you have sufficient space in front of any object, its height can be closely estimated by the following method. Hold your 45-degree drafting triangle upright so that the bottom edge is parallel to the ground. Using your eye to sight along the angled edge, walk backwards until you see the top of the object you wish to measure. If at this location you theoretically extended the edge of the triangle until it hit the ground, the distance from the ground point to the object would be close to the height of the object. (See Figure 10.13.)

Figure 10.14 shows the measurement of an exterior location using triangulation. Triangles were laid out and measured between the side of

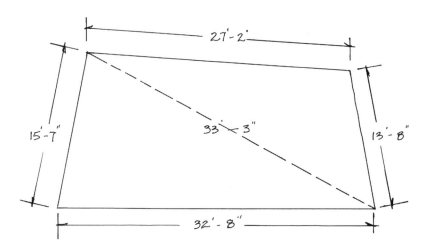

Figure 10.12 Use of triangulation to measure a room that is not square.

157

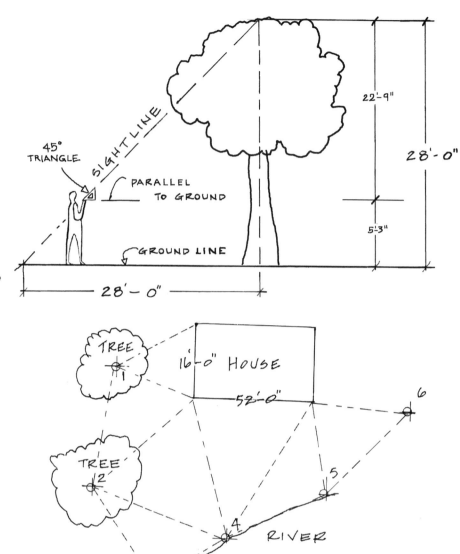

Figure 10.13 Using a 45-degree triangle to estimate the height of an object.

Figure 10.14 Measuring a landscape with triangulation.

the house and two trees. To plot the shape of the river beside the house, a series of numbered stakes were hammered into the ground. Triangulation can be used to measure very large sites. Figure 10.15 is a site plan for a large exterior set for *The Last of the Mohicans* (1992). You can see the dashed lines of the triangles that were used to measure the location.

Trigonometry

Trigonometric functions (the relationship between the angles and sides of triangles) can aid in site measurement and layout. For any oblique triangle, if you know any two angles and one side of the triangle, or any two sides and one angle of the triangle, you can solve for any of the remaining sides or angles using a trigonometric function. These functions can be looked up in a trigonometric table such as the one in *Architectural Graphic Standards*. A good quality builder's calculator will calculate trigonometric functions. If you do not have a trigonometric table, you can divide any oblique triangle into two right triangles. The trigonometric functions for right triangles can be easily memorized

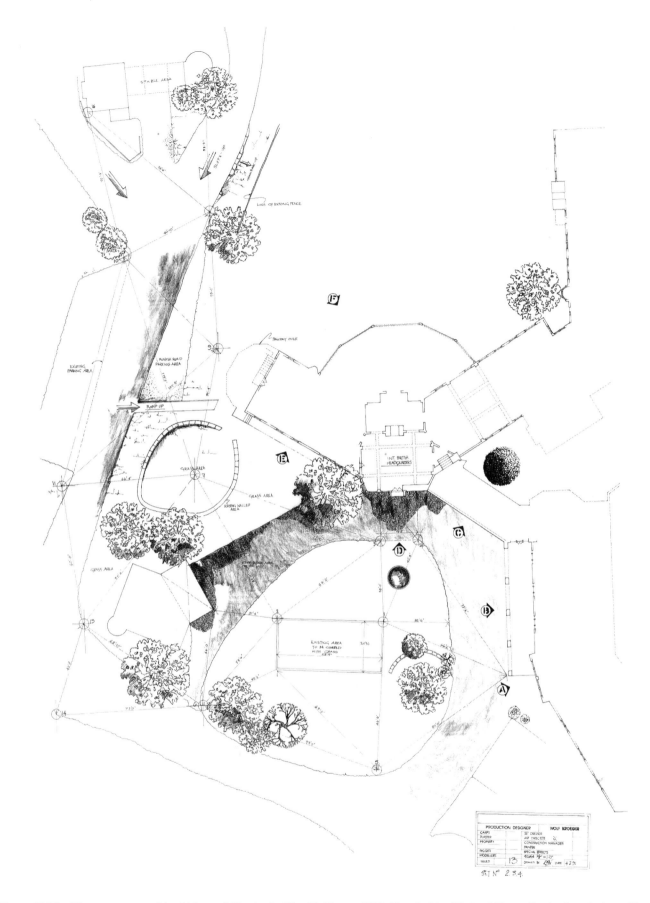

Figure 10.15   Site measurement for "Albany." *The Last of the Mohicans.* 1992. Directed by Michael Mann. Production designed by Wolf Kroeger. Drafting by Richard Holland. Drafting courtesy of Twentieth Century Fox.

with a simple mnemonic aid (think of an Indian village or banging your toe) SOH-CAH-TOA.

sine: opposite over hypotenuse
cosine: adjacent over hypotenuse
tangent: opposite over adjacent

Figures 10.16 to 10.18 provide examples of trigonometric solutions.

Laying Out Large Right Angles

When measuring or laying out the plan on a site it is often necessary to establish a perpendicular to a line. The following is a quick way to do this: The formula for a right triangle is the square of the hypotenuse equals the sum of the squares of the two sides. The simplest divisions of a right triangle are sides of 3 and 4 units with a hypotenuse of 5 units. Use any number to multiply 3, then 4 and 5 will create sides of a right triangle.

1. Multiply 3, 4, and 5 by any number to create a right triangle of a convenient size. Starting from the point where you want to establish a perpendicular, measure and mark one side of the triangle.

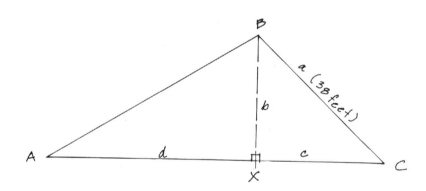

TO SOLVE FOR c

$$\cos = \frac{adjacent}{hypotenuse}$$

$$\cos 48° = \frac{c}{38 \text{ feet}}$$

$$c = \cos 48° \times 38 \text{ feet}$$

$$c = 25' - 5 \tfrac{1}{8}"$$

TO SOLVE FOR b

$$\sin = \frac{opposite}{hypotenuse}$$

$$\sin 48° = \frac{b}{38 \text{ feet}}$$

$$b = \sin 48° \times 38 \text{ feet}$$

$$b = 28' - 2 \tfrac{7}{8}"$$

TO SOLVE FOR d

$$\tan = \frac{opposite}{adjacent}$$

$$\tan 30° = \frac{28' - 2 \tfrac{7}{8}"}{d}$$

$$d = \frac{28' - 2 \tfrac{7}{8}"}{\tan 30°}$$

$$d = 48' - 10 \tfrac{61}{64}"$$

$$x = d + c$$

$$x = 48' - 10 \tfrac{61}{64}" + 25' - 5 \tfrac{1}{8}"$$

$$x = 74' - 4 \tfrac{5}{64}"$$

Figure 10.16   Solving for a side of an oblique triangle by dividing it into two right triangles.

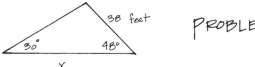

PROBLEM: SOLVE FOR SIDE X

$$X = a \sin(A + C) \div \sin A$$

$$X = 38 \text{ feet} \times \sin 78° \div \sin 30°$$

$$X = 74'-4\tfrac{5}{64}''$$

Figure 10.17 Solving for the side of an oblique triangle.

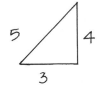 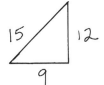 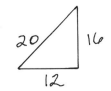

Figure 10.18 Simple right triangles.

2. Attach a string to a nail and drive the nail into the point on the line where you want the perpendicular. Measure the length of the second side of the right triangle along the string and use it as a compass to make a large chalk arc.
3. Remove the nail and repeat the process from the other end of the first line.
4. The point of intersection of the two arcs is the top of the right triangle.

Surveying the Proscenium Stage: Axis Lines and Sight Lines

In surveying for a plan we are concerned with width and depth measurements. On a proscenium stage the 0'-0" line for depth measurements is traditionally the plaster line, or the back edge of the proscenium. Depth measurements taken from the rear of the plaster line back on the stage are marked as plus measurements. The depth measurements from the plaster line into the orchestra are marked as minus measurements. The 0'-0" line for width measurements is always the centerline of the stage. This is the point exactly midway between the side edges of the proscenium.

To set the 0'-0" line for depth measurements, snap a chalk line at the plaster line between the left and right sides of the proscenium. Measure and mark the midpoint between the side walls. The Figure 10.19a uses a right triangle to establish the centerline of a stage, perpendicular to the proscenium line. A right triangle of 12, 16, and 20 feet was chosen as a convenient size. From the center point on the plaster line, 12 feet is measured in one direction. At the 12-foot mark, a 20-foot length of mason's line was attached to a piece of chalk. The string and chalk were used like a large compass to draw an arc. This procedure was repeated from the center point for the 16-foot side. The point at which the two arcs cross is perpendicular to the center of the proscenium line. A snap line was used to mark the centerline. If, in laying out your triangle on the location, it is necessary

161

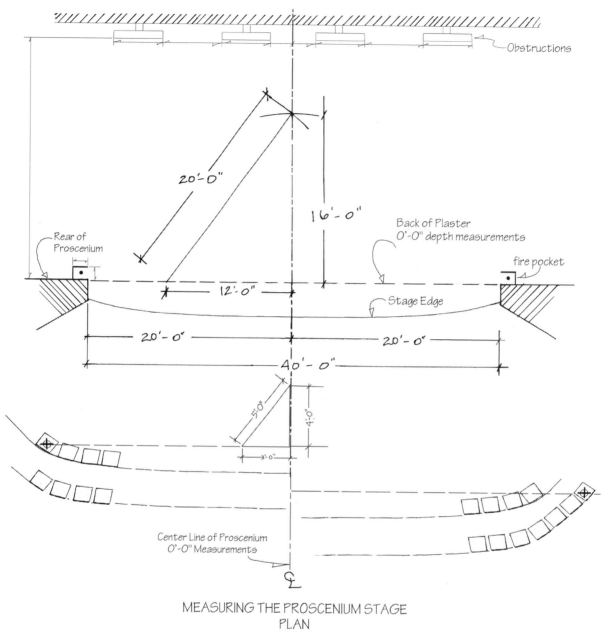

MEASURING THE PROSCENIUM STAGE
PLAN

Figure 10.19a Surveying the plan of a proscenium stage.

or more convenient to have a right triangle with a shorter leg, you could make one side 5 units and the other sides 12 and 13.

To plot the edge of a curved stage or the curve of an orchestra pit, take a series of depth measurements from the plaster line at measured intervals, such as every 4 feet.

To survey this proscenium stage the extreme left and right orchestra seats were also located and measured with the help of a right triangle. A length of mason's line with a string level was attached at the centerline of the stage, extended to the depth position of the extreme seats, and adjusted with the aid of the level until the line was even with the stage floor. A second length of line was located between the extreme edge seat on the left side and the centerline. A right triangle of 3, 4, and 5 feet was used to make certain the line was perpendicular to the centerline. Both lines were then measured, on the centerline from the plaster line to the perpendicular, and from the centerline to the extreme orchestra left seat. The procedure was repeated to measure the orchestra right sight line.

Figure 10.19b shows how the extreme right and left audience sight lines for the proscenium stage determine the visible acting and scenic areas of the stage as well as the widths of the backings behind the scenic openings.

Measuring Grid and Proscenium Heights and Pipe Positions

To locate the center position of each hanging pipe in a counterweight system, have them flown in to their lowest trim position. Measure their depth position from the plaster line back at the centerline. When determining the angle of skewed lines, snap two perpendiculars at the right and left edge of the plaster line and measure to each pipe at each end.

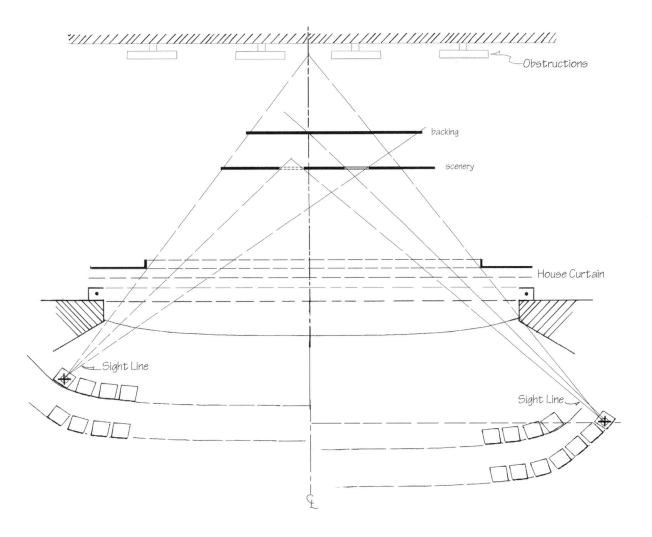

SIGHT LINES FOR THE PROSCENIUM STAGE
PLAN

Figure 10.19b   Plan sight lines for the proscenium stage.

Surveying the Cross-Section of the Proscenium Stage

In surveying the cross-section we are concerned with height and depth measurements. The 0'-0" line for depth measurements is the plaster line. The 0'-0" line for height measurements is the stage floor. The height of the proscenium will be measured with a steel tape measure. Carefully slide it up along the side reveal of the proscenium until it touches the top. To measure the maximum out trim of the house curtain, bring it in to its lowest trim, attach your tape to its bottom edge, and raise it to its highest trim. You can determine the maximum out trim of the pipes in the same manner. Next locate the most extreme audience sight lines, those closest to and furthest from the stage. To locate the closest sight line extend your mason's line with its string level along the centerline to the nearest seat and measure the location.

With orchestra seating the nearest seat to the stage edge (with the extreme vertical viewpoint of the stage) is usually not at centerline but towards the edge of the orchestra pit. In this situation you will need to locate and measure the position of the seat just as you did the orchestra extreme right and left sight lines.

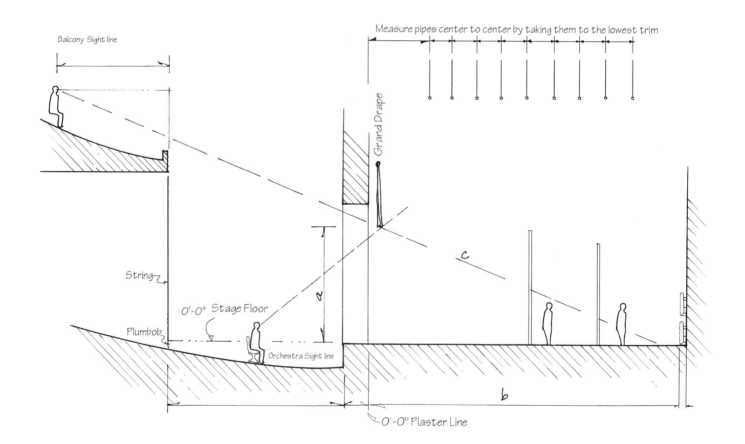

MEASURING THE PROSCENIUM STAGE
CROSS SECTION

Figure 10.20a   Surveying the cross-section of the proscenium stage.

The highest vertical sight line is usually the top row of the balcony. Plot the position of this seat by dropping a plumb bob attached to mason's line from the balcony edge at centerline and measuring to and from that point. With two surveyors you can use visual geometry to plot the balcony sight line. One person sits in the highest balcony seat and observes the stage. There will be a point where his or her line of sight is cut by a vertical obstacle: the edge of the proscenium, or the lowest position of a grand drape. The second person stands on the stage and marks the highest point on the rear wall (a ladder may be needed) or the deepest point on the stage floor that the balcony observer can see. Measure the height of the horizontal obstruction.

If there are several balconies you need to check if portions of the stage are blocked by a balcony edge and locate the horizontal obstruction.

Calculating the Minimum Height of a Backing

To calculate the minimum height for a backing, such as a drop outside a window or a hall backing behind a door, use the ground plan to determine the closest point of view. In the theater this will be the seat in the house closest to the opening. On the plan draw a line from this seat through the opening to the backing. Elevate this line to a cross-section showing the eye of the audience member in relationship to the stage, the height of the opening, and the position of the backing. Draw a line from the eye of the audience member to the top horizontal obstruction of the scenery and carry the line on until it hits the backing. Give a foot or so of extra height as "slush." The same principles apply to scenic backings for film and television. The camera is a moving sight line, so you will need to determine the closest position it will get to the opening, say about 3 feet from a window. The camera is usually about 5 foot 3 inches above the set floor. If you know the specific lens of the camera, you can plot that angle from the lens to the backing. If you don't know the exact lens, give it a rough 60-degree cone of vision and allow some added height to the backing.

Figure 10.20b shows how the extreme vertical sight lines for the proscenium stage determine the visible acting and scenic areas of the stage, the heights of backings, and the locations of electrics, flown scenery, and borders. The same principles apply to scenic backings for film and television.

Site Layout

When you are laying out a set on a landscape, you can rent fluorescent sprayed stakes from an architectural supply house or the shop can make pointed wooden sticks. Colored fluorescent plastic tape can be tied between stakes to indicate walls. If it is necessary to mark a straight line across a piece of land from one point to another, it is useful to have available 10 or more bamboo canes or thin straight sticks. The canes are then spaced, perhaps 8 to 10 feet or more apart, over a given distance. When five or six canes are in position, straighten the line by adjusting the intermediate canes between the two ends.

To lay out the centerline of a setting at a specific longitude and latitude as drawn on a topographical map you can use a pocket hand level, a protractor, and a compass. However, the most accurate method of laying out a set on a landscape is with an transit, which can be rented from an architectural supply house.

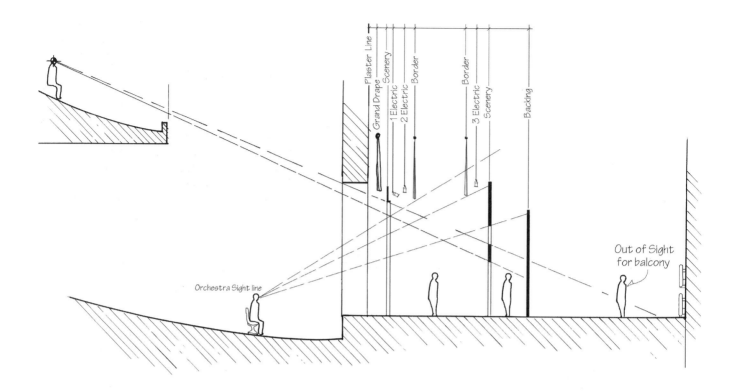

SIGHT LINES FOR THE PROSCENIUM STAGE
CROSS SECTION

Figure 10.20b   Vertical sight lines for the proscenium stage.

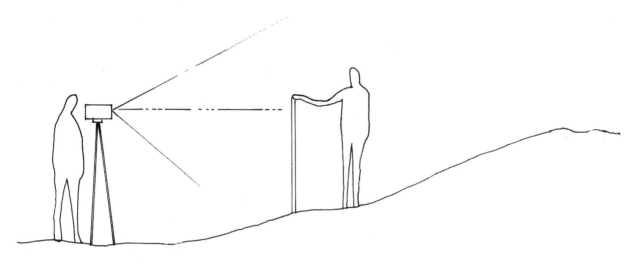

Figure 10.21   Measuring heights and depths with a transit.

The Engineer's Transit

There are simple, inexpensive tools and methods for surveying. The problem is that they lack precision and can take a lot of time. To obtain measurements that result in absolute accuracy and a minimum expenditure of time and effort, surveying is done with a transit. A transit is a complex measuring instrument used for precise field measurements.

Many construction coordinators on feature films own their own transits. Transits can also be rented. Surveying with a transit is a complex procedure taught in engineering schools, but it is helpful for the art director to have a simple understanding of what kinds of situations call for a transit.

The head of a transit contains a telescope on a horizontal axis mounted on a level that turns around a vertical axis. The head contains a bubble (a glass tube partially filled with a volatile spirit and an air bubble), and from its center is hung a plumb bob—both of which are used in leveling the instrument. The head is mounted on a tripod whose legs are adjustable, and small leveling screws in the head are used for precise adjustment. Two wheels below the telescope rotate independently and are used in measuring angles and in measuring from true North. The telescope contains focusing cross hairs and, with a level transit, a straight line from any point on the viewed image through the optical center of the lens will strike the object being viewed in a straight line. The transit is often used with a story or range pole to measure a series of heights and or depths from a horizontal 0'-0" line.

Measuring a Grade

It is possible to measure a grade using an optical level. From a level surface, sight through the highest point of the grade until the image of the bubble is level. At this height measure the height from the ground to the center of the lens. To measure a steep incline you can use the above method with a graduated measured rod or story pole moving the level from point. A transit provides a more accurate means of measuring a grade. (See Figure 10.22.)

A transit can be used to lay out a plan on a location by plotting specific angles and distances to the corners of a shape and relating that shape to due North. The same type of layout can be used to measure the topography of a landscape or the variations in depth on a surface such as the roof of a building.

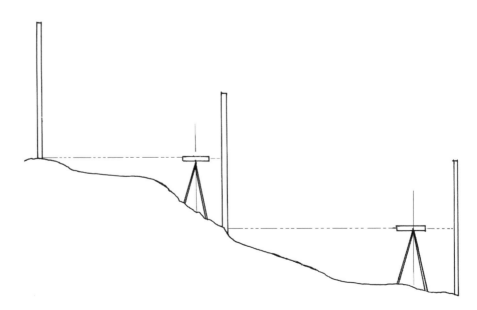

Figure 10.22   Measuring a grade.

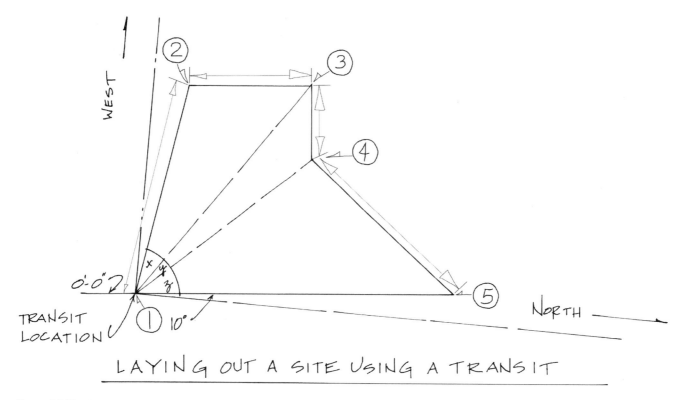

WEST

① 10°

② ③ ④ ⑤

0'-0"

TRANSIT
LOCATION

x y z

NORTH

LAYING OUT A SITE USING A TRANSIT

Figure 10.23   Laying out a plan with a transit.

Survey

For large exterior locations a survey company may be hired to measure and draw a site plan. Figure 10.24 shows the survey of a small town used in the film *To Wong Foo, Thanks for Everything, Julie Newmar* (1995). The survey was turned into a ground plan by adding the scenery, which consisted of the building facade of an old cinema, a garage, and an interior and exterior two-story hotel with wild walls.

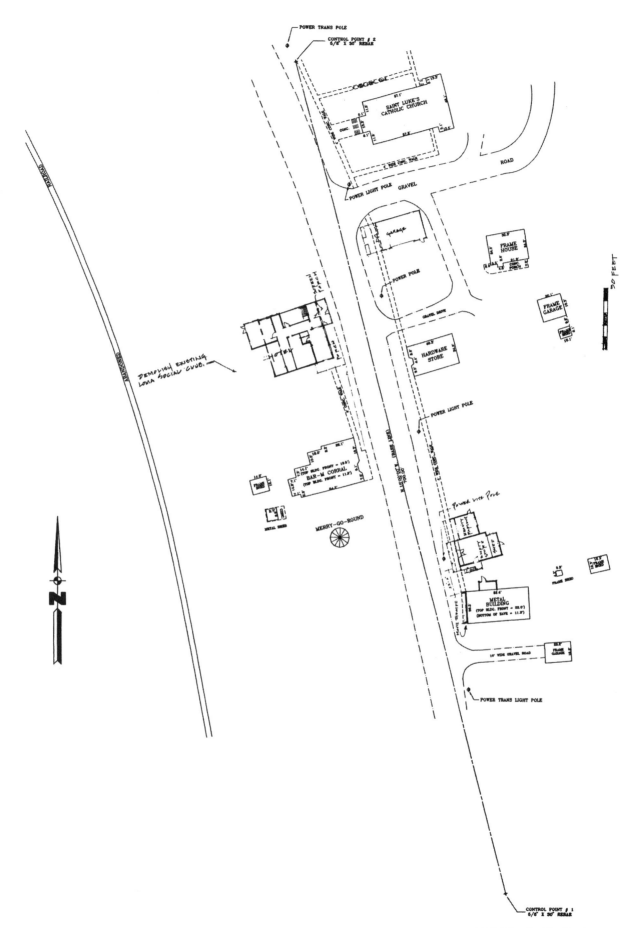

Figure 10.24   Site Survey from Loma, Nevada. *To Wong Foo, Thanks for Everything, Julie Newmar.* 1995. Directed by Beeban Kidron. Produced by Universal City Studio, Inc. Production Designed by Wynn Thomas. Used with permission.

11

Axonometric Drawing

Axonometric Drawing Defined

An axonometric drawing of an object is like a perspective drawing in that it can, in one view, simultaneously show three sides of an object. Unlike a perspective drawing, however, where the lines of projection converge to vanishing points, the projection lines of an axonometric object remain parallel. Axonometric sketches and draftings are used to quickly communicate a three-dimensional shape in a single view. They can be understood by a person who can't read orthographic projection, and quick axonometric sketches are often used in discussing how to construct a piece of scenery. Axonometric draftings can be drawn in scale and dimensioned, and are occasionally added to draftings as a supplementary view. (See Figures 11.1 to 11.3.)

Principles of Axonometric Projection

An axonometric drawing shows three sides of an object in a single view. Imagine a simple object angled behind a glass sheet. Rays of light travel from each corner of the object in straight lines, parallel to each other and perpendicular to the sheet. If each ray were to pierce the glass creating a small hole, and if the holes were connected with lines drawn on the glass,

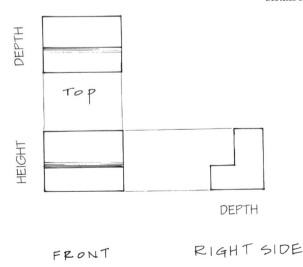

Figure 11.1 Orthographic projection: (1) Shows only one side of an object in each view; (2) Parallel lines remain parallel.

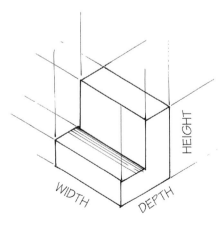

Figure 11.2 Axonometric drawing: (1) Shows three sides in one view; (2) Parallel lines remain parallel.

171

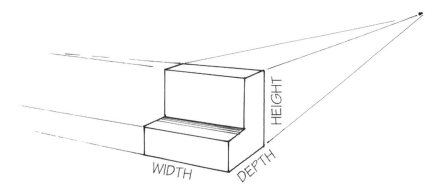

Figure 11.3 Perspective drawing: (1) Shows three sides in one view; (2) Parallel lines converge to a single point.

you would have an axonometric drawing. Since we are accustomed to three-sided views being drawn in perspective with foreshortened sides, a measured axonometric projection at first glance appears distorted.

In scenic drafting, we sometimes include an axonometric sketch in which the length of axonometric lines are not measured but drawn by eye to what feels proportionally pleasing. Such a sketch is marked with "no scale" as it is not measurable.

Common Axonometric Projections

Although an object can be rotated at any angle to the viewer, there are three types of projection that are commonly used in scenic drafting: isometric, cavalier, and military. The most commonly used axonometric projection is isometric. This type of projection is used to quickly sketch the explanation of a three-dimensional object. You will also find an isometric useful to hard-draft a measured isometric to explain a complex object in a single view. You may choose it instead of or in addition to an orthographic layout.

Occasionally, draftspeople construct an exploded isometric. This is done by pulling the sides or pieces of an object away to show more clearly how it is constructed. Professional decorators and scenic designers sometimes draw a complex isometric of a room or several rooms with see-through walls to explain the totality of a location.

Cavalier projection is used to explain the totality of a location as well. Cavalier projection is also used to explain objects with complex fronts and little on their sides. Cabinet projection is a modification of cavalier projection. Cabinet projection is used by professional decorators and scenic designers to quickly draw many pieces of cabinetry or other simple pieces of furniture.

Military projection gives a "bird's-eye-view" or "god's view" of a space. This axonometric projection is an underutilized view that is of great value in giving a film director a sense of the totality of a set or location.

Construction of Axonometric Drawings

The height, width, and depth lines of an object, also known as the x, y, and z coordinates, form the principle axis lines of an object. (See Figure 11.4.) In an axonometric drawing, any lines that fall on these axis lines, and lines that are parallel to them, are called axiometric lines and are measurable. Lines that are not on or parallel to the axis lines are not measurable.

The procedure for drafting an axonometric drawing is first to establish the axis lines, thus determining the angled position of the object you are viewing. Then, starting from the juncture of the axis lines, measure and draw the edges of the object. You cannot measure a nonaxiometric line but must enclose it inside a box and locate its end points. (See Figure 11.5.)

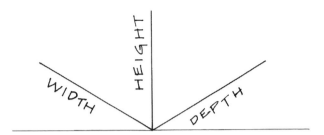

Figure 11.4 Primary axis lines.

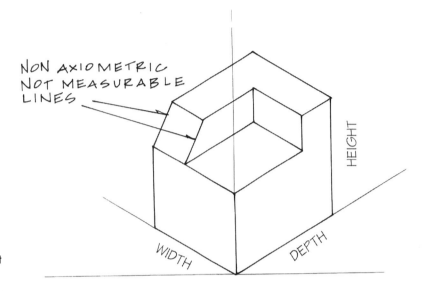

Figure 11.5 Axonometric drawing of an object containing nonaxiometric lines.

Isometric Projection

Isometric means "equal measure," and in the isometric projection the three major axis lines are at equal angles—120 degrees—to the plane of projection. Since all three sides of the object are seen with the same amount of distortion, this is the most commonly used axonometric projection.

Before drawing an isometric you need to consider how to position the object to emphasize the sides you want to describe. For example, if it is most important for you to describe the underside of an object, you need to position it so you see that side. The isometrics in Figure 11.6 show several positions of a six-sided object.

Rules of Isometric Drawing

1. The isometric axis lines may be placed in any position.
2. Each of the three angles between the axis lines must be 120 degrees.
3. Vertical lines remain vertical.
4. Parallel lines remain parallel.
5. Only axiometric lines are measurable.

Exploded Axonometric Projection

In an exploded axonometric, the parts of the object are pulled apart. Such a drawing may be used to explain how a complex object goes together or to show the inside of an object. The construction of an exploded view follows the same rules as that for any other isometric, but any of its parts may be pulled away from the others along an axis line. Often the axis lines between parts are left in as very light guidelines to show how the pieces connect. (See Figure 11.7.)

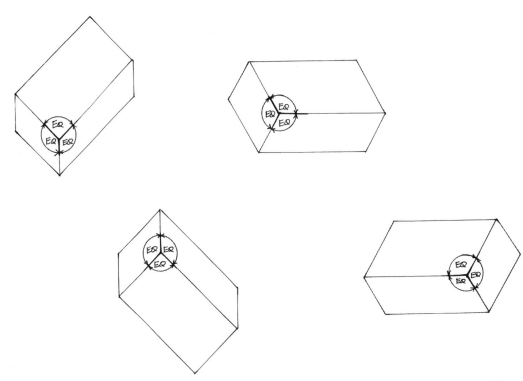

ALL 3 AXES ANGLES ARE EQUAL AND 120°

Figure 11.6 Positioning the object for isometric views.

ISOMETRIC VIEWS

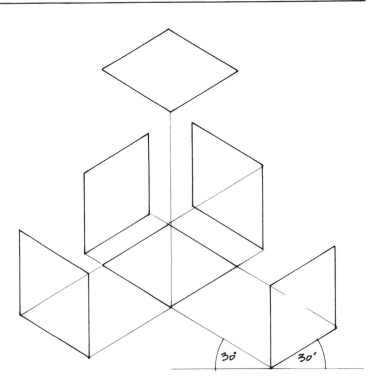

Figure 11.7 Exploded isometric drawing.

The isometric drawing in Figure 11.8 was done for a lighting grid structure designed by Mark Kruger of Kruger Associates for the Espre Centre in Rockville, Maryland. The illustration shows a perspective

174

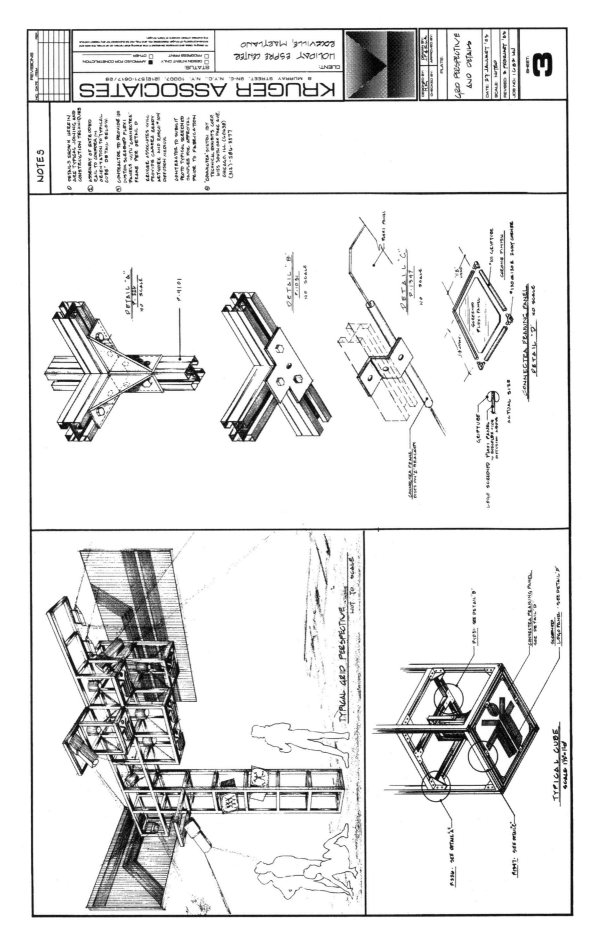

Figure 11.8 Scenic example of an isometric drawing. Grid perspective and details. Lighting grid for the Holiday Espre Center, Rockville, Maryland. Design by Mark D. Kruger Designs Light, Inc. Used by permission.

drawing of a typical section of the grid, an isometric drawing of a typical grid module, and a series of isometric drawings explaining the construction of the various joints. Detail "D," the "Connectra Framing Panel," is an exploded isometric. This is a special isometric in which the pieces of the object are pulled away from each other along the axis lines in order to show how an object is constructed.

Isometric Circles

A circle that is drawn in an isometric view becomes an ellipse. Ellipses in isometric drawing are difficult and time-consuming to construct. It is of great help to the scenic designer to collect a wide variety of ellipse guides and templates in various sizes and proportions. If you need to plot an isometric ellipse, it can usually be drawn with sufficient accuracy by using the four-center method, as illustrated in Figure 11.9.

The following list explains how to use the compass to draw an isometric ellipse.

1. Draw the isometric of a square containing the circle. This is an equilateral parallelogram whose sides are equal to the diameter of the circle.
2. Bisect each side of the square and connect each bisected side with the opposite corner as illustrated in Figure 11.9.
3. The lines you have drawn will intersect at four points, which will be the centers for the arcs of the ellipse. Draw the two large arcs and the two small arcs with the radii as indicated.

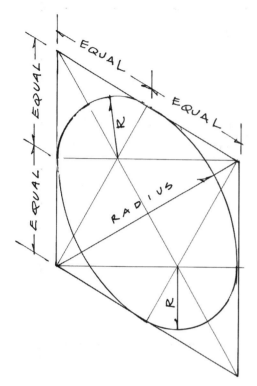

Figure 11.9 Isometric ellipse.

Cavalier Projection

In a cavalier projection the front face of the object becomes the plane of projection. It is drawn in its true size and shape, perpendicular to the line of sight. The receding lines can be drawn at any angle, but 45 degrees is common. (See Figure 11.10.) Many old Japanese prints are examples of cavalier drawings. Because of the extreme distortion of the receding sides in a cavalier drawing, it is best not to use cavalier projection to explain a wide object that has a great depth.

A cross-section using cavalier projection through the set can be used to illustrate a room or several rooms. In the same cross-section you can also show the style of architecture and its decoration. In such an illustration a cross-section through a room or series of rooms on the plan becomes the plane of projection. The side walls of the room recede, but the rear wall of the room will be parallel to the viewer. This view can show architectural details as well as the dressing of the room, such as curtains on windows and nearby furniture.

Cabinet Projection

This is a specific type of cavalier drawing where the receding sides in the cavalier drawing are drawn in half scale so the object will seem less distorted.

Rules of Cavalier Projection

1. The most complex face of the object becomes the plane of projection. This face will be perpendicular to the line of sight.
2. The receding sides of the object are drawn at any convenient angle, with 45 degrees being the most common.
3. Vertical lines remain vertical.

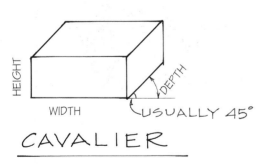

Figure 11.10 Cavalier drawing.

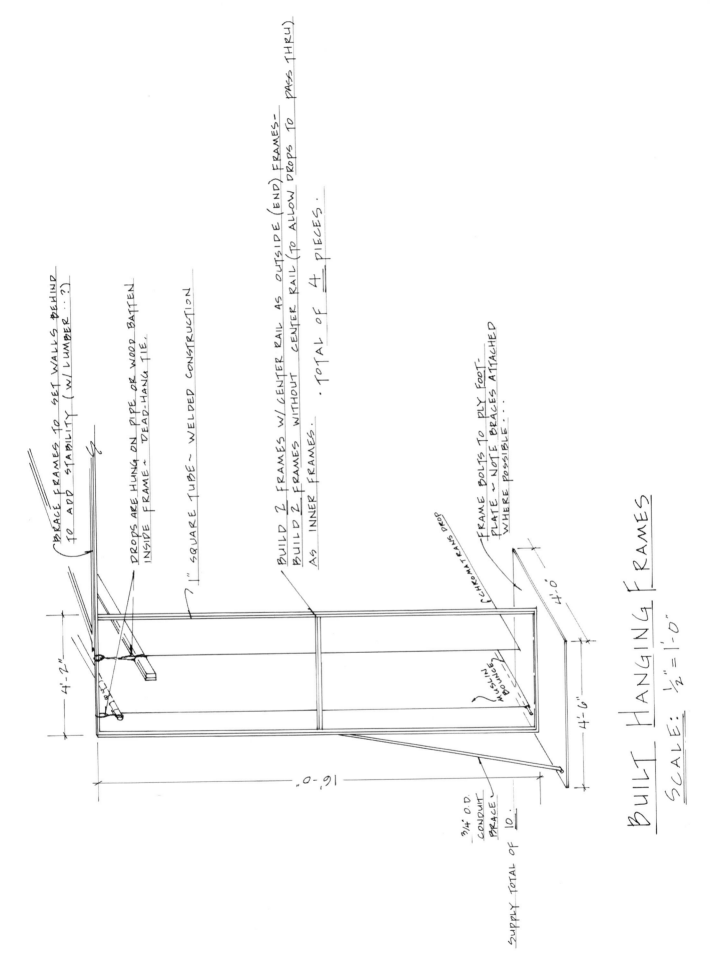

Figure 11.11 Scenic example of a cavalier drawing.

177

4. Parallel lines remain parallel.
5. Axiometric lines, which include everything on the face of the object, are measurable. Nonaxis lines are not measurable.

Military Projection

A military projection gives a clear bird's-eye view of a space. A perspective drawing distorts an object by projecting it to a vanishing point, but a military projection shows relative sizes in their true-scaled length. It allows the viewer to transcend a fixed viewpoint and to have the sense of moving through a particular space.

This underutilized view is a good choice for illustrating the overview of a complex ground plan, such as the relationship of several city blocks or the position of cars at an intersection. Because a military projection is developed vertically from a ground plan, it can be quickly constructed.

To avoid objects blocking each other in a military projection, solid areas are sometimes drawn as translucent, or they are drawn with a broken or sectioned edge and a removed section of wall.

Rules of Military Projection

1. The ground plan is rotated so its edge is 30 degrees from the ground line.
2. Vertical lines remain vertical.
3. Parallel lines remain parallel.
4. Axiometric lines, which include the ground plan, are measurable. Nonaxis lines are not measurable.

In Figures 11.13 and 11.14, the plan and the military drawing of the fort for feature film *The Last of the Mohicans* allowed the production designer, Wolf Kroeger, to plan the stages of destruction the fort would undergo during the battle.

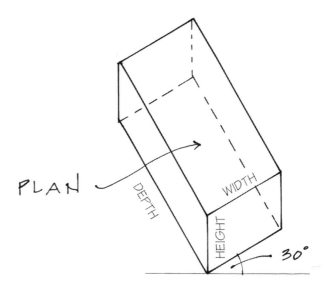

Figure 11.12 Military drawing.

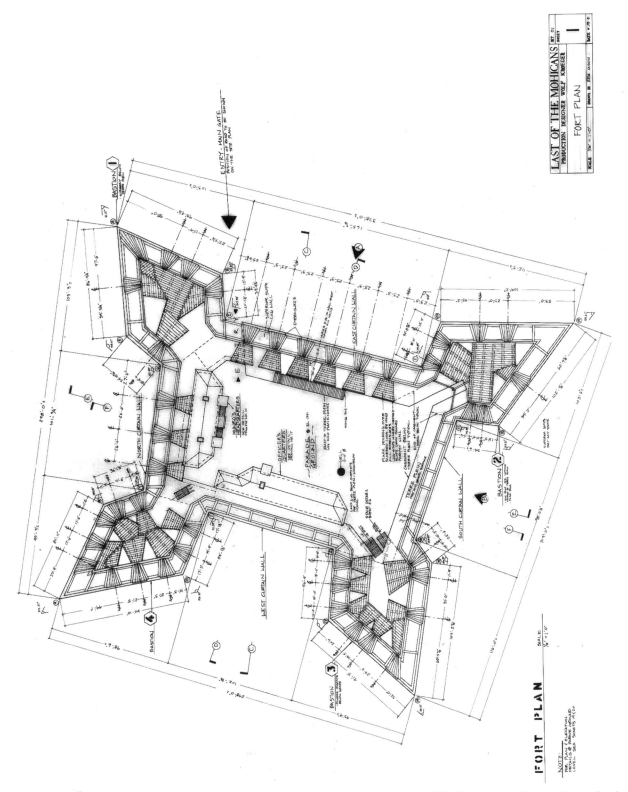

Figure 11.13   Drafting plan of the fort from the feature film *The Last of the Mohicans*. 1992. Directed by Michael Mann. Production designer Wolf Kroeger. Drafting by Erik Olson. Courtesy of Twentieth Century Fox.

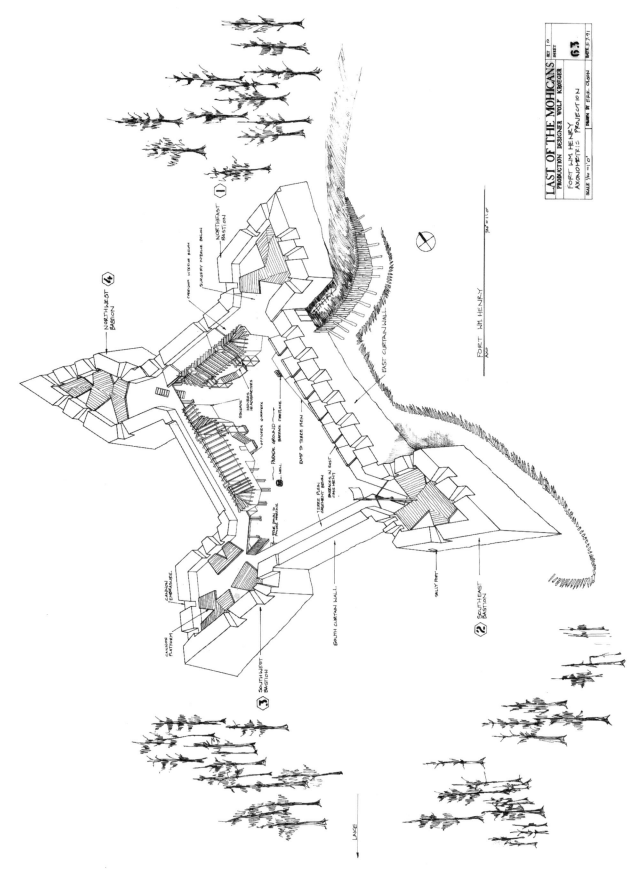

Figure 11.14   Military projection of the fort from the feature film *The Last of the Mohicans*. 1992. Directed by Michael Mann. Production designer Wolf Kroeger. Drafting by Erik Olson. Courtesy of Twentieth Century Fox.

Plate 1   Digital illustration of the Astra Pharmaceutical National Meeting. Scenic design and *AutoCAD* rendering by Carl Baldasso. ©1999 Hotopp Associates Limited.

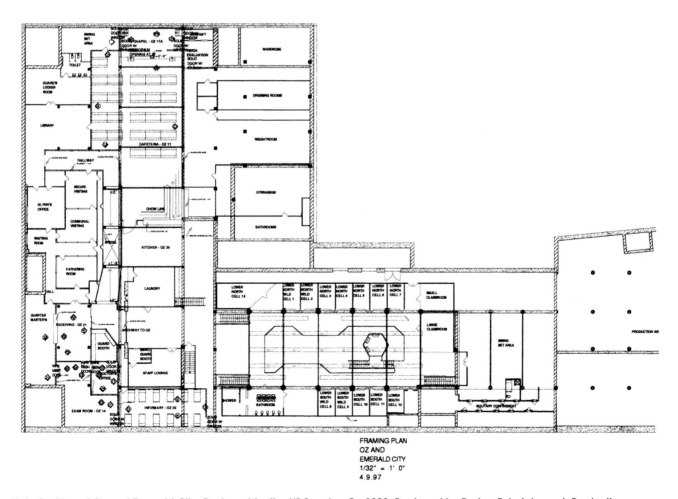

FRAMING PLAN
OZ AND
EMERALD CITY
1/32" = 1' 0"
4.9.97

Plate 2   Plan of Oz and Emerald City. Designed for the HBO series *Oz.* 1999. Produced by Rysher Entertainment. Production designed by Gary Weist. *ArchiCAD* drafting and renderings by Katherine Spencer. Used by permission.

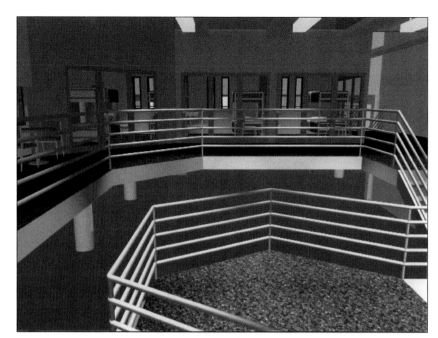

Plate 3   Guard tower looking towards upper balcony. Designed for the HBO series *Oz*. 1999. Produced by Rysher Entertainment. Production designed by Gary Weist. *ArchiCAD* drafting and renderings by Katherine Spencer. Used by permission.

Plate 4   Crane shot, looking into a cell on the upper balcony. Designed for the HBO series *Oz*. 1999. Produced by Rysher Entertainment. Production designed by Gary Weist. *ArchiCAD* drafting and renderings by Katherine Spencer. Used by permission.

Plate 5   Under balcony, looking towards guard tower with wild cell removed. Designed for the HBO series *Oz*. 1999. Produced by Rysher Entertainment. Production designed by Gary Weist. *ArchiCAD* drafting and renderings by Katherine Spencer. Used by permission.

Plate 6 Living room looking towards dining room. From the CBS Television pilot *Family Brood*. 1998. Produced by the Levinson/Fontana Company. Production designed by Gary Weist. *ArchiCAD* drafting and renderings by Katherine Spencer. Used by permission.

Plate 7 Dining room with kitchen in background. From the CBS Television pilot *Family Brood*. 1998. Produced by the Levinson/Fontana Company. Production designed by Gary Weist. *ArchiCAD* drafting and renderings by Katherine Spencer. Used by permission.

Plate 8 Print of chairs from Design Group, LTD, Photoshop Library.

Plate 9 Panoramic concept sketch of news set for WITI FOX Milwaukee. Design by James Fenhagen and Erik Ulfers. Sketch Artist, James Yates. Art Director, André Durette. Used by permission.

Plate 10 Sketch of the set for *Good Morning America*. 1998. Produced by ABC News. Design by James Fenhagen and Erik Ulfers. Sketch Artist, James Yates. Art Director, George Allison. Used by permission.

SPU OFFICES/MANATTAN   PANEL 1

SPU OFFICES/MANATTAN   PANEL 2

Plates 11 and 12   Computer-generated renderings of the feature film *Bait,* Castle Rock Entertainment. Fall 2000. Production Designer, Peter Jamison. Computer rendering by Peter Jamison. Used by permission.

Plate 13   Location photograph of a Soho Café, Tribeca, from the feature film *Bait,* Castle Rock Entertainment. Fall 2000. Used by permission.

Plate 14   Computer-generated rendering of a Soho Café showing digital addition of scenery, from the feature film *Bait,* Castle Rock Entertainment. Fall 2000. Production Designer, Peter Jamison. Computer rendering by Peter Jamison. Used by permission.

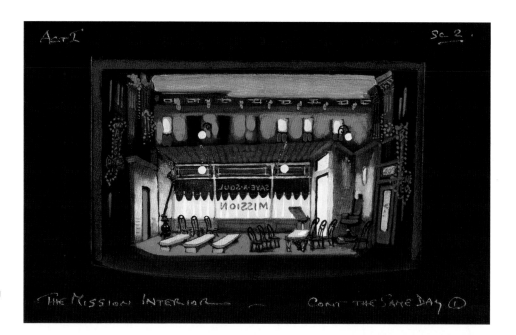

Plate 15 Act I sc.2-The Mission
Interior-Cont. The Same Day 1.
Sketch for the musical *Guys and
Dolls.* Directed by Jerry Zaks.
Designed by Tony Walton. Drafting
by Steve Olson and Ann Waugh.
Used by permission.

Plate 16 Act II-Crap Game in the
Sewer-Cont. That Night 3. Sketch
for the musical *Guys and Dolls.*
Directed by Jerry Zaks. Designed
and illustrated by Tony Walton.
Drafting by Steve Olson and Ann
Waugh. Used by permission.

Plate 17 Illustration of the set for the Morning
Show for the 1992 Barcelona Olympics. Design
and illustration by Jeremy Conway. Used by
permission of NBC Television Studios.

Plate 18   Photograph of the set for the Late
Night Studio for the 1992 Barcelona Olympics.
Design and illustration by Jeremy Conway.
Used by permission of NBC Television Studios.

Plate 19   The Nickelodeon Green Slime
Geyser. Conceptualized and designed by
Tom Hennes of Tom Hennes, Inc. Produced
by DeMartin-Marona-Cranstoun-Downes.
Used by permission.

Plate 20   The Imagination Machine. Designed by
Tom Hennes and David Sirola of Tom Hennes, Inc. for
KBD Innovative Arts, Marina Del Rey, CA, and East
Coast Theatrical Supply, Cornwall-On-Hudson, NY.
Used by permission.

Plate 21   Sony Electronics, Inc. Comdex '95.
Designed by Tom Hennes of Tom Hennes Inc. Used by
permission.

Plate 22   Photograph from *Discovery News.* ABC News/Discovery Channel. 1997. Directed by Roger Goodman. Scenic design by George Allison. Digital architecture by Jim Suhre. Lighting by Rita Ann Kogler. Courtesy of SMA VR Studio.

Plate 23   Virtual Studio. SMA VR Studios, Manhattan. Courtesy of SMA VR Studio. Courtesy of SMA VR Studio.

Plates 24 and Plate 25   Video still shots from *Vietnam: The Soldiers' Story.* 1997. ABC News/The Learning Channel. Produced by Ed Hersh. Directed by Bernie Hoffman. Set design by George Allison. Digital architecture, textures, and lighting design by Rita Ann Kogler. Sketch Artist, Kevin Locke. Courtesy of SMA VR Studio.

12

Mechanical Perspective

Principles of Perspective Drawing

A perspective drawing is a two-dimensional representation of the appearance of (or how we see) a three-dimensional object, as opposed to the reality (or what we know) about that object. The purpose of a perspective drawing is to show how things look, rather than to tell exactly and fully what they are.

Perspective occurs because the light rays that describe each point of an object travel to our eyes in straight lines. As these rays converge, those from furthest away travel the longest distance, creating a more acute angle as they approach the eye. The size of an object between rays from further away thus appears smaller then it would if the object were closer. (See Figure 12.1.)

Since objects of the same size appear to get smaller as they recede in space, we have the illusion that receding parallel lines appear to be converging to a single point at a distant line, the horizon, where the sky appears to touch the earth.

The classic example of this phenomenon of optical convergence is the illustration of a straight railroad track lined by telegraph poles as you would see it if you stood on the track looking into the distance. (See Figure 12.2.)

Although you know the lines of the track must remain parallel, they appear to converge at a central point. And although you know that the telegraph poles are all the same height, they appear to be getting smaller as they get further away.

We use orthographic drawing to show measurable size and the true shape of an object. We use perspective drawing to show many sides of an object at the same time, to depict objects in relationship to their surroundings, and to show them as the human eye would see them.

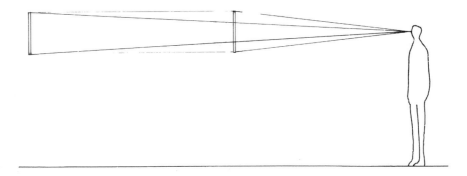

Figure 12.1   An object appears smaller if it is further away.

Figure 12.2   Optical convergence.

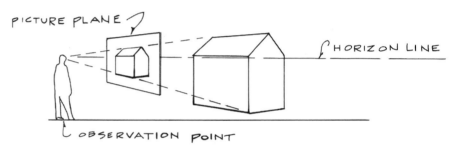

Figure 12.3   Elements of a mechanical perspective.

Elements of a Perspective Drawing

The flat, two-dimensional image of a perspective drawing mimics what the human eye sees by imposing an imaginary plane between the light rays streaming in straight lines from the object to a single point representing the eye of the observer. This plane on which the perspective is constructed is called the **picture plane.** The picture plane is placed perpendicular to the centerline of sight and perpendicular to the ground line on which the object or scene sits. To visualize how the picture plane allows us to create a two-dimensional perspective image of a three-dimensional object, imagine an observer looking at an object such as a house. From each corner point of the house, light rays stream in straight lines towards the observer's eye, their angles converging as they come closer. Imagine the picture plan as a clear sheet of glass placed between the house and the observer's eye with the rays of light piercing the glass as they pass through it. If each pierced dot on the glass were connected, the result would be a simple, two-dimensional perspective drawing of the object. (See Figure 12.3.)

When you observe anything, you observe it from a specific spot. Where you stand greatly affects the view you have of an object or of a scene, as you can view it from the right or left side, or from a higher or lower vantage point. The spot where you stand will be a certain distance away from the object or scene, and this distance from which you view will also affect the image you receive. In a perspective drawing, the spot from which you view an object or scene is called the **observation point**.

When you view any object or scene, there is an imaginary line in the distance towards which the edges of objects appear to recede. This line is called the **horizon line**, and its height is the height of your eyes above

182

the ground. It is also the height of a camera lens if you are sketching a camera view. Usually you view a scene from a standing position from which the horizon appears about 5 feet above the ground. But you may lie on the ground and view an object with the horizon line at about 18 inches, or you may draw a perspective from a bird's-eye view with the horizon 20 feet above the ground, or you may theoretically draw the underside of an object in which case the horizon would be below the ground line on which an object sits.

Perspective Variables

When you look at an object or scene its image is affected by how close you are to it, from how high or how low you view it, and from what angle you view it. When drawing a perspective, the following choices strongly influence the look of your drawing and should be carefully considered:

1. Location of Observation Point
2. Angle of View
3. Location of Picture Plane

Location of Observation Point

When you locate your observation point, you choose the distance from which you view an object or scene. The closer you stand to any object the more it appears distorted. Imagine standing 8 feet away from a house and looking at it, and then standing 20 feet away from the house and looking at it again. When you are very close, the house appears foreshortened and distorted. When you get a distance away, the house appears more natural. If you view the house from a great distance, such as 50 feet, you will notice that the depth of projections on the house, such as the porch or the roof eaves, appear to have flattened. The degree of perspective distortion is determined by the distance of the observation point from the object or scene observed. (See Figure 12.4.) **The closer the observation point is to the object or scene, the more distorted the object seems.**

When you locate your observation point, you also choose the height from which you view an object or scene, thus determining the horizon line. From a higher vantage point with its higher horizon line, you will see more of the ground and the relative distances between objects sitting on the ground; you will see less of the sky, and you will be more likely to see the tops of objects. From a lower observation point with its lower horizon line, an object will appear taller, more imposing, and more important. From a lower observation point the observer will see less of the ground and more of the sky; objects that are behind other objects will more likely be hidden. (See Figure 12.5.)

Angle of View

A setting can be observed from many different angles with each position of the observer resulting in a different picture of the same elements. Where you position your observation point determines the angle of view. If you are drawing the perspective of a room, you must first decide from which angle you wish to view the walls. You may decide, for example, that you don't want your centerline of vision to look directly into a corner of the room as this bisects the set in an unattractive manner. Therefore you might choose to locate your observation

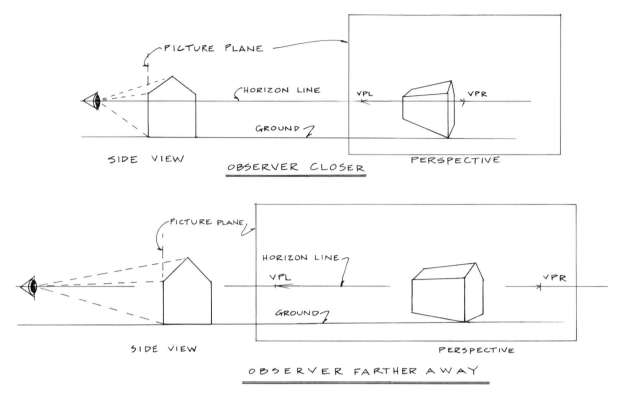

Figure 12.4   Distance of the observation point from the object.

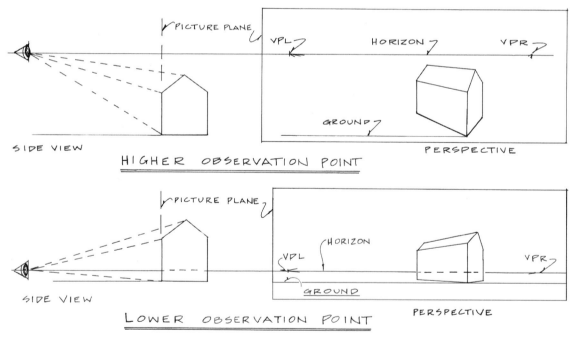

Figure 12.5   Height of observation point.

point so the centerline of sight angles towards the left or right of the corner. You may decide that you want the formality of a wall perpendicular to your line of sight, or you may decide that you want the dynamism of walls at an angle to the center of your line of sight.

The width of the angle of observation determines how much you will see, and in a perspective drawing sets the edges of your picture. Viewing a set from a wide angle allows you to see more of the scene, while view-

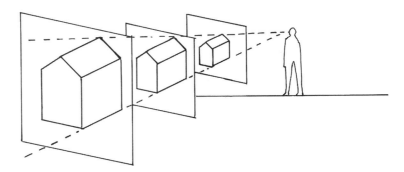

Figure 12.6 Distance of picture plane from the observation point.

ing a set from a narrow angle lets you see less of the scene. The human eye has a lens with a 60-degree cone of vision (30 degrees on each side of the centerline of vision), so to draw a picture with the feeling of a human perspective you should choose around 60 degrees. Perspective sketches can be drawn with wider angles of up to 90 degrees (45 degrees on each side of the centerline of vision), although with wider angles, distortion occurs at the edges. A true field of vision is circular, but in effect, we mask off a portion to create a rectangular picture. With a camera lens as the observation point of an illustration, the angle of vision will depend on the specific angle of each lens.

Location of Picture Plane

If you again visualize the picture plane as a glass sheet, you will see that if you locate the sheet very close to the observer's eye, you will have a tiny perspective image of the object you are observing. If you locate the glass sheet further away from the observer's eye, however, you will have the same image but much larger. (See Figure 12.6.) The proportions of both images will be the same. Thus, you see that **the distance of the picture plane from the observation point determines the size of the perspective image.** You can locate the picture plane any distance away from the observation point. Although the picture plane is often between the observation point and the scene, to create a larger image you could locate it behind the scene. Since the picture plane is theoretical, you can also locate it through or touching any object you are drawing.

Angle of View for Television and Film Perspectives

The edges of the image on a television screen are currently set at a ratio of 1.33 to 1. This proportion means that the width of the image on your television screen is approximately one-third greater than its height, a proportion that is good for viewing close-ups of people talking. When drawing the perspective of a television setting, use these proportions for the frame of your picture.

The anamorphic proportion for feature films is 2.35 to 1. The width of an anamorphic frame, defined as an optical image distorted by having a different magnification of the image in each of two perpendicular images, is approximately two and one-third times the height and is excellent for viewing landscapes or epic events.

The most common film screen proportion is wide angle, a ratio of 1.85 to 1. The width is almost twice the height, a good proportion for viewing a combination of close-up, middle, and wide-angle shots that compose most feature films. Since film usually has wider proportions than television, it necessitates that the edges of film be cropped for television viewing. The exception is Academy proportion, which is used mostly in Europe and for student films and has the same proportion as television.

Unlike the human eye, which essentially has one lens of 60 degrees, the television or film camera has a choice of lenses, each of which has a different angle of observation. To draw the perspective of a camera lens, you need to know the approximate position of the camera to set your observation point, and you need to know or pick a camera lens to draw the angle of observation. The angles for various lenses are listed in *The American Cinematographer's Manual* (see "Suggested Reading"). If you do many perspectives of film sets, you may find it helpful to purchase or make metal or plastic templates of various lens angles.

The Three Types of Perspective

The position of your observation point in relationship to an object you are viewing can create three distinctly different types of perspective, as illustrated in Figure 12.7.

- **Parallel Perspective** One Vanishing Point — If you look perpendicularly at a rectangular object, the edges of the side you are facing will appear parallel while the edges of the object's side will appear to converge towards a single, central vanishing point on the horizon.
- **Angular Perspective** Two Vanishing Points — If you look at a rectangular object with your line of sight angled to its face, the edges of the object's sides will appear to converge towards two vanishing points on the horizon, one to your left and one to your right.
- **Oblique Perspective** Three Vanishing Points — Normally, when constructing a perspective illustration, we let the vertical lines remain vertical. However, the vertical lines in a per-

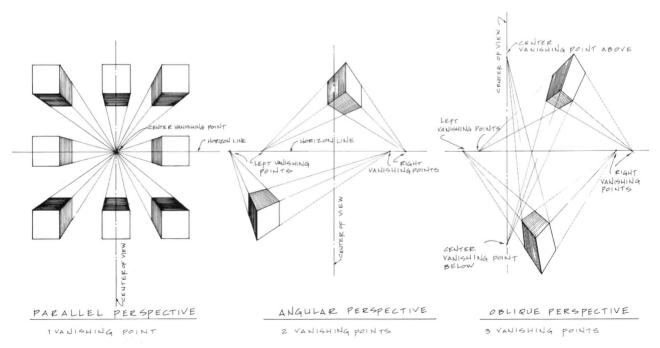

Figure 12.7 Three types of perspective.

Figure 12.8 Parallel perspective as shown in the sketch of the "Terrace of the Waldorf Towers" from the feature film *My Favorite Year.* 1982. Directed by Richard Benjamin. Designed and drawn by Charles Rosen. Used by permission.

spective actually appear to converge to a third point either above or below the horizon. Occasionally, we add the vertical vanishing point. It might be used by the scene designer to draw a backdrop, such as a bird's-eye view looking down at buildings, or for an expressionist style, where buildings seem to tower over the viewer.

Definition of Mechanical Perspective

Although the purpose of a perspective drawing is not to produce a measurable drawing, you can use measurement and geometry to create a perspective drawing from a plan and elevation. This method is known as mechanical as opposed to freehand or "eyeballed" perspective. A drawing done in this manner has a tight look caused by the mechanical nature of its process and by the fact that it is calculated from one viewpoint, as though the eyeball of the viewer were locked in position. We actually see the world through two eyes, set slightly apart, and this binocular vision creates two slightly overlapping points of view. In addition, our eyes usually move as we view an object or scene, and our visual experience is the blending of a series of overlapping images seen over a short period of time.

Understanding the principles and practice of mechanical perspective are important skills for design students to master. Because of the fixed

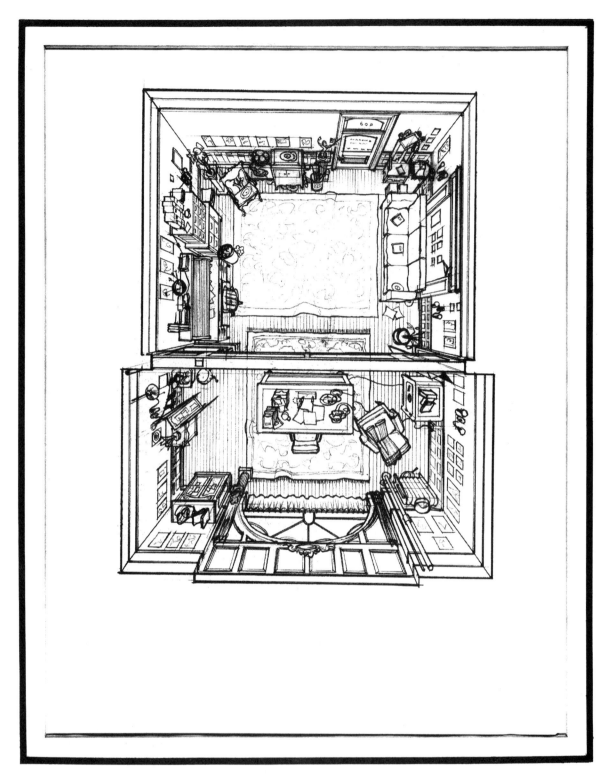

Figure 12.9 Parallel bird's-eye perspective as shown in the sketch for "Zero's Office" from the feature film *The Producers.* 1968. Directed by Mel Brooks. Designed and drawn by Charles Rosen. Used by permission.

nature of mechanical perspective, most designers use it as a skeletal armature on which to base a perspective drawing. For a scenic illustration, it is often enough to set a horizon line, and mechanically determine key vanishing points and the height of several walls. Then the mechanical perspective can be placed under a sheet of tracing paper and the illustration drawn freehand. (See Figure 12.13.)

Figure 12.10   Angular perspective as shown in the sketch for the "Farmhouse" from the feature film *The River*. Designed and drawn by Charles Rosen. Used by permission.

Figure 12.11   Angular perspective as shown in the sketch for "Charly's room" from the feature film *Charly*. Designed and drawn by Charles Rosen. Used by permission.

Figure 12.12 Oblique perspective in a theatrical backdrop. Designed and drawn by James Joy. Used by permission.

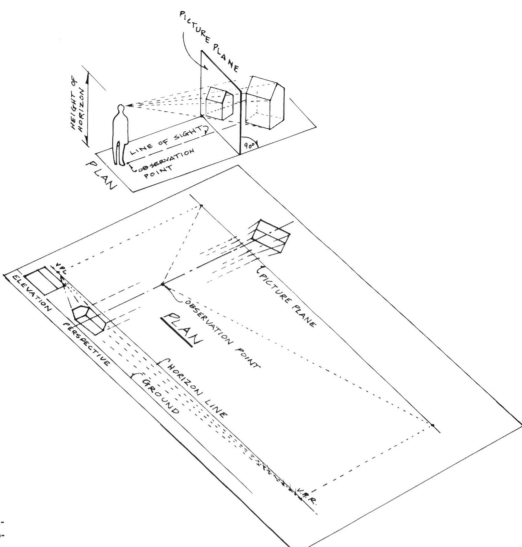

Figure 12.13 Three-dimensional perspective in a two-dimensional layout.

Three-Dimensional Layout on a Flat Surface

When you visualized the picture plane as a glass sheet between the observer and the object being observed, you saw the three-dimensional phenomenon of creating a two-dimensional perspective drawing.

When we construct a mechanical perspective, we have to convert the three-dimensional relationship onto a flat piece of paper. This is done by revolving the picture plane 90 degrees until it lies flat on top of the ground plan. In this position, the two views are on top of each other. Then the picture plan is pulled in a straight line away from the ground plan and located either above or below it. On the ground plan, the position of the picture plane remains as a straight line.

Having pulled the picture plane away from the ground plan, each corner point on the plan has to be "dropped" to the new location of the picture plane. That is why this method of drawing a mechanical perspective is known as "drop-point perspective."

To complete a perspective drawing we have to determine the perspective height of each corner of the object. We measure the true heights at the picture plane and project these heights towards the vanishing points.

The beautiful mechanical perspective of a Victorian house by the New York University Tisch alumnus Dan Kuchar clearly shows the two-dimensional layout of a mechanical perspective. (See Figure 12.14.) The position of the observer to the sides of the house and the location of the picture plane are chosen and drawn on the ground plan on the top half of the paper. The picture plane is rotated and pulled below the plan to develop the perspective. The orthographic projections of the front and side of the house, showing the true heights of the architecture, are located to the left and right of the perspective so that any height can be projected directly across to the line where the house touches the picture plane.

Laying out a Mechanical Perspective on a Sheet of Paper

1. In a situation involving a proscenium, a line on the plan perpendicular to the centerline of the stage will be the picture plane. This picture plane is usually at the front of the show portal or the back of the proscenium arch. The observation point for a proscenium set will be in the middle of the orchestra seating. In other stage situations such as a thrust theater or theater-in-the-round, you will need to pick the seat from which you want to view the set and choose the best position for the picture plane. When you illustrate movie sets, you will choose the observation point from which you want to view the set and choose the best position point for the picture plane, usually touching a part of the set so you can measure its height on the picture plane. Since the camera is moveable, you can view the set from any angle. Usually the height of the camera lens is at eyesight, about 5 feet and 3 inches above the floor. Occasionally you will want to illustrate a shot from a different height, such as a crane shot from above. When drawing an object or objects in perspective, you can observe the object or plane on which the object rests at whatever height or angle you feel is best for the illustration and position the picture plane accordingly.

   On your drafting board position the plan of the set or the plan of the object you are drawing so that the line of the picture plane is parallel to the edge of your T-square or parallel ruler, and the line of sight is perpendicular to the picture plane.

2. Draw a vertical line through the plan and the picture plane at the center of your line of sight. For a proscenium set, this will be at the centerline of the stage, but in other situations, you will choose the best location. Extend the vertical line to an empty area on the paper where you intend to construct the perspective drawing, either below or above the ground plan. Position and mark the observation point on the line of sight, choosing the distance from the picture plane. Draw and mark a horizontal ground line, the bottom of your perspective. (Many people like to locate the ground line at the observation point. This is the location that Dan Kuchar picked in Figure 12.14.)

3. Choose the height of your horizon line. On your perspective drawing, and in the scale of your ground plan, measure the height up from your ground line. Draw a horizontal line at the height and mark it as the horizon.

Locating Left and Right Vanishing Points in a Mechanical Perspective

In a perspective drawing, any lines on the plan parallel to the picture plane will remain parallel, but each angled line will have a particular vanishing point on the horizon line of the perspective drawing. Lines that are

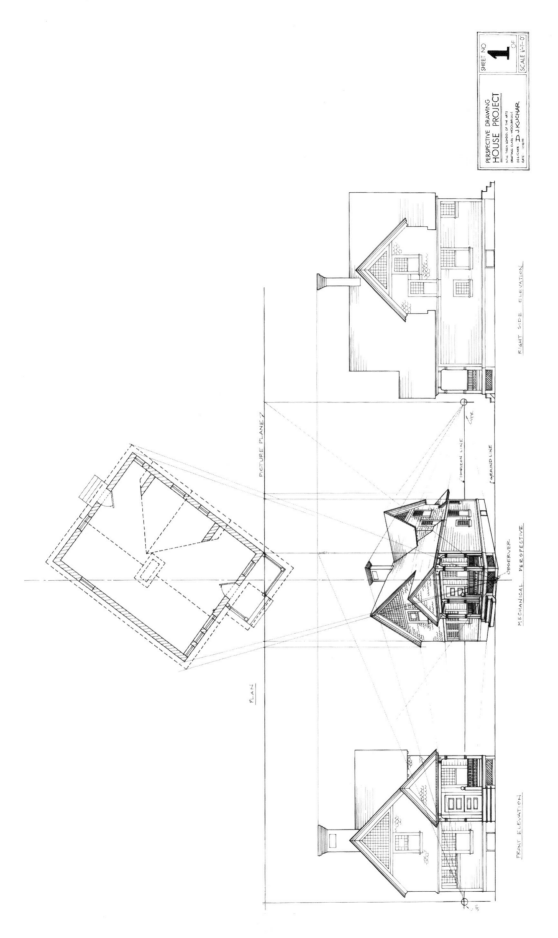

Figure 12.14 Mechanical perspective of a house. Designed and drafted by Dan Kuchar, New York University Tisch School of the Arts, 1990. Used by permission.

perpendicular to the picture plane on the plan will go to the center vanishing point, the point where the line of sight intersects the horizon line.

To locate the vanishing point for an angled line that is neither parallel nor perpendicular to the picture plane do the following:

1. From the observation point, draw a line at the same angle as the angle of the side of the object on the ground plan you are trying to draw. Both lines will be parallel.
2. At the point where this line intersects the picture plane, make a dot. From the dot, perpendicular to the picture plane, drop the line until it intersects your horizon line. This point on the horizon line is the vanishing point for that particular angled line on your plan and for all lines parallel to it. This applies to the top and bottom edges of the sides of your box.

To understand the characteristics of vanishing points, look at Figure 12.15 and, in your mind's eye, slowly rotate the rectangle to the left, keeping the sight line from the observation point perpendicular to the picture plane. You will see that as you turn the rectangle to the left, the vanishing point on the horizon line will move further away from the observer until the side of the rectangle is parallel to the picture plane, perpendicular to the centerline of sight,

Determining Heights in a Mechanical Perspective

Visualize the picture plane as a sheet between the observer and an object such as a large rectangular box. Rotate the box and push one vertical edge towards the observer until it touches the glass. From each cor-

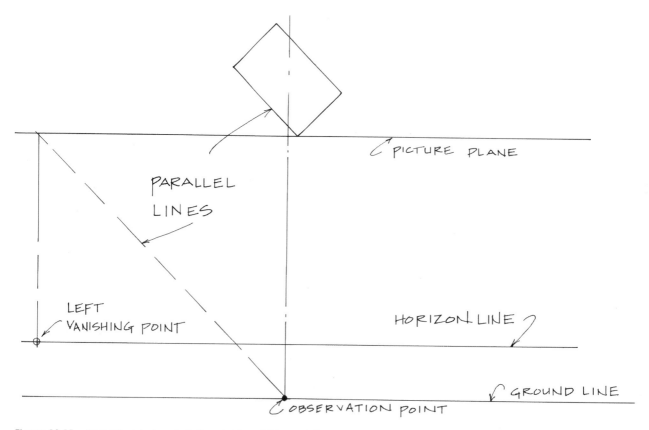

Figure 12.15   Procedure to locate left or right vanishing points.

ner point of the box, light rays stream in straight lines towards the observer's eye, their angles converging as they come closer to the eye of the observer. If rays of light were to pierce the glass as they pass through it, and their lines connected a "follow-the-dot" drawing, you would have a simple flat perspective drawing of the object.

In this perspective drawing on the glass, the height of the front edge of the rectangle would be measurable since it touches the glass sheet. The rear vertical edges of the rectangle would appear shorter than they are. In a mechanical perspective, the true height of any point can only be measured at the picture plane. If a rectangular box is positioned in front of or behind the picture plane, its height in the mechanical perspective can only be calculated by extending a side edge line of the rectangle until it intersects the picture plane. At that point its true height can be measured.

Determine the heights of the sides of an object in the following manner:

1. In Figure 12.16 the picture plane is drawn touching the front edge of a 48-inch high box. On the plan, drop the front edge point that touches the picture plane vertically to the ground line of the perspective drawing. Measure 48 inches up from ground level and draw the front edge of the rectangle.
2. On the plan, the two sides of the box that angle to the left will, in the perspective drawing, converge at the left vanishing point, and the two sides of the box that angle to the right will converge at the right vanishing point. On your perspective, draw light lines from the top and bottom of the front edge of the rectangle to each vanishing point.

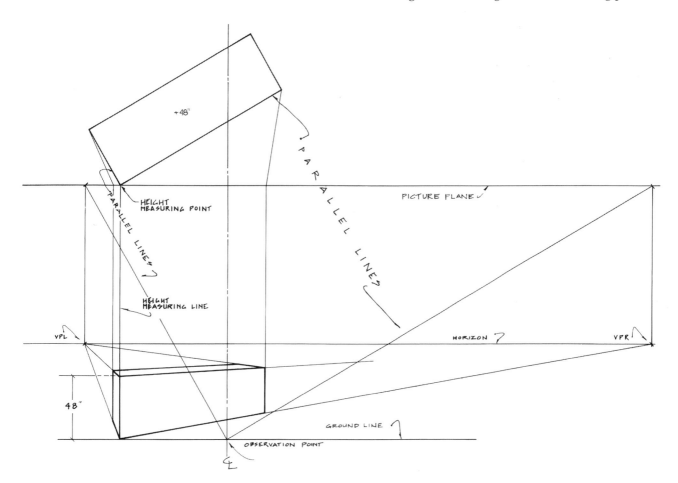

Figure 12.16   Determining the heights of an object touching the picture plane.

3. To locate the perspective height of the left rear vertical edge of the rectangle, on the plan, draw a light line from the left rear corner of the box towards the observation point until it intersects the picture plane. From the picture plane, drop the line vertically until it intersects the two lines converging towards the left vanishing point. The left side of the rectangle is now drawn in perspective.

4. To locate the perspective height of the right front vertical edge of the rectangle, on the plan, draw a light line from the right side corner towards the observation point until it intersects the picture plan. From the picture plane, drop the line vertically until it intersects the two lines converging towards the right vanishing point. The front of the box is now drawn in perspective.

5. In the perspective, the rear top edge of the rectangle will converge at the right vanishing point and the right top edge will converge at the left vanishing point. Draw them in lightly. The lines will intersect forming the top of the rectangle.

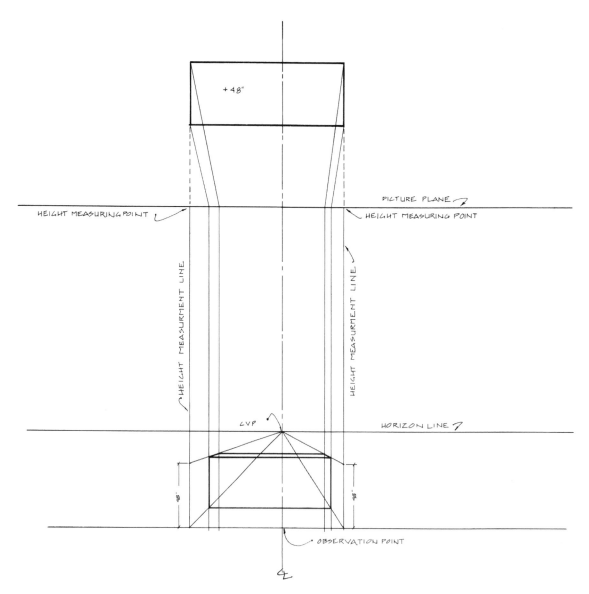

Figure 12.17 One-point perspective.

Determining the Height of an Object that Is Parallel to But Not Touching the Picture Plane

A picture plane may be located so that no edge of the object is touching it. To determine the perspective height of such an object a side edge of the object is extended to the picture plane where its height can be measured. In Figure 12.17 a 48-inch high rectangular box is parallel to and behind the picture plane. The mechanical perspective is drawn in the following manner:

1. On the plan extend two top-side edges of the rectangle until they touch the picture plane.
2. From the picture plane, drop the lines vertically to the ground line of the perspective drawing.
3. Measure 48 inches up from the ground line. As the top sides of the rectangle are perpendicular to the picture plane, they will converge at the central vanishing point.
4. From the top and bottom of the 48-inch high verticals, draw light lines to the center vanishing point.
5. To locate the vertical sides of the rectangle, on the plan, draw light lines from each corner of the object towards the observation point until they intersect the picture plane. From the picture plane, drop the lines vertically until they intersect the lines converging to the center vanishing point.

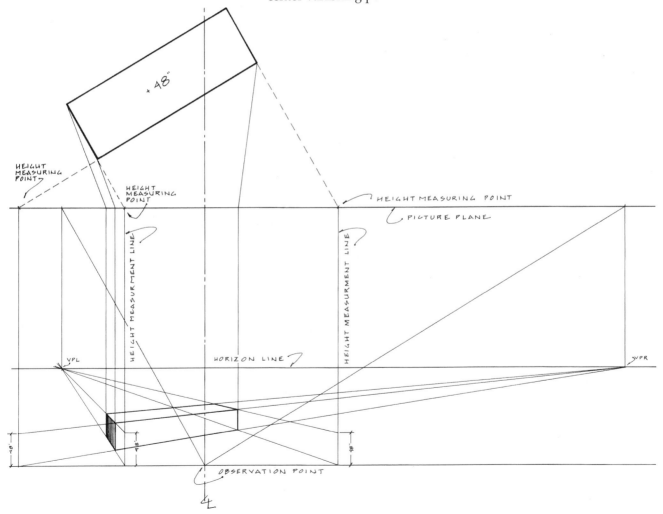

Figure 12.18   Two-point perspective of an object not touching the picture plane.

Drawing an Object Angled to and Not Touching the Picture Plane

If the object not touching the picture plane is angled to the viewer rather than parallel, its sides are still extended to the picture plane to be measured. In the following example a 48-inch high rectangle is angled to but not touching the picture plane. The mechanical perspective is drawn in the following manner:

1. On the plan extend the lines of the top front and side edges until they intersect the picture plane.
2. From the picture plane, drop the lines vertically to the ground line of the perspective drawing.
3. Measure 48 inches up from the ground line.
4. From the top and bottom of the 48-inch high vertical, draw light lines to the right or left vanishing point. If on your plan the side edge line is angled to the left, it will go to the left vanishing point; if it angled to the right, it will go to the right vanishing point.
5. To locate the vertical sides of the rectangle, on the plan, draw light lines from each corner of the object towards the observation point until they intersect the picture plane. From the picture plane drop the lines vertically until they intersect the lines converging to the vanishing points.

Locating the Vanishing Point of Inclined Lines

Parallel inclined lines in perspective also angle to a particular vanishing point. However, if the slope angles up, the vanishing point will be higher than the horizon line. If the incline angles down, the vanishing point will be lower than the horizon line.

Locate the vanishing point of an inclined line in the following manner (see Figure 12.19):

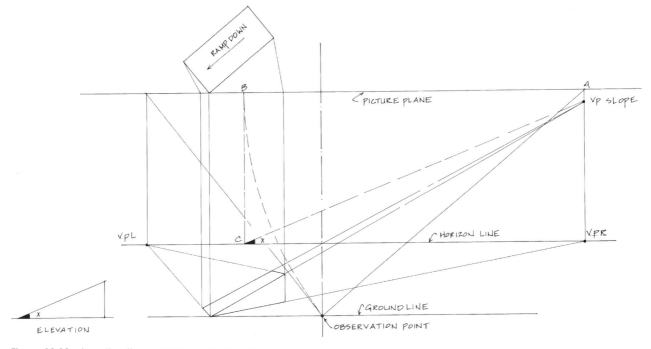

Figure 12.19 Locating the vanishing point for a sloping line.

1. From the observation point, draw a line parallel to the inclined line on the plan until it intersects the picture plane (point A). From the picture plane, drop the line vertically to the horizon line. Draw a light vertical line through this point.
2. Using a large compass with point A as the center, draw an arc from the observation point until it intersects the picture plane (point B).
3. From point B, draw a vertical line until it intersects the horizon line (point C).
4. From point C on the horizon line, draw a line at the angle of your inclined line (angle x). Extend this line until it intersects the vertical drawn through the vanishing point. The intersection of these two lines is the vanishing point for the inclined line.

Using the Vanishing Point of Sloped Lines to Aid in Drawing Stairs

The vanishing point for an inclined line can also be located by determining the height of each end, and connecting and extending the endpoints until they intersect a vertical drawn through the vanishing point. This method is useful when drawing stairs in perspective, as connecting the top points of the rises creates an inclined line to a vanishing point. While it is easy to make a mistake calculating the many edge points of stairs, a line to the vanishing point of the incline quickly checks the perspective height of each rise. The stair railing will converge to the same vanishing point. (See Figure 12.20.)

The Glass Box Method of Calculating Perspective Heights

By adding an extra step to the process of calculating the heights in a mechanical perspective, the glass box method solves the problem of distant vanishing points off the page. It also allows all height measurements to be measured from one or two lines at the edges of a perspective sketch where they won't confuse the drawing. Although at first it may seem complicated, it can speed up the process of constructing a perspective sketch. As it doesn't use side vanishing points, it is an excellent method if you are drawing the perspective of a set with walls in forced perspective, where the top of the walls are not parallel to the base. A glass box perspective is drawn in the following manner:

1. Lay out your mechanical perspective on a sheet of paper in the normal manner, locating the ground plan, observation point, picture plane, horizon line, and ground line.
2. Draw two vertical lines, one to the left and one to the right of your plan, and extend them to the ground line of your perspective. In Figure 12.21 these lines are marked as "measuring perpendiculars."
3. On the plan, mark the left front corner as A. Draw a light line from this corner towards the observation point until it intersects the picture plane. From the picture plane, drop the line vertically to the perspective.
4. Measure the height of A on the measuring perpendicular from the ground line up. From the top and bottom of this line, draw light lines to the center vanishing point.
5. On your plan, from the left front corner of the rectangle, draw a horizontal line until it intersects the measuring perpendicular on the left. From the intersection with the measuring perpendicular draw towards

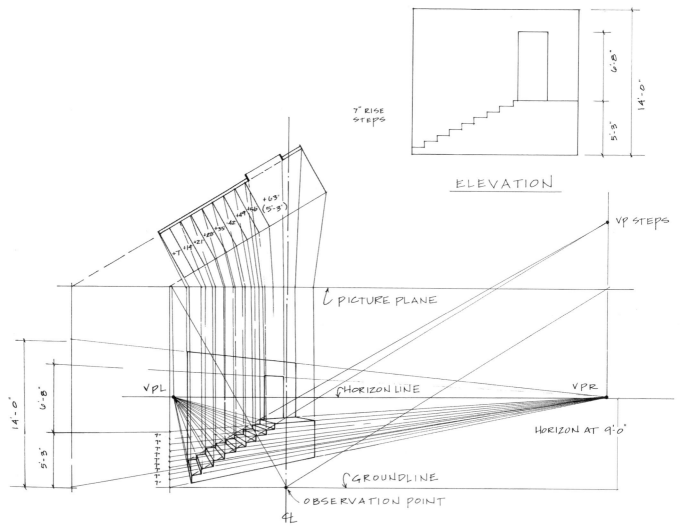

Figure 12.20   Mechanical perspective of a staircase.

the observation point until the line intersects the picture plane. At the picture plane, drop the line vertically. The dropped line will cross the two lines converging towards the center vanishing point. The vertical created at the point of intersection is the height of the left front edge.

6. From the top and bottom of this vertical, draw two light horizontal lines. These lines intersect the line drawn in step 3. The line created from this intersection is the left front edge of the rectangle in perspective. Finish the perspective by dropping the remaining corners of the rectangle in a similar manner.

If you have a complex sketch, rather than measuring each height from the ground line up on the perspective, dimension the measuring perpendicular from the ground line up. To keep track of numerous lines, mark each point on your ground plan with a letter and mark each projection of the point with the same letter or use colored pencils to differentiate the steps.

Mechanical Perspective for a Proscenium Setting

When drawing the mechanical perspective of a proscenium set, the picture plane is usually located at the show portal or the front edge of the

200

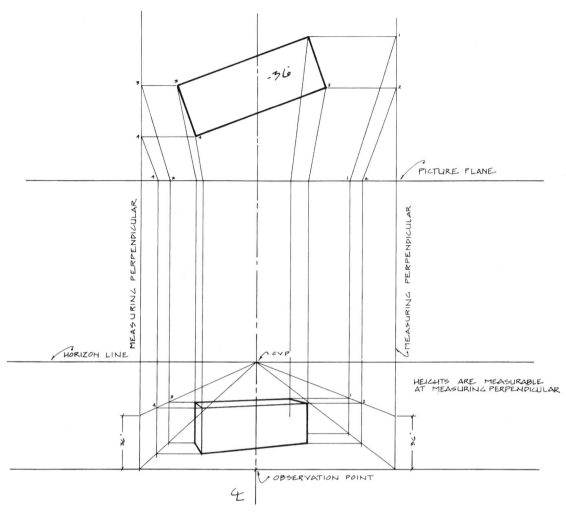

Figure 12.21 Two-point perspective: glass box method.

proscenium. Since either the proscenium or the show portal touches the picture plane, it can be drawn in its true size and immediately frame the picture and give a sense of the space.

In a proscenium theatre the observation point will be on the centerline of the stage. Usually it is at a 60-degree angle from the front corner of the proscenium edge. This maintains the feel of the human angle of vision, while including the entire set.

If the horizon line is located 6 feet above the stage floor, the perspective sketch is low enough to simulate an orchestra viewpoint but high enough to include enough of the floor and the arrangement of the furniture to give a sense of the ground plan. With a 6-foot high horizon line, a 6-foot man will always touch the horizon line. This makes it simple to quickly sketch in a human figure at any position in the perspective, giving an immediate sense of scale and depth. (See Figure 12.22.)

Combining Methods to Draw a Mechanical Perspective

Often a designer will use several methods to calculate the heights in a mechanical perspective. The mechanical perspective in Figure 12.23 is for Ben Edwards' design for the 1985-86 season Broadway production

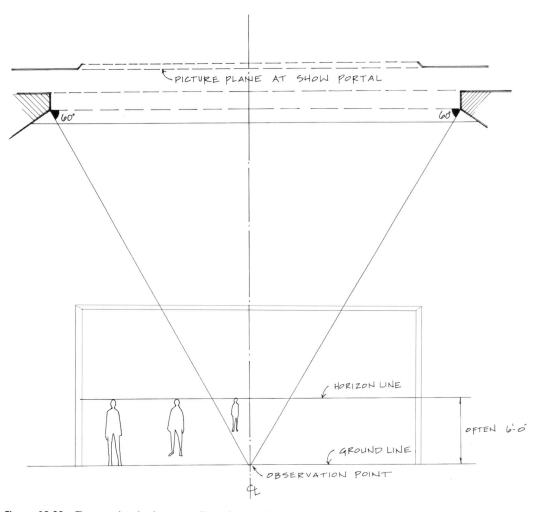

PICTURE PLANE AT SHOW PORTAL

60° 60°

HORIZON LINE

OFTEN 6'-0"

GROUND LINE

OBSERVATION POINT

CL

Figure 12.22 The mechanical perspective of a proscenium stage setting.

of *The Iceman Cometh.* Many of the draftings from this show are reproduced in Chapter 17, "A Box Set on a Proscenium Stage." The set had a raked deck and walls in forced perspective, so the height of each end of a wall had to be calculated separately. The glass box method was used to determine most heights, but the left and right vanishing points helped plot walls at acute angles to the centerline of the set.

To calculate the many heights of the raked deck and perspective walls, a composite cross-section was drawn to the right of the plan. Any point on the plan could be projected horizontally to the cross-section, and its height measured and transferred to the measuring line at the perspective.

To keep track of the lines and points of each coordinate, the coordinates for points and lines were identified with small letters. In Figure 12.23, one set of projected lines is identified with a dark dash.

Mechanical Perspective of an Interior

The illustration in Figure 12.24 is the mechanical perspective of an interior. The method of calculating the mechanical perspective of an interior is the same as any other. However, care is required in choosing the location of the observation point and the point of view.

The picture plane can be located at any position in front of the observation point. It may be in front of the room or behind the room, the difference being that the further away the picture plane is from the

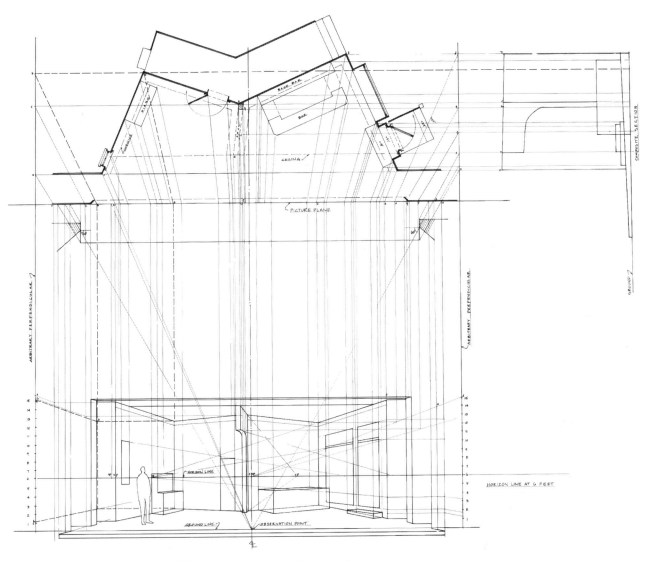

Figure 12.23 Combining methods to draw a mechanical perspective.

observer, the larger the size of the resulting perspective sketch. Perspective construction is easiest if you locate the picture plane so it touches a wall where heights can be measured directly.

Removing the Distortion at the Sides of a Perspective

The curve of the human eye means that the sides of a scene are slightly closer to us than the center. When laying out the plan for a mechanical perspective we usually ignore this curvature and draw the picture plane as a straight line. This results in increasing distortion at the edges of the perspective. To eliminate this distortion, curve the picture plane according to the following method. From the observation point, draw the 60-degree angle of human vision, 30 degrees on each side of the center of the line of sight. Place the needle end of your beam compass at the observation point and the lead tip at the point where your 60-degree angle intersects with your picture plane. This creates a curved picture plane with the center deeper than the sides. (See Figure 12.25.) Construct the mechanical perspective in the usual manner.

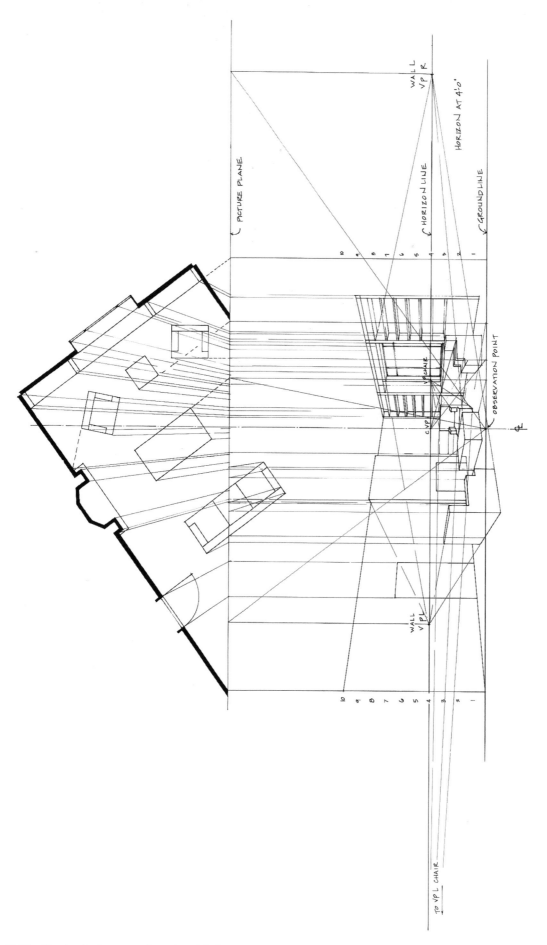

Figure 12.24 Mechanical perspective of an interior.

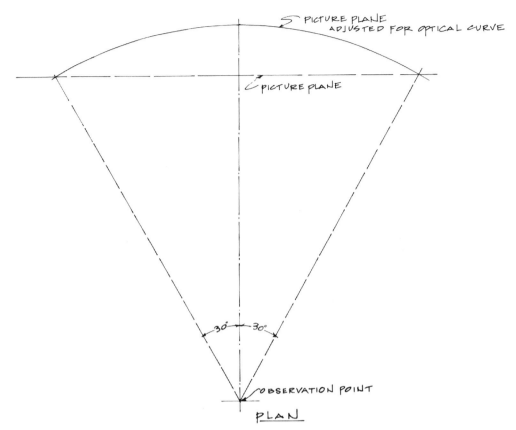

Figure 12.25 Curving the line of the picture plane.

Quickly Locating Key Perspective Points

With experience in perspective sketching, a horizon line and the calculation of few key points on the plan may be all that is needed to make a fairly accurate illustration of a setting. Any point on a plan can be quickly drawn in perspective. From a key point on the plan drop a vertical line to the ground line of the perspective and measure its height at that point. From the top and bottom of the measured line, draw light lines to the center vanishing point. On the plan, from the same key point, draw a light line towards the observation point until it intersects the picture plane. At the picture plane, drop the line vertically. The line will cross the two lines converging towards the center vanishing point. The vertical created is the height in perspective at that point.

Estimation and Freehand Drawing with Mechanical Perspective

Most designers use mechanical perspective as a tool to begin the outlines of a set. At a comfortable point, they start freehand sketching, eyeballing the location of vanishing points on the horizon and using them to keep parallel lines in perspective. In freehand perspective sketching, as vanishing points are located further away from the centerline, it becomes less critical to the perspective drawing to draw their exact position. It is usually enough to visually aim a line to its approximate vanishing point.

Perspective heights can often be drawn by estimating their size against heights that have been calculated. For example, having drawn in the perspective of a 10-foot wall, and the angle of its edge on the floor and ceiling, the height of a 7-foot-high door in that wall can be visually estimated and its top edge drawn to the same vanishing point. A hand-drawn perspective illustration needs to be visually accurate. It is not a mathematical drawing.

Perspective Grid

A perspective grid is another method of drawing a mechanical perspective. The grid shows in perspective equal divisions of height, width, and depth as seen from a particular observation point and horizon height. (See Figure 12.26.) Diagonals are used to draw equal divisions in perspective. Since a grid takes time to draw and is applicable only to one set of viewing conditions, it is most useful for repeated views from the same vantage point. It might be used to draw many different productions in the same proscenium, or the different scenes of one production. Following is the method for creating a perspective grid:

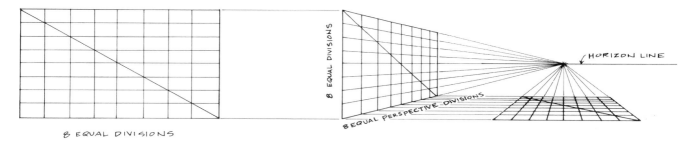

Figure 12.26   Use of diagonals to make proportional divisions.

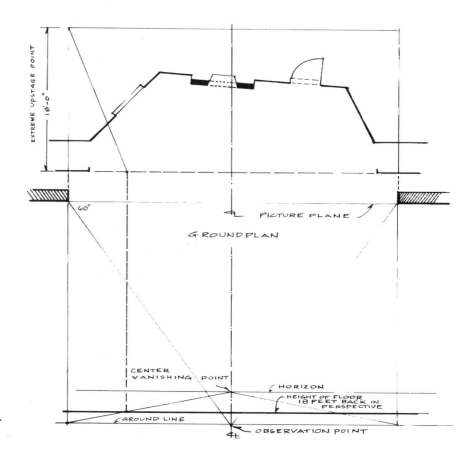

Figure 12.27   Sheet layout for a perspective grid.

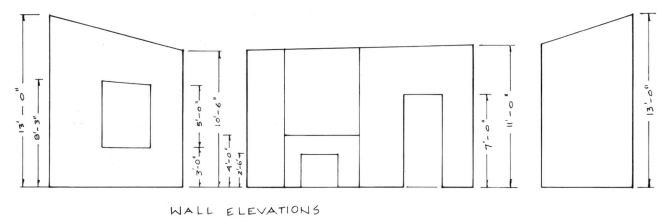

WALL ELEVATIONS

Figure 12.28   The elevations for the example.

1. Locate your plan, observation point, ground line, horizon line, and picture plane as you would for a mechanical perspective.
2. At the plan, on the line of the picture plane, and at the perspective along the ground line, measure and dimension equal divisions on either side of center. For a 1/2-inch-scale grid, mark one-foot divisions. For a 1/4-inch-scale grid mark every 2 feet. The divisions should extend the width of the scenery on your plan, and there should be an equal number of divisions on both sides of the center. (See Figure 12.29.)
3. At the furthest mark, draw a perpendicular to the picture plane. Along this line, to the deepest point on your plan, measure and dimension divisions equal to those along the front. Use the marks to draw a grid of equal squares across your plan.
4. Extend the lines at the edges of the grid to the ground line of the perspective. From the ground line up measure and dimension the numerical divisions with which you gridded your plan. The total height of the divisions should be at least as high as the highest point on your scenery, often the height of the show portal. There must be the same number of vertical divisions as depth divisions on the plan.

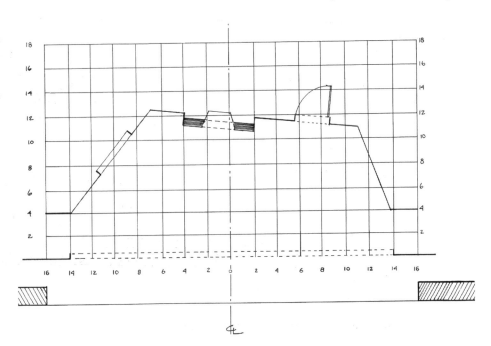

Figure 12.29   The ground plan grid.

Either increase the number of vertical divisions or the number of depth divisions to make them equal. Draw a horizontal line connecting the top marks on both sides, creating a rectangle.

5. On the perspective, draw a line from each front corner of the rectangle to the center vanishing point. (See Figure 12.30.)

6. At the plan, draw lines from the two rear corners of the grid towards the observation point until they intersect the picture plane. From the picture plane, drop the lines vertically until they intersect the lines converging to the center vanishing point. The vertical lines created are the rear side edges of the perspective grid. Draw horizontal lines connecting their top and bottom corners.

7. On the perspective, from each measured vertical and horizontal division, draw lines towards the center vanishing point until they intersect the rear edges of the perspective grid.

8. Draw a light diagonal line through one side wall of your grid, from the lowest front edge corner to the rear corner.

9. On the side wall of the perspective grid, draw a vertical line at each point where the diagonal intersects the lines converging to the center vanishing point.

10. When each line intersects the side edge of the floor, draw it horizontally to the other side. At the far side of the floor, draw each point vertically to the top of the perspective grid. This completes the perspective grid.

11. Now, draw the set. Locate the corners of the set on the floor of the perspective by counting the squares on the plan and an equal number of squares on the perspective floor. In this manner, draw the plan on the floor of the perspective. (See Figure 12.31.)

12. Draw a vertical line from each corner of the perspective plan. Plot the height of each vertical by measuring the height along the dimensioned side edge of the perspective grid and tracing its perspective path back along the side wall of the grid. When you reach the depth of the point on the plan, project the line horizontally to the edge of the wall.

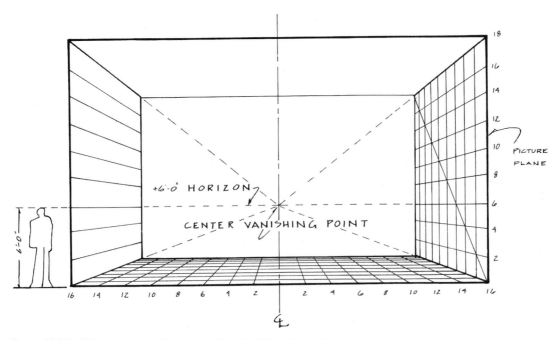

Figure 12.30   Using a diagonal to proportionally divide the grid.

208

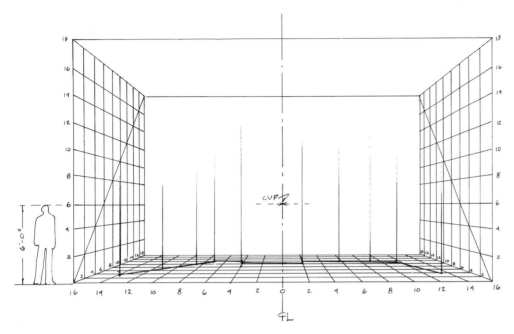

Figure 12.31   Plotting the ground plan on the grid.

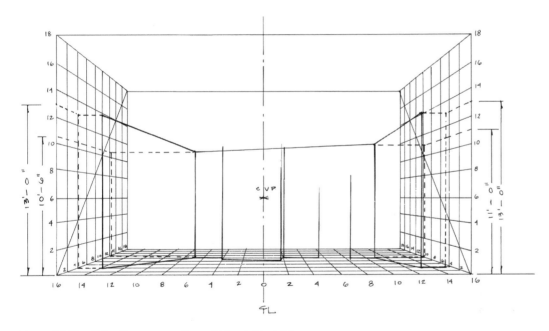

Figure 12.32   Using the perspective grid to plot heights.

13. Once the planes of major architectural elements are drawn, their vanishing points can be located by extending their top and bottom edges to the horizon line. (See Figure 12.33.) These vanishing points can be used to complete the sketch. (See Figure 12.34.)

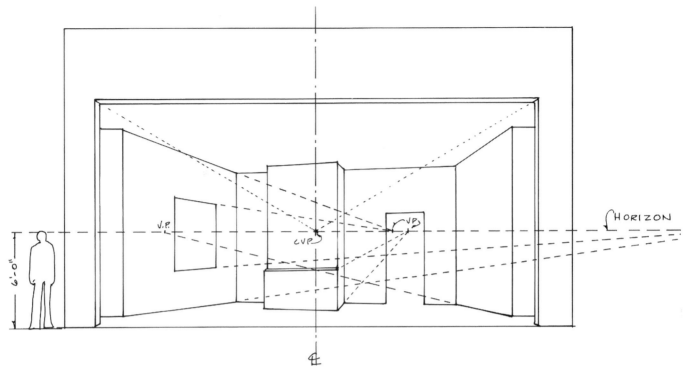

Figure 12.33   Using vanishing points to check the grid.

Figure 12.34   The perspective sketch.

13

Forced Perspective

Definition of Forced Perspective Scenery

Forced perspective is scenery that has the perspective built into it. Forced perspective scenery is primarily a theatrical convention, although some film designers employ it for special effects.

When scenery is forced, either the vertical scenery lines or the horizontal scenery lines that would normally be parallel are angled towards a vanishing point. A forced design may also take repeating units of scenery that are the same size and proportionally decrease their widths as they get further away from the viewer and closer to the vanishing point.

In general, forcing scenery makes it appear taller than it is. A slight force that is not immediately noticeable can "soften" the look of the set. A more extreme force may be able to make a setting appear humorous, forbidding, or powerful. A theatrical setting in forced perspective can also make the acting space appear deeper than it is while still allowing the actors to remain close to the audience. Since forced perspective was an early style of scenery design, it can also have an "old-fashioned look," which may be used to evoke the sense of an earlier time.

Vertical Forced Perspective

In Figure 13.1, the first picture shows the elevation of a simple building with no forced perspective. The second picture shows the same building forced vertically, with all vertical lines angled to a single vanishing point above the building. The third picture is also forced vertically, but

Figure 13.1   Vertical forced perspective.

in addition the higher window units and the divisions between them have been proportionally decreased in height.

Horizontal Forced Perspective

The illustrations in Figure 13.2 show the elevation of a wall with three repeating arched entrances. The first picture in Figure 13.2a is drawn with no forced perspective. But in the second picture in Figure 13.2a, the horizontal lines above the height of a person are angled towards a single vanishing point. In Figure 13.2b, the lines are angled and, in addition, the arches decrease their width and height proportionally as they recede.

A Box Set with the Ground Plan in Forced Perspective

In Figure 13.3, the left illustration shows the ground plan of a rectangular room on a normal proscenium stage. With the fourth wall of the room removed to allow the audience to see inside, the extreme right and left seats in the audience are unable to see the side walls of the set or any action near the walls. This visibility problem was traditionally solved by angling the side walls of the room. Once the side walls were angled, to maintain an illusion of reality required that all other lines on the ground plan, normally parallel to the side walls, would now be angled in a gradual transition from the center outward, as shown in the illustration on the right in Figure 13.3.

The method of calculating such a transition on the ground plan is to extend the lines of the angled side walls until the two walls intersect at a point known as a vanishing point. All lines that formerly were parallel to the side wall, whether floorboards or other interior walls, are drawn at an angle from their furthest down stage point to the vanishing point.

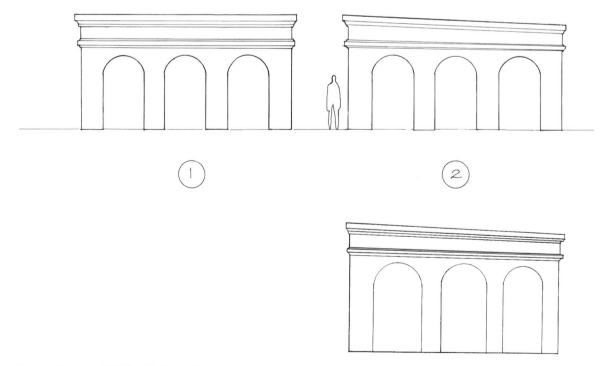

Figures 13.2a and 13.2b   Horizontal forced perspective.

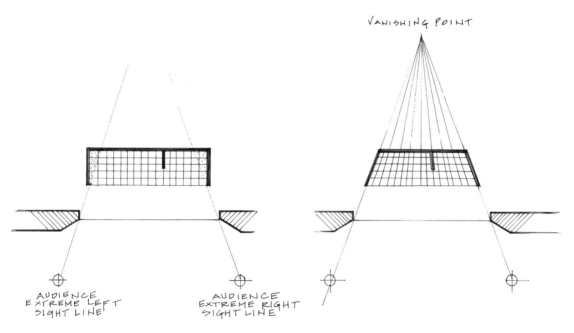

Figure 13.3   Raking the walls of a box setting to increase visibility.

The Ground Plan of a Three-Sided Set with Two Vanishing Points

In addition to angling the side walls of a three-sided set, the designer may angle the rear wall. An angled rear wall gives the set a more informal feeling and creates a more dynamic pattern of actor movement.

In this situation the side walls are extended until they intersect at the first vanishing point. The second vanishing point is found by first drawing a horizontal line at the front edge of the set, parallel to the proscenium wall. This horizontal line is extended until it intersects with the edge line of the rear wall, which has been extended in the same direction.

All up and down stage lines or walls on the plan, which would normally be parallel, are drawn towards the first vanishing point. All horizontal lines or walls on the plan that would normally be parallel to the proscenium are drawn to the second vanishing point. (See Figure 13.4.)

Forcing the Ceiling and Walls of a Set

When the design of a box set had a ceiling, it became the convention to angle it as well as the side walls, making the walls and ceiling stylistically complementary. Angling the ceiling also allowed the maximum amount of ceiling while keeping downstage electric pipes out of balcony sight lines, yet able to wash the entire setting with light. (See Figure 13.5.) The degree of rake of the ceiling was a critical design choice. The more extreme the rake, the more stylized the design looked. The less extreme, the more naturalistic the setting appeared. Once the ceiling was angled, to maintain the illusion of reality, other horizontal lines near the ceiling needed to be angled as well in a gradual transition.

To assure that all the walls of a set are forced in a similar manner, first draw the cross-section of the entire set and determine the angle of the ceiling. If you do not have a ceiling and want your wall elevations in forced perspective, in the cross-section determine the angle of the top edge of your walls.

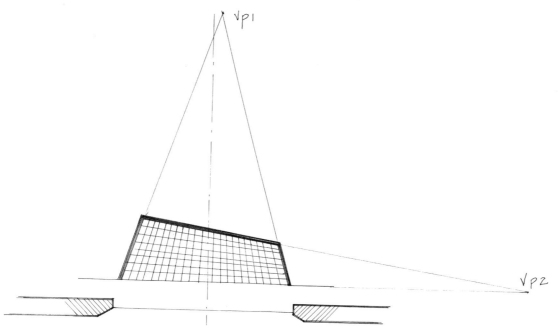

Figure 13.4 Use of two vanishing points on the ground plan.

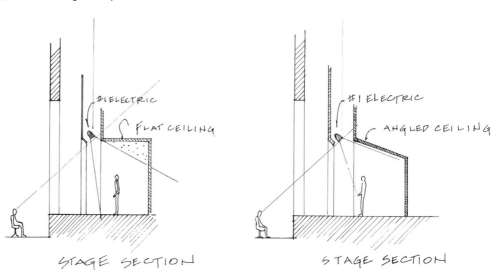

Figure 13.5 Angling the ceiling to allow access for the #1 electric.

Second, decide the height of your horizon line, a line parallel to the stage floor. Above this horizon line, all lines that would normally be horizontal and parallel to the stage floor will be built in perspective, angling towards a vanishing point. Below the horizon line, all lines that would normally be horizontal will remain so.

To locate the vanishing point on the cross-section of the set, extend the line of the ceiling or the top edge of the walls until they intersect with the horizon line. This point of intersection is the vanishing point for the scenic elevations.

Choosing the Height of the Horizon Line in a Forced Perspective Set

As the actor moves upstage, he or she will obviously not decrease in height, so it is common in a naturalistic setting to attempt to keep the

214

forced perspective lines above the height of the an actors' heads. This puts the horizon line above 7 feet from the stage floor, or, if there is a staircase, at least 7 feet above the top platform.

The height of the horizon line and the integration of lines of forced perspective in a set are complex variables. Very small adjustments in the angle of the ceiling or the height of the horizon line will result in major changes in the look of a set. You may also need to consider that lower horizon lines result in more complex and therefore more costly building.

Lower horizon lines feel more stylized and may be used to help create mood. Tony Walton in his design for the 1988-89 season Broadway musical *Lend Me a Tenor* sets his horizon line at a low 4 feet 6 inches, and this choice of visual dislocation works well with farce, in which the seemingly normal has gone awry.

Drawing Wall Elevations in Forced Perspective

After you have determined the vanishing point for the entire set on the cross-section, you can draw the elevations of each wall. Measure the width of each wall on the ground plan and transfer it to your sheet of elevations. Measure the heights of the sides of each wall on the cross-section and transfer the heights to each wall elevation. Draw the top edge of the wall as a line connecting the two side heights. The top edge of the wall will be at the correct angle for your perspective.

In Figure 13.6, in the example for Wall 1, the height at A and the height at B are measured on the cross-section and transferred to the elevation. With the side heights A and B drawn, the angled top edge of the wall is determined.

On each wall elevation, lightly draw in the horizon line at the height at which you have set it on the cross-section. Extend the angled top edge of each wall until it intersects at the vanishing point for that wall. All lines above the horizon line, which would normally be parallel to the stage floor, are drawn to the vanishing point. **All lines horizontal below the horizon line remain parallel.**

In Figure 13.6, the horizon line was set at 7 feet above the stage floor. Note that the mullion lines of the window angle to the vanishing point above the horizon line but remain parallel below it.

Drawing the wall elevations for a box set in forced perspective require you to calculate a separate vanishing point for each wall.

Calculating Proportionally Decreasing Widths

As objects in perspective appear to decrease in width as well as height, the designer may wish not only to build in a forced perspective but also to proportionally decrease the width of same-sized objects as they sit further away from the audience.

This is illustrated in Figure 13.7 and calculated by the following method:

1. First, draw the elevation of the wall without any forced perspective. Divide its length into equal divisions that relate to the architectural elements of the piece of scenery. In Figure 13.7, the width of each of the 3 arches is 3 times the length of the wall between, before, and after the openings. This elevation was divided into 13 equal divisions.
2. Draw a line the length of the wall at an angle to a centerline. Call this Line A. Extend Line A until it touches the centerline at a vanishing

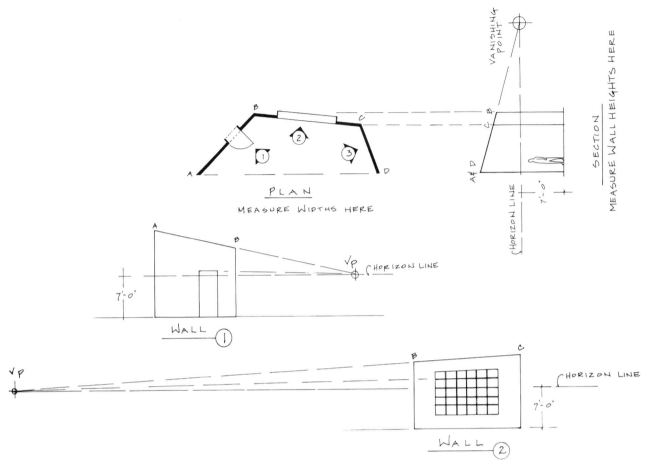

Figure 13.6 Determining heights of forced perspective walls.

point. The angle of Line A is not the angle of the wall on the ground plan. It is a design choice that you want to experiment with.

3. From the upstage front edge of Line A, draw a horizontal to the centerline, Line B. From the front edge of Line A, draw another horizontal to centerline, Line C. Divide Line C into a number of equal spaces totaling the divisions of the wall—13 equal spaces in Figure 13.7. Draw lines from each division mark on Line C to the vanishing point. Draw a diagonal, Line D, from the front corner of Line C to the rear of Line B.

4. The diagonal Line D will intersect with each of the lines converging to the vanishing point. Make a point at each intersection and draw horizontal lines from each point of intersection until they intersect with Line A.

5. Line A is now divided into proportionally decreasing divisions. If you play with adjusting the angle of Line A, you will find that as Line A becomes more parallel to the centerline, the proportional divisions become more similar and the wall appears more naturalistic.

These divisions are used in drawing the front elevation of the wall.

Examples of Forced Perspective Scenery

The first example of forced perspective scenery, in Figure 13.8, shows a vertical and a horizontal force. It is a sheet of elevations for the walls of the wood-framed house for August Wilson's 1979 play *Fences*. It was

Forced Perspective

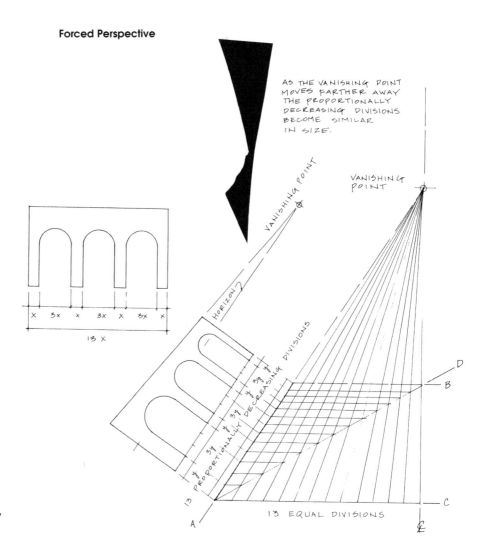

AS THE VANISHING POINT
MOVES FARTHER AWAY
THE PROPORTIONALLY
DECREASING DIVISIONS
BECOME SIMILAR
IN SIZE.

Figure 13.7 Calculating proportionally decreasing widths.

designed and drafted by Patricia Woodbridge for the Cincinnati Playhouse in the Park. As this is a very naturalistic setting, the horizon line is very high: 18 feet 6 inches above the stage floor. In addition to a horizontal vanishing point, the vertical side walls of the house rake in slightly: 3 inches on one side and 4 inches on the other. The upper windows, though similar in style to the lower, are 4 feet 9 inches rather than 5 feet, which contributes to the feeling of the forced perspective.

The second example, in Figure 13.9, is a set of elevations from Tony Walton's design for the 1988-89 Broadway farce *Lend Me a Tenor* by Ken Ludwig. The walls are in forced perspective with a very low horizon line: 4 feet 6 inches above the stage floor. Although there is no ceiling, the angle of the top of the walls is acute, contributing to the stylization of the setting. *Lend Me a Tenor* was built by Showtech in Norwalk, Connecticut. The shop foreman used a trigonometric function to mathematically calculate all of the forced perspective heights. The most complex construction on this show was the cornice dentils, whose horizontal lines angled to the vanishing point while the widths decreased in size as they receded. The dentils could not be mass-produced; each dentil had to be individually crafted. The forced perspective of the cornice required that each dentil proportionately decrease in size. As each dentil was a different height and width, the full-size detail was drawn without perspective at the size of the largest dentil. The dentils in forced perspective were laid out in full-size in the shop. The intricate drafting for this forced perspective was done by Charles Beal.

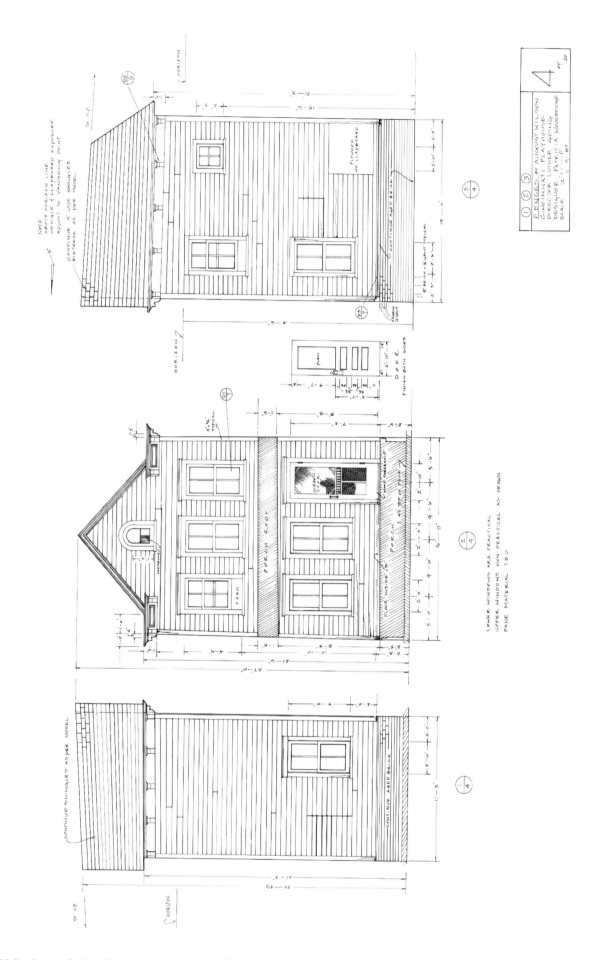

Figure 13.8 *Fences* for the Cincinnati Playhouse. Written by August Wilson. Designed and drafted by Patricia Woodbridge.

218

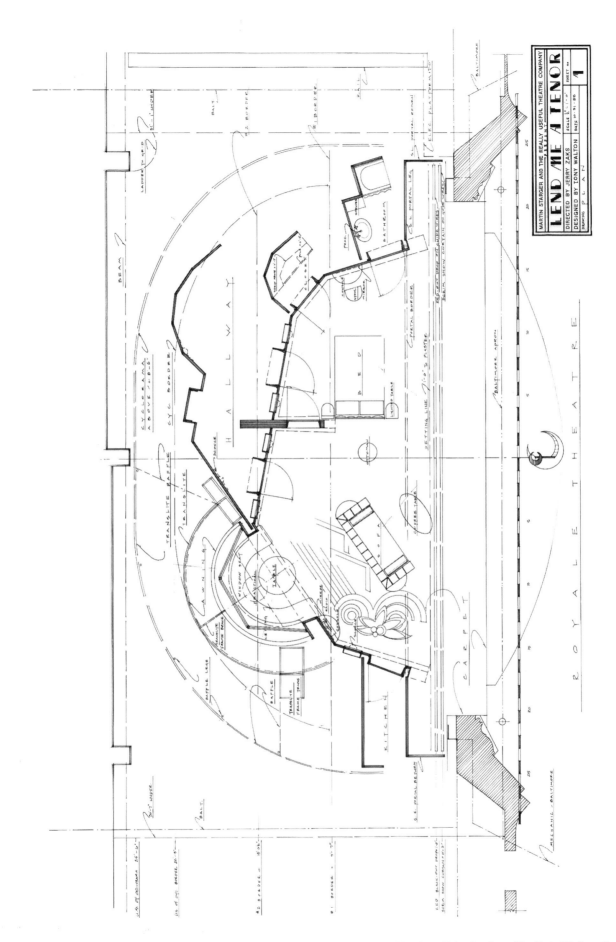

Figure 13.9a Sheet 1. Director's plan. Draftings from *Lend Me a Tenor*. Directed by Jerry Zaks. Designed by Tony Walton. Drafting by Charles Beal. Used by permission.

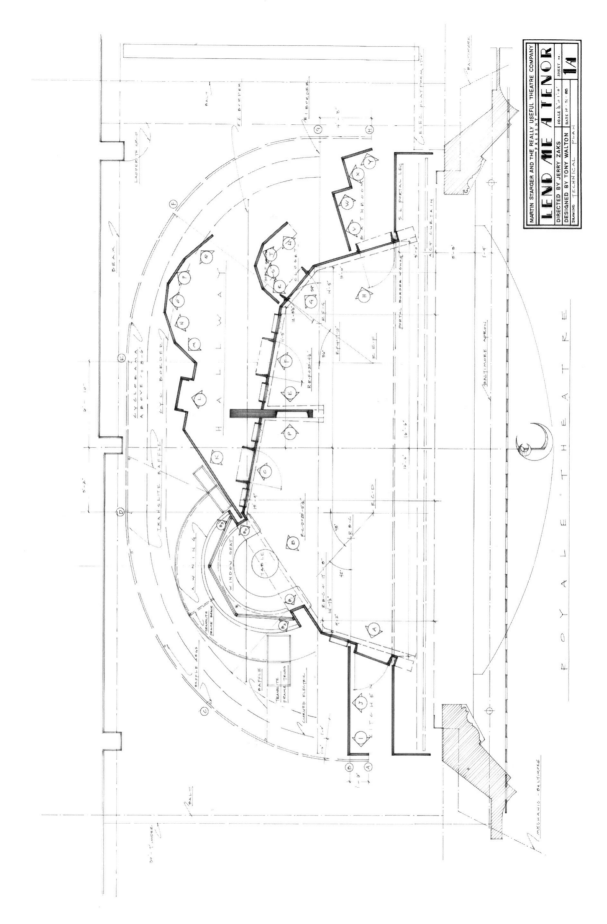

Figure 13.9b Sheet 1A. Technical plan. Draftings from *Lend Me a Tenor*. Directed by Jerry Zaks. Designed by Tony Walton. Drafting by Charles Beal. Used by permission.

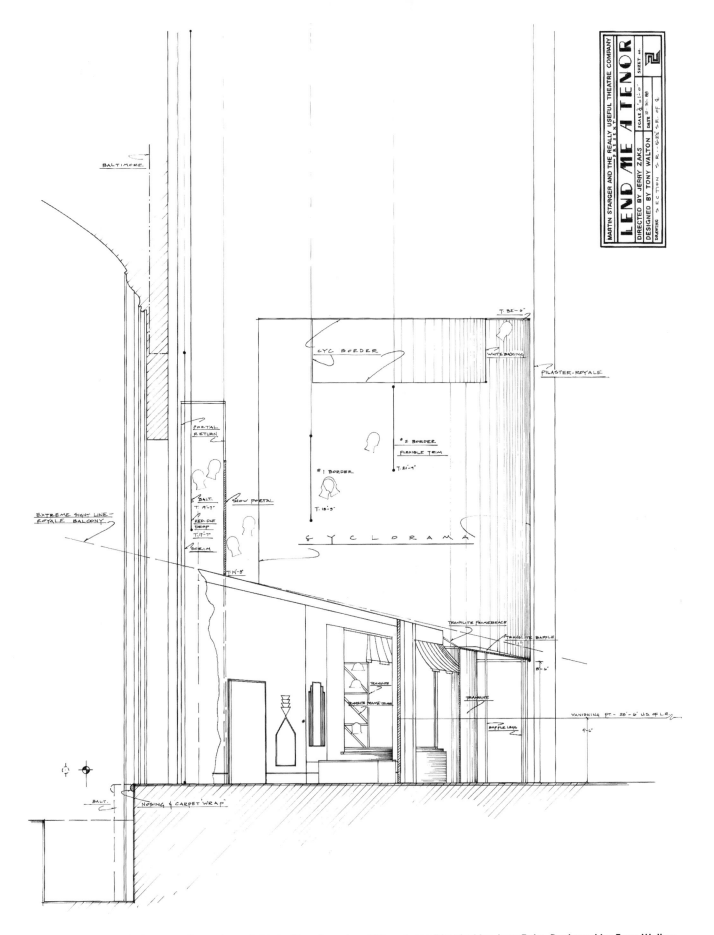

Figure 13.9c   Sheet 2. Cross-section—stage right draftings from *Lend Me a Tenor*. Directed by Jerry Zaks. Designed by Tony Walton. Drafting by Charles Beal. Used by permission.

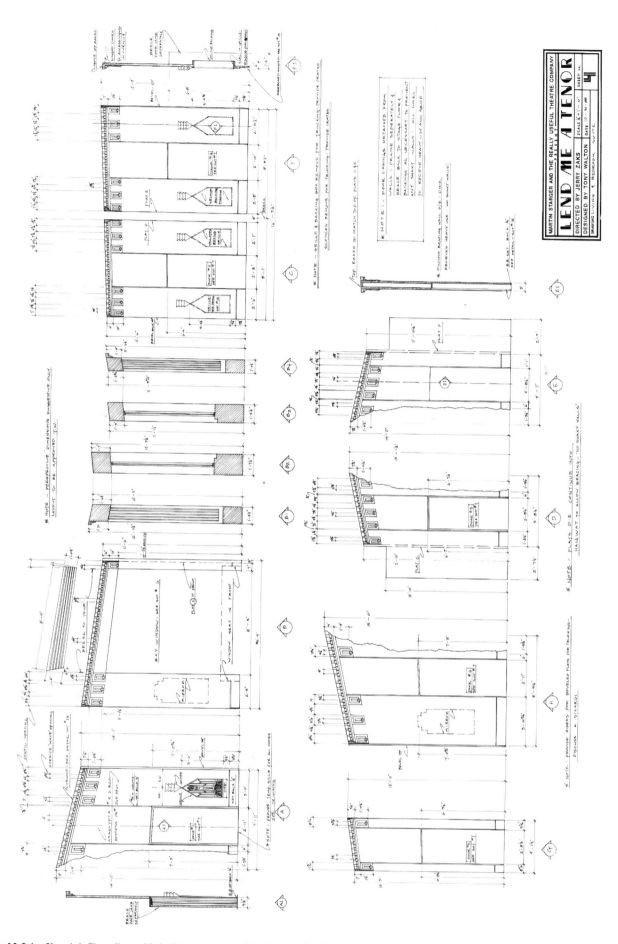

Figure 13.9d Sheet 4. Elevations: Main living room and bedroom. Draftings from *Lend Me a Tenor*. Directed by Jerry Zaks. Designed by Tony Walton. Drafting by Charles Beal. Used by permission.

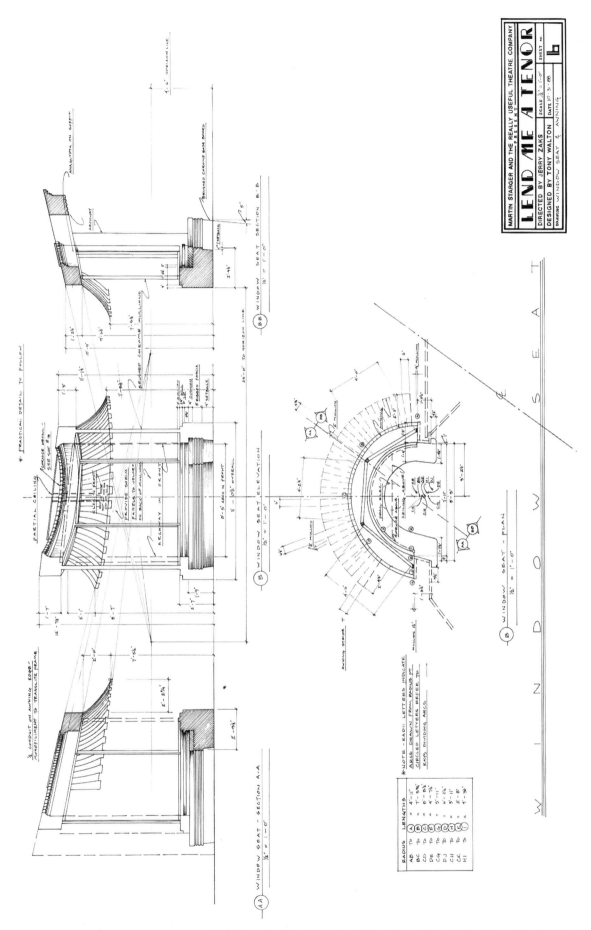

Figure 13.9e   Sheet 6. Elevations: Window seat and awning. Draftings from *Lend Me a Tenor*. Directed by Jerry Zaks. Designed by Tony Walton. Drafting by Charles Beal. Used by permission.

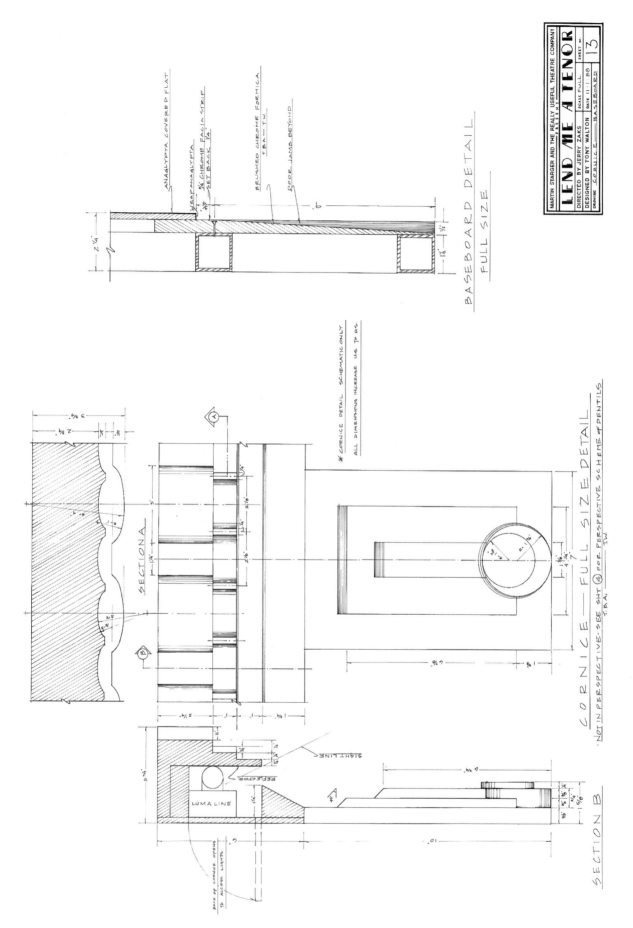

Figure 13.9f   Sheet 13. Dentil and baseboard details. Draftings from _Lend Me a Tenor_. Directed by Jerry Zaks. Designed by Tony Walton. Drafting by Charles Beal. Used by permission.

14

Multisheet Sets and Coding

Description of Coding

Coding is the method of labeling and cross-referencing different views of sets and the parts and details that relate to them. On a multiset production, coding identifies each set or location. On a large feature film, scenic coding is also used to track set costs. The object of coding is for the reader of a drafting to be able to locate easily and quickly a specific view and understand its position to the whole.

Coding is an area where it is obvious that scenic drafting is not systematized. Scenic draftspeople use numbers and letters in different ways to identify pieces of scenery. Whatever method you choose to code a production should be appropriate for the complexity of the design, should be logical, and should be consistent for all the draftings of a production.

Naming Pieces of Theatrical Scenery

When drafting a theatrical production with multiple pieces such as a multiset musical, the clearest method of identification is to give them short descriptive names that are easy to remember, such as "Tree," "Tavern," "Rose Drop, "Winter Sky Translucency," "Winter Sky Bounce Drop," "Stage Right Border #3," "Stage Left Tab #2" (a tab is a soft, full masking that usually runs upstage and downstage), "Show Portal," and so on. Having simple names for pieces of scenery makes it easy to refer to them when building and installing the show. The name of each piece of scenery and of each piece of masking should be clearly labeled wherever the piece is drawn.

Labeling by View

Labeling by orthographic view is best for a simple object whose views fit on a single sheet. The most complex side is labeled as the front, and then the sides are laid out and labeled in the standard orthographic manner: right-side view to the right, left-side view to the left, rear view to the left of the left-side view, plan below, and the top view above the front view. (See Figure 14.1.)

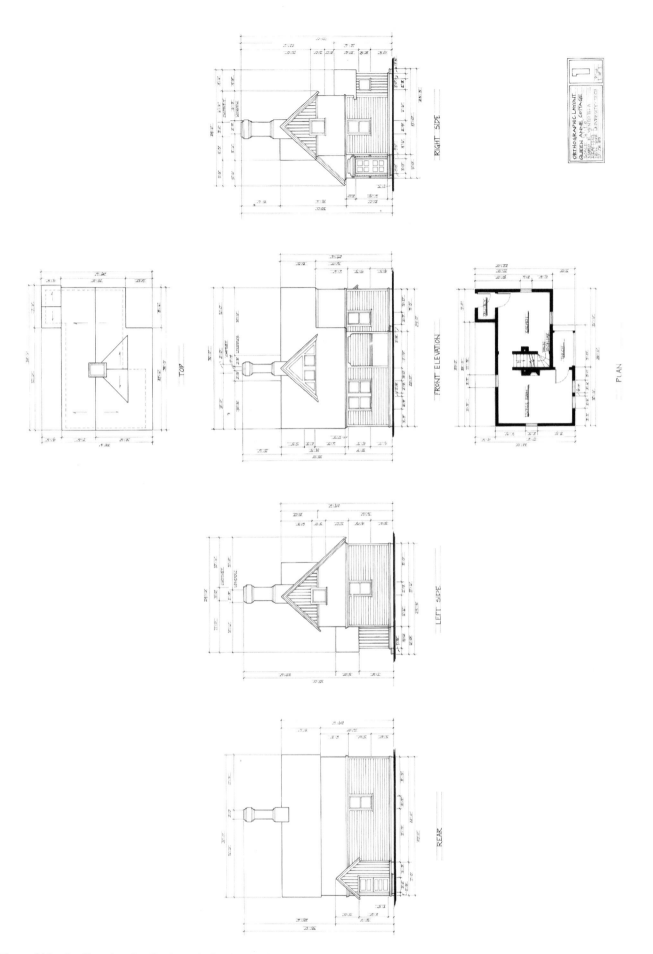

Figure 14.1 Drafting showing the layout of a simple object—Exterior of a house. Designed and drafted by Mario Ventenilla, New York University Tisch School of the Arts. Used by permission.

Multisheet Layout

All the draftings of a production should be the same size, with the exception being the master ground plan or studio plan, which may be larger. A pack of drafting of different sized sheets is difficult to handle, and the smaller draftings tend to get lost. The most common size for drafting sheets is 24 inches by 36 inches, with 36 inches by 42 inches used for large scenic productions.

When a single set requires multiple sheets, carefully consider which views you need to draw and the clearest way to organize the layout so the information fits logically and attractively on equal-sized sheets. Deciding the best way to separate a set into views and how to arrange the views on consecutive sheets should be done before beginning to draft finished sheets. Done correctly it prevents errors and omissions and speeds up the drafting process. The beginning draftsperson often finds it helpful to plan the layout by sketching it on small sheets.

Labeling Views with Letters

Figures 14.2a and 14.2b show the same views of the house on two sheets. Each view is positioned on a sheet so that it relates to the neighboring view.

Sheet 1 Places the plan below the most complex front elevation with the right-side elevation to its right.

Sheet 2 Places the left-side elevation to the right of the rear elevation and the top view above it.

Figures 14.3a, 14.3b, and 14.3c show the same house laid out on three sheets:

Sheet 1 Shows the ground plan of the house elevation with the roof to its right.

Sheet 2 Shows the front elevation with the right-side elevation to its right.

Sheet 3 Shows the rear elevation with the left-side elevation to its right.

Coding Views with Numbers or Letters

Most theatrical draftspersons use letters of the alphabet to identify walls. Each wall is labeled on the plan and again below its elevations, as shown in Figure 14.4. The walls should be coded from left to right so elevations can be laid out in sequence with common edges adjacent. In theatrical drafting, sections are often labeled with double letters to distinguish them from single-lettered elevations: "Section A-A," "Section B-B," and so on.

As complex film sets may have more than twenty-six walls, wall elevations in film are often numbered. Some film draftspeople identify sections with numbers, but it seems clearest to use letters to distinguish them from elevations: "Section A," "Section B," and so on. Some draftspersons differentiate elevations from sections by placing an "S" with a dash preceding the number of the section.

Many draftspeople feel that in addition to coding views it is important to verbally identify them, as in "Section through Wainscoting," "Elevation Wall B," "Plan Detail Window Casing."

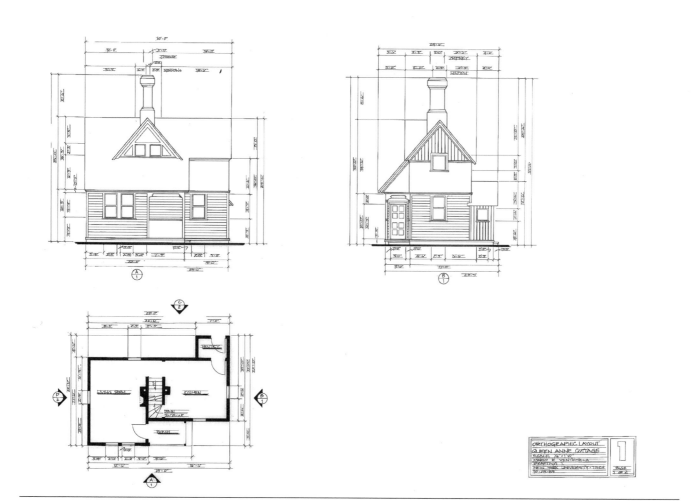

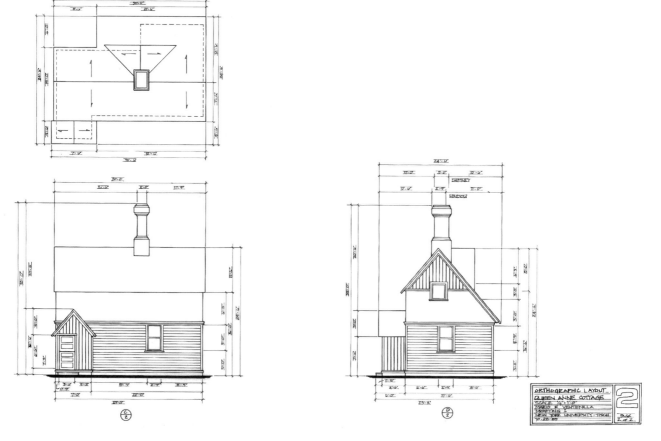

Figures 14.2a and 14.2b Drafting showing a double-sheet layout of the house. Designed and drafted by Mario Ventenilla, New York University Tisch School of the Arts. Used by permission.

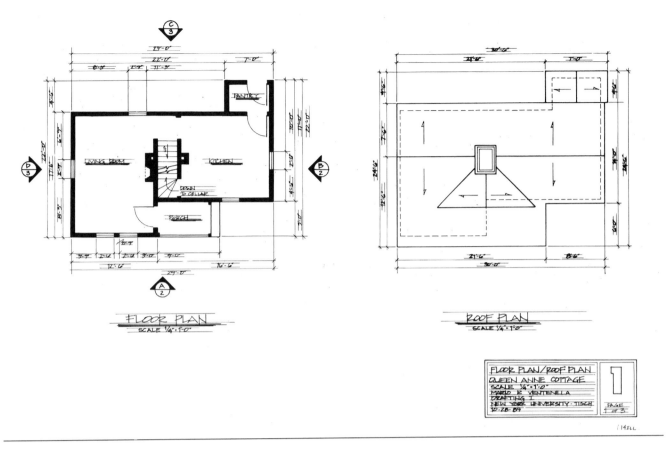

FLOOR PLAN
SCALE ¼"=1'-0"

ROOF PLAN
SCALE ¼"=1'-0"

FLOOR PLAN/ROOF PLAN
QUEEN ANNE COTTAGE
SCALE ¼"=1'-0"
MARIO R. VENTENILLA
DRAFTING I
NEW YORK UNIVERSITY-TISCH
10-28-89

1

PAGE 1 of 3

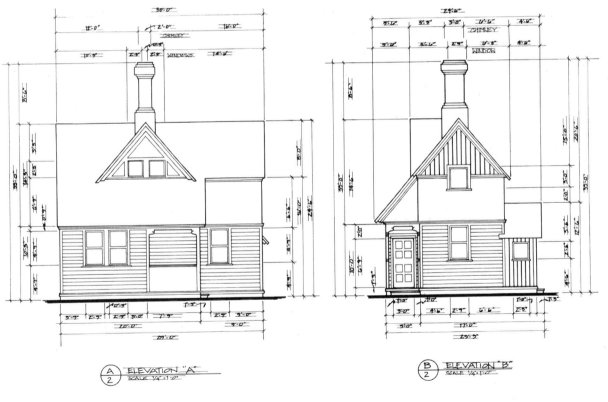

ELEVATION "A"
SCALE ¼"=1'-0"

ELEVATION "B"
SCALE ¼"=1'-0"

ELEVATIONS "A"/"B"
QUEEN ANNE COTTAGE
SCALE ¼"=1'-0"
MARIO R. VENTENILLA
DRAFTING I
NEW YORK UNIVERSITY-TISCH
10-28-89

2

PAGE 2 of 3

Figures 14.3a and 14.3b Drafting showing a triple-sheet layout of the house. Designed and drafted by Mario Ventenilla, New York University Tisch School of the Arts. Used by permission.

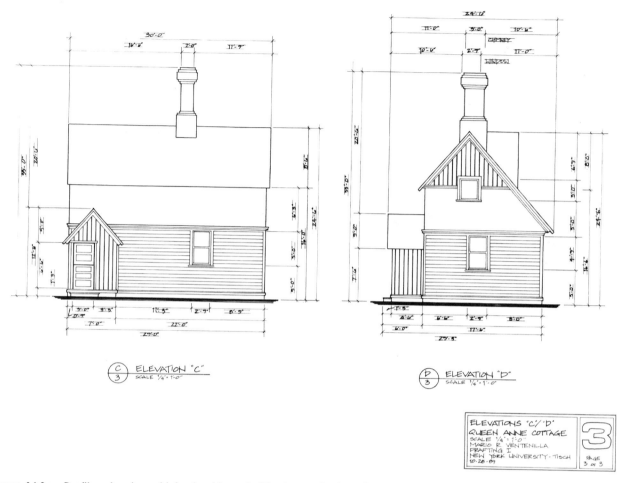

Figure 14.3c   Drafting showing a triple-sheet layout of the house. Designed and drafted by Mario Ventenilla, New York University Tisch School of the Arts. Used by permission.

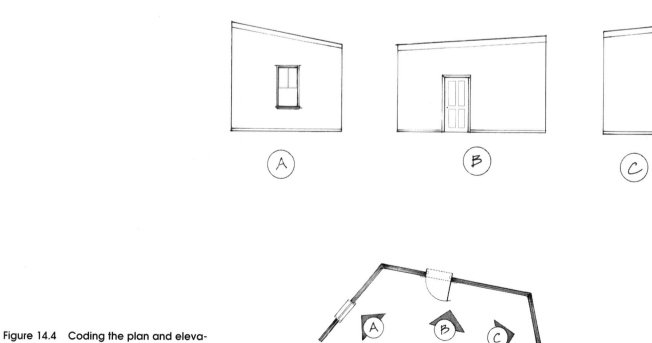

Figure 14.4   Coding the plan and elevations of a simple box set.

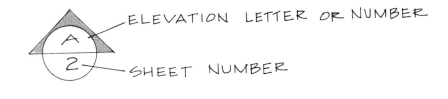

ELEVATION LETTER OR NUMBER

SHEET NUMBER

Figure 14.5 Graphic symbol for coding a plan.

Graphic Symbol for Coding Plan Views

The clearest and most commonly used graphic symbol for coding the ground plan of a set is a circle, called the bubble, inside an arrow that points in the direction of the point of view, perpendicular to the elevation. The circle is divided in two, its top half identifying the view and its bottom half identifying the sheet on which the view appears. This graphic symbol is illustrated in Figure 14.5.

The quickest way to draw this symbol on the plan is to draw two light lines parallel to and perpendicular to each wall at the place where you wish to locate the symbol. Use a template to draw a circle where the lines intersect. To draw the arrow, set your adjustable angle parallel to the wall and, placing a small 45-degree triangle on top of the adjustable angle, draw two 45-degree lines to the centerline of the circle. Lightly but solidly, shade the inside of the arrow around the circle.

On a plan, views will be at different angles to the reader, but their identifying numbers or letters should all be horizontal.

Graphic Symbols for Labeling Elevation and Section Views

A bubble with the same code that identifies a view on the plan is drawn below the elevation of that view. A bubble with the same code that identifies the cutting line of a section is drawn below the section. Bubbles below the elevation or section should not have an arrow.

Coding the Details of a Sectional View

A section removed to the side of an elevation is sometimes coded by circling the areas to be enlarged and drawing lines to the identifying bubble. Figure 14.6 shows many details coded on the section beside the elevation. Additional details that are needed but don't show in the section are coded directly on the elevation.

Coding Details on Sections and Elevations

Details are identified with numbers. Sometimes they are just identified with a code number and the sheet on which they appear. Often a detail view is identified by writing "FSD" (full-size detail) or "DT" (detail) before its number.

If elevations are lettered, a detail may be further identified by preceding its number with the letter of an elevation to which the detail refers: "A-1," and "A-2," and so on. Figure 14.6 is an example of this kind of detail coding.

Figures 14.7 to 14.9 show three coding systems.

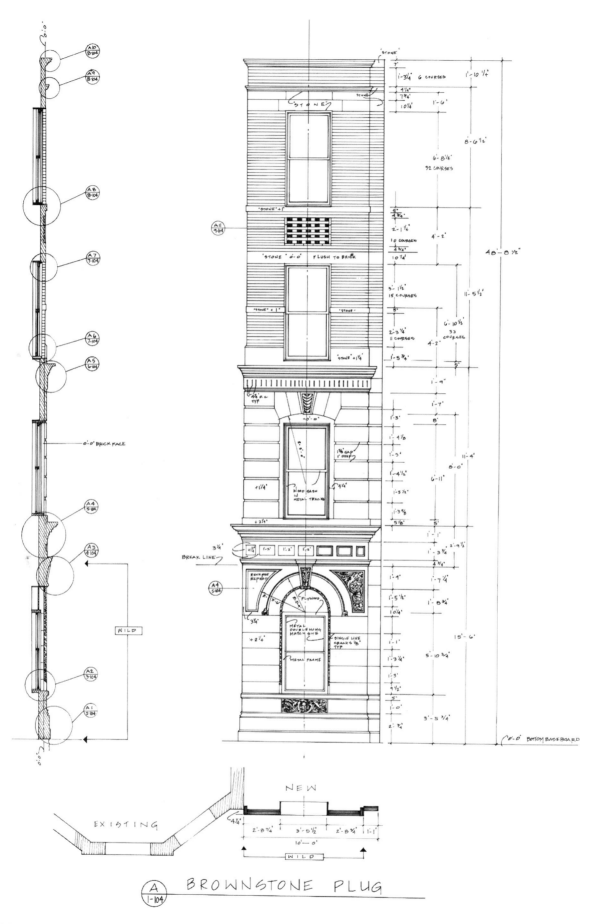

Figure 14.6 Coding the details of a sectional view.

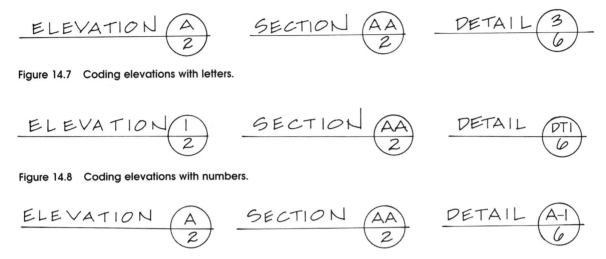

Figure 14.7   Coding elevations with letters.

Figure 14.8   Coding elevations with numbers.

Figure 14.9   Coding each room with a letter.

Coding a Feature Film

Most feature films have many different locations and sets. The art director, often in collaboration with the location manager, the production accountant, and the assistant director, will name and number the sets in the film. The accounting department has a range of numbers in their spreadsheet available for sets. These numbers will be used by all departments to identify sets, and to budget and track costs.

Art directors have different ways of numbering sets. At the start of a film, sets are often in flux. One method of setting up a numbering system that has the flexibility to accommodate changes is to organize the set list in clusters around set names, starting with 010 for the first cluster and jumping in 10-number increments for each additional cluster.

Coding and Naming Sets for a Feature Film

Most feature films have many different scripted set locations. The names for these sets first appear in the scripts but often change as the production evolves. For example, "Joe's Delightful Deli" can become "Paul's Yummy Pizza Hut." To avoid the confusion of constant changes it is a good idea to use generic names such as "Eatery in the Bronx" or "School Cafeteria." When possible it is best to use character names to identify their places: "Sue's apartment," "Joe's Bar," or "Mr. Picking's Office."

One of the initial jobs for the art director is to generate a numbered set list. These numbers and names are used to help identify each set, organize budgeting, and cost tracking. This seemingly simple job is quite difficult and very important. The names and locations of the sets are always in flux, and people quickly start generating their own names for things. The final decision on the name of each set will be chosen by the AD (assistant director) and will appear in the shooting schedule. Unfortunately, the shooting schedule is generated long after the art and locations departments have been in preproduction. Occasionally an inexperienced AD will also generate a mess of names in the schedule that are entirely different from what the art, location, and billing departments have been working with. It is recommended that the art director work with the location manager, accountant, and AD to generate the set list. If everyone gets together early enough it is possible to develop a set list that can be used not only by the art department but by all departments to identify, budget, and track the costs of sets.

A good method of setting up a numbering system that has the flexibility to accommodate changes is shown in the following table. The set list is organized in clusters around character names and numbers, starting with 010 for the first cluster and jumping in 10-number increments for each additional cluster. In this table the exterior of "Sue's Apartment" is a location. The hallway to the apartment is an interior set built in a studio, while the interior of Sue's Apartment is a set built in the same studio. If the script was rewritten to require the interior basement of Sue's Apartment, this numbering and naming system would make it easy to include the basement in the "Sue" cluster without renumbering all the sets. (Note that built sets on a set list are differentiated from locations by italics.)

#	L/S	E/I	SET	SET LOCATION	
010		**L**	**E**	**River Edge**	**Hudson River & 135 St.**
020		**L**	**E/I**	**Restaurant/Bar**	**Ave. B, Bet. 6 & 7**
	021	L	E	Restaurant	Ave. B, Bet. 6 & 7
	022	L	I	Restaurant	Ave. B, Bet. 6 & 7
	023	L	I	Bar	Ave. B, Bet. 6 & 7
030		**L/S**	**E/I**	**Sue's Apartment**	**West End Ave. at 84 St.**
	031	L	E	Front & Street	West End Ave. at 86 St.
	032	S	I	*Hallway*	*Studio A*
	033	S		*Apartment*	*Studio A*
040		**L**	**E**	**Dry Cleaning Store**	**Broadway at 68 St.**
050		**L**	**E/I**	**Cab w/Streets**	
060		**L**	**E**	**Church**	**St. Anthony's, W.E.A.**

Each sheet of drafting on a feature film includes a space to include the set number on the title block.

Occasionally it clarifies a situation to include the set number in the bubble surrounding the view number. For example, a large elaborate set may be divided into pieces for cost tracking with each view identified by a set number following the view number as in the title bubble of Figure 14.6.

Coding Special Items

If a set has similar elements such as columns, snow mounds, or gymnasium lockers, they can be identified by number. Figure 14.10 shows two template shapes that are often used for specialized identification.

If a built set has many doors and windows, they are often identified on plan and elevation by numbers preceded by D for door or W for window. The hexagonal template shape is often used for this purpose. (See Figure 14.11.)

Figure 14.10 Specialized coding symbols—doors, windows, and so on.

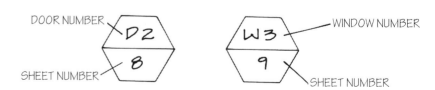

Figure 14.11 Coding doors and windows.

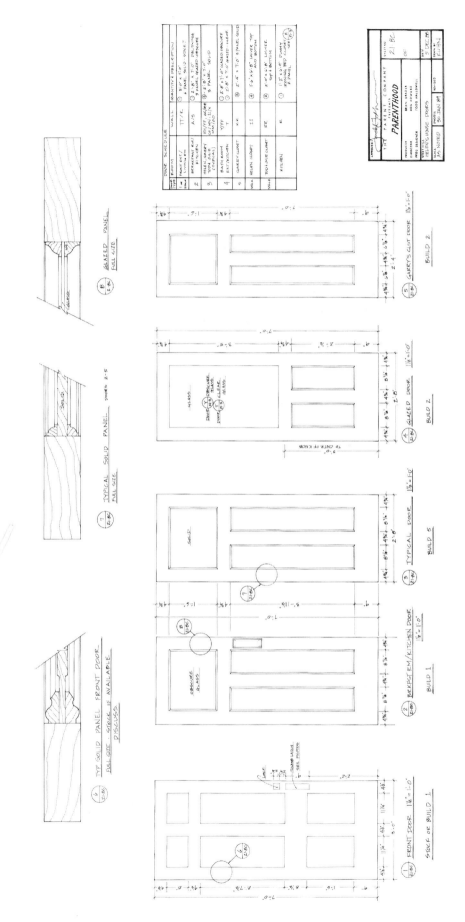

Figure 14.12   Specialized door coding for the feature film *Parenthood*. 1989. Directed by Ron Howard. Designed by Todd Hallowell. Drafted by Beth Kuhn. Courtesy of Universal City Studio, Inc.

Figure 14.13   Practical lighting symbol.

In film drafting doors and windows, only the height and width dimensions of the inside of the reveal appear on wall elevations. A separate sheet shows the door or windows in a larger scale along with their full-size details. A written door or window schedule lists the type of each door, the wall it appears on, the hardware it needs, and sometimes its paint treatment. Figure 14.12 shows a drafted sheet of doors with their details and a door schedule.

Practical Lighting Symbol

The symbol in Figure 14.13 is traditionally used in the theatre to locate positions of practical lights on the ground plan and of sconces on the walls. These locations are important to the director and the lighting designer. On a fabric-covered theatrical flat this symbol indicates that a built support is needed on the back. A number inside refers to a list of lighting practicals that the set designer needs to buy.

15

Period Shapes
and Scenic Details

Scenic Detailing

Details are enlarged views of small areas of a drafting. Areas chosen for detailing are often those that typify the construction of a part of the set, such as a section through a baseboard that runs around a room. A detail of a complex area of an elevation such as the intersection of a door casing, plinth, and baseboard may be needed to explain how the shapes come together. A full-size detail showing the profile of a baluster may be needed in order to fabricate it.

Details may be drawn in any large scale, but they are most often drawn full-size as that shows the builder the true profile of each piece. While some draftspeople draw just the profile of a detail, it is often required that the draftsperson show the size and shape of each piece of material that composes the shape. Such detailing requires an understanding of methods of scenic construction, as well as knowledge of scenic construction materials and the sizes they come in. A combination of technical knowledge and design sensibility is needed for good detailing.

Surface Detailing and Structural Detailing

Surface detailing involves the replication of moldings and surfaces that mimic architectural details, often period details, using contemporary scenic building materials and methods of scenic construction. Usually surface detailing is a process of layering materials together, most often stapling and gluing materials on a flat to create a surface profile that mimics the size and shape of real objects. The surface is often heavily textured and painted so that its scenic construction doesn't show. If it is to be stained or kept raw, the draftsperson should note this so care will be taken during construction not to let glue or staples show. The detail will need to be designed and built to avoid unattractive edges that would not take stain well.

Structural detailing is detailing in which the structure is part of the design. In such detailing, materials such as wood or metal are used for their structural ability to support a load or stress, or to span a space, or to take a specific shape—which only that material is able to do. Such detailing may require a dialogue between the draftsperson and the construction coordinator or technical director. If the construction requires a knowledge of engineering, the draftsperson may work with a construction coordinator in film, or the technical director or shop owner in theatre, or with a structural engineer who is hired both as a consultant and to guarantee the safety of the construction.

Period Details

In a building, as the earth shifts over time and changes in weather expand and contract different materials at different rates, gaps and cracks occur in areas of architectural transition. Moldings were developed to span and hide such areas: a cornice to cover the transition between a wall and the ceiling, a baseboard to cover the transition between a floor and a wall, and a casing to cover the juncture between a plaster wall and a wood window frame. Primitive buildings had simple moldings. Like the architecture to which they were attached, the simple shapes reflected the climate and the type of building materials specific to the area. Over time, these simple shapes became increasingly embellished and ornate, reflecting the style of each period and of each geographical area.

Unlike an architect who deals with contemporary form, the scenic designer often creates illusions mimicking different periods and places. A scenic design may reflect the social level and personality of the characters in the drama. A room or building may be aged and show changes that have occurred over time.

The shapes and proportions of the details of a set need to reflect the same sensibility as the design. If you were designing a stage, film, or television set for an adaptation of Edith Wharton's novel *Ethan Frome,* the door casing of the house in which Ethan lives would probably be simple, as he is poor. It would be wide and thick, as wood was plentiful at that time in New England, and it would have a touch of American Federal design, as that was the prevalent style of the period. The education of a scenic designer/draftsperson should include comparative regional and historical styles of architecture. Many books show historical and contemporary architecture and their details. A beginning library might start with:

A History of Architecture on the Comparative Method, by Banister Fletcher, Charles Scribner's Sons, New York, 1967.
Styles of Ornament, by Alexander Speltz, Dover Publications, Inc., New York, 1957.
Miniature Rooms: The Thorne Rooms at the Art Institute of Chicago, by Kathleen Aquilar, Abbeville Press, New York, 1983.

Historical Detailing

The architectural orders are the systems used by the architects of the classic period to proportion the various parts and details of their buildings. Each of the orders possesses a distinctive period and style, and each has a clear set of rules that govern the proportional relationships of its parts. The three orders, Doric, Ionic, and Corinthian, were originated by the Greeks. The Romans modified each of the three Greek orders as well as developing two of their own, the Tuscan and the Composite. A design student should study the classic orders as they have influenced architectural details through the ages.

A scenic draftsperson also needs to understand the shapes, names, and uses of architectural elements and how they are constructed scenically. The drawings in Figures 15.1 to 15.6 illustrate the scenic construction of some simple, common American Victorian architectural elements.

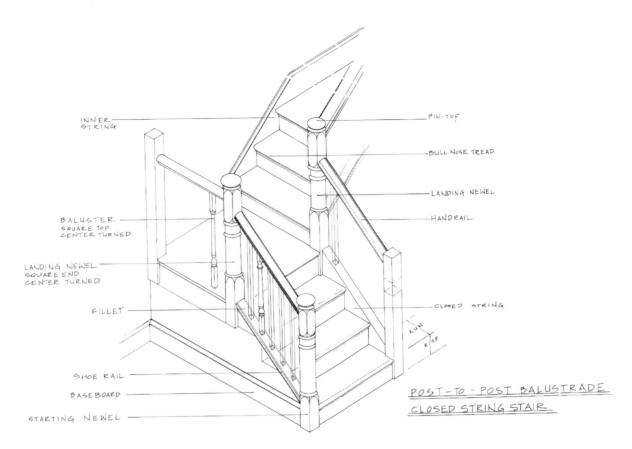

INNER STRING

BALUSTER
SQUARE TOP
CENTER TURNED

LANDING NEWEL
SQUARE END
CENTER TURNED

FILLET

SHOE RAIL

BASEBOARD

STARTING NEWEL

PIN-TOP

BULL NOSE TREAD

LANDING NEWEL

HANDRAIL

CLOSED STRING

RUN
RISE

POST-TO-POST BALUSTRADE
CLOSED STRING STAIR

Figure 15.1   Post-to-post balustrade—closed string stair.

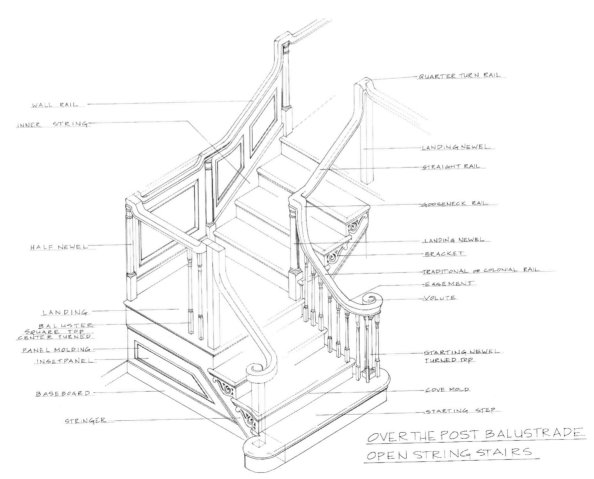

WALL RAIL

INNER STRING

HALF NEWEL

LANDING

BALUSTER
SQUARE TOP
CENTER TURNED

PANEL MOLDING

INSET PANEL

BASEBOARD

STRINGER

QUARTER TURN RAIL

LANDING NEWEL

STRAIGHT RAIL

GOOSENECK RAIL

LANDING NEWEL

BRACKET

TRADITIONAL OR COLONIAL RAIL

EASEMENT

VOLUTE

STARTING NEWEL
TURNED TOP

COVE MOLD.

STARTING STEP

OVER THE POST BALUSTRADE
OPEN STRING STAIRS

Figure 15.2   Over-the-post balustrade—open string stair.

239

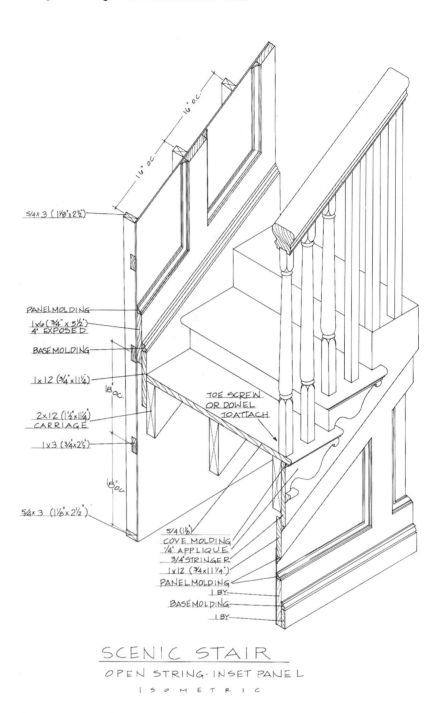

5/4 x 3 (1⅛"x 2½")

PANEL MOLDING
1x6 (¾" x 5½")
4' EXPOSED

BASE MOLDING

1x12 (¾"x 11¼")

2x12 (1½"x 11¼")
CARRIAGE

1x3 (¾"x2½")

5/4 x 3 (1⅛"x 2½")

TOE SCREW
OR DOWEL
TO ATTACH

5/4 (1⅛)
COVE MOLDING
¼" APPLIQUE
3/4 STRINGER
1x12 (¾"x 11¼")
PANEL MOLDING
1 BY
BASE MOLDING
1 BY

SCENIC STAIR
OPEN STRING · INSET PANEL
I S O M E T R I C

Figure 15.3 Scenic stair—isometric open string with inset panel.

Interconnecting Details

A common mistake in detailing room molding is to design each detail separately without designing them to interconnect gracefully. The draftsperson needs to analyze each situation to see where details join. For example, a door casing may have to be thick enough to accept a baseboard and chair rail running into it. Or wood paneling at the top of a stair may need to be designed so that the center of its stile accepts a connecting handrail.

A complex detail may include a full-size drawing of a part of an elevation with a plan below and a section to the side, or with revolved plans and sections drawn on top of the elevation. Break lines are often used to remove noncritical areas of the full-size drawing, allowing more details to show in a single drawing. If it is important to show a continuous detail and it won't fit on a single sheet, match lines can be used to code where the two images join.

240

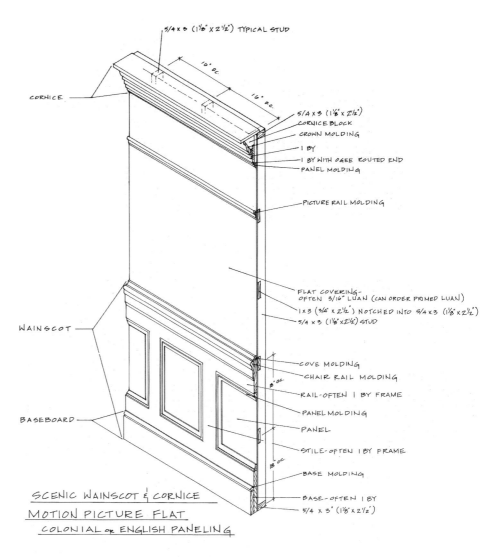

5/4 x 3 (1⅛" x 2½") TYPICAL STUD

16" O.C.

16" O.C.

CORNICE

5/4 x 3 (1⅛" x 2½") CORNICE BLOCK

CROWN MOLDING

1 BY

1 BY WITH OGEE ROUTED END

PANEL MOLDING

PICTURE RAIL MOLDING

FLAT COVERING—OFTEN 3/16" LUAN (CAN ORDER PRIMED LUAN)

1 x 3 (3/4" x 2½") NOTCHED INTO 5/4 x 3 (1⅛" x 2½")

5/4 x 3 (1⅛" x 2½") STUD

WAINSCOT

COVE MOLDING

CHAIR RAIL MOLDING

RAIL—OFTEN 1 BY FRAME

PANEL MOLDING

PANEL

STILE—OFTEN 1 BY FRAME

BASE MOLDING

BASEBOARD

BASE—OFTEN 1 BY

5/4 x 3" (1⅛" x 2½")

SCENIC WAINSCOT & CORNICE

MOTION PICTURE FLAT

COLONIAL OR ENGLISH PANELING

EAST COAST WALL FRAMING

I S O M E T R I C

Figure 15.4 Typical scenic wainscot and cornice—motion picture flat.

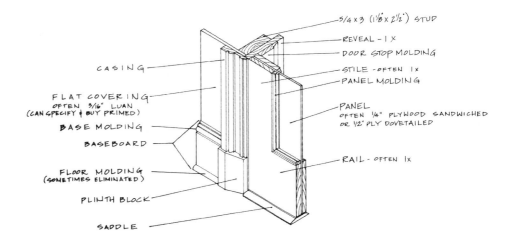

5/4 x 3 (1⅛" x 2½") STUD

REVEAL — 1 X

DOOR STOP MOLDING

STILE — OFTEN 1X

PANEL MOLDING

CASING

FLAT COVERING OFTEN 3/16" LUAN (CAN SPECIFY & BUY PRIMED)

PANEL OFTEN ¼" PLYWOOD SANDWICHED OR ½" PLY DOVETAILED

BASE MOLDING

BASEBOARD

RAIL — OFTEN 1X

FLOOR MOLDING (SOMETIMES ELIMINATED)

PLINTH BLOCK

SADDLE

TYPICAL SCENIC DOOR & JAMB

MOTION PICTURE FLAT

ONSTAGE OPENING DOOR

I S O M E T R I C

Figure 15.5 Typical scenic door and jamb—motion picture flat.

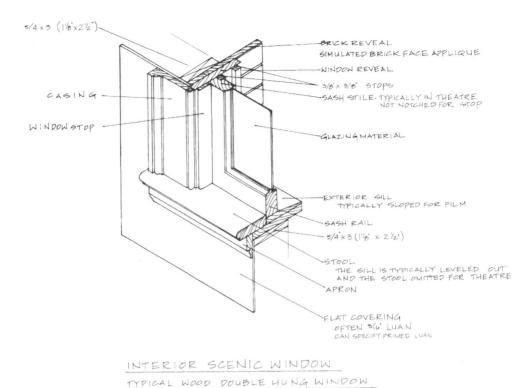

Figure 15.6 Typical scenic double-hung window—motion picture flat.

Detailing Molding

When detailing a piece of molding such as the cornice of a room, the overall size of the detail is determined in the small-scale elevation, insuring that the detail will be in proportion with the other architectural elements of the set. The overall size is measured in the larger scale of the detail, and then the pieces and shapes of the detail are designed to fit. The profile of the entire detail should be roughly designed before choosing the specific molding shapes that will compose the detail.

A three-dimensional sense of the molding can be had by making a cavalier drawing of the detail. Parallel lines are projected from each corner of the profile of the molding, and light shading is used to define shapes.

After the profile is set, with the shape of each piece of molding or other material tightly drawn, the catalogue moldings are noted by number. Special-order shapes, such as a purchased preformed length of shaped Styrofoam, are noted by the company that sells them. The sales contact and phone number are also noted. Dimensions are the last thing to be added to the detail. Since pieces of molding are drawn full size, they are not dimensioned. The dimensions that are required are any that the carpenter needs in putting the pieces together, such as the spacing between two shapes that are attached.

Milled Lumber Sizes

Scenic detailing often involves using stock pieces of lumber. Milled lumber varies in size from supplier to supplier and, occasionally, even in different shipments from the same supplier. For purposes of simplicity and clarity, it has been agreed by the building industry that standard sizes of lumber refer to approximate rather than actual sizes. In full-size detailing, you draw the actual size of the wood.

When noting sizes of lumber in a drawing, it is important to be clear when your dimension means a stock size versus an exact size. A 1 x 4 refers to a piece of wood that is, when milled, approximately 3/4 inches thick and 3 1/2 inches wide. If, as draftsperson, you specify a 1 x 4, it means that the carpenter can use the approximate size. If you specify 3/4 inches by 3 5/8 inches, it means that the carpenter has to rip down a board to the exact size you specified.

Following is a list of the actual sizes of softwood lumber from a prominent New York lumber company that guarantees these sizes.

You Order	Actual Size
1 x 4	3/4 by 3 1/2
1 x 6	3/4 by 5 1/2
1 x 8	3/4 by 7 1/2
1 x 10	3/4 by 9 1/4
1 x 12	3/4 by 11 1/4
2 x 4	1 1/2 by 3 1/2
2 x 6	1 1/2 by 5 1/2
2 x 8	1 1/2 by 7 1/4
2 x 10	1 1/2 by 9 1/4
2 x 12	1 1/2 by 11 1/4
4 x 4	3 1/2 by 3 1/2
4 x 6	3 1/2 by 5 1/2
4 x 8	3 1/2 by 7 1/2
4 x 10	3 1/2 by 9 1/4
4 x 12	3 1/2 by 11 1/4

In addition, this company sells 5/4-inch stock (which is approximately 1 1/8-inch thick), 1/2-inch square stock, and various strips of particular sizes, such as 25/32 inches by 1 3/4 inches, or 1 3/8 inches by 2 3/4 inches, their width measurements being dependent on how logs are milled.

Common Scenic Building Materials

To draw scenic details the draftsperson needs to know the characteristics of common scenic building materials and the thicknesses in which they come. Following is a basic list:

Material	Thickness	Use
Luan	3/16″	Basic hard flat covering.
Primed Luan	3/16″	Basic hard flat covering primed with a basecoat.
Homosote	1/2″ or 3/8″	A heavy soft covering that can be gouged or carved or textured.
Plywood	1/4″, 1/2″, 3/4″, or 1″	Has a heavy grain, which usually needs to be primed, sanded, and sealed before painting.
Birch Plywood	1/4″, 1/2″, 3/4″, or 1″	A light grain that takes stain in an attractive manner.
Sheet Rock	5/8″	Used to build real as opposed to scenic walls.
Medium-Density Fiberboard	3/8″, 1/2″, 3/4″, or 1″	A very smooth surface without a grain. Can be painted directly without priming and sanding. Does not take stain in an attractive manner.
High-Density Fiberboard	3/8″, 1/2″, 3/4″, or 1″	An extremely smooth surface without a grain. Usually used for lacquer finishes.
Masonite	1/8″ or 1/4″	Smooth on one side, textured on the other. Brittle.
Wiggle Board	3/8″	Takes curves easily. Has a slight texture.
Bending Poplar	1/8″	Takes curves easily and can be stained.

Stock Wood Molding

Scenic details often use wood molding, which can be purchased from various suppliers, including lumber companies. At the beginning of a job, a draftsperson usually gets a molding catalogue from the lumber company that the construction foreman uses. A molding catalogue organizes wood moldings by type and shows their profiles in full size.

While scenic designers often combine contemporary molding in unusual ways to create historical shapes, a scenic design student should get a molding catalogue and learn the traditional use of each molding shape. For example, crown moldings are part of the top moldings of objects such as the cornice of a room, the crown of a cabinet, or the top of a chest. Base moldings are combined with boards to form the base of objects such as the baseboard around a room or around a cabinet or chest. Sash molding forms the frames of windows and is designed to hold glass, and so on.

Router Shapes

In addition to using purchased moldings, a carpenter can shape the edge of a wood board with a hand tool called a router that accepts various shaped bits. Woodworking tool catalogues often show full-size shapes and sizes of router bits. These can be xeroxed onto acetate sheets as part of a draftsperson's equipment. The construction foreman can let the draftsperson know what bits he or she has.

Some shops own a machine called a cutter that accepts different knives that shape lengths of wood. This tool comes with a catalogue of the full-size knife profiles.

Prefabricated Ornamental and Architectural Pieces

Companies sell prefabricated architectural pieces such as balustrades or fireplaces, architectural details such as elaborate cornices, and various shapes in special materials such as extruded or cast plastics. Experienced draftspeople collect useful catalogues and organize them by categories such as: Architectural Elements—Large, Architectural Ornaments—Small, Backdrop, Bathroom, Doors and Windows, Kitchen, Fencing and Grating, Flooring and Wall Covering, Hardware, Metal Shapes, Moldings, Plastics, Pressed Metal, Signage, and so on.

In detailing metal construction it helps to have a catalogue from a metal company such as Ryerson in Chicago, which organizes metal by shape and lists stock sizes. You can purchase plastic templates of scaled stock metal shapes.

Examples

Many of the draftings in this book show examples of detailing. Figures 15.7 and 15.8 contain two examples of detailing molding. Figures 15.9 and 15.10 show two examples of structural detailing.

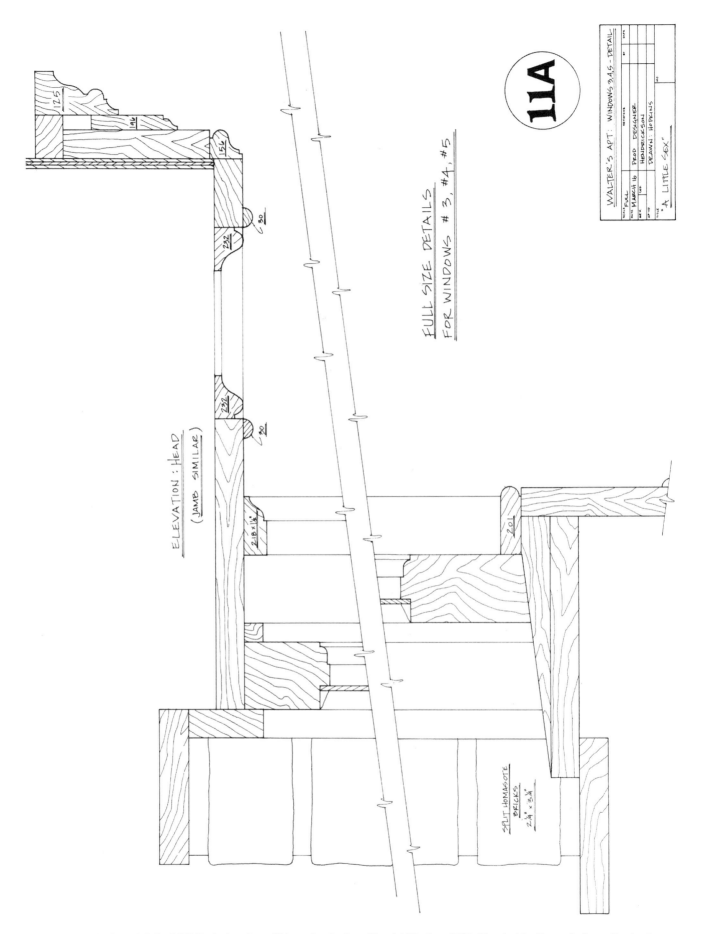

Figure 15.7   Window detail of "Walter's Apartment" from the feature film *A Little Sex*. 1982. Directed by Bruce Paltrow. Production designed by Stephen Hendrickson. Drafting by Speed Hopkins. Designs courtesy of MTM Enterprises, Inc.

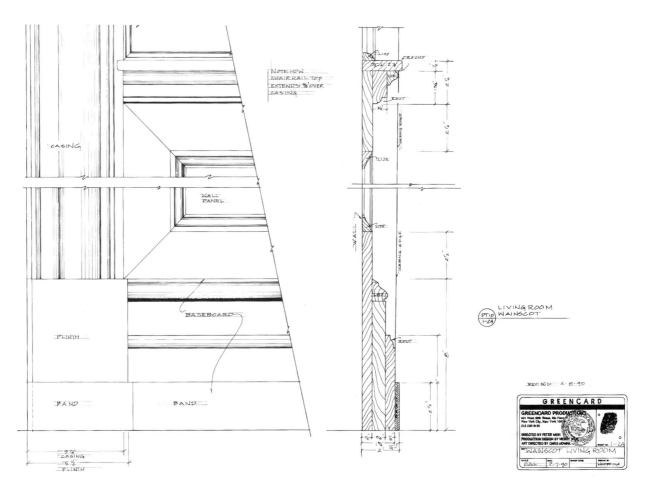

Figure 15.8 Wainscot detail of the "Living Room" from Touchstone Pictures' feature film *Green Card*. 1990. Directed by Peter Weir. Production designed by Wendy Stites. Drafting by Patricia Woodbridge. Used by permission from Disney Enterprises, Inc.

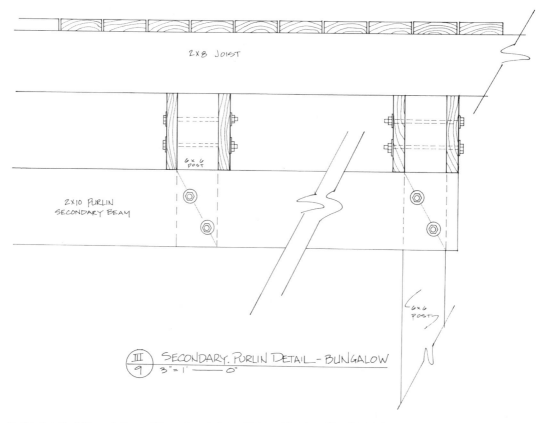

Figure 15.9 Purlin detail of "Beach House" from Touchstone Pictures' feature film *My Father, The Hero*. 1994. Directed by Steve Minor. Production designed by Christopher Nowak. Drafting by Christopher Nowak. Used by permission from Disney Enterprises, Inc.

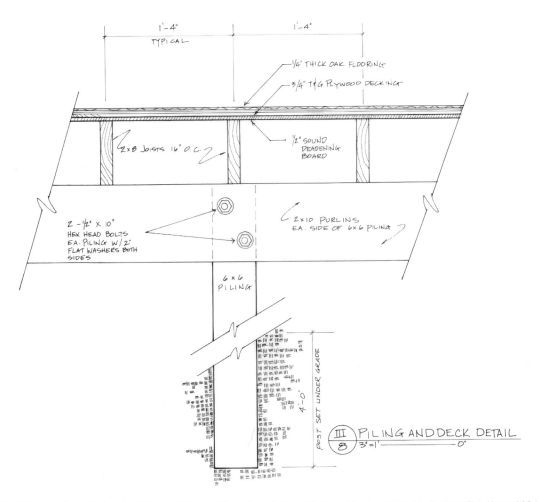

Figure 15.10   Piling and deck detail of "Beach House" from Touchstone Pictures' feature film *My Father, The Hero.* 1994. Directed by Steve Minor. Production designed by Christopher Nowak. Drafting by Christopher Nowak. Used by permission from Disney Enterprises, Inc.

16

Computer Drafting
and Rendering

Moving on to Digital

Computer aided drafting, commonly referred to as CAD, is an alternative to hand drafting. Several CAD programs are available for both Macintosh and Windows computers. Although commands differ within each program, all programs draw lines and shapes using exact mathematical coordinates known as vectors. This means that no matter in what size the object will ultimately be printed, it will maintain sharp, crisp edges.

The precise nature of CAD drawing is both its blessing and its curse. There is no ambiguity in CAD drafting, no messy confusing lines. However, while exact tight lines are needed at the final stage of drafting, many designers feel that loose, soft lines that gradually discover a shape are an important part of the design process. Although hardware and software for digital graphics are evolving towards more natural ways of drawing, they aren't there yet.

The current method of digital drawing eliminates eye-hand coordination. Eye-hand coordination is basic in the training of graphic artists as learning how to see is integrated with learning how to physically manipulate a pencil. Eventually drawing becomes partially a "left brain" function, and choice in drawing becomes somewhat subconscious. The neatness of digital drawing eliminates ambiguity, but it also eliminates the ability to create what Tony Walton refers to as "lucky accidents."

CAD lines and shapes are drawn by choosing from a tool palette and then manipulating them, either by typing in dimensions or by moving points. Shapes are located on the monitor screen by selecting and moving them visually or by typing in mathematical coordinates. The ability to erase or move sections of a drafting makes for easier changes to an existing drawing without the mess or the time spent redrawing a clean sheet or a different layout. This makes CAD drafting ideally suited for drafting plans, which often go through many changes and are essentially schematic drawings. Like text blocks in a word processing program, digital drawing allows images to be copied and pasted, which is useful in situations with repeating elements such as a row of columns. Digital designers can create personal libraries from pieces of drawings, incorporate old work into new designs, or choose CAD-drafted items from commercial libraries. Increasingly, manufacturers of products such as windows and doors are supplying CAD drawings of their products.

Digital design allows one to easily enlarge or reduce a drawing. In a CAD drafting, zooming in to see a detail or out to see the whole picture manipulates the view of the drawing without affecting the scale of an image. The areas of a drafting that need to be explained in a larger view can be drawn in more detail rather than redrawing them. Individual drawings are organized on sheets in common scales, including metric, before printing.

Digital graphics also use layers. Layers function somewhat like sheets of tracing paper. Similar elements of a drawing or pieces of a drawing can be isolated on a layer and identified by its own nonprinting color. For example, in CAD, all the dimensions can be on a separate layer. In drafting specs, furniture and director notes can be on their own layer. Layers can be turned on or off so you can see them or not; they can also be printed or not printed, as well as joined in combinations for printing. If you have a color printer or plotter, color can be added to draftings and becomes an additional way of organizing information for the viewer.

When dimensioning, CAD works in two ways. You can type in dimensions when creating a shape or line, or you can click on points of a line and the computer will generate the dimensions between points. In a CAD drafting, the points to which a dimension refers are always clear, eliminating confusion. CAD dimensions are associative; that is, as the size of an object is changed, the dimension adjusts. This eliminates dimension errors. CAD allows the draftsperson to set dimension tolerances and styles, to do direct or sequential dimensioning, and to convert instantly between metric and American Standard measurement.

One of the most exciting aspects of computer drafting is the ability to move from two-dimensional to axonometric and perspective views of an object or set. This is done by dimensioning or extruding the height of an object from its width and depth. The three-dimensional image of an object can be created after drawing in two dimensions or at the same time—essentially drafting in 3-D. Once a set or object has been drafted in 3-D, it can be rotated to any angle and viewed from any position. This eliminates the tedium of dropping points in a mechanical perspective and of redoing the perspective for another or a better view.

The linear or "wire-frame" two- or three-dimensional views can be turned into an illustration by what is called texture mapping. In texture mapping a colored flat pattern or texture is developed in a digital graphic program such as Photoshop. The flat-surface design is then imported into a three-dimensional CAD program and "wrapped" around a three-dimensional shape. The process is somewhat like wallpapering a room.

Once textured, objects or sets are lit much as they would be in theatrical lighting. CAD renderings, unlike hand-drawn ones, can show exactly what a set will look like rather than an artist's interpretation of how it will appear. Although this eliminates ambiguity—what you see is what you get—it also eliminates personal artistic style and means that all digital renderings have a similar look. With a mechanically created structure, color, texture, and lighting become even more critical in conveying a particular mood.

A 3-D digital set is a virtual model, which allows the viewer to move or "fly-through" the space, allowing a "previsualization" of scenery before it is constructed. Such a model can be viewed not only from the angle of the human eye but also from any camera angle—and can simulate the pans, swoops, and tilts of a movie camera. The addition of animation software allows the movement of scenery or objects so that you can see a virtual figure walk through the space, revolve a piece of scenery, or move a virtual car. Finally, built scenery can be totally eliminated, as live actors can move in front of blue screen walls while digital scenery surrounds them inside the camera.

We are still in the infancy of the computer revolution, and the use of the computer for digital drafting and rendering of scenery is steadily increasing. The expense of hardware, the amount of time needed initially to draft a production in CAD, and the lack of good designers with high CAD skills are all factors slowing down its acceptance. Change is occurring so rapidly that any book will be dated, lists of hardware and software will be obsolete, and examples of artists' digital work will seem primitive as their computer skills keep evolving. Nevertheless, it should be helpful to give a general rundown of the hardware and software used for scenic work and to see examples of digital drafting and rendering.

Computer Hardware

Computer: CAD and digital image manipulation require machines with enough speed and power to process massive amounts of information. Computer speed is measured in megahertz. Computer memory and storage capacity are measured in megabytes. Whether you choose to purchase a PC or a Macintosh computer, you need to get the fastest and most powerful machine you can afford.

Monitor: To see as much of a CAD drafting as possible, you need at least a 19-inch monitor, although a 21-inch monitor is preferable. The more expensive monitors reduce or eliminate screen distortion and have a higher resolution resulting in a crisper picture.

Scanner: An essential piece of hardware for anyone working with graphic imagery is a flatbed scanner, which allows an image to be digitized into a computer. More expensive scanners have better software, are more color correct, and have a higher scanning resolution, which gives clearer images.

Printer: Large-format ink jet printers are increasingly replacing plotters for outputting CAD.

External File Storage: Since images take up a huge amount of memory, you will need a way to externally store and transmit large files. Zip, Jazz, and SyQuest are companies that sell external storage systems. All these systems allow you to open files, make changes, and save files with changes back onto the same disk or tape. Increasingly, CDs are being used for storage. CDs are very low in cost and are readable by both Macintosh and PC platforms. A program such as *Toast* for the Macintosh allows you to burn text, graphics, or sounds onto a disk. The process of burning information onto a CD is very simple to learn. Currently, CDs, unlike other storage mediums, are "read only," meaning that it is not possible to change information on the disk once it has been burned.

Graphics Tablet: An additional computer tool that you may want to purchase is a graphics tablet and pen, which eliminate drawing with the mouse. Some pens are pressure sensitive, and you can purchase pens that airbrush. Wacom recently introduced a graphics tablet that allows you to see the image on the tablet as you draw, and includes drawing tools and palettes at the edges of the tablet.

Digital Camera: Digital cameras are another way of getting images into your computer. The more expensive cameras have higher resolutions, which give you clearer pictures. They can plug in directly to the computer or transfer the images via a memory card.

File Formats for Graphic and CAD Images

When you save a software file you choose a specific file format in which to save it. You can think of formats as languages that keep evolving. Software programs such as *Adobe Illustrator* usually have their own native language. There are formats that work between specific programs; for example, *Photoshop* and *Illustrator* now read back and forth. There are also formats that are used by most people and have become standard, just as English and Spanish have evolved into international languages. There are also formats that are rarely used and eventually die. As formats keep evolving some of them will become outdated, but a brief description of the current graphic formats in use should be helpful.

DWG	Native to *AutoCAD* programs.	
DXF	A vector-based format.	This is currently the standard format to translate between different CAD programs such as *AutoCAD* and *MiniCAD*.
TIFF	Translates both pixel-based (raster images) and vector-based programs.	This is currently the standard format for graphic translation between pixel-based programs such as *Photoshop* and vector-based programs such as *Illustrator* or CAD programs.
EPS	Encapsulated Postscript format also translates between pixel-based vector-based programs.	This is a dying language.
3-DS	Native to 3-D *AutoCAD* programs.	
JPEG	Internet file format.	Originally developed as a way to make any file smaller for Internet translation. Also makes files readable by any program or operating system. This format is rapidly becoming the most used. The JPEG format allows a choice of file compression from 0 to 12; 0 being the most compressed with the most rapid transmission. The more compressed the JPEG file, the more a graphic image is degraded in transmission. Even 12, the highest JPEG resolution, has a slight degradation.

Computer Graphics Software

Photoshop, by Adobe. This graphic program is the industry standard for digital image enhancement, photo retouching, and image compositing. In this program, images are manipulated by selecting and changing individual dots known as pixels. Since an image is composed of a fixed number of pixels, as an image is magnified its edges may appear jagged. This program is the best choice for representing gradations of shades and colors as in photographs or paintings.

Illustrator, by Adobe. This is a 2-D design and illustration program. Like CAD programs it uses vectors, or mathematical coordinates, to describe objects according to their geometry. Vector graphics can be printed at any size or resolution without losing detail or clarity, and are used to design signs, logos, and graphic images with crisp shapes.

CADtools, by Hot Door. This is an illustrator plug-in (i.e., purchased separately and added to your program) that allows you to draw and dimension in scale and with associative dimensions that adjust when you change the size of an image. Dimensioned graphics are often used in designing signs.

CorelDRAW, by Corel Corp. This is a vector-based eight-component illustration program.

It includes 2-D drawing, writing software, a texture generator, a full 3-D modeling and rendering package, a paint program, a charting program, an auto-tracing program, a media cataloger, and huge libraries of type and clip-art.

CAD, Modeling, and 3-D Lighting Programs

AutoCAD, by Autodesk. This is the predominant CAD program for architecture and engineering. Autodesk's programs are developed for the IBM-compatible PC only and are not portable to the Macintosh platform unless you have enough speed and storage capacity to run an emulation program like *Virtual PC*. The full program is huge and has many features that are not intelligible to nonengineers and not needed by set designers. Autodesk has its own proprietary file format, which is not easily interpreted by other CAD programs, and errors can occur in trying to read *AutoCAD* draftings in other CAD programs or in importing from other CAD programs.

AutoCAD LT for *Windows*, by Autodesk. This is a reduced version of *AutoCAD*. *AutoCAD LT* has fewer 3-D capabilities than the full program.

3D Studio Max, by Autodesk. This is a sophisticated and powerful modeling, rendering, and animation program that creates high-quality 3-D stills with lighting effects. It integrates well with other Autodesk CAD systems and works on the Windows interface.

Lightscape, by Discreet. This is an advanced light-rendering and previsualization program. Its technology has the ability to mimic physically based lighting specifications, add and position lighting fixtures, and create photographic-quality realism. This program works on the Windows platform. It imports multiple translation formats, including 3-DS, DXF, TIFF, EPS, and JPEG, and works in conjunction with current 3-D modeling programs such as *AutoCAD*, *3-D Studio*, *Cadvance*, *ArchiCAD*, and Form·Z.

MiniCAD or Vectorworks, by Diehl Graphsoft Inc. This program works on both Macintosh and Windows and is the CAD program most used by Macintosh-based scenic designers. It includes 3-D modeling capabilities, basic 3-D lighting, and a theatrical lighting designer's tool kit for designing light plots and standard lighting design reports.

ArchiCAD, by Graphisoft. This is an expensive CAD program with excellent 3-D, lighting, and camera fly-through capability. Developed for architects rather than engineers, it is an intuitive, easy to learn and use CAD program.

Ray Dream Studio, by Fractal Design Corporation. This is a relatively inexpensive, simple, easy to use modeling program with limited animation and fly-through abilities.

Infini-D, by MetaCreations. This is an excellent mid-priced modeling, rendering, and animation program.

Form·Z, by Auto des sys, Inc. This pure modeling program does not have the ability to do animation. It is an unusual modeling program in that it allows a fluid blending together of shapes that is somewhat like sketching, and it can be paired with the animation system Electric Image, Inc.

Electric Image, by Electric Image, Inc. This is a high-end, 3-D modeling, lighting, and animation program.

CAD Drafting and Rendering for Corporate Design

Currently, computers are most used for drafting scenery in permanent production situations. CAD drafting and rendering have a contemporary look that suits the presentation of scenic designs for many corporate applications such as industrials, trade shows, and commercials. Hotopp Associates Limited is a company that specializes in corporate design, sometimes also called "Industrial Theatre." They design scenery for special events, industrials, exhibits, trade shows, and television. The primary function of their designs is to convey a corporate message. While some of this type of scenery takes place on a traditional stage and involves moving and flying scenic pieces, much of it takes place in nontheatrical spaces that must be adapted for theatrical use with the addition of lighting trusses, seating, a stage, and sometimes dining or schoolroom tables.

Hotopp Associates does not usually work directly with a client but is hired by a production company with its own creative director and technical director. The work that Hotopp Associates does often involves a two-step process of first submitting a design proposal, usually of sketches and groundplans, which competes against other firms. Only after they get a job do they draft elevations. Design presentation is critical to the success of this company.

Carl Baldasso is vice president of the firm and drafts many of the projects. He first learned to draft in *CorelDRAW*, a vector-based illustration and rendering program that works on both Macintosh and PC machines. Although it is a drawing program, *CorelDRAW* allows you to dimension and to draw in scale. Carl liked the ease of use of this program and that its shading and multiple line weights give his elevations a graphic rather than technical look. Figure 16.1 is a sheet of drafting in *CorelDRAW* for the scenery for a new product launch for Gillette. The audience, consisting of sales managers, first entered a space and sat on risers facing a large wall with a logo. The logo wall flew out while sidewalls traveled left and right, revealing three large screens on which they saw a video presentation. Finally, a tunnel was revealed, leading to a large room with product displays. (See Figure 16.2.)

Carl increasingly drafted in *AutoCAD LT*. Although it took more time to draft a ground plan of 3-D elements, once done he could fairly quickly create multiple perspective views for presentation. And if Hotopp Associates got the job, he already had a good start on doing the elevations. As *AutoCAD* is the industry standard, Carl often receives the initial plans of a venue in *AutoCAD*, and technical directors and lighting designers increasingly want him to submit draftings in *AutoCAD*. Carl sometimes imports *Photoshop* raster or pixel-based images into his *AutoCAD* draftings. He also has imported vector images from *CorelDRAW*, but *AutoCAD* does not allow the importing of Corel's shading or variations in line weight.

Figures 16.3a to 16.3d show some of the *AutoCAD LT* draftings that Carl did for a national sales force meeting of Schering Laboratories that

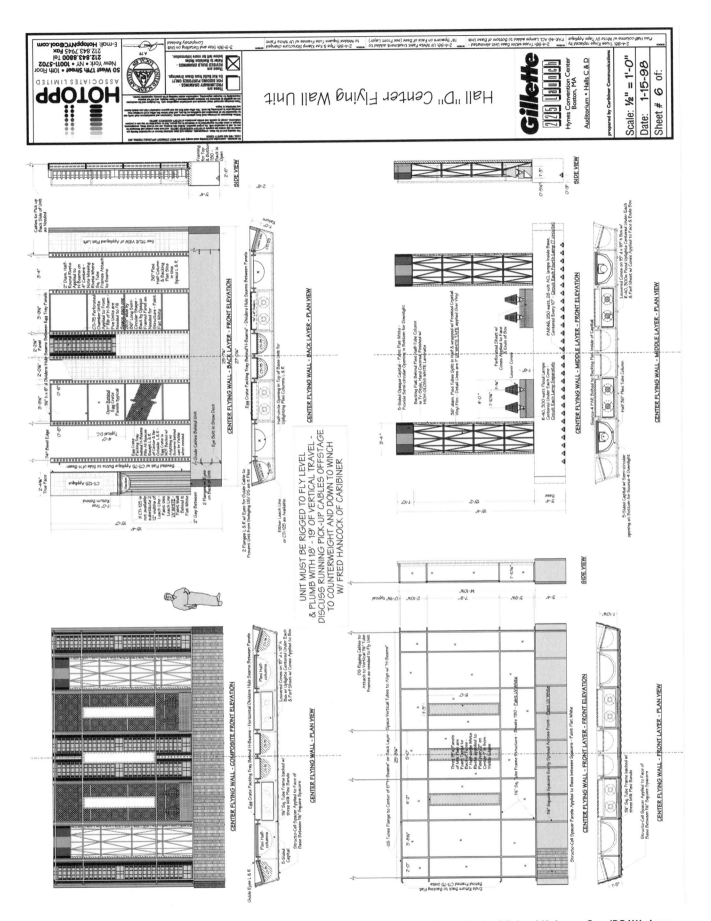

Figure 16.1 CAD drafting of flying center wall for a Gillette product launch. Scenic design by Michael Hotopp. *CorelDRAW* elevation by Carl Baldasso. ©1998 Hotopp Associates Limited.

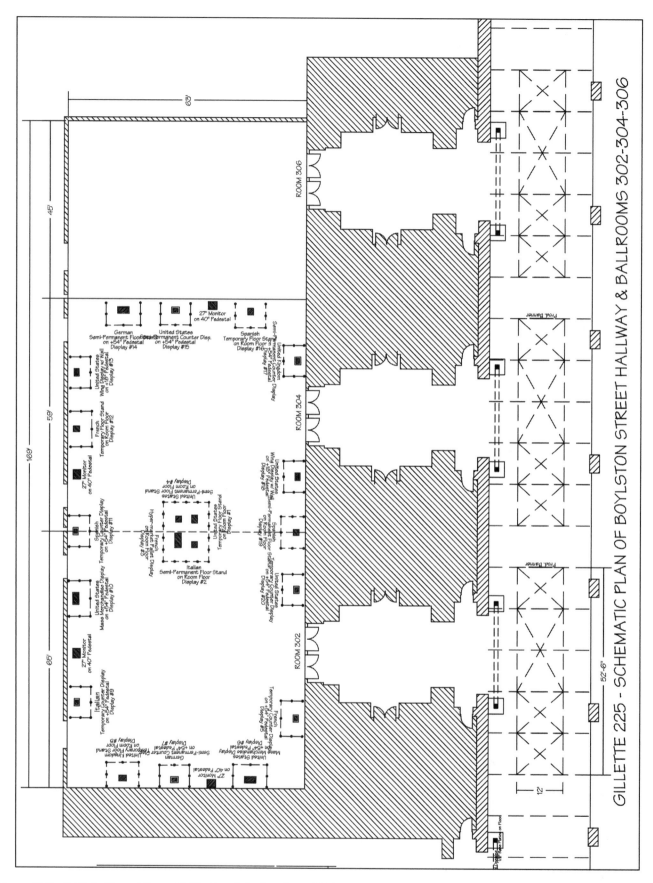

Figure 16.2 CAD drafting of the exhibit hall and displays for a Gillette product launch. Scenic Design by Michael Hotopp. *AutoCAD LT* Plan by Carl Baldasso. ©1998 Hotopp Associates Limited.

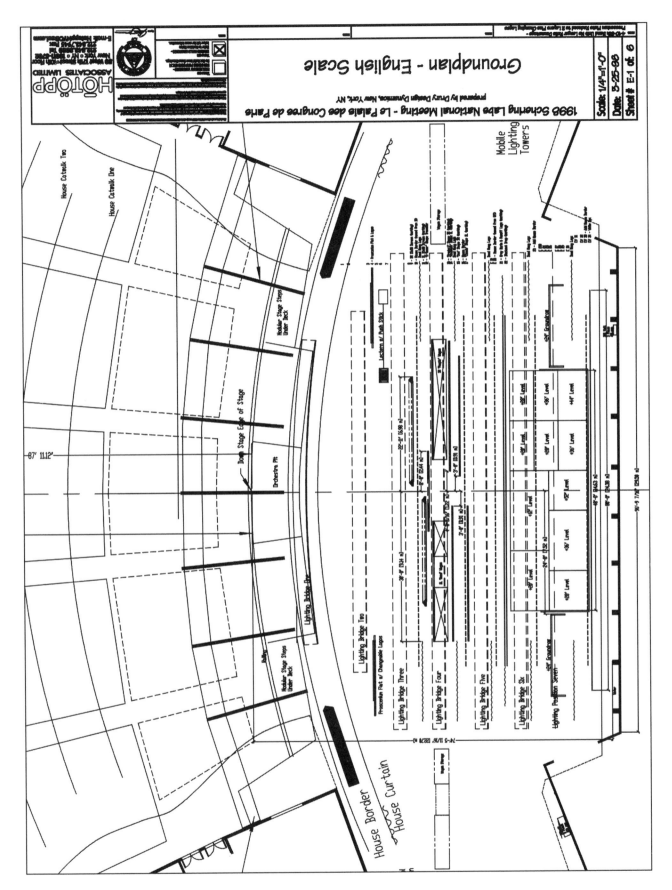

Figure 16.3a   Ground plan. Draftings for the 1998 Schering Labs national meeting. Scenic Design and *AutoCAD LT* Plan, Section, and Elevations by Carl Baldasso. ©1998 Hotopp Associates.

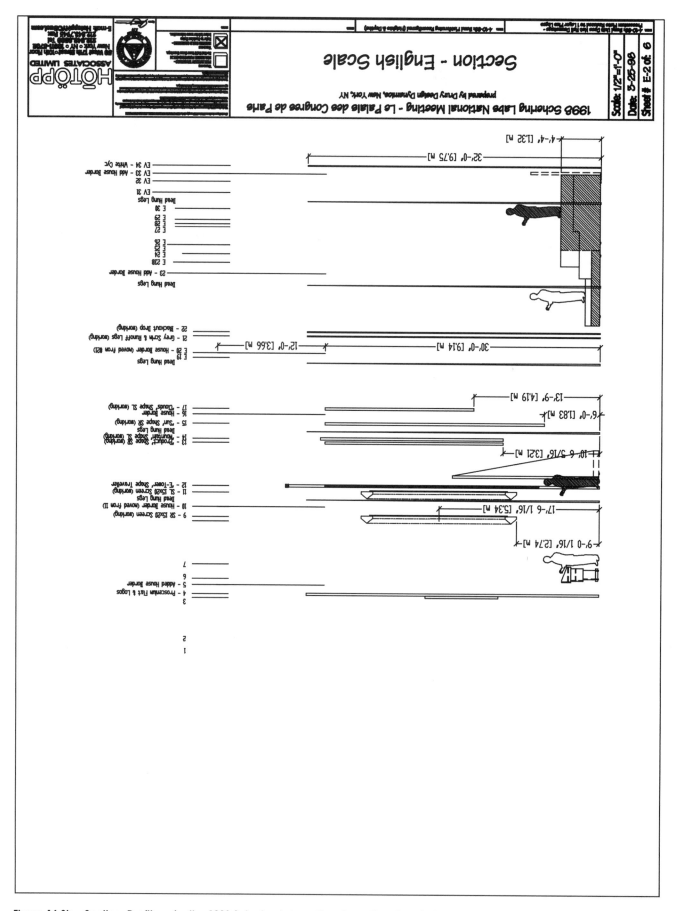

Figure 16.3b   Section. Draftings for the 1998 Schering Labs national meeting. Scenic Design and *AutoCAD LT* Plan, Section, and Elevations by Carl Baldasso. ©1998 Hotopp Associates.

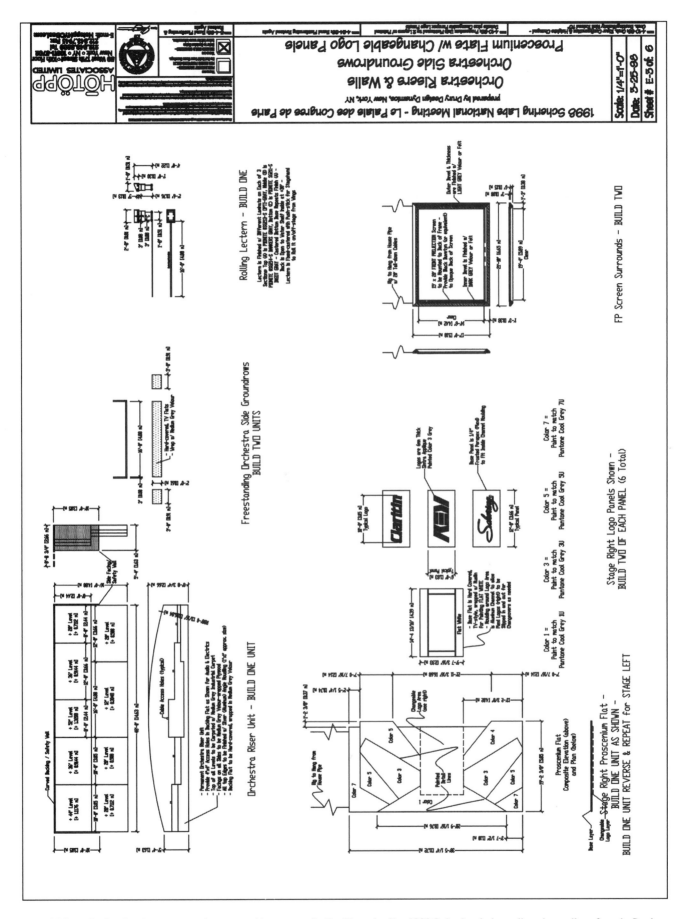

Figure 16.3c Orchestra risers, ground rows, and logo panels. Draftings for the 1998 Schering Labs national meeting. Scenic Design and *AutoCAD LT* Plan, Section, and Elevations by Carl Baldasso. ©1998 Hotopp Associates.

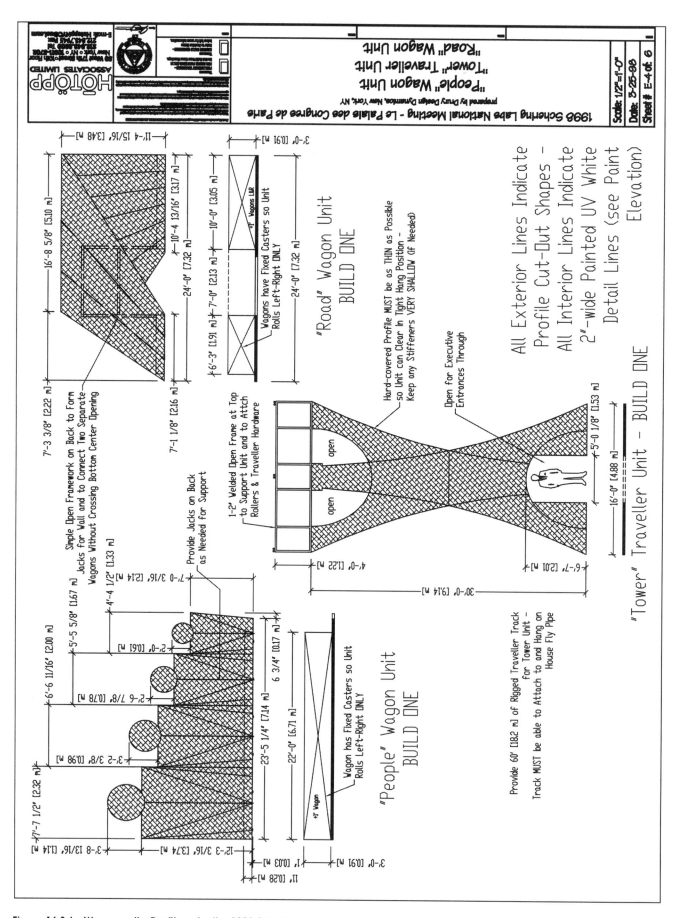

Figure 16.3d Wagon units. Draftings for the 1998 Schering Labs national meeting. Scenic Design and *AutoCAD LT* Plan, Section, and Elevations by Carl Baldasso. ©1998 Hotopp Associates.

took place in a theatre in Paris. The design consisted of moving, tracking, and flying scenic pieces. *AutoCAD* allowed him to dimension in both metric and American Standard simultaneously.

Figure 16.4 is an *AutoCAD* perspective sketch that Carl drafted for a proposal for a new drug launch. The design concept was that of a multilevel set representing areas in and around a hospital.

As his CAD skills increased, Carl switched to a full *AutoCAD* program using *CorelDRAW* only for pure graphics. He currently drafts each of the scenic elements on separate layers but in three dimensions so each object has vertical depth as well as length and width. He often incorporates stock elements such as trusses, chairs, stage light fixtures, and human bodies from the library of work he has created for other projects.

Drafting pieces in three dimensions allows Carl to create a virtual set model and the orthographic drawings at the same time. After dimensioning the pieces of the model in one file, he prints out different sheets of drafting based on what layers he has turned on or off. Within the *AutoCAD* program, he can render the virtual model much as one would light a set, and assign finishes and textures to the surfaces of objects. See Figure 16.5 for a rendering of one of his more recent designs.

CAD-Drafting a Television Soap Opera

Scenic design for television leads in the use of CAD and digital rendering. CAD is now used to draft many news sets, talk shows, and game shows.

Figure 16.4 RPR (Rhône-Poulenc-Rorer) drug launch proposal sketch. Scenic design and *AutoCAD LT* sketch by Carl Baldasso. ©1998 Hotopp Associates Limited.

Figure 16.5   Digital illustration of the Astra Pharmaceutical National Meeting. Scenic design and *AutoCAD* rendering by Carl Baldasso. ©1999 Hotopp Associates Limited. Also see Plate 1 of the color insert.

CAD drafting is especially helpful in drafting daytime drama where small sets are reused and rearranged on the same stage. Here CAD eliminates the repetition of redrawing, and its database function helps in the tracking and reuse of sets, flats, and scenic elements such as doors and windows.

Tarrent Smith computer-drafted all the scenery designed by Bill Mickley for the soap opera *All My Children*, produced by ABC (American Broadcasting Companies, Inc). At the time, *All My Children* shot each weekday, as it still does, and required a new studio plan each day. There were an average of six sets in the studio each day, four of which were usually new sets. The new sets often reused walls or architectural units from previously built sets. They had approximately 150 sets in storage that could be reused.

Drafting the scenery on computer allowed Tarrant to quickly reconfigure the studio plan, adding or subtracting sets as needed. It also allowed him to track and quickly retrieve sets or portions of sets as needed. For CAD-drafting soap opera sets, Tarrant developed many macros, or computer actions that follow in automated sequence, to speed up repetitive actions. For example, Tarrant individualized his digitized pad, allowing him to call up a French door with the click of his mouse. A macro automatically kicks in that asks him for the height and width of the door and the direction of the swing. It then asks him how many muntins he would like the door to have and generates the plan and elevation of the door.

The *AutoCAD* program that Tarrant used to do the plans and elevations also allowed him to generate a perspective armature of the set. With the perspective generated he had unlimited choices in picking a station point from which to view the perspective. (See Figures 16.6a to 16.6c.)

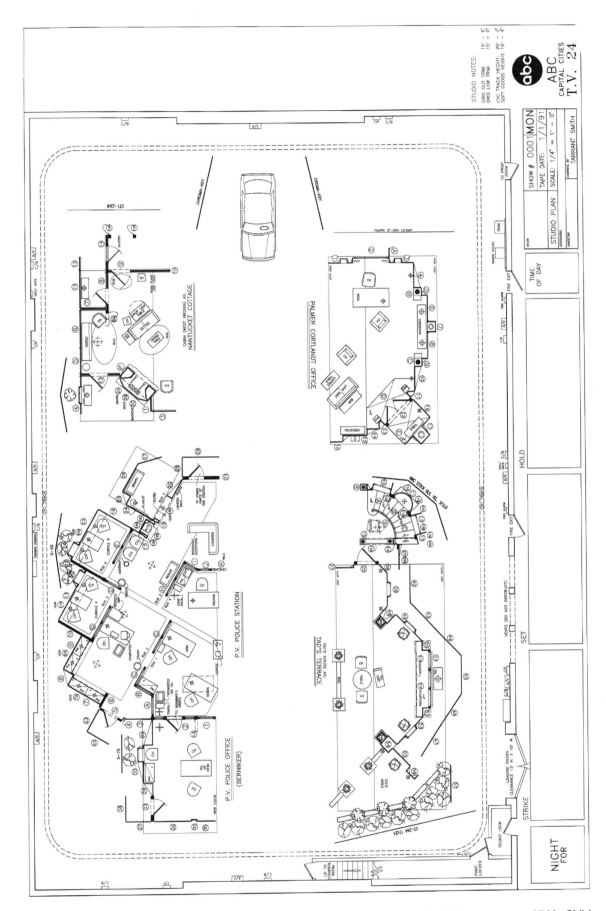

Figure 16.6a *AutoCAD* drafting elevations. Draftings of the "Pine Valley Police Station" for the ABC soap opera, *All My Children*, 1993. Designed by William Mickley. Drafting by Tarrant Smith. Used by permission from American Broadcasting Companies, Inc.

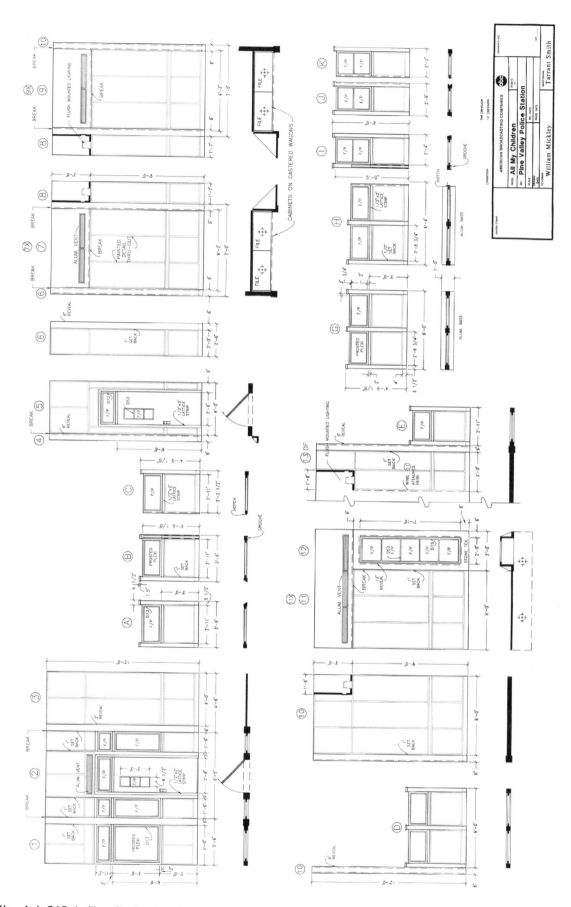

Figure 16.6b *AutoCAD* drafting. Studio plan. Draftings of the "Pine Valley Police Station" for the ABC soap opera, *All My Children*. 1993. Designed by William Mickley. Drafting by Tarrant Smith. Used by permission from American Broadcasting Companies, Inc.

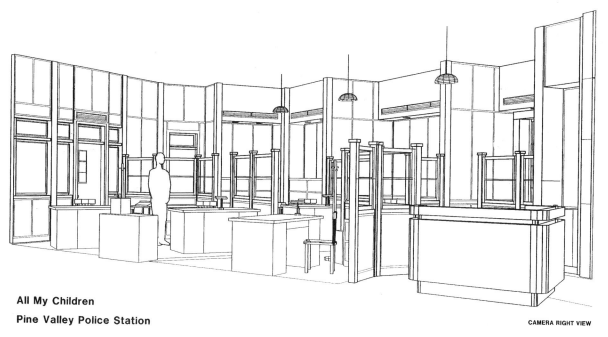

All My Children

Pine Valley Police Station

CAMERA RIGHT VIEW

Figure 16.6c *AutoCAD* perspective. Draftings of the "Pine Valley Police Station" for the ABC soap opera, *All My Children*. 1993. Designed by William Mickley. Drafting by Tarrant Smith. Used by permission from American Broadcasting Companies, Inc.

CAD Drafting and 3-D Visualizations for Television Design

Gary Weist is a production designer who uses *ArchiCAD*'s 3-D rendering capabilities as a visualization tool for himself and to help him sell his concepts to directors and producers. Gary says that he had worked with pencil for many years but became tired of sketching and drafting and then resketching and redrafting. Although there was a big learning curve in switching over to CAD, he found that working on a computer revitalized his interest in drafting. After mastering CAD, he quickly became convinced of its advantages when the design for the renovation of some offices required multiple revisions.

Although Gary is skilled at hand-sketching perspectives, he finds that 3-D CAD sketching is now a faster way for him to try out design ideas. Further, it lets him simulate moving through a possible set. He has come to prefer the accuracy of size and scale relationships in a CAD perspective to the mathematical uncertainty of a hand sketch.

Gary has discovered that many of his clients like his CAD visualizations, especially those who have difficulty imagining drawings as built sets. Others, though, mostly those who have a hard time committing to a design, don't like it at all.

Figures 16.7a to 16.7d show several renderings from Gary's designs printed from fully colored and textured 3-D visualizations, with accompanying CAD ground plans. The draftings and 3-D renderings were done by Katherine Spencer, who trained in scenic design at Carnegie Mellon University and who is fluent in *AutoCAD*, *ArchiCAD*, and *MiniCAD*.

The first group of renderings in Figures 16.7a to 16.7d are from the HBO television program *Oz*. The examples include selected views from a huge contiguous prison set covering 54,000 square feet. The set had two distinct areas. The first part of the prison, referred to as the "Emerald City," was designed as a contemporary construction where inmates inhabit a fishbowl structure with all their moves under the

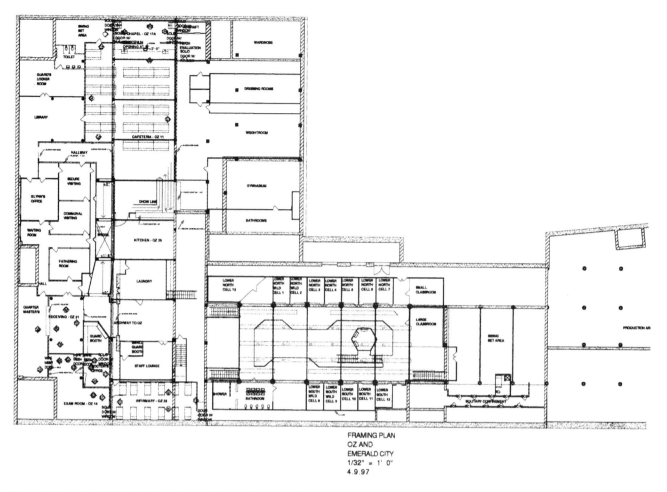

Figure 16.7a *ArchiCAD* drafting. Plan of Oz and Emerald City. Also see Plate 2 of the color insert. Designed for the HBO series *Oz.* 1999. Produced by Rysher Entertainment. Production designed by Gary Weist. *ArchiCAD* drafting and renderings by Katherine Spencer. Used by permission.

observation of guards. The second area was designed as an older-looking part of the prison where the inmates are in control and anarchy rules. The illustrations are from the newer area of the prison.

The second group of renderings in Figures 16.8a to 16.8c is from a television CBS pilot called *Family Brood.* The design was for a classic Sears mail-order house from the turn of the century: a simple structure with basic, almost generic appointments such as bay windows, fireplaces, archways, and built-in cabinetry.

CAD-Drafting a News Set, and a Personal Style of Digital Rendering

James Fenhagen and Erik Ulfers are partners in the company Production Design Group, Limited. They design for stores, restaurants, industrial theatre, and theatre, but their specialty is sets for television news shows.

Jim Fenhagen has evolved a personal style of rendering that reflects his design sensibility: a unique combination of hand and computer work. Jim feels that the rendering is of primary importance in his design process, both as a visualization tool for himself and to sell ideas to clients.

While he was studying theatre design his rendering process often incorporated collaged elements—xeroxing found photographs onto sticky-back film, then drawing and painting on them. As Jim became

266

Figure 16.7b   *ArchiCAD* 3-D visualization. Guard tower looking towards upper balcony. Also see Plate 3 of the color insert. Designed for the HBO series *Oz.* 1999. Produced by Rysher Entertainment. Production designed by Gary Weist. *ArchiCAD* drafting and renderings by Katherine Spencer. Used by permission.

Figure 16.7c   *ArchiCAD* 3-D visualization. Crane shot—looking into a cell on the upper balcony. Also see Plate 4 of the color insert. Designed for the HBO series *Oz.* 1999. Produced by Rysher Entertainment. Production designed by Gary Weist. *ArchiCAD* drafting and renderings by Katherine Spencer. Used by permission.

Figure 16.7d *ArchiCAD* 3-D visualization. Under balcony looking towards guard tower with wild cell removed. Also see Plate 5 of the color insert. Designed for the HBO series *Oz*. 1999. Produced by Rysher Entertainment. Production designed by Gary Weist. *ArchiCAD* drafting and renderings by Katherine Spencer. Used by permission.

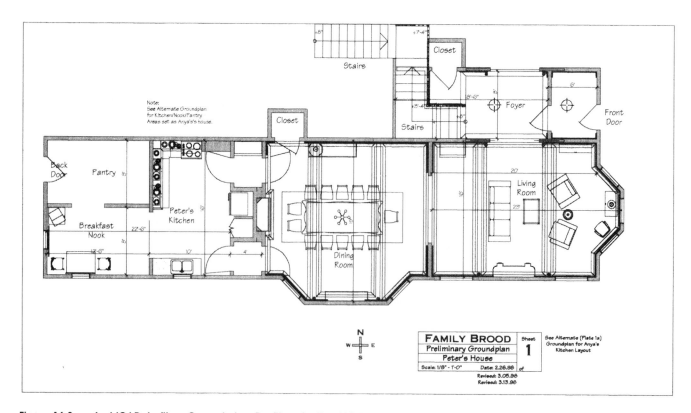

Figure 16.8a *ArchiCAD* drafting. Ground plan. Draftings for the CBS Television pilot *Family Brood*. 1998. Produced by the Levinson/Fontana Company. Production designed by Gary Weist. *ArchiCAD* drafting and renderings by Katherine Spencer. Used by permission.

Figure 16.8b   Living room looking towards dining room. Also see Plate 6 of the color insert. Draftings for the CBS Television pilot *Family Brood*. 1998. Produced by the Levinson/Fontana Company. Production designed by Gary Weist. *ArchiCAD* drafting and renderings by Katherine Spencer. Used by permission.

Figure 16.8c   *ArchiCAD* 3-D visualization. Dining room with kitchen in background. Also see Plate 7 of the color insert. Draftings for the CBS Television pilot *Family Brood*. 1998. Produced by the Levinson/Fontana Company. Production Designed by Gary Weist. *ArchiCAD* drafting and renderings by Katherine Spencer. Used by permission.

more familiar with computers, he found computer-scanned images could replace the xeroxing/sticky-back approach. The graphic program *Photoshop* also allowed him infinite possibilities in manipulating visual elements. In Jim's work today, his sketch artist, James Yates, hand draws the architectural framework and scans it into a Macintosh for texturing and shading. Additional scenic and dressing elements are scanned, sized, and layered into the rendering. These elements might include a truss from a truss catalogue, the photo of a rug from a magazine, some elements from digital photographic clip-art, lighting fixtures and light beams, the head of a news anchorman plunked onto a found photographic body, or some textures and materials from the CD-ROM that comes with *Surfaces*, a reference book by Judy Juracek.

Over time, James Yates has created an extensive *Photoshop* library of images he can use or reuse. The resulting rendering has a very individual, quirky, hyper-realistic look. Because the rendering is a computer image, it has the flexibility to evolve with ease, as ideas are developed or changes required. Since the image is digital, even when Jim has to be out-of-town, James can E-mail him a current version of the design for additional input. Figure 16.9 is a page of chairs from the extensive digital library that James has created.

Jim tried *Form·Z*, a 3-D modeling program, to render some of his designs, but he found the pure computer illustrations cold. He disliked the "hard" nature of the pure computer design process, and the fact that in a CAD rendering all the design decisions have to be made before an illustration occurs. He wants flexibility and looseness, time to let a design evolve without every nut and bolt specified.

Jim often shows his clients the initial rendering in black and white to allow them to concentrate on the form. He also prefers that his illustrations *not* be mathematically accurate, often employing forced perspec-

Figure 16.9   Print of Chairs from Design Group, Limited, *Photoshop* Library. Also see Plate 8 of the color insert.

tive or other exaggerations and "twistings of reality" to find and convey his particular vision. "Scenic designers," he says, "don't deal with reality but with drama." Jim feels that his current combination of hand drawing and computer graphics is a way of keeping his work more human. Rather than creating a 3-D "fly-through," he prefers to do sketches of multiple points of view, sometimes combining them into a single wrap-around view that is like a camera pan. Only after a design is quite evolved does he have it drafted in *MiniCAD*. Figure 16.10 is an example of one of his panoramic renderings.

Another news set Jim designed was for *Good Morning America*. Figure 16.11a is a sketch and Figures 16.11b to 16.11g are selected *MiniCAD* draftings.

Previsualization of Feature Film Scenery

Peter Jamison is a production designer for film who uses a variety of computer rendering and animation programs to create a single illustration of a set to be built or scenic additions to add to existing locations. Peter calls his illustrations "previsualizations." He feels that a traditional sketch is not accurate enough and only gives an indirect interpretation of the direction in which a designer wishes to go. His digital illustrations, on the other hand, give a clear image of what he wants to make before it is built. In addition, rather than showing a single viewpoint, his computer-generated images can allow a plethora of different viewpoints as well as film pans, tilts, and other camera moves.

Being fluent in computer rendering allows Peter to design the picture with and for the director rather than leaving it to an assembler. He says, "I didn't want to leave the final image up to chance or the digital effects house." He adds, "Once directors get a taste of it, they demand a hard previsualization."

Figure 16.10 Panoramic concept sketch of news set for WITI FOX Milwaukee. See also Plate 9 of the color insert. Design by James Fenhagen and Erik Ulfers. Sketch Artist, James Yates. Art Director, André Durette. Used by permission.

Figure 16.11a   Sketch of the set. See also Plate 10 of the color insert. Sketch and *MiniCAD* draftings of the set for *Good Morning America.* 1998. Produced by ABC News. Design by James Fenhagen and Erik Ulfers. Sketch Artist, James Yates. Art Director, George Allison. *MiniCAD* drafting by Tarrant Smith. Used by permission.

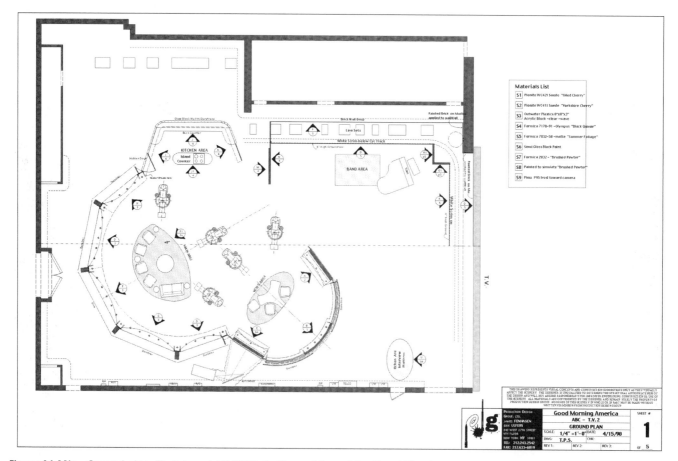

Figure 16.11b   Ground plan. Sketch and *MiniCAD* draftings of the set for *Good Morning America.* 1998. Produced by ABC News. Design by James Fenhagen and Erik Ulfers. Sketch Artist, James Yates. Art Director, George Allison. *MiniCAD* drafting by Tarrant Smith. Used by permission.

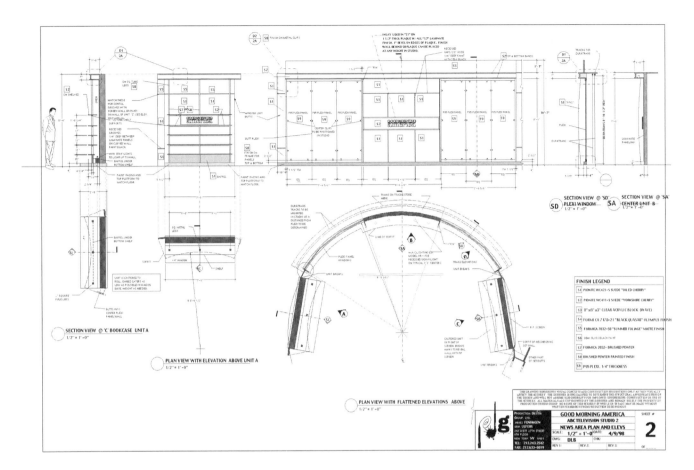

Figure 16.11c   News area plan and elevation. Sketch and *MiniCAD* draftings of the set for *Good Morning America*. 1998. Produced by ABC News. Design by James Fenhagen and Erik Ulfers. Sketch Artist, James Yates. Art Director, George Allison. *MiniCAD* drafting by Tarrant Smith. Used by permission.

Peter started working with computer imaging in 1985 when he wanted to control the look of a simulated tank attack. At that time, unlike now, the man on the street couldn't afford the bulky, highly sophisticated hardware and software required for high-end digital effects. Working at Twentieth Century Fox, Peter used a Power Macintosh and *Electric Image*, the highest-end of the Macintosh platform animation and rendering software.

Peter currently owns and uses multiple software programs to create digital illustrations. He develops the armature of the set using *Modular Pro* or *Electric Image* and then uses *Photoshop* to render and correctly scale the textures of the surfaces.

Figures 16.12a and 16.12b are two digital perspective renderings of Peter's virtual model of the set for The Special Projects Unit, an office complex for the film *Bait*. The image was generated in *Electric Image* and finished in *Photoshop*. Peter says that in model rendering his early training in theatrical lighting helps him enormously in choosing lighting angles, colors, and specials.

Figure 16.13a is a photograph of a location in New York City's Soho district that was turned into a Café for the film *Bait*. Scenic additions of a large sign, plugs in the windows, and cafe tables and chairs were digitally added to the photograph to show the director exactly what was planned (Figure 16.13b). Peter generated the three-dimensional frame in *Modular Pro*, used *Photoshop* to manipulate the textures, and animated the tablecloths in *Electric Image* to get them to drape correctly.

273

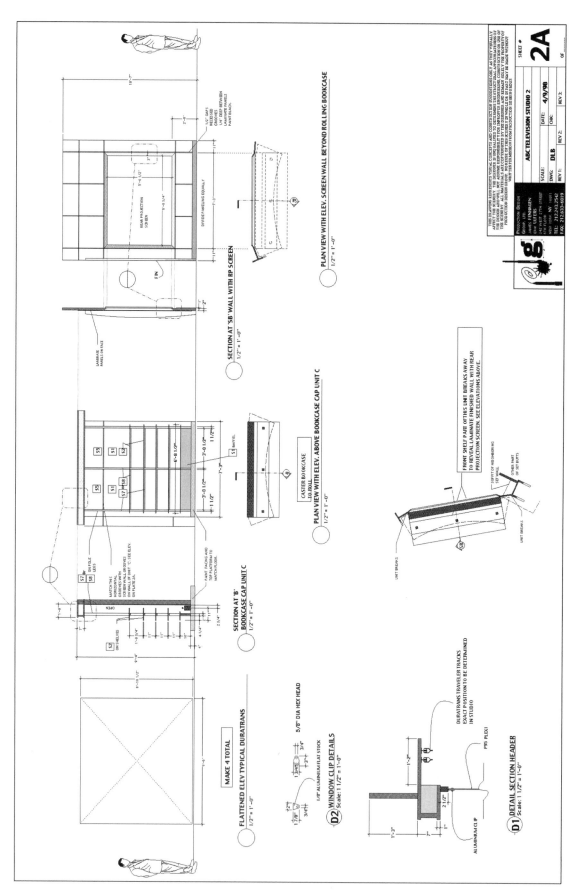

Figure 16.11d Elevations—News area. Sketch and *MiniCAD* draftings of the set for *Good Morning America*. 1998. Produced by ABC News. Design by James Fenhagen and Erik Ulfers. Sketch Artist, James Yates. Art Director, George Allison. *MiniCAD* drafting by Tarrant Smith. Used by permission.

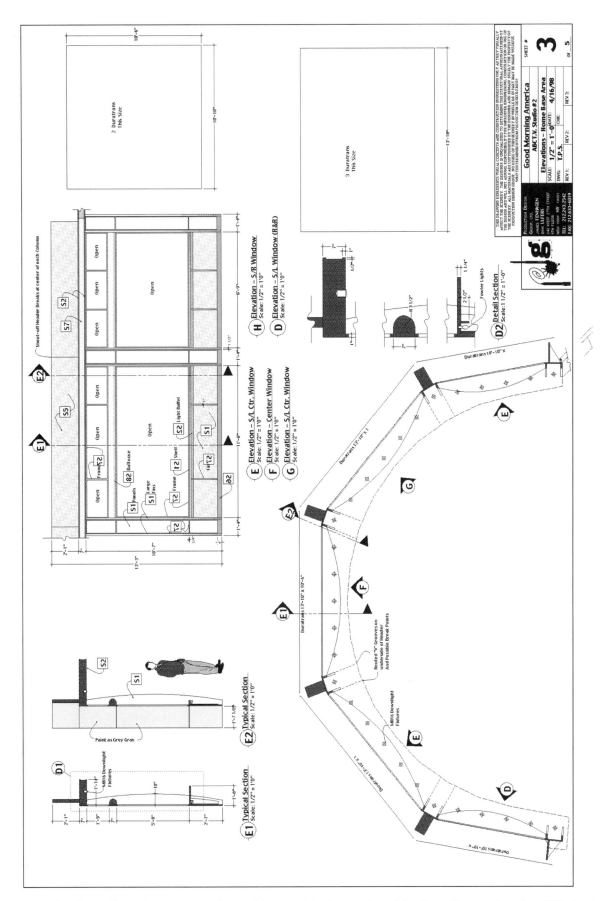

Figure 16.11e   Elevations—Home base area. Sketch and *MiniCAD* draftings of the set for *Good Morning America*. 1998. Produced by ABC News. Design by James Fenhagen and Erik Ulfers. Sketch Artist, James Yates. Art Director, George Allison. *MiniCAD* drafting by Tarrant Smith. Used by permission.

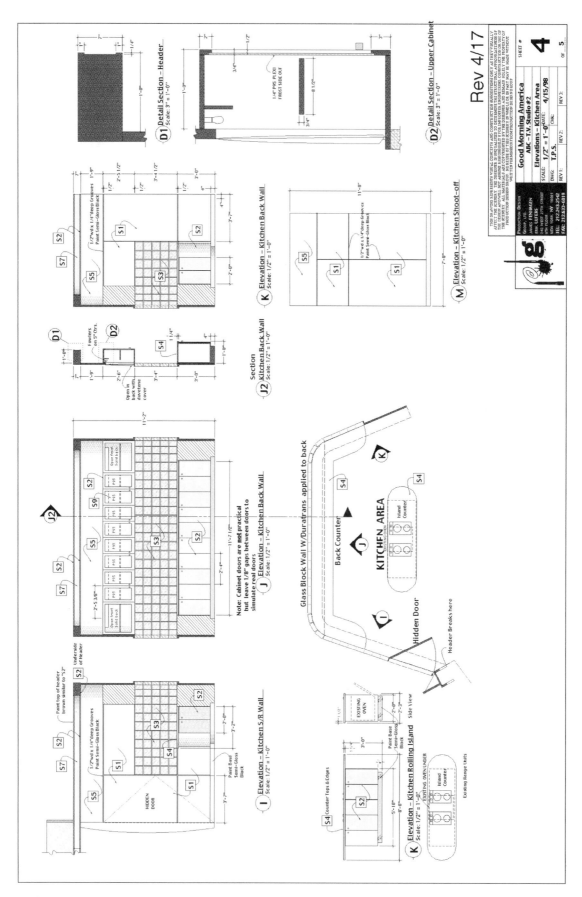

Figure 16.11f Elevations—Kitchen area. Sketch and *MiniCAD* draftings of the set for *Good Morning America*. 1998. Produced by ABC News. Design by James Fenhagen and Erik Ulfers. Sketch Artist, James Yates. Art Director, George Allison. *MiniCAD* drafting by Tarrant Smith. Used by permission.

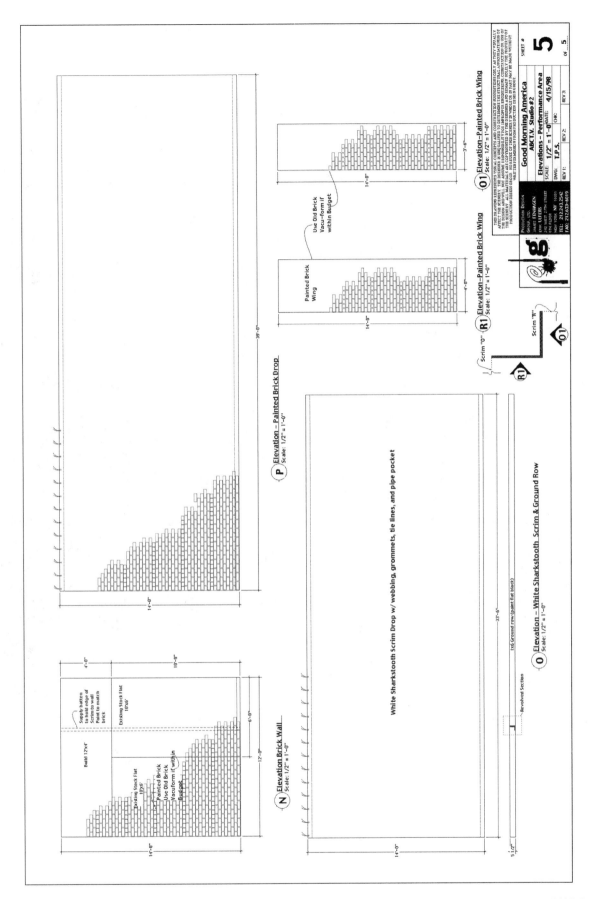

Figure 16.11g   Elevations—Performance area. Sketch and *MiniCAD* draftings of the set for *Good Morning America*. 1998. Produced by ABC News. Design by James Fenhagen and Erik Ulfers. Sketch Artist, James Yates. Art Director, George Allison. *MiniCAD* drafting by Tarrant Smith. Used by permission.

SPU OFFICES/MANATTAN   PANEL 1

SPU OFFICES/MANATTAN   PANEL 2

Figures 16.12a and 16.12b   Computer-generated renderings of "The Special Projects Unit" for the feature film *Bait*, Castle Rock Entertainment. Fall 2000. See also Plates 11 and 12 of the color insert. Production Designer, Peter Jamison. Computer rendering by Peter Jamison. Used by permission.

Figure 16.13a   Location photograph of a Soho Café, Tribeca. See also Plate 13 of the color insert. Images from the feature film *Bait,* Castle Rock Entertainment. Fall 2000. Production Designer, Peter Jamison. Computer Rendering by Peter Jamison. Used by permission.

Figure 16.13b   Computer-generated rendering of a Soho Café showing digital addition of scenery. See also Plate 14 of the color insert. Images from the feature film *Bait,* Castle Rock Entertainment. Production Designer, Peter Jamison. Computer Rendering by Peter Jamison. Used by permission.

Part II

Professional Applications

17

A Box Set on a Proscenium Stage

Ben Edwards was a designer of scenery for both theatre and film who during his career designed over fifty box sets. Ben was a master at using forced perspective to create the illusion of an interior on a proscenium stage. His design for *The Iceman Cometh* in the 1985-86 Broadway season is an example of this skill. Although the setting is seemingly a four-walled room with one wall removed, to increase visibility for the edges of the audience, to allow dynamic patterns of actor movement, and to give the set thrust and power, the ceiling and the side walls are angled and the floor is raked. The rear wall of the room, rather than being straight and static, is split slightly off center stage, and the parts angle in two directions as though around an odd exterior structure. The angled rear walls force the action into opposing patterns of movement. They also partially divide the large space, allowing the direction to focus on a small local area or widen to include the entire room. Although the overall structure of the room is highly stylized, a feeling of realism is reinforced by meticulous attention to period details including heavily ornate built molding. A high horizon line for the forced perspective makes the design theatrical while maintaining the illusion of naturalism.

The complex draftings were done by Beth Kuhn. The full-size details reflect her extensive knowledge of period molding shapes and scenic construction. Figures 17.1 to 17.7 are representative sheets from a large set of drawings.

The ground plan in Figure 17.1 shows the width and depth relationship of the set and its masking to the stage and to the extreme audience sight lines. Only large, built-in pieces of scenic furniture are shown on this sheet as a separate director's plan with all furniture and practical lights was drawn at a later date.

The cross-section in Figure 17.2 shows the height and depth relationship of the set and masking to the stage space and to the lowest, closest audience sight line. Balcony sight lines were calculated on separate, 1/4-inch-scale sections as part of the design process. By angling the downstage border, this design with its deep but only slightly raked ceiling allows two light pipes, the first and second electrics, to cover the set. A hard black velour "horn" above the side walls of the set is an elegant way to mask the gap at the edges of the hard border.

The floor plan in Figure 17.3 describes the raked floor, platforms, steps, and their surface treatments.

In Figure 17.4, each piece of masking, hard and soft, is drawn along with dimensions and specifications as to their construction. Since these are large, simple shapes, they are drawn in the smaller scale of 1/4 inch to the foot.

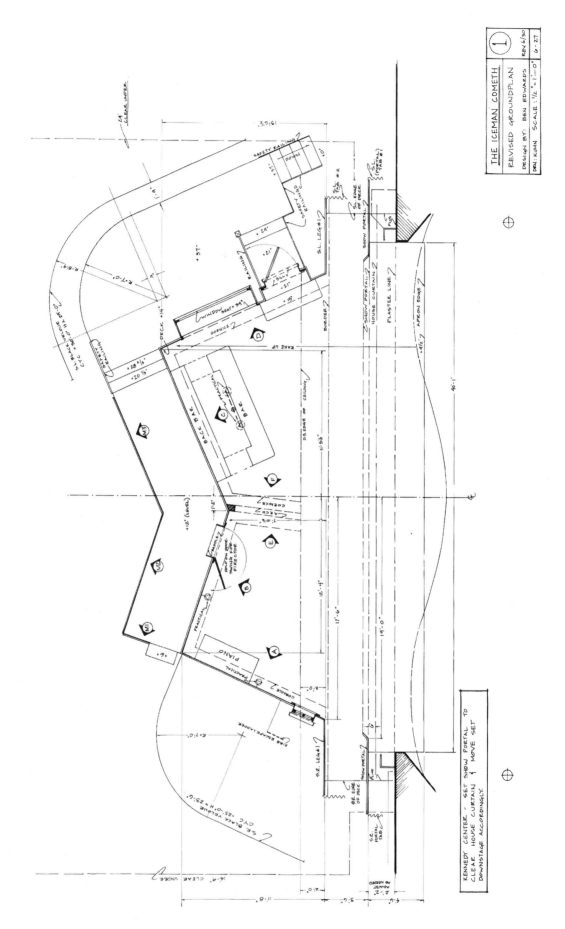

Figure 17.1   Sheet 1—Ground plan. Drafting of the theatrical set for *The Iceman Cometh*. Directed by Jose Quintero. Designed by Ben Edwards. Drafting by Beth Kuhn.

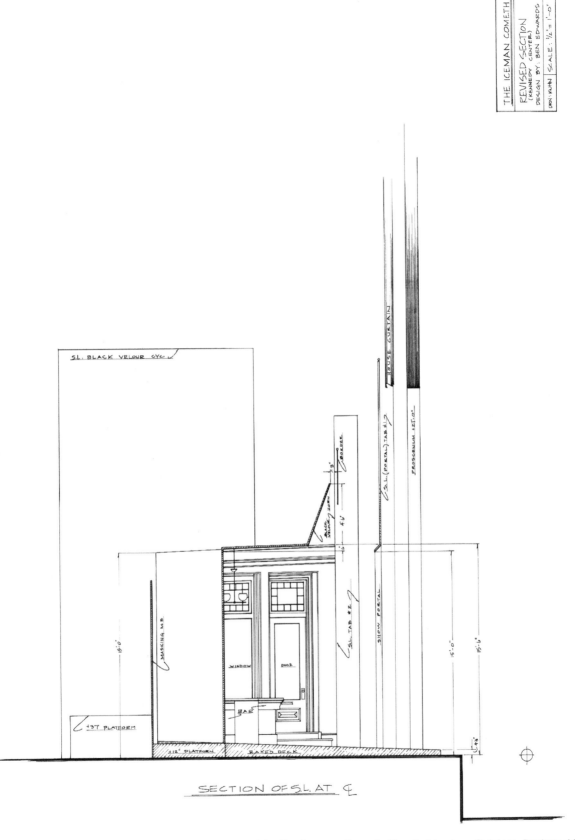

Figure 17.2 Sheet 2—Section. Drafting of the theatrical set for *The Iceman Cometh*. Directed by Jose Quintero. Designed by Ben Edwards. Drafting by Beth Kuhn.

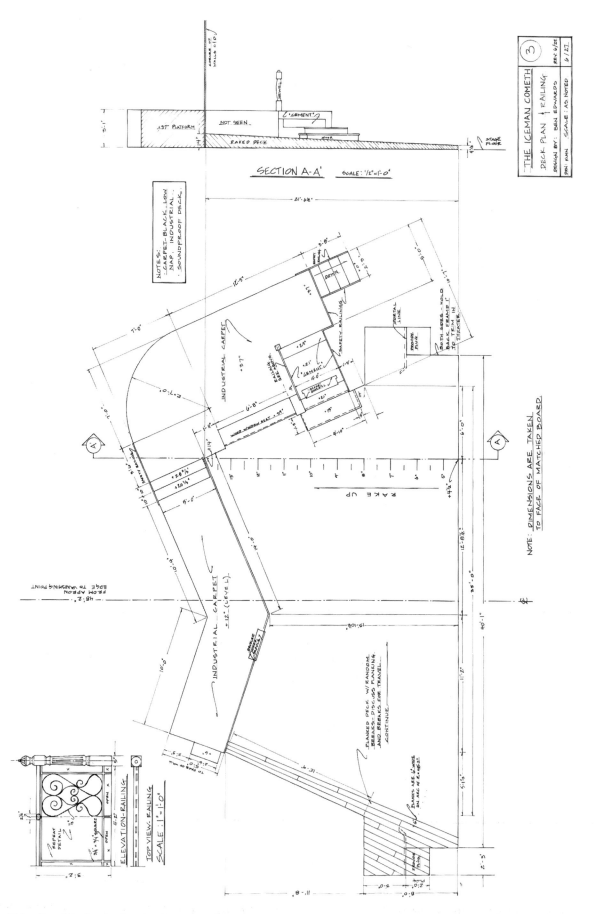

Figure 17.3   Sheet 3—Deck plan. Drafting of the theatrical set for *The Iceman Cometh*. Directed by Jose Quintero. Designed by Ben Edwards. Drafting by Beth Kuhn.

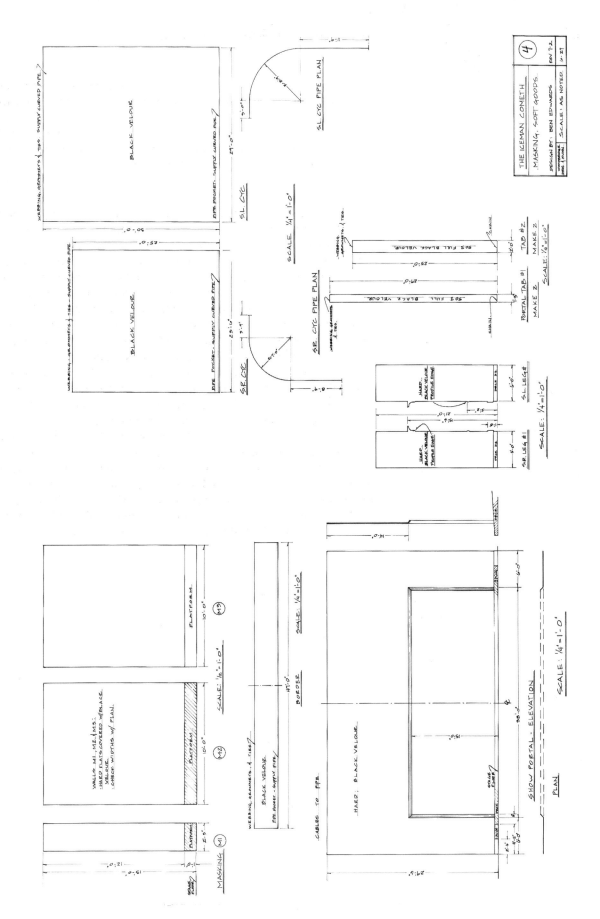

Figure 17.4 Sheet 4—Masking. Drafting of the theatrical set for *The Iceman Cometh*. Directed by Jose Quintero. Designed by Ben Edwards. Drafting by Beth Kuhn.

One of the many sheets of wall elevations is illustrated in Figure 17.5. All walls are drawn to the 0'-0" floor level, with a section of the rake drawn below the elevation.

The sheets in Figure 17.6 illustrate two pages of the many full-sized detail sheets required for this set. Each large-size detail is coded to refer to its position on the smaller-scale elevations.

The ceiling in Figure 17.7 is drawn as a reflected view rather than a true view.

A true view shows the actual size and shape of an angled plane. You would calculate the true view of this ceiling by projecting each corner across to the section, projecting them again to an empty area on the sheet, and then measuring the true widths from centerline to each corner. (Calculating the true view of an inclined shape is covered in the Chapter 7 section on Skewed Planes.) In addition to showing its true size and shape, drawing the true view of a ceiling demands that you flip it over so that what is downstage becomes upstage. To clarify this, think of the true view of the ceiling as a drawing of the ceiling as though it were sitting on the shop floor waiting to be painted.

You might need to draw the true view of a ceiling if the ceiling were covered with ornate decoration and acutely angled, but in most drafting situations you can draw the reflected rather than the true view.

A reflected-plan view is drawn as though you put a large mirror flat on the stage floor and drew the reflection of the ceiling upon it. A reflected view is essentially a tracing of the plan of a room or set with the addition of ceiling elements and notes specifying ceiling surface treatments. Often, especially if the ceiling is angled, overall sizes are not dimensioned and parts are dimensioned independently of total ceiling lengths. The true size of a ceiling is calculated by the construction department after the built walls are in position.

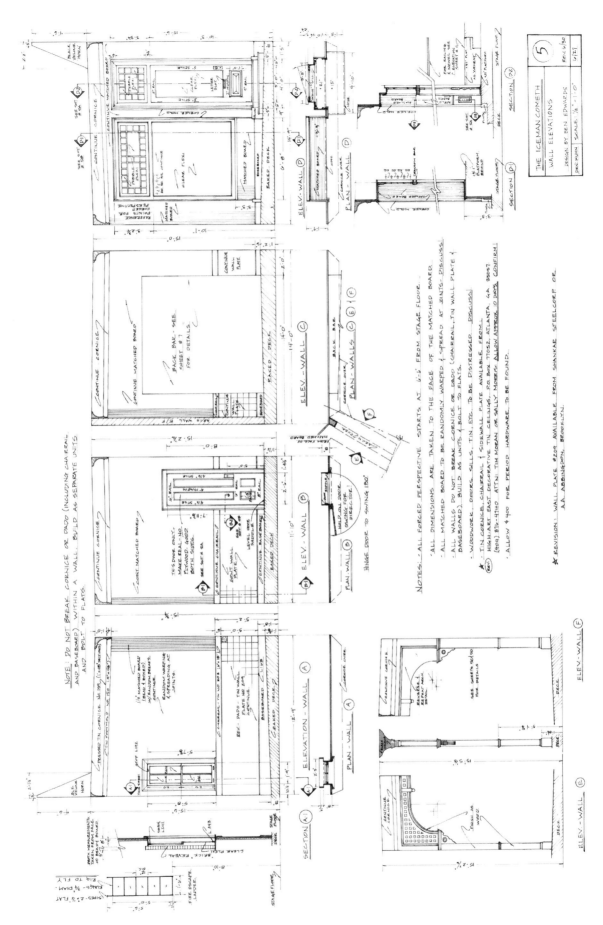

Figure 17.5   Sheet 5—Wall elevations. Drafting of the theatrical set for *The Iceman Cometh.* Directed by Jose Quintero. Designed by Ben Edwards. Drafting by Beth Kuhn.

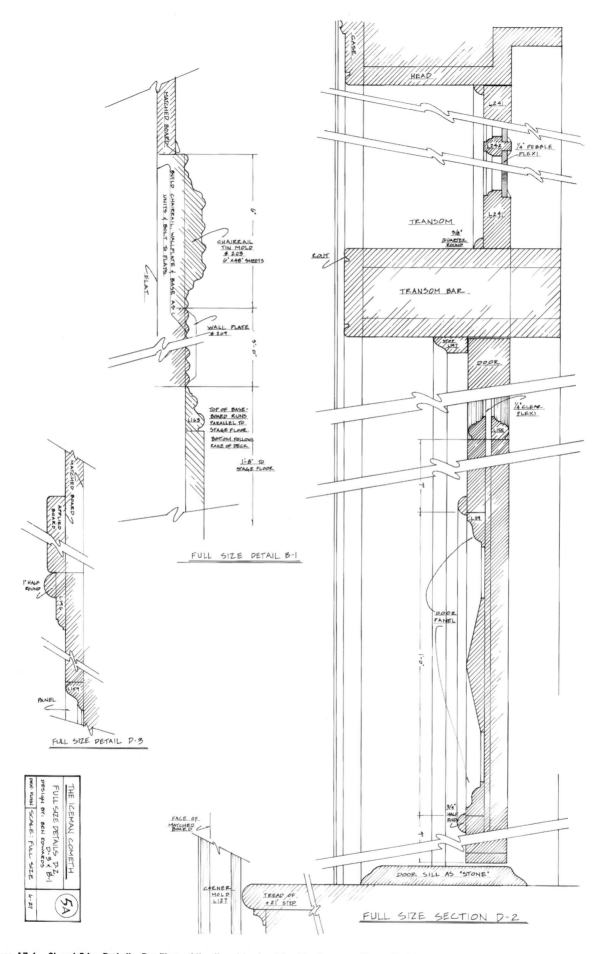

Figure 17.6   Sheet 5A—Details. Drafting of the theatrical set for *The Iceman Cometh*. Directed by Jose Quintero. Designed by Ben Edwards. Drafting by Beth Kuhn.

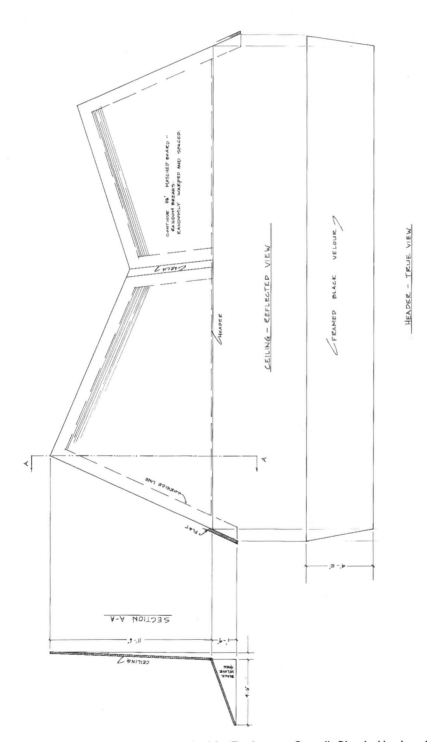

Figure 17.7   Sheet 6—Ceiling. Drafting of the theatrical set for *The Iceman Cometh.* Directed by Jose Quintero. Designed by Ben Edwards. Drafting by Beth Kuhn.

18

Architectonic Scenery

Theater embraces a wide spectrum of scenic drafting styles—styles determined by the nature of the scenic designer, by the type of scenery he or she is designing, and by the process by which the scenery is constructed.

If structural or engineering drafting is at one end of the scenic continuum, architectonic or sculptural scenery is at the other. The drafting of architectonic scenery, although it is drawn in scale and follows the usual layout rules of plan, section, and elevation, is more like freehand drawing, relying on line and shading to capture qualities of age and texture as well as shape. This type of design and drafting is most often seen in the set designs for operas, although it also can be found on some musicals or even box settings. Such drafting is usually accompanied by a finished model, fully textured and painted, that is a three-dimensional scaled miniature of the set.

The drafting for an architectonic design may have few dimensions or no dimensions at all, as it is usually redrafted in the scenic shop with the expectation that the drawings and the model will be interpreted by a skilled technical director. The nature of architectonic scenery is such that it is beautiful, intricate, and time-consuming to construct.

Ming Cho Lee is, perhaps, the most skilled of this type of draftsman. Although he sometimes hires a draftsperson to help him draft more geometric designs, the intricate and personal nature of his work usually demands that, to get the look he wants, he must do his own drafting.

The draftings in this book have, for purposes of clarity, been reproduced by first tracing them with ink on Denril paper and then photographing them. Because of the impossibility of copying the sketch-like nature of Ming Cho Lee's draftings, they have been photographed directly from the original pencil drawings.

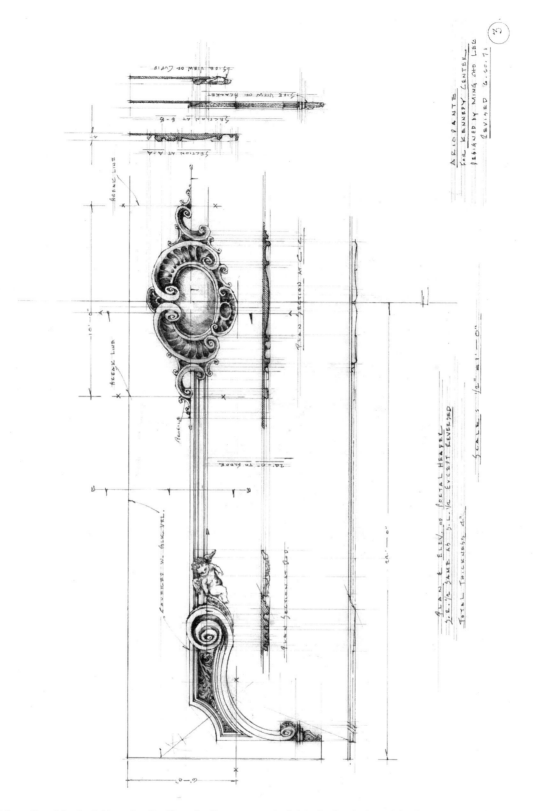

Figure 18.1a   Sheet 3—Portal header. Draftings for the opera set of *Ariodante,* designed for the Kennedy Center. 1971. Directed by Tito Capobianco. Designed and drafted by Ming Cho Lee. Used by permission.

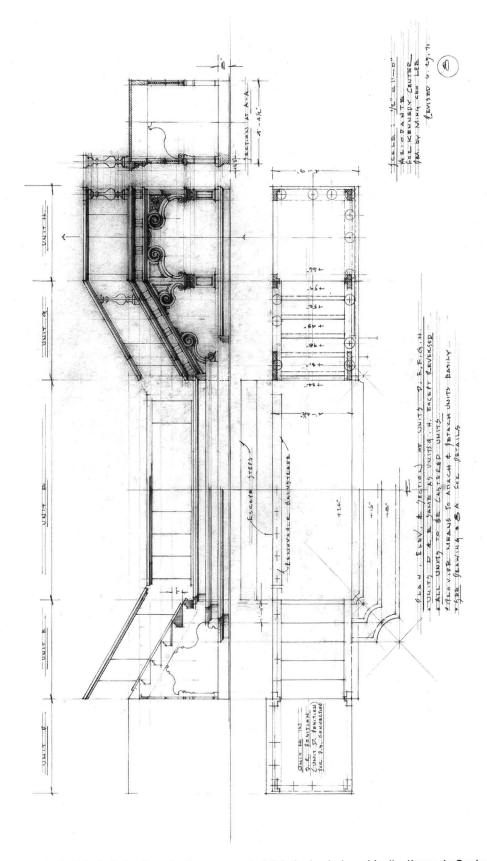

Figure 18.1b   Sheet 8—Units D, E, F, G, H. Draftings for the opera set of *Ariodante*, designed for the Kennedy Center. 1971. Directed by Tito Capobianco. Designed and drafted by Ming Cho Lee. Used by permission.

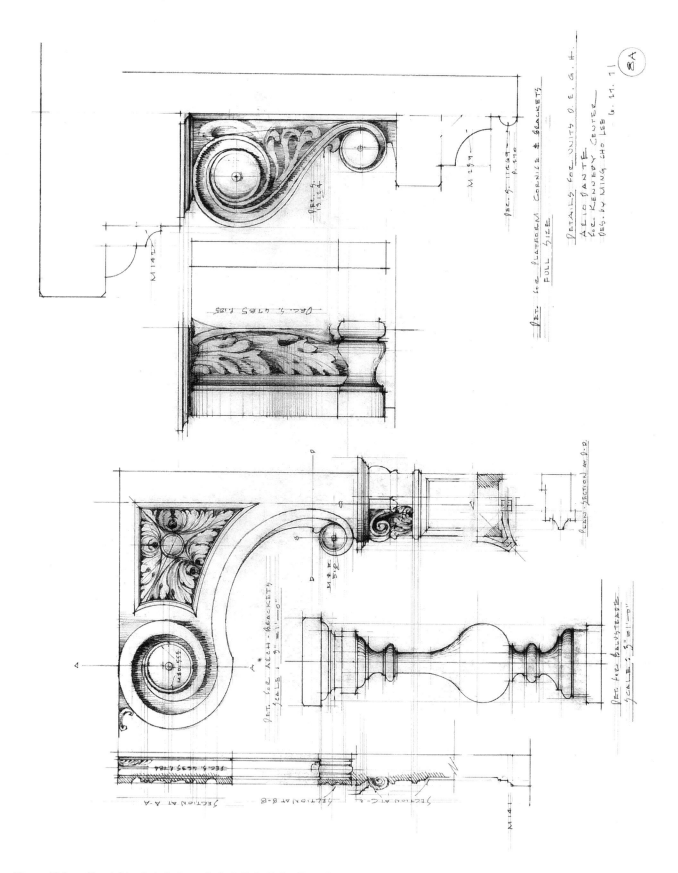

Figure 18.1c   Sheet 8A—Details for units D, E, F, G, H. Draftings for the opera set of *Ariodante,* designed for the Kennedy Center. 1971. Directed by Tito Capobianco. Designed and drafted by Ming Cho Lee. Used by permission.

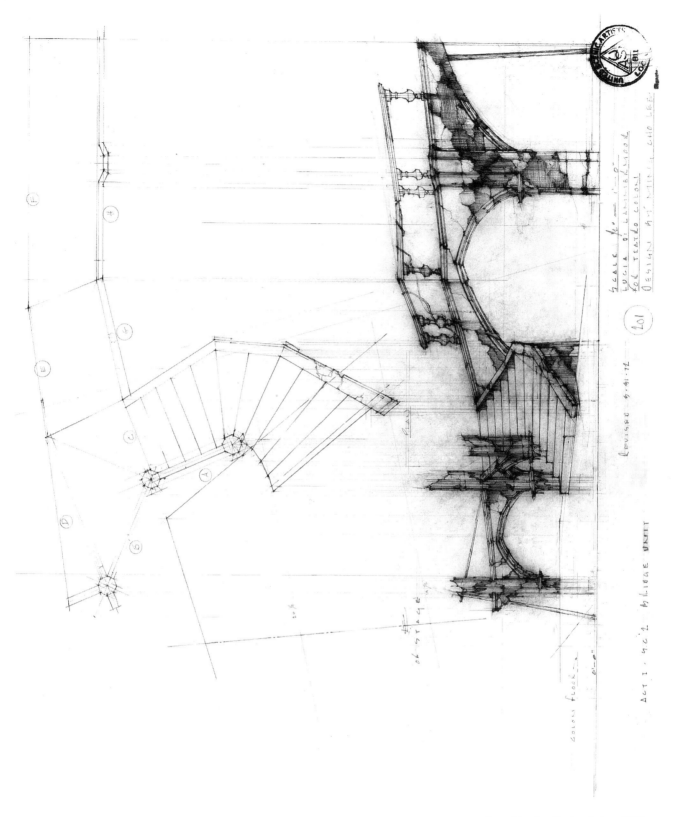

Figure 18.2a   Sheet 201—Bridge unit. Draftings for the opera set of *Lucia Di Lammermoor,* designed for the Teatro Colon. 1972. Directed by Tito Capobianco. Designed and drafted by Ming Cho Lee. Used by permission.

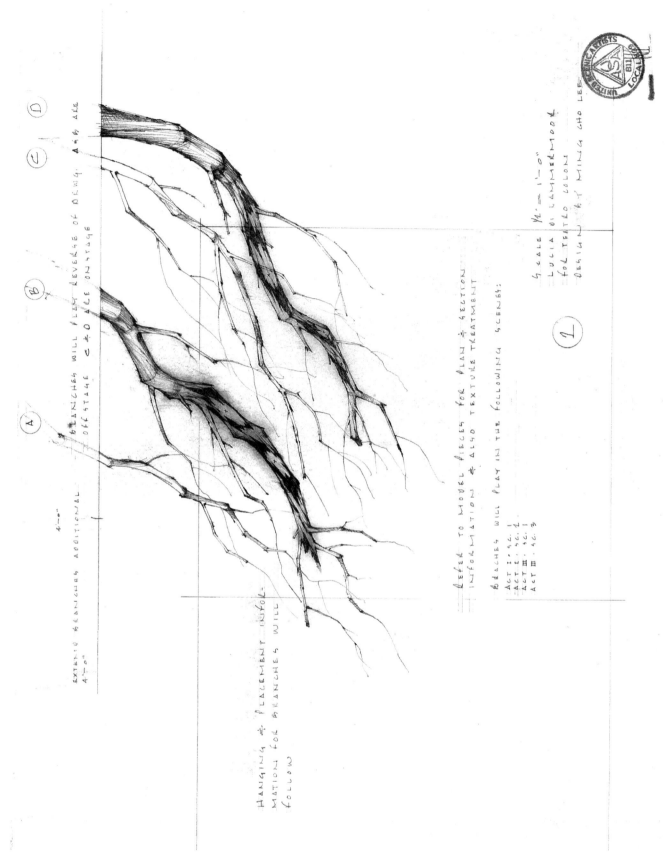

Figure 18.2b   Sheet 2—Hanging branches. Draftings for the opera set of *Lucia Di Lammermoor*, designed for the Teatro Colon. 1972. Directed by Tito Capobianco. Designed and drafted by Ming Cho Lee. Used by permission.

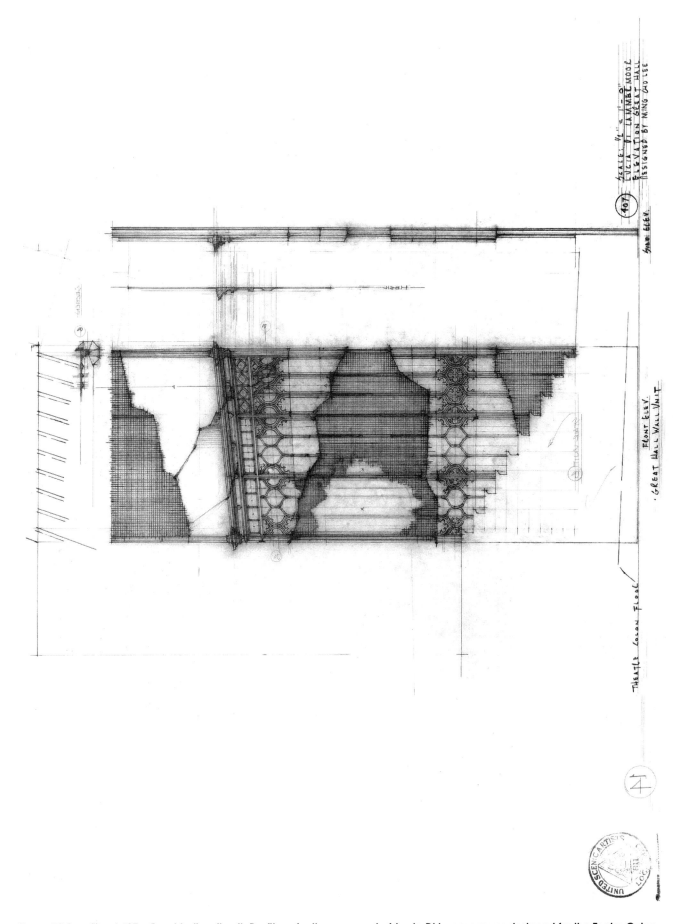

Figure 18.2c   Sheet 407—Great hall wall unit. Draftings for the opera set of *Lucia Di Lammermoor,* designed for the Teatro Colon. 1972. Directed by Tito Capobianco. Designed and drafted by Ming Cho Lee. Used by permission.

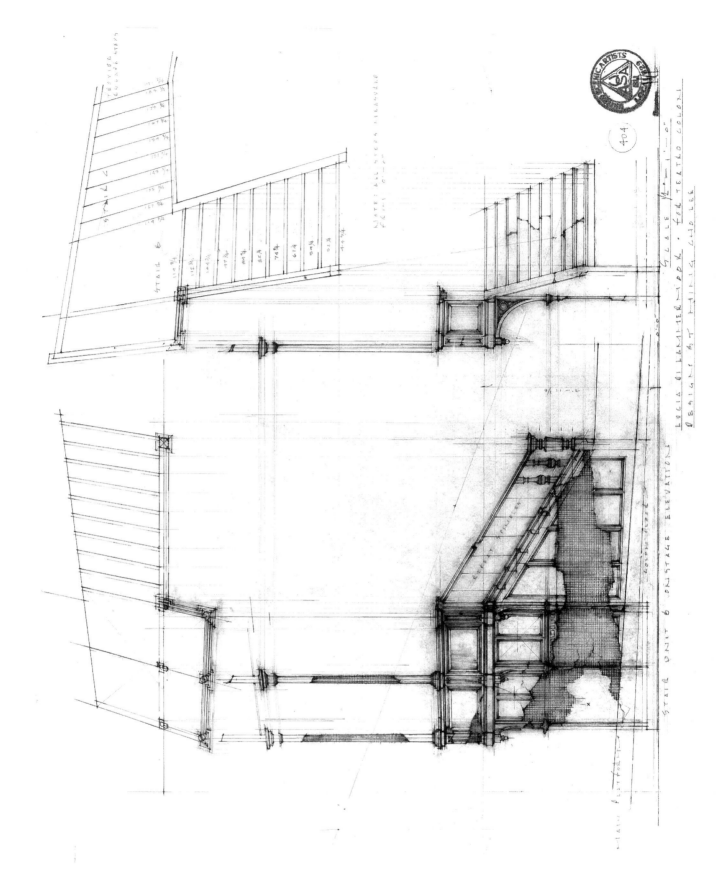

Figure 18.2d   Sheet 404—Stair unit. Draftings for the opera set of *Lucia Di Lammermoor,* designed for the Teatro Colon. 1972. Directed by Tito Capobianco. Designed and drafted by Ming Cho Lee. Used by permission.

19

A Musical

The musical *Guys and Dolls* was designed by Tony Walton and directed by Jerry Zaks in the 1991-92 Broadway season. Tony designed this production as a typical old-fashioned musical, combining drops with built pieces of scenery that track onstage into their playing positions. Although the overall design concept is familiar, the style of the scenery is distinctly modern in both design sensibility and sophistication. The draftings were done by Steve Olson and Anne Waugh and combine lovely drawing with technical specifications.

The master ground plan in Figure 19.1a shows the position of all permanent scenery, masking, light ladders, and storage positions in relationship to the stage and the extreme right and left audience sight lines. The silhouettes of moving scenery and flying drops are drawn with solid lines in their storage position and dashed lines in their playing position. Each drop and every piece of scenery and masking are labeled. On the left side of the sheet, in Figure 19.1b, a schematic pipe grid shows what is on each pipe and the depth of each pipe from the base or 0'-0" line positioned at the show portal.

The Cross-Section in Figures 19.2a and 19.2b is taken on the centerline of the stagehouse looking towards the most informative side of the stage. It shows the height and depth positions of all permanent pieces of scenery, and the masking and lighting positions in relationship to the stage and to the lowest, closest audience sight line. All drops and flying pieces of scenery are drawn in solid line in their storage positions and again in dashed line in their playing position. Dashed silhouette outlines indicate the playing positions of major pieces of scenery. Each drop and every piece of scenery and masking is labeled. Trim heights are given for borders and flying scenery. At the top of the sheet the schematic pipe grid is drawn, showing what is on each pipe and its depth from the 0'-0" line positioned at the show portal. The maximum heights the pipes can trim are noted.

The Deck plan, Sheet 3, in Figure 19.3, shows the position of the track lines for the winched scenery units.

We have here reproduced several representative sheets from the large packet of elevations and detail sheets required to build the many pieces of scenery and drops for this design.

On a show this complex it is necessary to draft shift plots to keep track of all the scenic changes. A small, 1/8-inch-scale plan of the theatre and the permanent scenery was drawn for each visual phase of the production and labeled as to act and scene number. The playing position of scenery and furniture is drawn in solid outline for each phase. Scenery storage positions relevant to the preceding or following phase are indicated with a dashed outline. Arrows are used to indicate the movement of scenery both onstage and offstage. Notes indicate what pieces of scenery enter and exit. (See Figures 19.5a and 19.5b.)

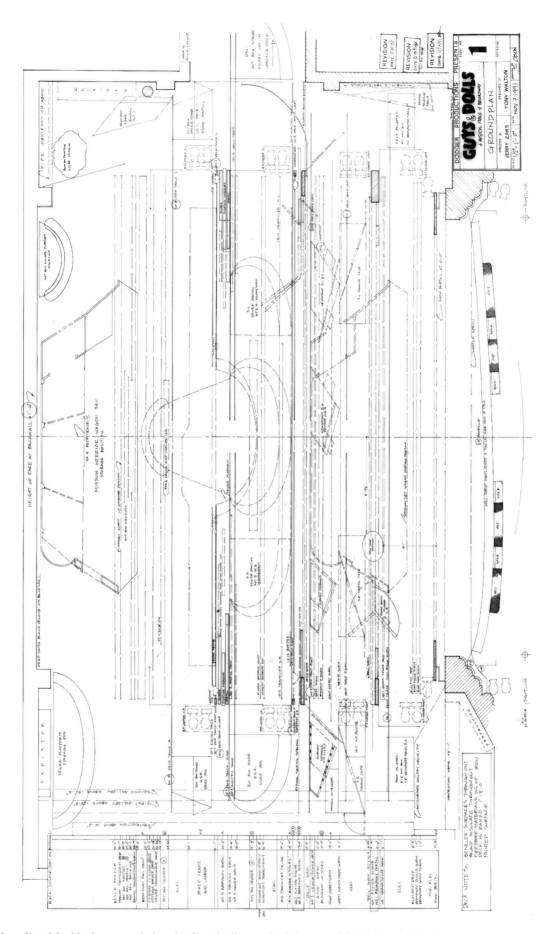

Figure 19.1a   Sheet 1—Master ground plan. Drafting for the musical *Guys and Dolls*. Directed by Jerry Zaks. Designed by Tony Walton. Drafting by Steve Olson and Ann Waugh. Used by permission.

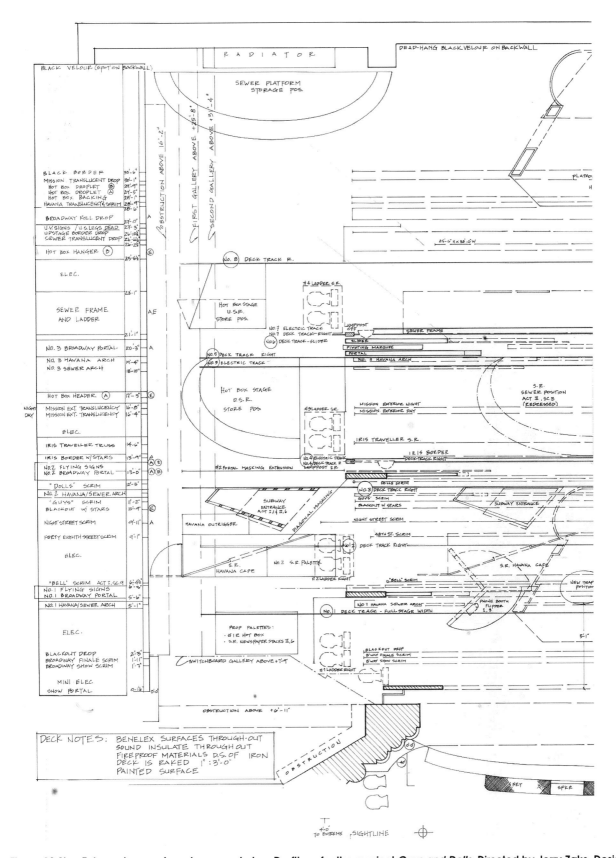

Figure 19.1b Enlarged area of master ground plan. Draftings for the musical *Guys and Dolls*. Directed by Jerry Zaks. Designed by Tony Walton. Drafting by Steve Olson and Ann Waugh. Used by permission.

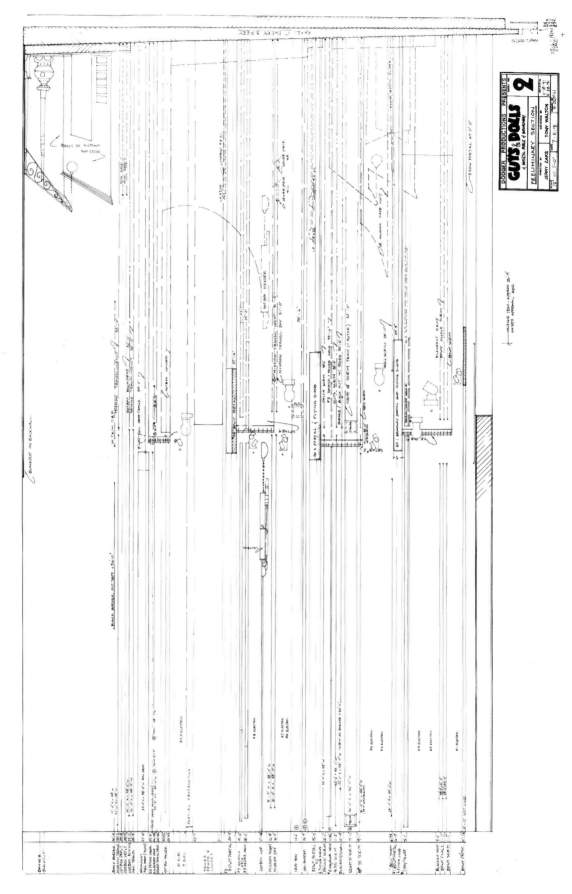

Figure 19.2a   Sheet 2—Preliminary section. Draftings for the musical *Guys and Dolls.* Directed by Jerry Zaks. Designed by Tony Walton. Drafting by Steve Olson and Ann Waugh. Used by permission.

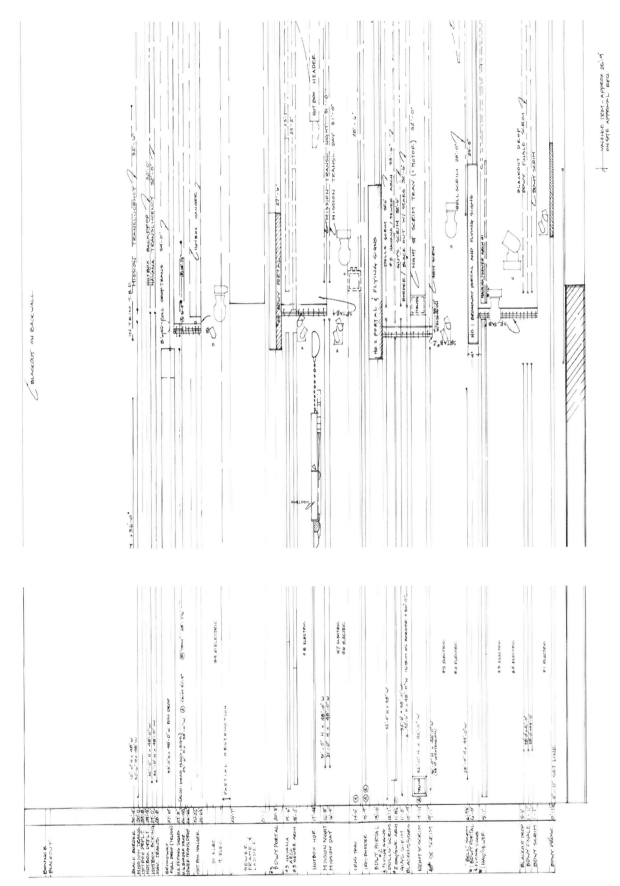

Figure 19.2b Enlarged area of preliminary section. Draftings for the musical *Guys and Dolls*. Directed by Jerry Zaks. Designed by Tony Walton. Drafting by Steve Olson and Ann Waugh. Used by permission.

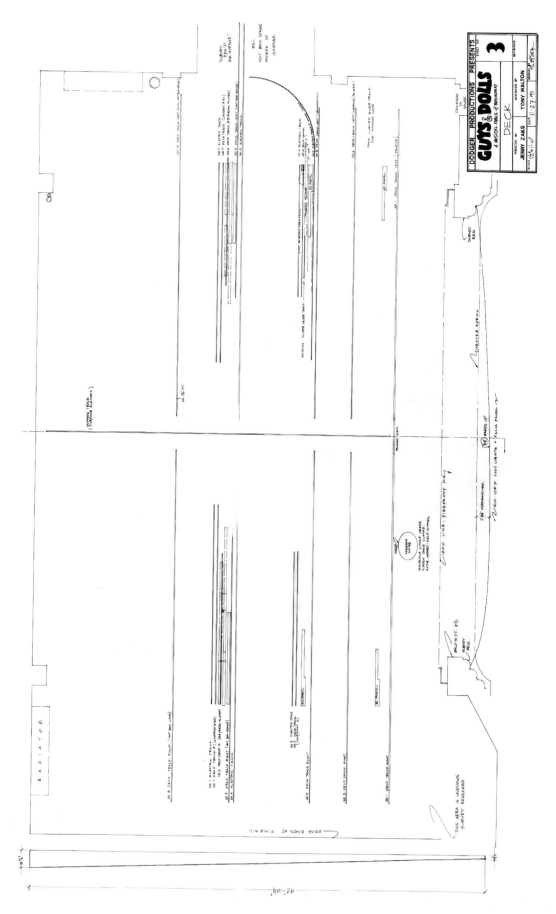

Figure 19.3 Sheet 3—Deck plan. Drafting for the musical *Guys and Dolls*. Directed by Jerry Zaks. Designed by Tony Walton. Drafting by Steve Olson and Ann Waugh. Used by permission.

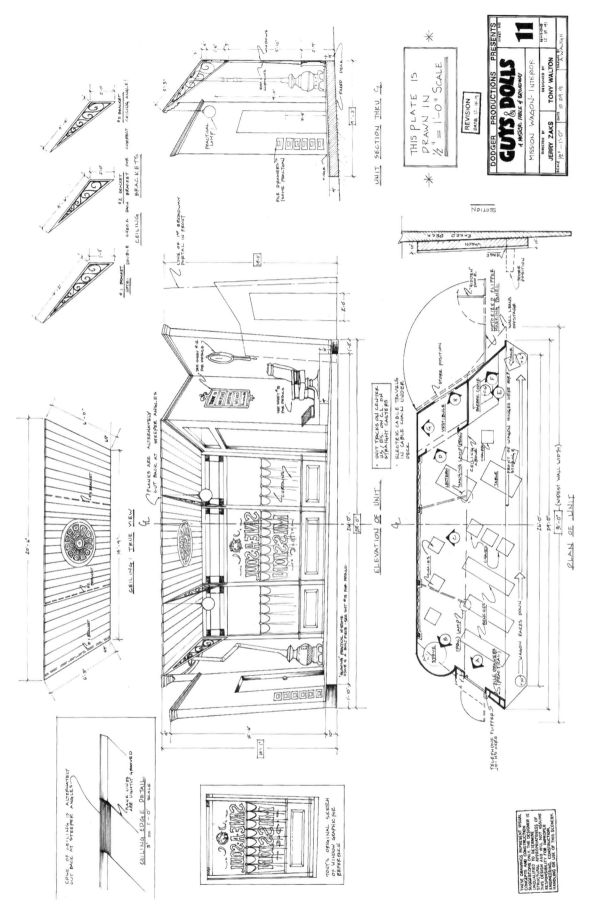

Figure 19.4a   Sheet 11—Mission wagon interior. Draftings for the musical *Guys and Dolls.* Directed by Jerry Zaks. Designed by Tony Walton. Drafting by Steve Olson and Ann Waugh. Used by permission.

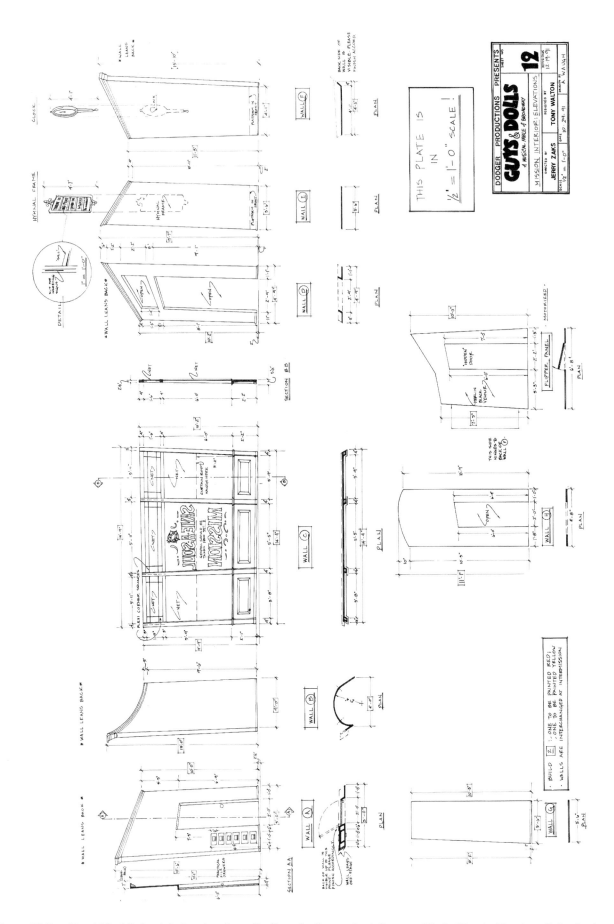

Figure 19.4b   Sheet 12—Mission interior elevations. Draftings for the musical *Guys and Dolls*. Directed by Jerry Zaks. Designed by Tony Walton. Drafting by Steve Olson and Ann Waugh. Used by permission.

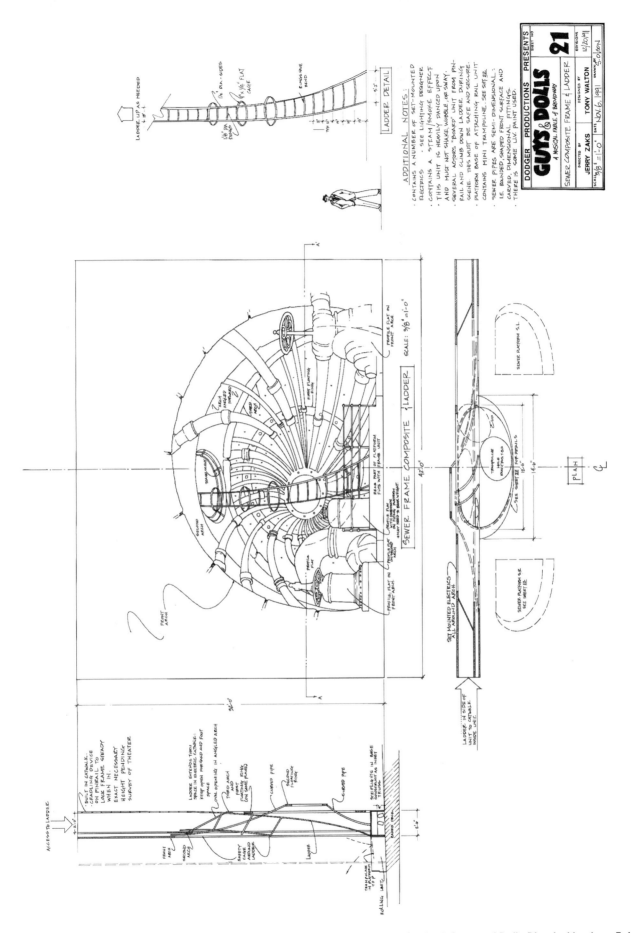

Figure 19.4c   Sheet 21—Sewer composite—frame and ladder. Draftings for the musical *Guys and Dolls*. Directed by Jerry Zaks. Designed by Tony Walton. Drafting by Steve Olson and Ann Waugh. Used by permission.

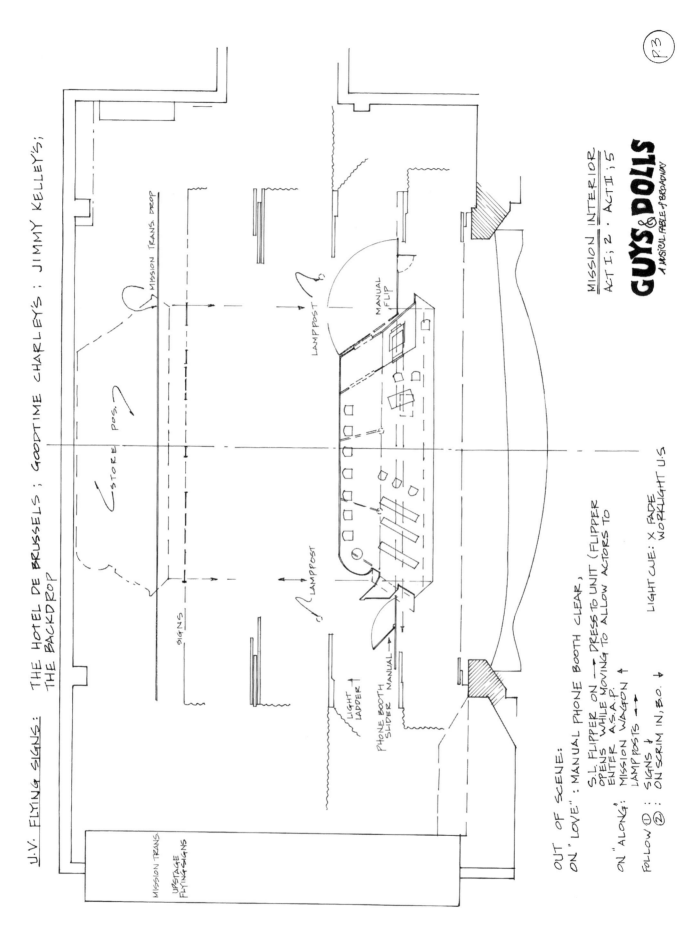

Figure 19.5a   Shift plot. Page 3—Mission Interior. Act I sc. 2; Act II sc. 5. Draftings for the musical *Guys and Dolls*. Directed by Jerry Zaks. Designed by Tony Walton. Drafting by Steve Olson and Ann Waugh. Used by permission.

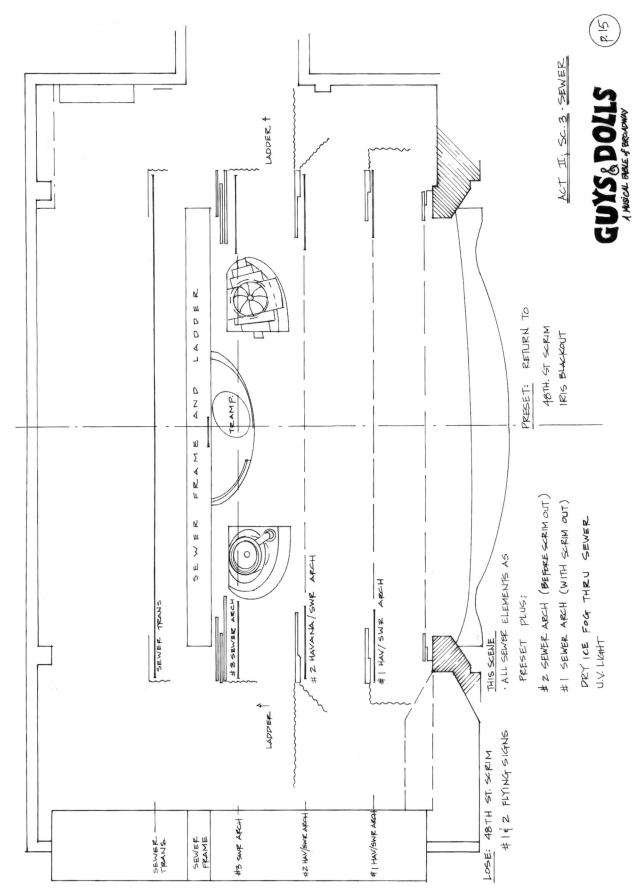

Figure 19.5b   Shift plot. Page 15—48th St./Sewer Ext. Act II sc. 3. Draftings for the musical *Guys and Dolls*. Directed by Jerry Zaks. Designed by Tony Walton. Drafting by Steve Olson and Ann Waugh. Used by permission.

Figure 19.6   Act I sc.2—The Mission Interior—Cont. The Same Day 1. See Plate 15 in the color insert. Sketch for the musical *Guys and Dolls.* Directed by Jerry Zaks. Designed and illustrated by Tony Walton. Drafting by Steve Olson and Ann Waugh. Used by permission.

Figure 19.7   Act II—Crap Game in the Sewer—Cont. That Night 3. See Plate 16 in the color insert. Sketch for the musical *Guys and Dolls.* Directed by Jerry Zaks. Designed and illustrated by Tony Walton. Drafting by Steve Olson and Ann Waugh. Used by permission.

20

Television Scenery

For the NBC television coverage of the 1992 Barcelona Olympics, Jeremy Conway designed four televisions studios to be built in the Olympic Village in Barcelona, Spain. Three of the studios housing the Prime Time, Late Night, and the Pay-Per-View Programs were built to fit into existing rooms. The fourth studio, designed for the Morning Show program, was built on top of the roof of an existing building called the Torre Mapfre.

Jeremy's design for the Morning Show studio consisted of a wall-to-floor arc of curving glass that looked out over the Mediterranean. This design was not only striking and elegant; the large amount of natural light the glass transmitted also meant that less artificial light was required within the studio to balance inside with the outside views. Because of the temporary nature of the installation, a requirement of the design was that the structure be self-supporting rather than anchored to the existing building. This was accomplished by a series of interlocking trusses whose legs mounted on top of the deck and within a large trench surrounding the deck. The trench was weighted with sandbags for ballast.

The finished drafting for the project was primarily done by Jeff McDonald, who has a background in architecture and engineering, and also by Jeff Sage, who is experienced in carpentry and comes from a theatrical background. The construction specifications were reviewed and stamped by a structural engineer. We have reproduced selected drawings from the many required for this large project.

The B sheets in Figures 20.1a to 20.1c are for the Late Night Studio, a more traditional design for a television news studio than that of the roof-top studio.

The D sheets in Figures 20.2a to 20.2c are for the Morning Show. Because of the architectural nature of this design, the draftings are excellent examples of structural drafting.

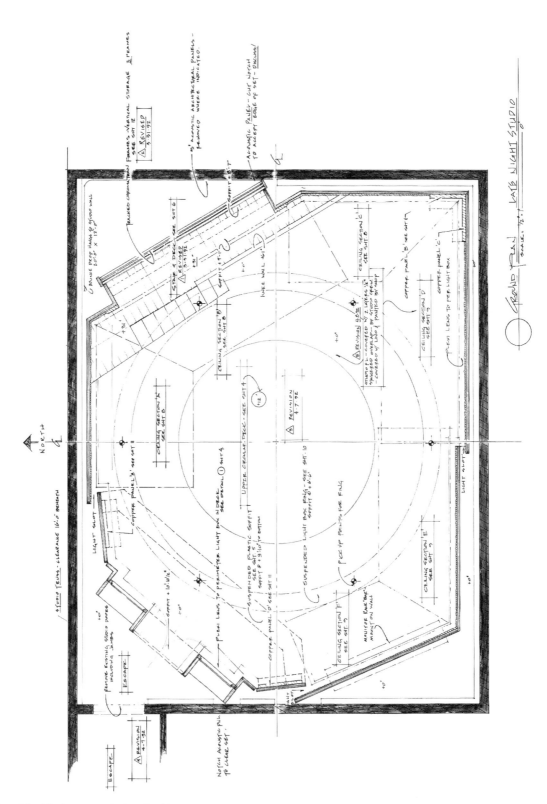

Figure 20.1a   B1—Master ground plan. Draftings of the set for the Late Night Studio for the 1992 Barcelona Olympics. Designed by Jeremy Conway. Art Direction by Kim Jennings. Drafting by Jeff McDonald and Jeff Sage. Used by permission of NBC Television Studios.

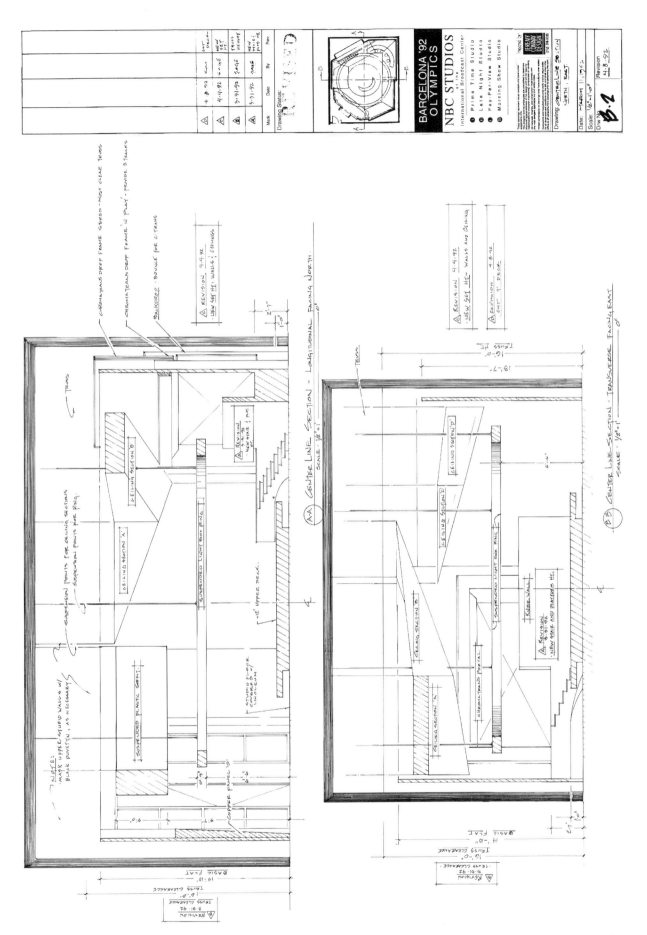

Figure 20.1b   B2—Centerline section North East. Draftings of the set for the Late Night Studio for the 1992 Barcelona Olympics. Designed by Jeremy Conway. Art Direction by Kim Jennings. Drafting by Jeff McDonald and Jeff Sage. Used by permission of NBC Television Studios.

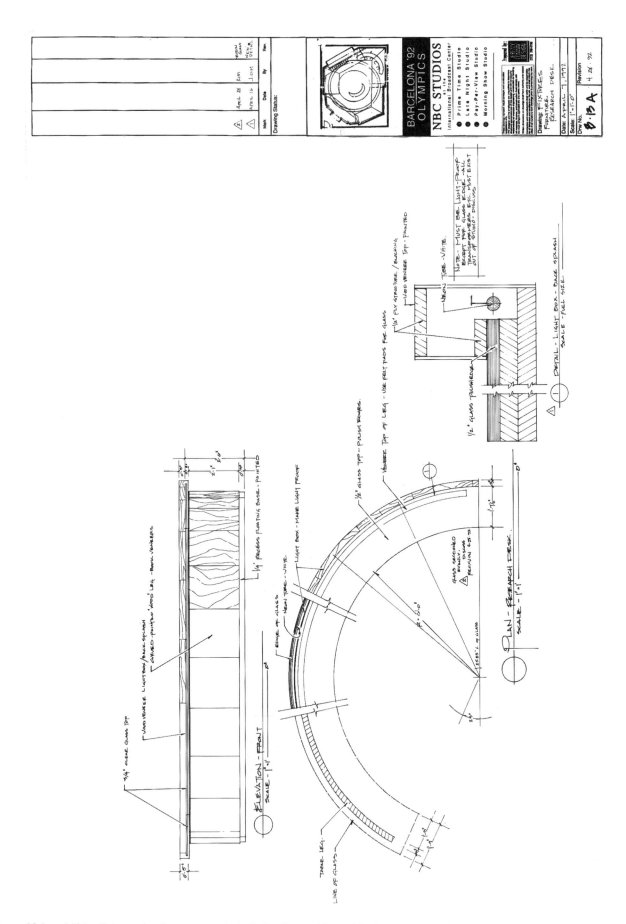

Figure 20.1c   B13A—Fixtures, furniture, research desk. Draftings of the set for the Late Night Studio for the 1992 Barcelona Olympics. Designed by Jeremy Conway. Art Direction by Kim Jennings. Drafting by Jeff McDonald and Jeff Sage. Used by permission of NBC Television Studios.

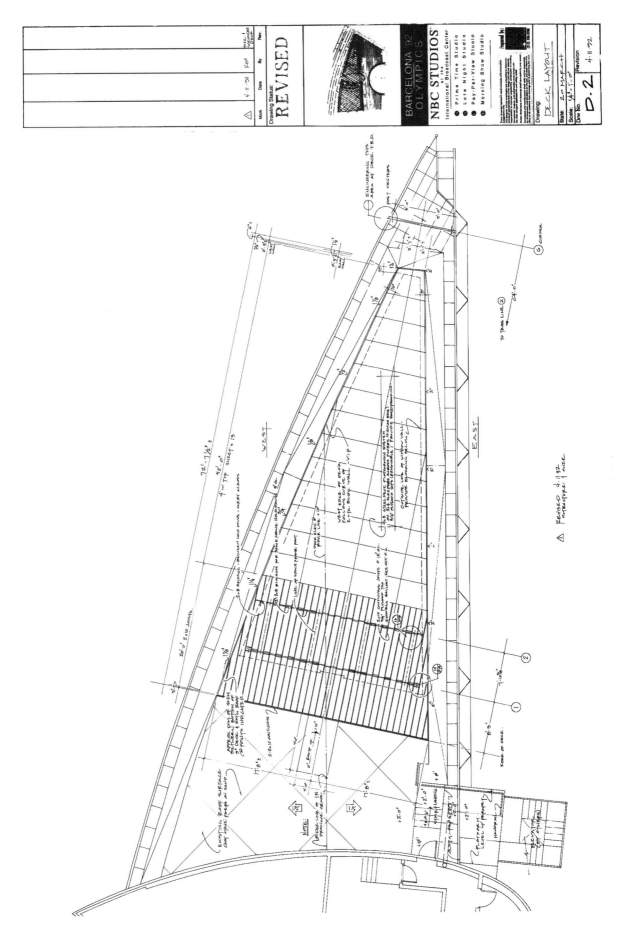

Figure 20.2a D2—Deck Layout. Drafting of the Morning Show for the 1992 Barcelona Olympics. Designed by Jeremy Conway. Art Direction by Kim Jennings. Drafting by Jeff McDonald and Jeremy Conway. Used by permission of NBC Television Studios.

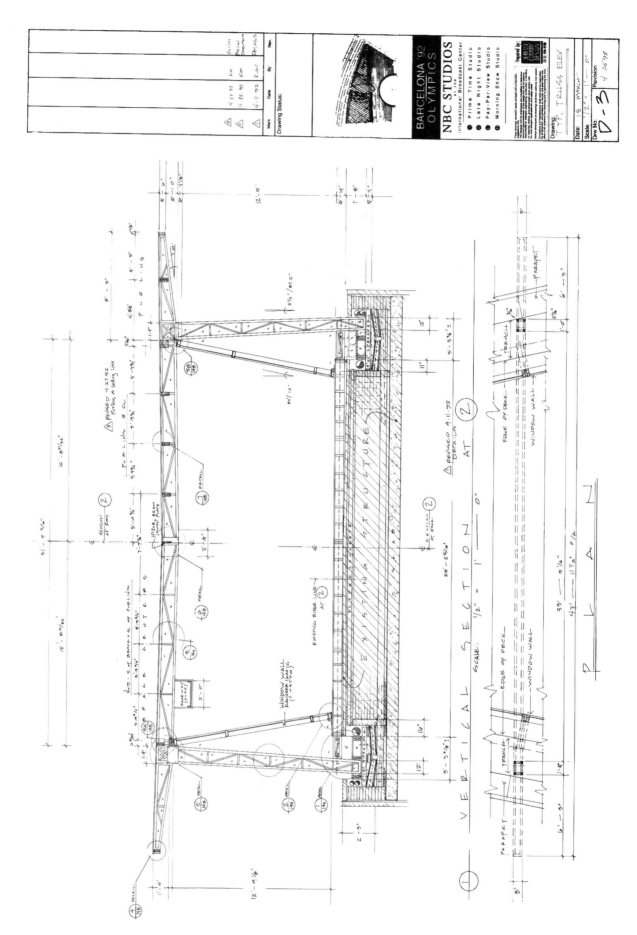

Figure 20.2b D3—A Typical Truss Elevation. Drafting of the Morning Show for the 1992 Barcelona Olympics. Designed by Jeremy Conway. Art Direction by Kim Jennings. Drafting by Jeff McDonald and Jeremy Conway. Used by permission of NBC Television Studios.

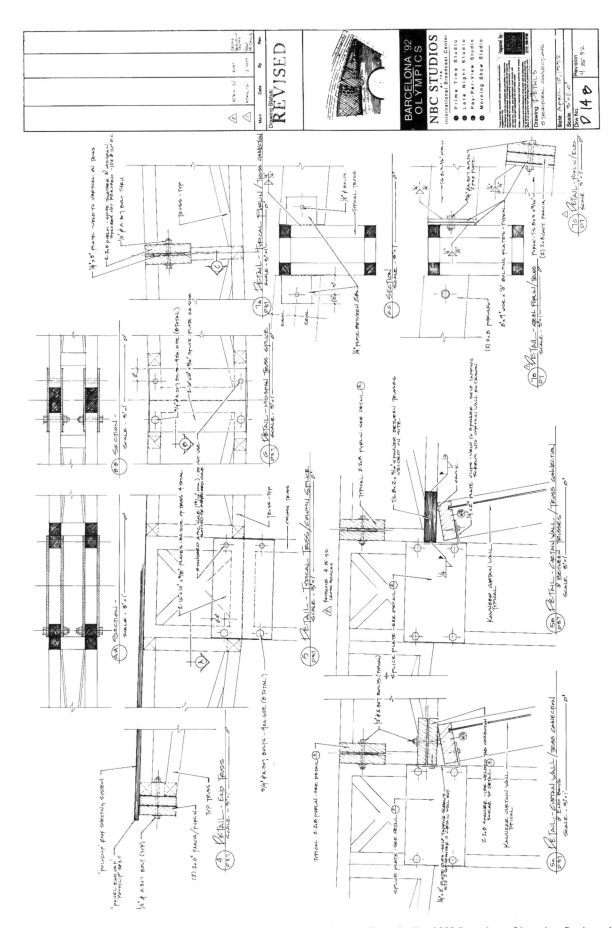

Figure 20.2c   D14B—Detail—Structural Connections. Drafting of the Morning Show for the 1992 Barcelona Olympics. Designed by Jeremy Conway. Art Direction by Kim Jennings. Drafting by Jeff McDonald and Jeremy Conway. Used by permission of NBC Television Studios.

Figure 20.3   Illustration of the set for the Morning Show for the 1992 Barcelona Olympics. See also Plate 17 of the color insert. Design and illustration by Jeremy Conway. Used by permission of NBC Television Studios.

Figure 20.4   Photograph of the set for the Late Night Studio for the 1992 Barcelona Olympics. See also Plate 18 of the color insert. Design and illustration by Jeremy Conway. Used by permission of NBC Television Studios.

21

Motion Pictures

Two Styles of Drafting

On the West Coast most film draftspeople come from an architectural background and are used to working in large film studios, and on the East Coast many film draftspeople come from a theatrical background, do much location work, and work with different material suppliers. This has resulted in two distinct styles of film drafting. Each method has certain advantages over the other in different scenic situations. Certain complicated sets would probably be best drafted in an East Coast manner, while most soundstage sets would probably be best drafted in the West Coast style. With increasing bicoastal movement of draftspeople and designers, hybrid forms of drafting are already appearing as draftspeople choose the method best suited to the job at hand.

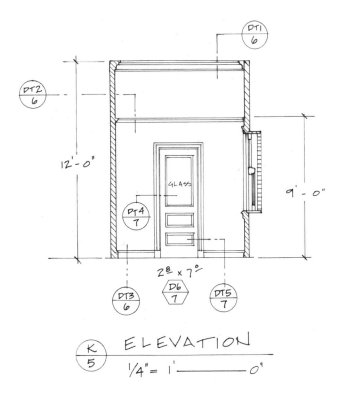

Figure 21.1   A West Coast drafting style.

West Coast

Most film draftspeople on the West Coast are used to working in a large film studio where there is an established procedure for building an interior on a sound stage. The ground plan of the set, drafted in 1/4-inch-to-the-foot scale and completely dimensioned, is drawn out full-size on the studio floor. As the widths of scenic pieces are built to fit the floor, wall elevations are dimensioned only for height. As most interiors are fairly simple, the elevations are drawn in 1/4-inch scale and coded detail bubbles refer directly to the elevations rather than to a portion of the plan and removed vertical section. As most molding comes from the studio supply, details are done full-size with no dimensioning but with numbers identifying wood and other specialized cast shapes that the studio has in its stock. Doors and windows are coded and drawn in a larger scale on a separate sheet with accompanying details.

On the West Coast, it is also common for a set to be drafted as a series of cross-sections through the entire set. This can be seen in the draftings for the film set for the feature film *Broadcast News*. (See Figure 21.5a.)

East Coast

Because most East Coast draftspeople come from a theatrical tradition they are used to scenery built in a shop and then trucked and loaded into a performance space. Separate portions of a single set may be built

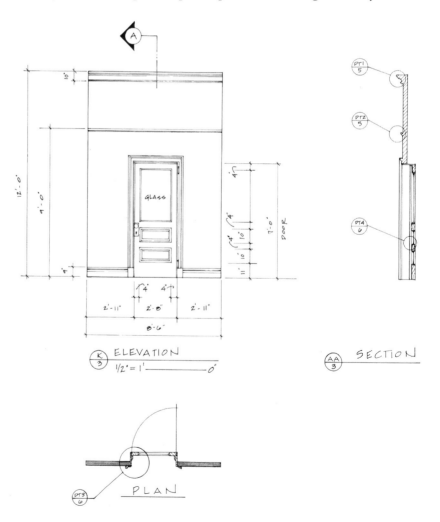

Figure 21.2   An East Coast drafting style.

by different groups, who may be in different shop spaces, and there may not be a shop setup of the set prior to the load-in. Although there are exceptions, individual pieces of theatrical scenery tend to be more complicated than pieces of film scenery; they may be in forced perspective, or mechanized, or built in unusual ways with unusual materials. The East Coast lacks the large Hollywood soundstages, and often sets for film or television are prebuilt in a shop space, separate from the studio space. Building pieces of scenery in a shop and then installing them into a location is common. And in the East, wood molding and scenic shapes do not come from a single studio shop but are purchased from different suppliers or made by carpenters using router bits.

If scenery is elaborate, draftspeople on the East Coast are used to drafting elevations in 1/2-inch scale, the scale for drafting theatrical elevations, rather than 1/4-inch scale. In addition to dimensioning widths on the ground plan of a set, they usually dimension both the heights and widths of each elevation. In drawing a complicated elevation, they often include its plan. Often sections are taken through informative parts of wall elevations and placed beside the elevation. Details are coded on the plan below the elevation and on removed sections rather than directly on top of the elevation. Details are usually drawn full-size and internally dimensioned. Pieces that are purchased from suppliers are identified. Shapes needing to be formed by routing are indicated.

Studio Scenery

Figures 21.3a and 21.3b show one of several studio sets built for *Carlito's Way*. The drafting is extremely clean and well organized and a fine example of the West Coast drafting style.

The sets for *Carlito's Way* were positioned in the studio on a studio plan drafted on a Macintosh computer by the Art Director, Gregory Bolton. Only those dimensions that position the sets into the studio location and the dimensions that set the distance between sets were required. Curved, dashed lines indicate "wild walls," pieces of a set that are built to be removed. (See Figure 21.4.)

The draftings in Figures 21.5a to 21.5c, although they were drafted some time ago, are also exceptionally lucid. They illustrates the typical West Coast method of drafting elevations as a series of cross-sections and of coding details by pointing to their location on an elevation.

Figure 21.6 is another example of a West Coast drafting style.

Location Scenery

Drafting scenery to fit into an existing location requires a tight survey of the space, including the size of the openings and passages that scenery needs to fit through as it is loaded. The drafting for location building needs to clarify existing structures on the basis of built scenery.

The draftings in Figures 21.7a to 21.7c are for an interior location in New York City. The ground plan on Sheet 1 in Figure 21.7a differentiates the existing architecture from the pieces that were added by shading one and cross-hatching the other. It also includes a work list for the setup, a list of restoration requirements, and the dates and time the space is available. The scenery, a large framed painting behind the altar, has been designed to enter in pieces that fit through a small door. It is also designed to be self-supporting so that it will not harm the existing papered walls. The plan in Figure 21.7b shows the dimensions of each

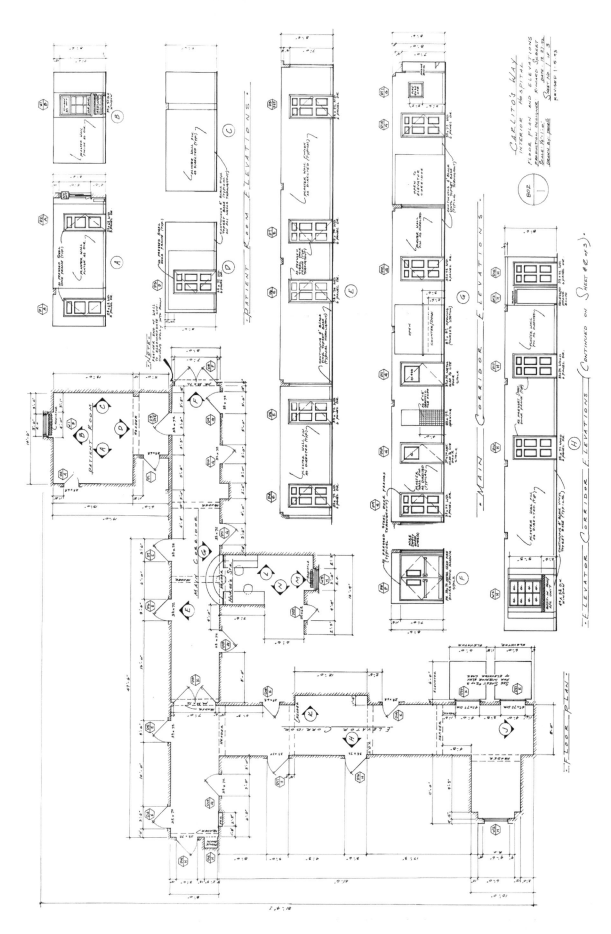

Figure 21.3a   Sheet 1—Floor Plan and elevations. Draftings of the "Interior Hospital" for the feature film *Carlito's Way*. 1993. Directed by Brian DePalma. Production design by Dick Sylbert. Drafting by Joseph Pacelli. Used by permission of Universal City Studio, Inc. and Amblin Entertainment, Inc.

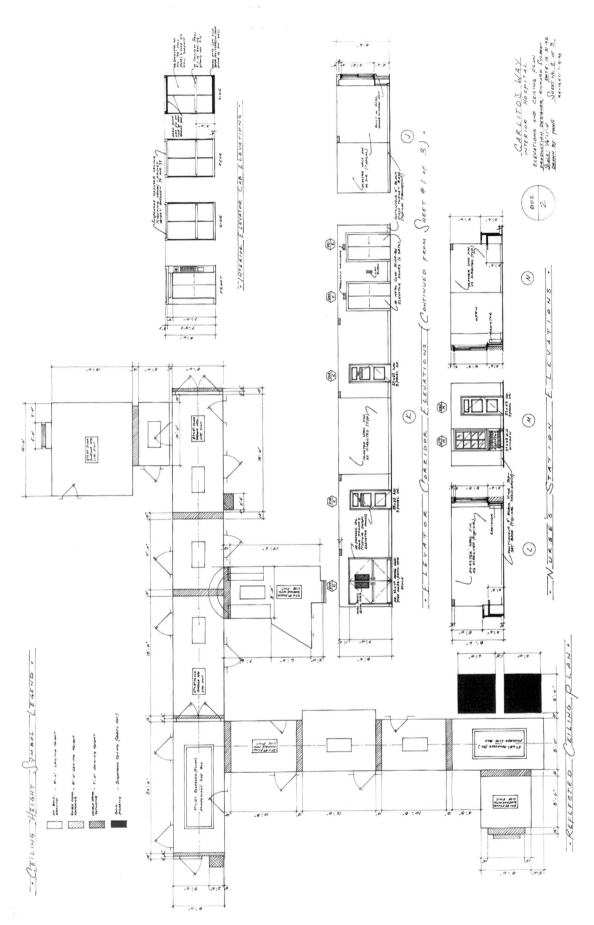

Figure 21.3b Sheet 2—Ceiling Plan and Elevations. Draftings of the "Interior Hospital" for the feature film *Carlito's Way*. 1993. Directed by Brian DePalma. Production design by Dick Sylbert. Drafting by Joseph Pacelli. Used by permission of Universal City Studio, Inc. and Amblin Entertainment, Inc.

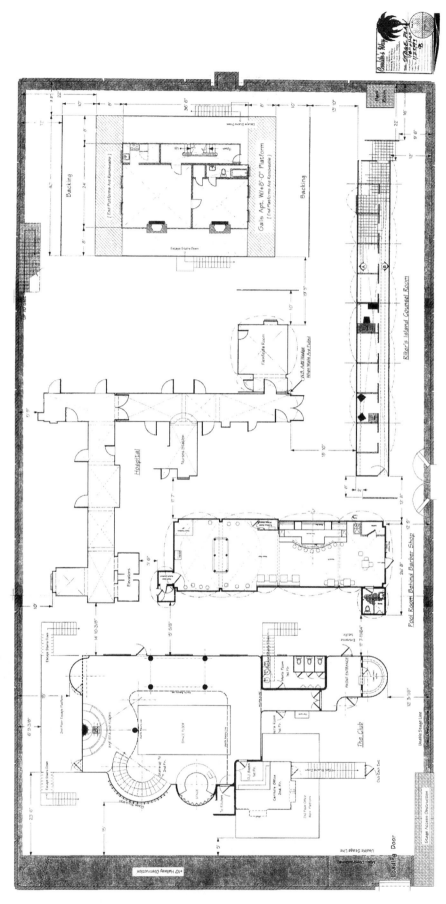

Figure 21.4   Studio Plan. For the feature film *Carlito's Way*. 1993. Directed by Brian DePalma. Production design by Dick Sylbert. Computer drafting by Gregory Bolton. Used by permission of Universal City Studio, Inc. and Amblin Entertainment, Inc.

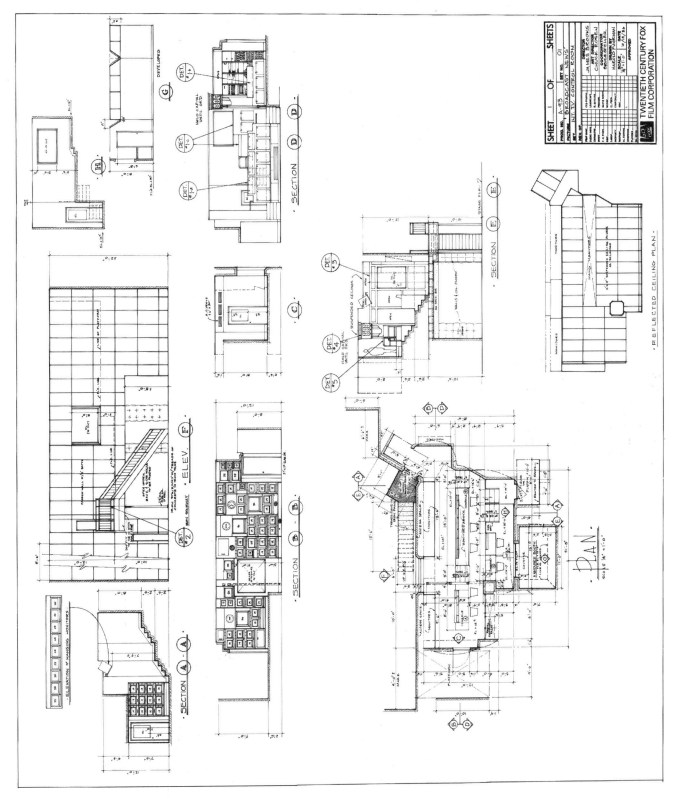

Figure 21.5a Int. T.V. Control Room Plan and Elevations. Draftings for the feature film *Broadcast News.* 1987. Directed by James L. Brooks. Production design by Charles Rosen. Drafting by Harold Fuhrman. Drafting courtesy of Twentieth Century Fox.

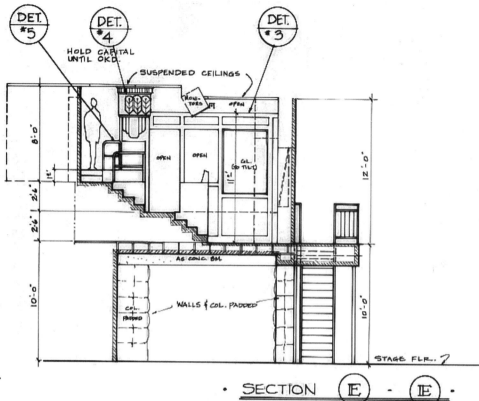

Figure 21.5b   An enlarged area of Figure 21.5a. Draftings for the feature film *Broadcast News.* **1987. Directed by James L. Brooks. Production design by Charles Rosen. Drafting by Harold Fuhrman. Drafting courtesy of Twentieth Century Fox.**

of the pieces that comprise the casing. A Xerox from a molding catalogue showing the face of a piece of embossed molding was attached to the sheet by sticky-back.

Scribing Scenery

Scribing is a technique often used in location construction when a piece of scenery must butt against an existing wall that has complex surface molding or other projections. The scenic wall is built with the framing of the flat held back from the edge of its surface covering. At the location, the carpenter uses a scribing tool to draw the contour of the existing wall's profile on the surface of the edge of the scenic wall. After he or she cuts the profile, the scenic wall can fit tightly against the existing wall without harming it.

A Built Set on an Exterior Location

Figures 21.8a to 21.8d provide examples of a location set that does not fit within an existing location but is built outside on an empty lot. This two-story hotel built in a small town in Nebraska is especially interesting because it is scenery that must be architecturally self-supporting. The span of the joists has been calculated so that several of the walls on the first floor, below the picture rail, can be wild. These wild walls are indicated by drawing a dashed-x on top of the elevation and writing "wild" at the center. The complex, two-story, multiwall set has been coded in an unusual manner. Bubbles with consecutive letters around the exterior perimeter of the buildings plan indicate the position of primary walls. The same coding identifies these walls on the exterior and interior elevations, helping the viewer read the drawings.

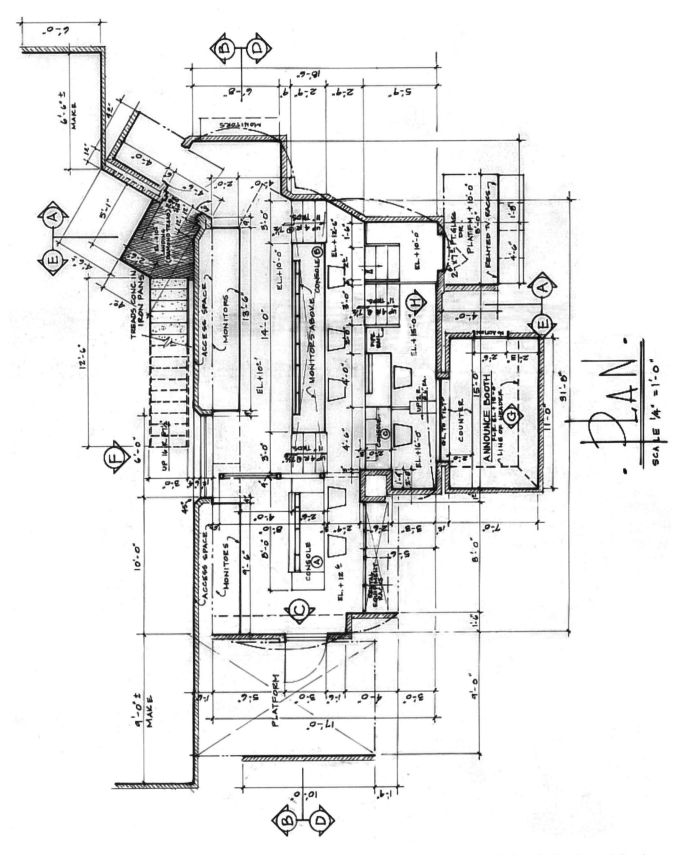

Figure 21.5c   An enlarged area of Figure 21.5a. Draftings for the feature film *Broadcast News*. 1987. Directed by James L. Brooks. Production design by Charles Rosen. Drafting by Harold Fuhrman. Drafting courtesy of Twentieth Century Fox.

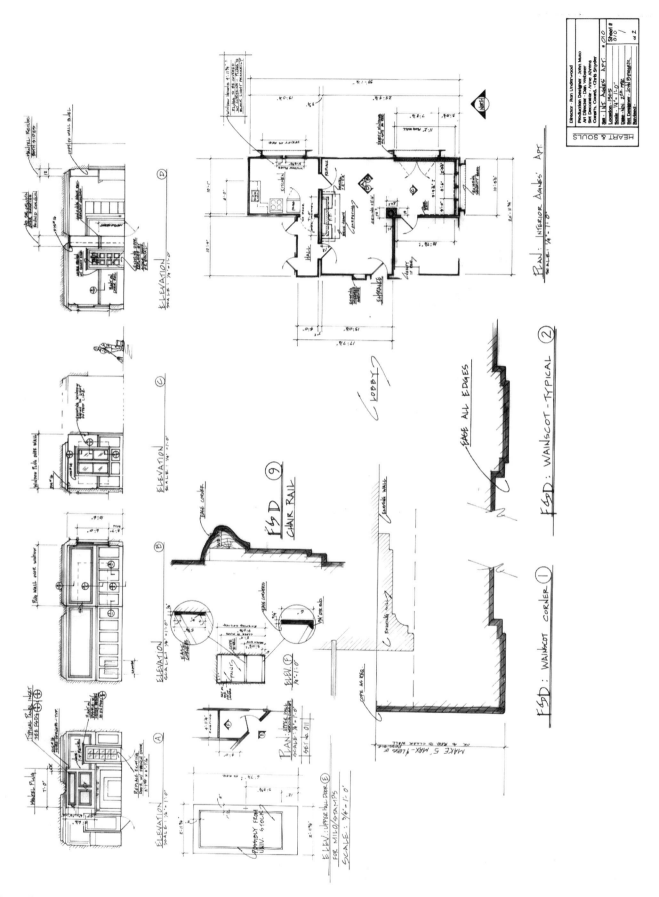

Figure 21.6 Sheet 1—Int. Drafting of "Agnes Apartment" for the feature film *Heart and Souls.* 1993. Directed by Ron Underwood. Production designed by John Muto. Set design by John Berger. Used by permission of Universal City Studio, Inc. and Amblin Entertainment, Inc.

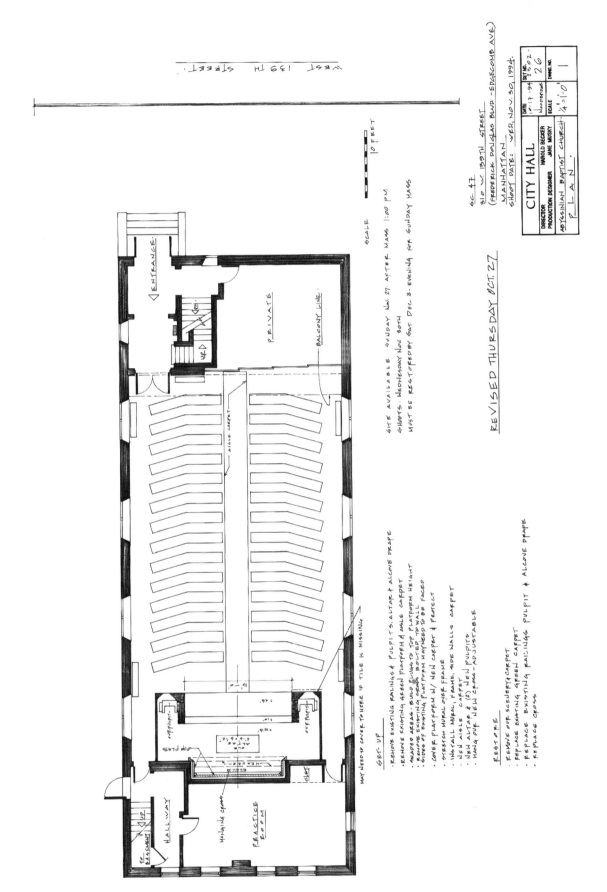

Figure 21.7a   Sheet 1—Plan. Draftings of the "Abyssinian Baptist Church" from the feature film *City Hall.* 1996. Directed by Harold Becker. Production design by Jane Musky. Drafting by Patricia Woodbridge. Reproduction with permission from Castle Rock Entertainment.

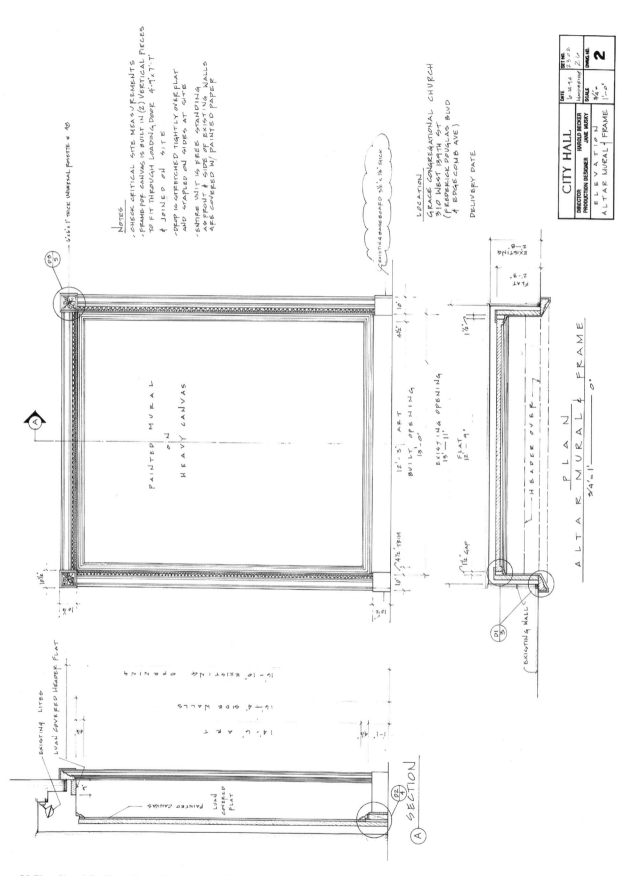

Figure 21.7b   Sheet 2—Elevation altar mural and frame. Draftings of the "Abyssinian Baptist Church" from the feature film *City Hall.* **1996. Directed by Harold Becker. Production design by Jane Musky. Drafting by Patricia Woodbridge. Reproduction with permission from Castle Rock Entertainment.**

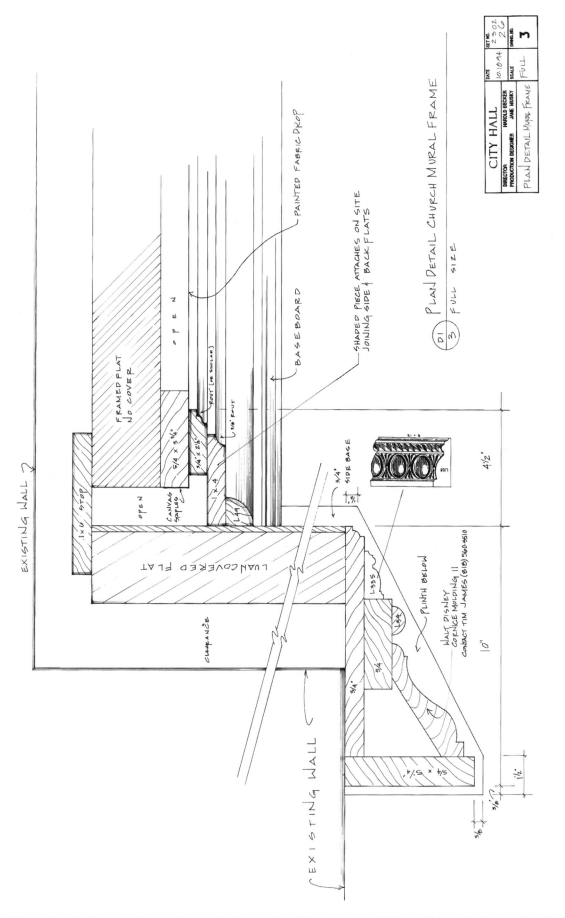

Figure 21.7c   Sheet 3—Plan detail, mural frame. Draftings of the "Abyssinian Baptist Church" from the feature film *City Hall*. 1996. Directed by Harold Becker. Production design by Jane Musky. Drafting by Patricia Woodbridge. Reproduction with permission from Castle Rock Entertainment.

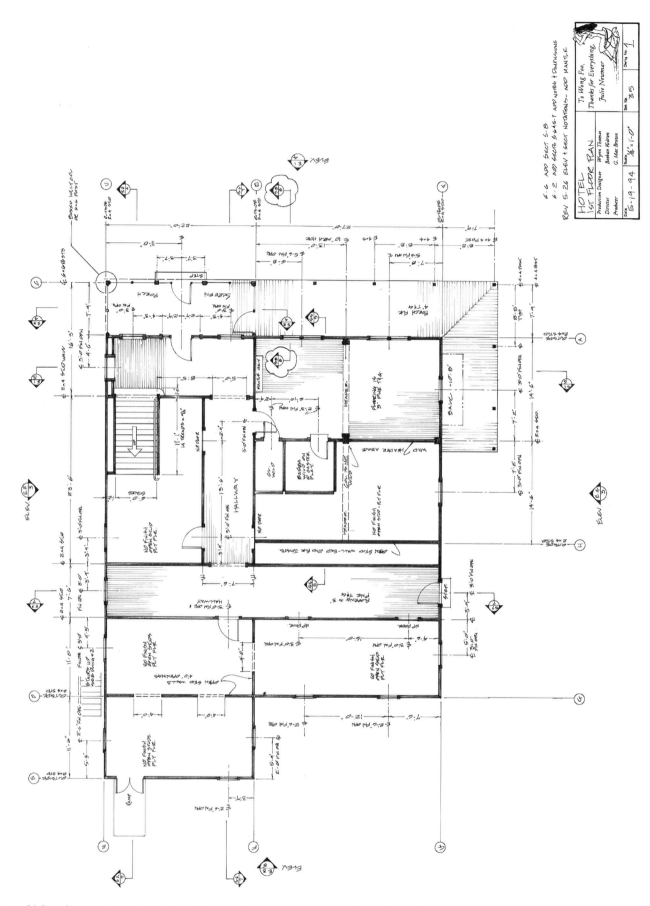

Figure 21.8a   Sheet 1—Hotel—First Floor Plan. Draftings from the feature film *To Wong Foo, Thanks for Everything, Julie Newmar.* 1995. Directed by Beeban Kidron. Produced by Universal City Studio, Inc. Production design by Wynn Thomas. Drafting by Bob Guerra. Used by permission of Universal City Studio, Inc. and Amblin Entertainment, Inc.

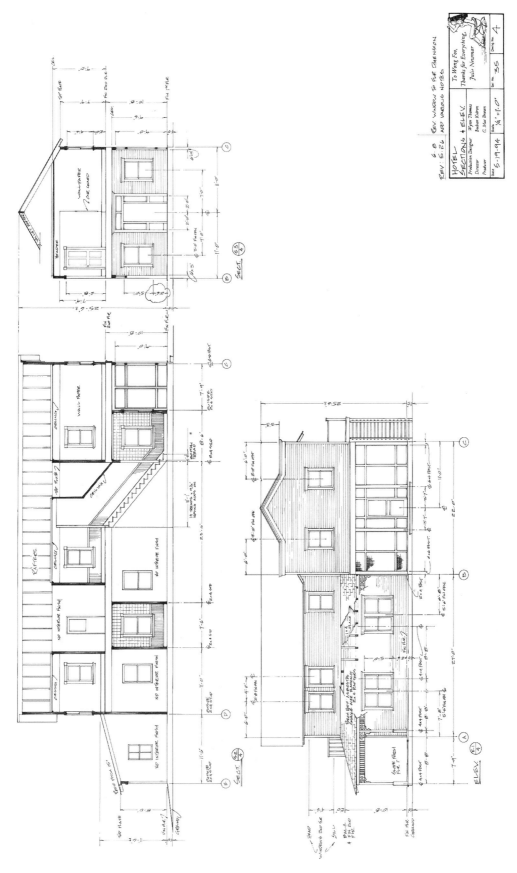

Figure 21.8b   Sheet 4—Hotel—Sections and Elevations. Draftings from the feature film *To Wong Foo, Thanks for Everything, Julie Newmar.* 1995. Directed by Beeban Kidron. Produced by Universal City Studio, Inc. Production design by Wynn Thomas. Drafting by Bob Guerra. Used by permission of Universal City Studio, Inc. and Amblin Entertainment, Inc.

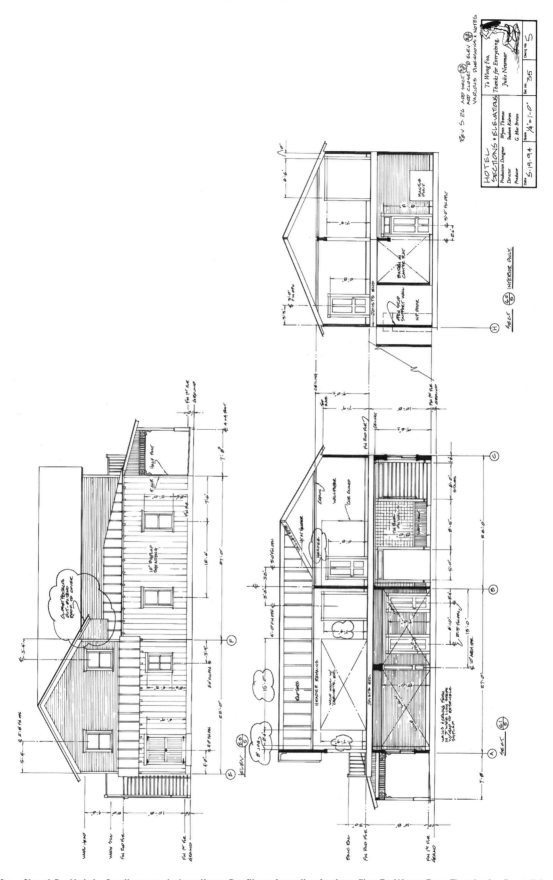

Figure 21.8c   Sheet 5—Hotel—Sections and elevations. Draftings from the feature film *To Wong Foo, Thanks for Everything, Julie Newmar.* 1995. Directed by Beeban Kidron. Produced by Universal City Studio, Inc. Production design by Wynn Thomas. Drafting by Bob Guerra. Used by permission of Universal City Studio, Inc. and Amblin Entertainment, Inc.

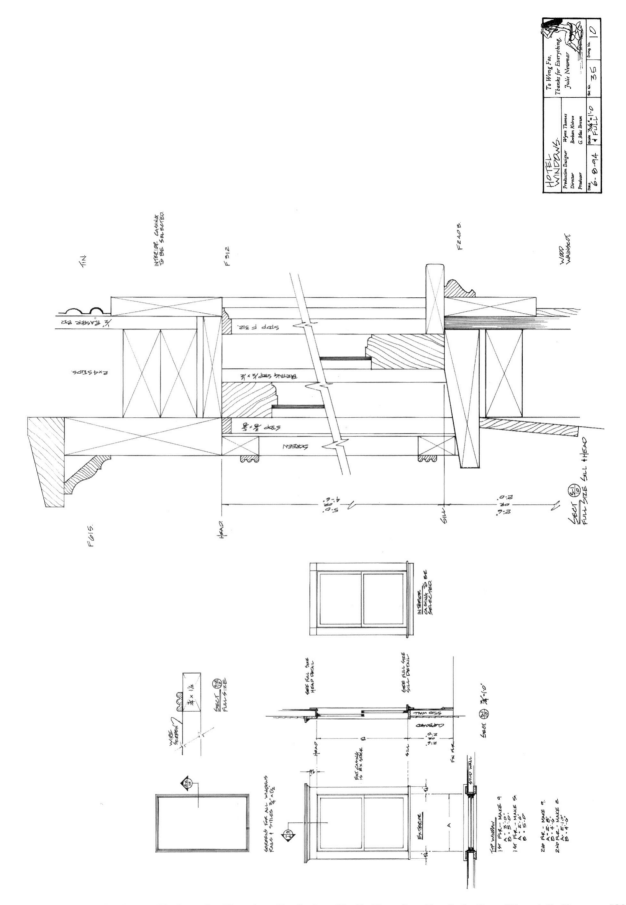

Figure 21.8d Sheet 10—Hotel—Windows. Draftings from the feature film *To Wong Foo, Thanks for Everything, Julie Newmar*. 1995. Directed by Beeban Kidron. Produced by Universal City Studio, Inc. Production design by Wynn Thomas. Drafting by Bob Guerra. Used by permission of Universal City Studio, Inc. and Amblin Entertainment, Inc.

22

Trade Shows
and Amusement
Park Scenery

There are many applications for scenic design other than creating designs around scripts for theatre, film, and television. These applications include music video, commercials, industrials, trade shows, fashion shows, exhibit design, restaurant and store design, window displays, and still shots for print. The drafting conventions are the same as for any other scenic design project, although, since the draftings may be shown to a client or agency, presentation may be stressed.

Tom Hennes has a company called Tom Hennes, Inc., that specializes in what he calls "exhibit and attraction design." His projects encompass a wide range of applications, some of which are very theatrical and textural, and others that are high-tech and architectural.

Although Tom was a German major at Kalamazoo College in Michigan, he spent most of his time in the theatre department. His field of specialization was in theatrical lighting, and he joined United Scenic Artists Local 829 as a lighting designer in 1981. His lighting background is central to his designs, which integrate scenery, lighting, and often projections.

One of Tom's more unusual designs was the "Green Slime Geyser" (Figure 22.1), a scenic attraction for Nickelodeon Networks, part of a tour at Universal Studios, Florida. "Green Slime" is a popular image in children's comedy, and this set was conceived by the network as a "Slime Depurification Plant" that would supply green slime for television by removing "purities" and retaining "impurities." This attraction utilized sixty-five different mechanical effects and multiple sound tracks with a green slime geyser that bubbled and erupted every 15 minutes.

Another unusual project that Tom conceptualized and designed was an apparatus called "The Imagination Machine" (Figure 22.2) to sell a client's creative services for amusement park rides. Designed to look like an antiquated Jules Verne submarine, whirring, churning, and belching smoke, the design was a theatrical spoof with a story line and stage props. Characters would brainstorm for new amusement park rides while the imagined rides appeared in three dimensions.

One of Tom's early projects was the design of a ride for an amusement park called Playland in Rye, New York. (See Figures 22.3a and 22.3b.) This children's ride passed by a series of caves with trolls, a smoke-breathing dragon, and a large glowing eyeball with a moving iris. (See Figure 22.3b.) Designed within a limited budget and constructed by a puppet-builder

Figure 22.1 The Nickelodeon Green Slime Geyser. Conceptualized and Designed by Tom Hennes of Tom Hennes, Inc. Produced by DeMartin-Marona-Cranstoun-Downes. Used by permission. See also Plate 19 of the color insert.

rather than an animatronics firm, the characters had very little motion—just a characteristic twist or turn—but were only seen for a moment. Tom says that the big benefit of designing a ride over designing for the theatre is that the audience point of view is very closely controlled: each scene needs to do only one thing, and the designer can decide how long the visitor gets to see it. In that way, it is much more like designing for film in that you can create a strong impression with limited means if the audience cannot examine it too closely.

Tom has a current staff of fourteen full-time employees, including draftspeople and model-makers. In the early years of his company, however, he not only did the designing but much of the surveying and drafting himself. Before he could design the ride at the Rye Playland, Tom and an assistant did a two-day survey of the existing curved track. The major part of the survey consisted of an enormous amount of triangulation from a series of regular spaced points along the track to several structural posts.

Although the site plan had to be extremely exact, the nature of Tom's

Figure 22.2 The Imagination Machine. Designed by Tom Hennes and David Sirola of Tom Hennes, Inc., for KBD Innovative Arts, Marina Del Rey, CA, and East Coast Theatrical Supply, Cornwall-On-Hudson, NY. Used by permission. See also Plate 20 of the color insert.

design—caves and trolls—was sculptural and anthropomorphic. This was reflected in his draftings, most of which were shaded soft drawings with few dimensions. Specific information, such as the elliptical shapes of the mirrored backdrops for "Sparkle's Cave," was drawn tightly. Each section of the ride was given a name reflecting its scenery, and each section was drafted as a separate entity. Figures 22.3a and 22.3b represent a selection from the many drawings for this project.

A more recent work of Tom's, stylistically high-tech and thus completely different from the amusement ride, was an exhibit design for Sony Electronics, Inc., in the Comdex 1995 Exhibit. (See Figure 22.4.) With this design Sony wanted a dominant exhibit at a major United States computer-technology show, one that would firmly position Sony as an important and innovative player in the industry.

Tom's design incorporated product display and demonstrations, conference rooms, a domed, 3-D high-definition video, and a laser theatre seating 160 people. Central to this design were thirty-four interactive computer stations surrounded by an environment of changing photographic images. The stations were designed to be open to the exhibition area while allowing a personal, quiet interaction with the technology. The seats had stereo sound built into the headrest, and the trackball was a sleek device (a backlit translucent orange ball in a purple fiberglass hand rest) mounted on a swiveling monitor. The theatre had two screens with three-dimensional laser effects about the convergence of the consumer electronics and computing industries. The three-dimensional glasses that the audience wore were specially designed as a glasses/visor set.

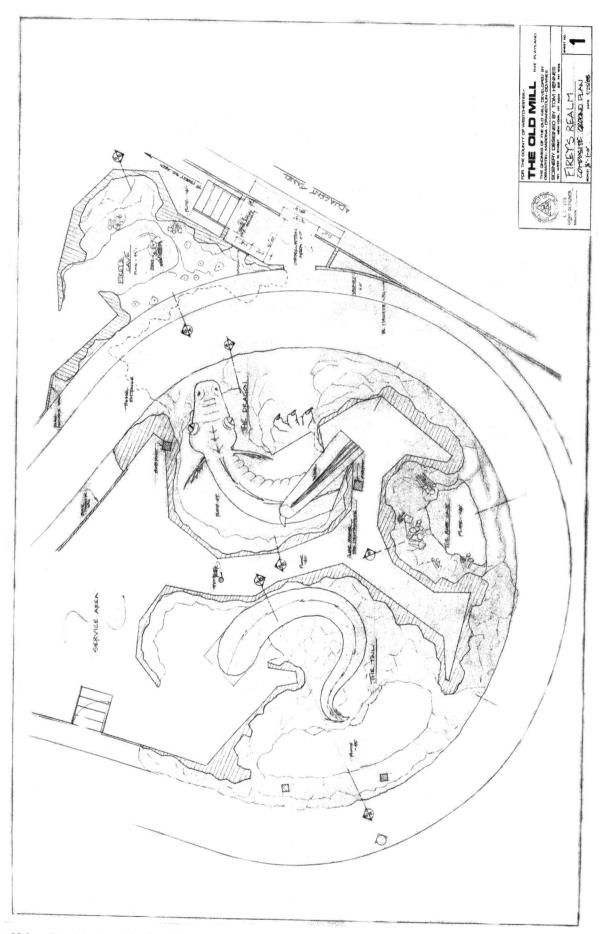

Figure 22.3a Sheet 1—Firey's Realm—Composite Ground plan. Draftings for "The Old Mill" for Rye Playland, for the County of Westchester, New York. Designed and drafted by Tom Hennes of Tom Hennes, Inc. Produced by DeMartin-Marona-Cranstoun-Downes, New York. Used by permission.

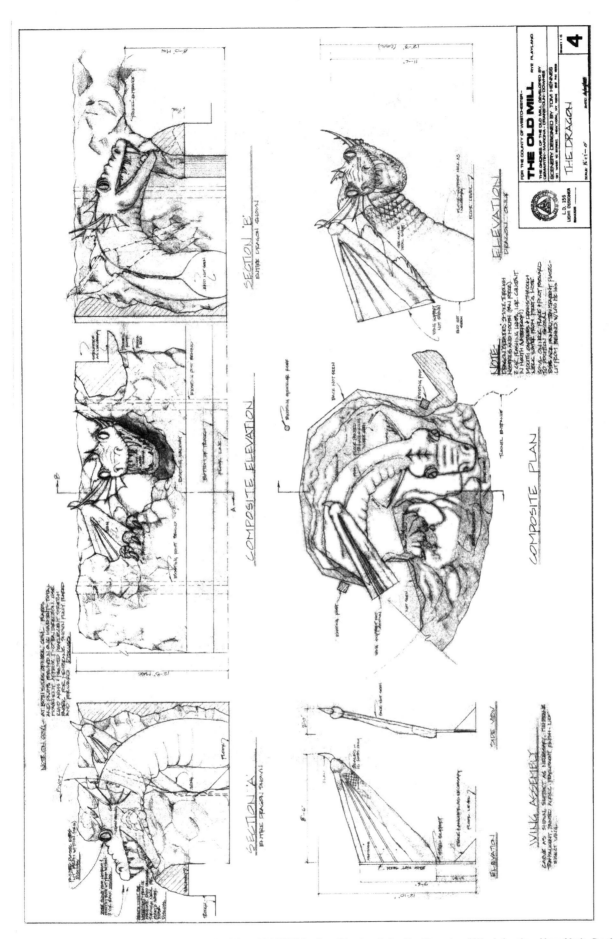

Figure 22.3b   Sheet 4—The Dragon. Draftings for "The Old Mill" for Rye Playland, for the County of Westchester, New York. Designed and drafted by Tom Hennes of Tom Hennes, Inc. Produced by DeMartin-Marona-Cranstoun-Downes, New York. Used by permission.

Figure 22.4   Sony Electronics, Inc. Comdex '95. Designed by Tom Hennes of Tom Hennes, Inc. Used by permission. See also Plate 21 of the color insert.

Tom felt that the Comdex design, while being high-tech, should not be cold and stark but attractive and welcoming. To this end the distinctive forms of the design had soft finishes and dyed woods were used for much of the exhibitory. The sliding doors to the conference rooms were curved and comfortable, and the overhead projection surfaces were scrims, which provided a soft architectural ceiling and a human scale to the exhibit. The projections were in a similar vein: they contained active and edgy lifestyle imagery but suggested leisure, comfort, and ease of use.

The slick, technical draftings for this project reflect the commercial nature of the design and were done by architecturally trained drafts-people. A few of the many draftings for this project may be found in Figures 22.5a to 22.5c.

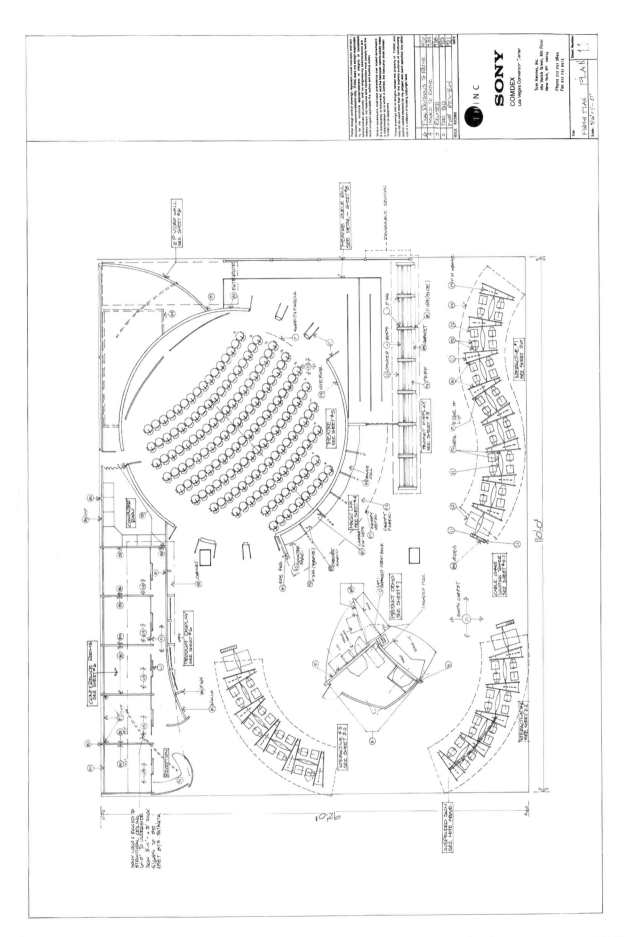

Figure 22.5a Sheet 2—Finish Plan. Draftings for Sony Electronics, Comdex '95. David Sirola, Project Head. Norman Clark, Detailing. Ken Saylor, Detail Design of Interactive Stations. Designed by Tom Hennes of Tom Hennes, Inc. Used by permission.

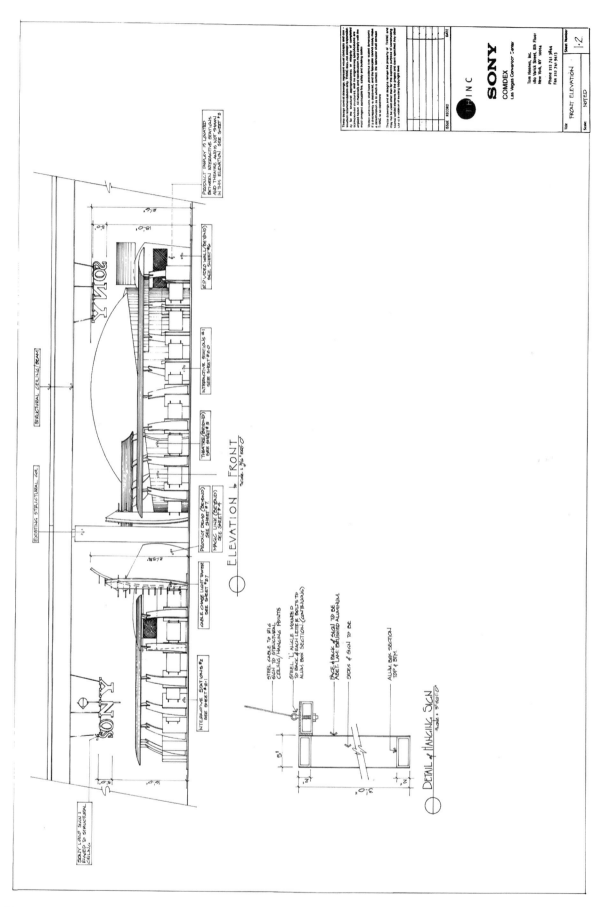

Figure 22.5b Sheet 1.2—(Interactive Stations)—Front Elevation. Draftings for Sony Electronics, Comdex '95. David Sirola, Project Head. Norman Clark, Detailing. Ken Saylor, Detail Design of Interactive Stations. Designed by Tom Hennes of Tom Hennes, Inc. Used by permission.

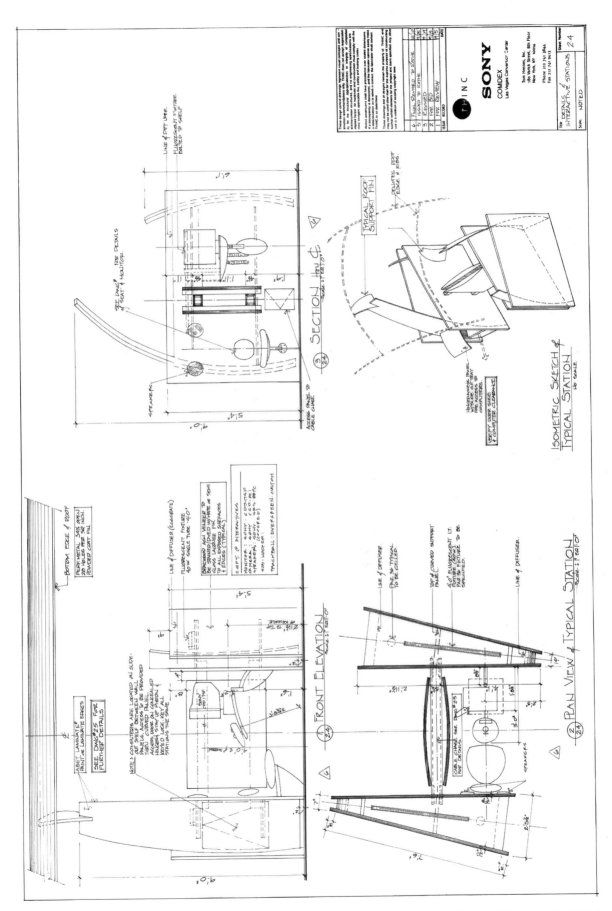

Figure 22.5c   Sheet 2.4—Interactive Stations—Details. Draftings for Sony Electronics, Comdex '95. David Sirola, Project Head. Norman Clark, Detailing. Ken Saylor, Detail Design of Interactive Stations. Designed by Tom Hennes of Tom Hennes, Inc. Used by permission

23

Virtual Scenery and Lighting

At the frontier of set design is the emerging world of virtual scenery. Virtual scenery exists solely in the computer and not in the real world. A fully textured and lit 3-D digital set is fed into a computer—with massive power and number-crunching ability—that is then integrated with a television camera. The camera shoots live actors in a blue-screen studio. (This is a studio painted a shade of blue that "falls out" of the image, thus allowing the insertion of digital scenery.) The power of the computer is such that as actors move, and the camera pans or moves forward and back, the computer recalculates the scenic image in real time.

Virtual scenery can include not only backgrounds but also set dressing that actors use, such as tables or stairs. A blue-painted simulation of similar size and shape to the virtual image is constructed for the shoot. One of the advantages of the blue-screen studio is that the actual shooting space can be quite small while the virtual set appears as large as the designer's imagination. For example, a 15-foot-wide blue-screen studio can convey the image of a set that is 75-feet wide. On one virtual project it was estimated that creating the virtual scenery cost one-tenth the projected cost of building, painting, setting up, and lighting identical scenery in the real world. Numbers like these guarantee a rising demand for technically savvy designers.

Like all design, the world of virtual design involves the collaboration of the director and scenic and lighting designers. Virtual sets, even more than physical sets, require skilled lighting if they are to look good, convey a particular mood, and appear real. The "dead" look of many computer-rendered 3-D sets is often caused by their being lit by a computer modeler rather than by a skilled lighting designer. Television is leading the move into virtual scenery. It is a type of media that often demands only limited mobility by its actors and thus requires smaller virtual set-up than does film. Two of the designers currently working in virtual design are husband and wife. Both attended the New York University Tisch School of the Arts, where they had traditional theatre training: Rita Ann Kogler as a theatrical lighting designer, and George Allison as a scenic designer. George is now head of Scenic Design for ABC News and has designed scenery for *Nightline* and *World News Tonight*. Rita Ann Kogler is a freelance digital lighting designer. Occasionally they collaborate on a project, such as the design of the virtual set for *Discovery News*, a weekly news show featuring science in the news. In Figure 23.1, only the anchor at his desk was real. The entire scenic background is virtual, including revolving panels and video feeds into virtual televisions. What this 2-D illustration can't convey to you is that the television

Figure 23.1   Photograph from *Discovery News.* **1997. ABC News/Discovery Channel. Directed by Roger Goodman. Scenic design by George Allison. Digital architect by Jim Suhre. Lighting by Rita Ann Kogler. Courtesy of SMA VR Studio. See also Plate 22 of the color insert.**

camera could pan and tilt in any direction and have the computer-generated virtual scenic image adjust in real time.

Rita Kogler has worked as an associate lighting designer for many years. She assisted Pat Collins on the Broadway productions of *Once Upon a Mattress* and *An American Daughter,* and on the national tours of *The Sisters Rosensweig* and *The Pointer Sisters' Ain't Misbehavin'.* Her work also includes assisting on lighting designs for European opera houses, where she found the metric-conversion capabilities of CAD extremely helpful. Rita says that Europe is much more CAD-savvy than America, and she is used to receiving house plans and returning light plots by E-mail.

Rita, disliking the commercial computer lighting symbol sets—"their accurate lighting contours were too busy," she says—created her own set, basing the shapes on the old plastic lighting templates. Using recognizable forms made it easier for electricians to make the transition to reading computer-generated light plots. Rita also reconfigured the database configuration that relates the information on each light to the master hook-up sheet, orienting it to the needs of the designer rather than the electrician.

Increasingly, Rita's work is not in the theatre but as a freelance digital lighting designer in the fast-expanding field of virtual scenery. Her current work reflects her traditional theatre design training combined with a mastery of computer skills.

A small virtual set for *Vietnam: The Soldiers' Story*, for an ABC News/The Learning Channel production that Rita and George designed, is a good design to examine because of its simplicity. The architecture of the virtual set was initially created for another production. The Vietnam virtual set consisted of simple, square poles holding panels of graphic imagery that were changed for each show to reflect the different topics. George said the purpose of the scenery was as a background for the talking lead-in to various segments of the program. As the lead-ins were short and quick, the design was intentionally simple. George says that many virtual sets are garish and overdesigned as it is easy to get carried away with the technology.

The Project

Vietnam: The Soldiers' Story was produced by Ed Hersh of ABC News with an extremely limited budget of around $2,000. The flexible nature of the virtual scenery is that its architecture could easily be adapted by the addition of new texturing and new lighting. A change in the graphics on the virtual panels further modifies the look. To sell the idea to The Learning Channel, Ed asked George for a sketch. (See Figure 23.2.)

VIETNAM: SOLDIERS IN BATTLE

Figure 23.2 Sketch for *Vietnam: The Soldiers' Story.* 1997. ABC News/The Learning Channel. Produced by Ed Hersh. Directed by Bernie Hoffman. Set Design by George Allison. Digital Architect/Textures and Lighting Design by Rita Ann Kogler. Sketch Artist, Kevin Locke. Courtesy of SMA VR Studio.

The Studio

Virtual set systems for television production include one or more cameras working in a blue-screen studio with a powerful computer. The studio for *Vietnam: The Soldiers' Story* consists of one or more cameras facing a blue wall and a floor with a white-plaid grid pattern. The blue wall and grid, like any television blue screen, will not be seen in the final image as the video controller has been programmed to "drop out" the color blue. The intersecting lines of the grid give the computer guidance as it mathematically plots the moving relationships between the real studio and actor and the virtual studio. The virtual scenery could depict a man standing in front of the Grand Canyon but, says George Allison, the movement of the actor is limited by the actual walls of the studio space. Larger blue-screen studios can easily adapt to additional camera setups and allow for more actor movement. Figure 23.3 shows the real blue-screen television studio that was used for *Discovery News* program in Figure 23.1.

The Camera System

The best virtual camera/computer systems in the spring of 1998 cost around $700,000. A lower-cost system using *Windows NT* can dip below $100,000. ABC Television didn't have its own virtual studio, so they hired the facilities at SMA Video, in Soho in New York City. SMA uses a virtual set system by a company called ORAD with a computer program called *Cyberset*. This particular system works by pattern-recognition technology, which was originally developed for the Israeli army. Rita sometimes works on an independent contract as the virtual lighting director at SMA Video. In the virtual graphics department where she works, there are seven computers: two PCs, two Macintosh, and three UNIX from Silicon Graphics.

Figure 23.3 Virtual Studio. SMA VR Studios, Manhattan. Courtesy of SMA VR Studio. See also Plate 23 of the color insert.

Drafting and 3-D Modeling

In any virtual set, the architectural form called the "wire frame" is drafted in a CAD program such as *AutoCAD*, *MiniCAD*, or *ArchiCAD*. It is then modeled in a program, such as *Game Gen*, *Form·Z*, *3D Studio Max*, or *Soft Image*. The wire frame forms the underlying structure of the virtual set; it might be thought of as the 2 x 4 framing of built scenery. Figures 23.4 and 23.5 show the *AutoCAD* drafting and the *Game Gen* wire-frame structure for *Vietnam: The Soldiers' Story*.

Texture Mapping

Covering the surface of a wire frame is called "texture mapping." Some people refer to it as "wallpapering." Usually the set designer supplies the textures, but in this case Rita designed both textures and lighting. Basic textures often consist of found graphic imagery scanned into the computer. Rita says that most generic collections of textures include some source of light reacting on the surfaces that is usually not the way she wants to light the set, therefore she can end up shooting the textures herself. In this design, Rita wanted the back wall to have a rough granite stone surface with a pattern of helicopters. She shot a picture of a stone surface that she liked and scanned it into the computer. She also found various pictures of helicopters and scanned them in as well. The shadow of the panels was created by "screen-grabbing," selecting or capturing, a reflected view of an actual panel. (We call this a "screen-grab" because we are "grabbing" it on the screen and manipulating it.) Rita uses *Adobe Photoshop* and/or *Fractal Design* to process textures. She

Figure 23.4   Wire-frame illustration. Drafted by Rita Ann Kogler. Courtesy of SMA VR Studio.

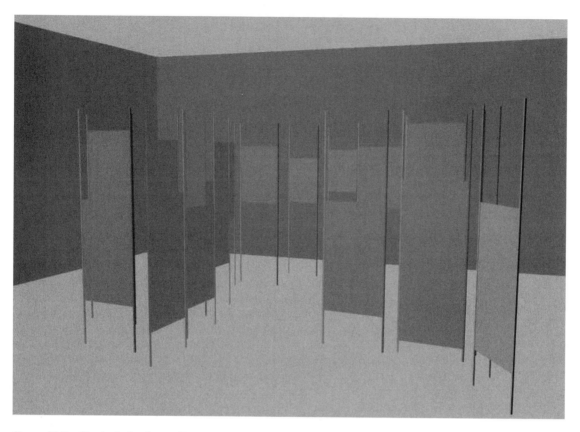

Figure 23.5 Shaded wire-frame illustration. Modeled by Rita Ann Kogler. Courtesy of SMA VR Studio.

manipulates the graphic imagery in various ways, using different features and filters inherent in the program, as well as *Kai's Power Tools* and *Photoshop* plug-ins to simulate various effects, such as depth of field, lens flares, water ripples, noise, and so on.

Rita also "lights" the textures much as you would paint light onto the surface of a paint elevation. For example, the floor-surface texture has a down-center soft highlight and the edges are ombreyed darker. Rita constructed shadows under and behind the panels but left their size and angle to be adjusted later in the model. Because the shadows in the virtual model need to be transparent, dark and light are reversed in the textures, as they would be in a photographic negative. An essential effect from *Photoshop* is the gaussian blur filter, which allows Rita to apply an overall wash to the set that ties the whole image together, much as footlights do in the theatre. "I enjoy discovering the digital tools that are analogous to the tools and effects I would be using in—for lack of a better term—real life," she says.

Figure 23.6 shows some of a collection of the textures that Rita developed for the Vietnam Project. Figure 23.7 shows them combined.

All 3-D wire-frame structures contain mathematical coordinates that allow flat surfaces to be molded over them. If, for example, you had a wire frame of a sphere and picked a 2-D digital texture of chrome, after texture-mapping you would have what looked like a chrome ball. Rita "mapped" the textures onto the wire frame many times before she was satisfied with them. Textures that Rita liked as 2-D images weren't always appropriate as sculptural forms. The "lighting" on the textures needed adjustments as well. Rita says that during the construction and texturing process, different programs and operating systems can work together. You could, for example, have *AutoCAD* draftings for *Windows NT*; *Form·Z* modeling on a

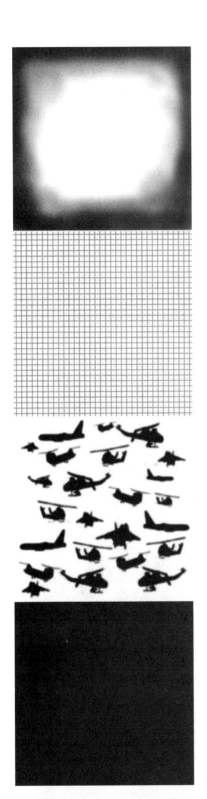

Figure 23.6   Wall texture selection for *Vietnam: The Soldiers' Story*. Modeled by Rita Ann Kogler. Courtesy of SMA VR Studio.

Figure 23.7   Composite wall texture for *Vietnam: The Soldiers' Story*. Modeled by Rita Ann Kogler. Courtesy of SMA VR Studio.

Macintosh or PC; *Photoshop* texturing on PC, Macintosh, and UNIX (Silicon Graphic) Computer; and *Lightscape* for a PC and UNIX on one project—as long as you use the common file formats of DXF and TIFF as a translation tool. A graphic translation program such as *DeBabelizer* allows you to view images even if the program or computer platform that created them isn't installed. This means that you can E-mail your director and producer versions of the design and they can view the image without having CAD or graphic software on their own computers.

Prerendering the Textured Forms

With the wire frame constructed and covered with the textured surface, Rita converts the file to a TIFF file, a common computer graphic language for saving and transferring images. She then imports the digital set into a PC version of a program called *Lightscape*, by Lightscape Technologies.

Lightscape is an advanced lighting and previsualization program that can duplicate the refractive qualities of light, including ambient light, transparency, shadows, reflections, and interreflections, as well as the refractive qualities of different textural material. With this program, you light a virtual set in much the same way as you would light a set in a real theatre. Digital 3-D spotlights, Fresnels, or other types of lights can be placed, aimed, colored, and focused to create directional light and bounce light. This program, however, goes far beyond theatrical lighting, offering a large variety of types of light, including neon, fluorescent, HMI, sodium vapor—and basically anything else. By inputting longitude and latitude (where you are on the earth's surface), the direction you are facing, the current month, day, and year, as well as weather conditions, the program can calculate the appropriate light of the sun or moon.

Using *Lightscape* Rita completed prelighting the composite textures for each surface a number of times, one for each lighting effect she wanted in the final version. The shadow that would fall beneath the panels was created as a separate, prelit image, its shapes to be adjusted later in the full model. Because the shadows beneath the panels needed to be transparent, they were created as negative images appearing, as they would be in a photographic negative, as white, positive shapes. All the images were saved in a TIFF file. Figures 23.8 and 23.9 show two lighting cues in the prelit virtual set.

Lighting the Virtual Set

The next step was importing the TIFF file into a powerful computer running a program that could hold the virtual set with its multiple prelit textures and let it change camera angles on cue with *Cyberset*, the computer-driven camera system. Although virtual set systems interface with *3D Studio Max*, *Soft Image*, and *Alias/Wavefront*, Rita says that they felt the program with the best interface with *Cyberset* was a UNIX version of *Game Gen*, an animation program used for developing computer games. Rita had needed to prelight the wallpaper textures because, as powerful as UNIX on the SGI computer was, it only allowed eight virtual lights to be turned on at one time. By using *Game Gen* switches to cue up prelit textures, she was able to include a wealth of lighting detail.

Lighting the Real Set

Rita used about twelve studio lights to light the real person in the blue screen studio, programming the changes into *Game Gen*. She points out that an advantage of lighting virtual scenery is that you have complete

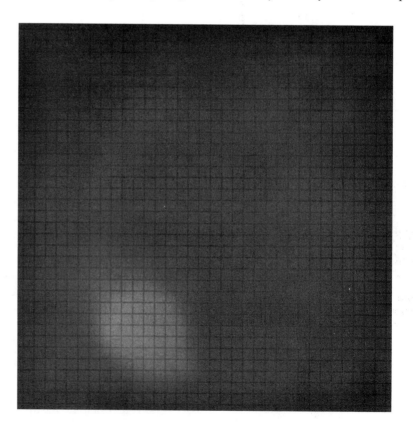

Figure 23.8   Composite floor with pre-light. Modeled by Rita Ann Kogler. Courtesy of SMA VR Studio.

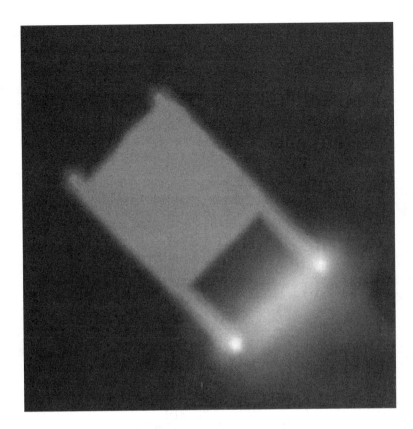

Figure 23.9   Panel shadows. Modeled by Rita Ann Kogler. Courtesy of SMA VR Studio.

separation between the lighting of the scenery and of the Talent. The only ambient light on either is that which you, the designer, choose to create.

The Shoot

When the actual television shoot occurred, Rita, in her graphics room, was cued from the control room. She switched on and off the different lighting effects on *Cyberset* much like, in her days in the theatre, she used to move the switches on the old dimmer boards. In Figures 23.10a and 23.10b are two different camera angles of the virtual set. Notice how the scenery has adjusted.

Figures 23.10a and 23.10b   Video still shots from *Vietnam: The Soldiers' Story.* 1997. ABC News/The Learning Channel. Produced by Ed Hersh. Directed by Bernie Hoffman. Set design by George Allison. Digital architecture, textures, and lighting design by Rita Ann Kogler. Sketch artist, Kevin Locke. Courtesy of SMA VR Studio. See also Plates 24 and 25 of the color insert.

Suggested Reading

Drafting

Browning, Hugh C. *Principles of Architectural Drafting: A Sourcebook of Techniques and Graphic Standards.* New York: Whitney Library of Design, 1996.

Giesecke, Frederick E., et al. *Technical Drawing,* 7th ed. New York: Macmillan Publishing, 1985.

Sadamatsu, Shuzo, and Junko Sadamatsu. *Design Drafting.* New York: Van Nostrand Reinhold, 1982.

Sutherland, Martha. *Lettering for Architects and Designers,* 2d ed. New York: Van Nostrand Reinhold, 1989.

Wiggins, Glenn E. *Manual of Construction Documentation: An Illustrated Guide to Preparing Construction Drawings.* New York: Whitney Library of Design, 1989.

Perspective

Ching, Frank. *Architectural Graphics,* 2d ed. New York: Van Nostrand Reinhold, 1985.

Cole, Rex Vicat. *Perspective for Artists.* New York: Dover Publications, 1976.

Morgan, Sherley W. *Architectural Drawing: Perspective, Light and Shadow, Rendering.* New York: McGraw-Hill, 1950.

Pile, John. *Perspective for Interior Designers: Simplified Techniques for Geometric and Freehand Drawing.* New York: Whitney Library of Design, 1985.

Vredemad de Vries, Jan. *Perspective: With a New Introduction by Adolf K. Placzek.* New York: Dover Publications, 1972.

General Reference

Carter, Paul. *Backstage Handbook: An Illustrated Almanac of Technical Information,* 3d ed. Louisville, KY: Broadway Press, 1994.

De Chiara, Josep, et al. *Time-Saver Standards for Interior Design and Space Planning.* New York: McGraw-Hill, 1991.

Fleming, John, Hugh Honour, and Niklaus Pevsner. *Penguin Dictionary of Architecture,* 4th ed. London: Penguin, 1991.

Graf, Don. *Data Sheets.* New York: Reinhold Publishing, 1944.

Kidder, Frank E., and Harry Parker. *Kidder-Parker Architects' and Builders' Handbook,* 18th ed. New York: John Wiley & Sons, 1946.

Kissam, Philip. *Surveying: Instruments and Methods for Surveys of Limited Extent.* New York: McGraw-Hill, 1947.

Ramsey, Charles G., and Harold R. Sleeper. *Architectural Graphic Standards,* 3d ed. New York: John Wiley & Sons, 1941.

———. *Architectural Graphic Standards,* 4th ed. New York: John Wiley & Sons, 1953.

———. *Architectural Graphic Standards,* 5th ed. New York: John Wiley & Sons, 1957.

———. *Architectural Graphic Standards,* 6th ed. New York: John Wiley & Sons, 1970.

———. *Architectural Graphic Standards,* 7th ed. New York: John Wiley & Sons, 1981.

———. *Architectural Graphic Standards,* 8th ed. New York: John Wiley & Sons, 1992.

———. *Architectural Graphic Standards,* 9th ed. New York: John Wiley & Sons, 1998.

———. *Architectural Graphic Standards,* 10th ed. New York: John Wiley & Sons, 2000.

Reznikoff, S. C. *Interior Graphic and Design Standards.* New York: Whitney Library of Design, 1986.

Scharff, Robert. *Workshop Math.* New York: Sterling Publishing, 1989.

Construction

Boyne, Colin, and Lance Wright. *Best of Architects' Working Details, Volume 2: Internal.* New York: Architectural Press, 1982.

Ching, Frank, Francis D. Ching, and Cassandra Adams. *Building Construction Illustrated,* 2d ed. New York: John Wiley & Sons, 1991.

di Cristina, George R. *Simplified Guide to Custom Stairbuilding and Tangent Handrailing.* Fresno, CA: Linden Publishing, 1994.

Graham, Frank D., and Thomas J. Emery. *Audell's Carpenters & Builders Guide.* New York: Theo. Audell & Co., 1923.

Knobloch, Phillip G. *A Treasury of Fine Construction Design : 104 Detailed Plates of Early Twentieth Century Interior & Exterior Elements.* Mendham, NJ: Astragal Press, 1995.

Martin, Clarence A. *Details of Building Construction.* Boston: Bates & Guild, 1899.

Mowat, William, and Alexander Mowat. *Treatise on Stairbuilding and Handrailing: The Classic Text for Joiners, Architects and Restorers.* Fresno, CA: Linden Publishing, 1985.

Newlands, James. *Carpenter & Joiner's Assistant.* London: Blackie and Son, 1869.

Schuttner, Scott. *Basic Stairbuilding.* Newtown, CT: Taunton Press, 1990.

Thallon, Rob. *Graphic Guide to Frame Construction: Details for Builders and Designers.* Newtown, CT: Taunton Press, 1991.

Historical Research

Amery, Colin. *Period Houses and Their Details.* Oxford: Butterworth–Heinemann, 1989.

Aquilar, Kathleen. *Miniature Rooms: The Thorne Rooms at the Art Institute of Chicago.* New York: Abbeville Press, 1983.

Bicknell, A. J. *Bicknell's Victorian Buildings : Floor Plans and Elevations for 45 Houses and Other Structures.* New York: Dover Publications, 1980.

Fletcher, Sir Banister. *History of Architecture on the Comparative Method,* 17th ed. New York: Charles Scribner's and Sons, 1967.

Goldberger, Paul. *A Monograph of the Works of McKim, Mead and White, 1879-1915.* New York: Da Capo Press, 1985.

Juracek, Judy A. *Surfaces: Visual Research for Artists, Architects, and Designers.* New York: W.W. Norton & Company, 1996.

Kelly, Frederick J. *Early Domestic Architecture of Connecticut.* New York: Dover Publications, 1963.

Meyers, Franz Sales. *Handbook of Ornament: A Grammar of Art, Industrial and Architectural Designing in All Its Branches for Practical as Well as Theoretical Use.* New York: Dover Publications, 1957.

Roberts, E. L. *Roberts' Illustrated Millwork Catalog: A Sourcebook of Turn of the Century Architectural Woodwork.* New York: Dover Publications, 1988.

Speltz, Alexander. *Styles of Ornament.* New York: Dover Publications, 1957.

Staebler, Wend W. *Architectural Detailing in Residential Interiors.* New York: Whitney Library of Design, 1990.

Strange, Thomas Arthur. *French Interiors, Furniture, Decoration, Woodwork and Allied Arts: During the Last Half of the Seventeenth Century, the Whole of the Eighteenth Century and the Early Part of the Nineteenth.* New York: Crown, n.d.

Tunstall, Small, and Christopher Woodbridge. *Houses of the Wren and Early Georgian Periods.* London: Architectural Press, 1928.

Wallace, Philip B. *Colonial Ironwork in Old Philadelphia.* New York: Dover Publications, 1998.

Ware, William. *American Vignola: A Guide to the Making of Classical Architecture.* New York: W. W. Norton & Co., 1997.

Theatre

Gillett, A. S., and J. Michael. *Stage Scenery: It's Construction and Rigging,* 3d ed. New York: Harper & Row, 1982.

Parker, W. Oren, and Harvey K. Smith. *Scene Design and Stage Lighting,* 7th ed. New York: Holt, Rinehart & Winston, 1996.

Pecktal, Lynn. *Designing and Drawing for the Theatre.* New York: McGraw-Hill, 1995.

———. *Designing and Painting for the Theatre.* New York: Holt, Rinehart & Winston, 1975.

Film

Fielding, Raymond. *Techniques of Special Effects Cinematography,* 4th ed. Boston: Focal Press, 1985.

Malkiewicz, Kris, and Jim Fletcher. *Cinematography,* 2d ed. New York: Simon & Schuster, 1992.

Preston, Ward. *What an Art Director Does: An Introduction to Motion Picture Production Design.* Beverly Hills, CA: Silman-James Press, 1994.

Ryan, Rod. *American Cinematographer Manual,* 7th ed. Hollywood, CA: The ASC Press, 1993.

Selected Catalogues

20th Century Fox
Fox Studios Operations
Production Services
Building 99
10201 W. Pico Boulevard
Los Angeles, CA 90035
(310) 369-7053
(310) Fox-Info
www.foxstudios.com
Catalog includes plastic formed surfaces (such as brick), pine mouldings, vacuum formed surfaces, flex resin moulding, rosettes and plant-ons.

Anderson Corp.
100 Fourth Avenue North
Bayport, MN 55003-1096
(888) 888-7020
www.andersoncorp.com
A complete guide to Anderson windows and patio doors.

Chadsworth
P.O. Box 2618
Historic Wilmington, NC 28402-2618
(800) COLUMNS [(800) 486-2118]
or (910) 763-7600
www.columns.com
Wood columns.

Cumberland Woodcraft Company, Inc.
P.O. Drawer 609
Carlisle, PA 17013-0609
(717) 243-0063
www.cumberlandwoodcraft.com
Period style wood details.

Decorators Supply Corporation
3610-12 South Morgan Street
Chicago, IL 60609
(773) 847-6300
www.decoratorssupply.com
Catalog #124 – Composite
Catalog #127 – Period capitals and brackets
Catalog #129 – Wood fiber Carvings
Catalog #130 – Plaster ornaments
Catalog #131 – Wood mantels

Federal Cabinet Company
409 Highland Avenue
Middletown, NY 10940
(914) 342-1511
Custom turned wood such as spindles.

Fisher & Jirouch Company
4821 Superior Avenue
Cleveland, OH 44103
(216) 361-3840
Interior and exterior decorative plaster ornaments in period styles.

Flex Moulding Inc.
16 East Lafayette Street
Hackensack, NJ 07601
(201) 487-8080
www.flexiblemoulding.com
Flexible moulding and plant-on decorations in simulated wood carving.

Garrett Wade Company
161 Avenue of Americas
New York, NY 10013
(800) 221-2942
www.garrettwade.com
Carpenters tools. Catalog has full size sections of router bit shapes.

J. P. Weaver Company
941 Air Way
Glendale, CA 91201
(818) 500-1740
Architectural Decoration for Interiors with Composition Ornaments
    Vol. II.

Marvin
P.O. Box 100
Warroad, MN 56763
(800) 346-5128
www.marvin.com
Residential catalog of Marvin windows and doors.

Paramount Pictures
5555 Melrose Avenue
Hollywood, CA 90038-3197
(323) 956-4242
www.emoulding.com
The Staff Shop. Wall facings (skins) in fiberglass, vacuum form,
    and/or fiber reinforced gypsum. Also wood mouldings.

Scenery West
1126 North Citrus Avenue
Hollywood, CA 90038
(213) 467-7495
Vacuumed formed surfaces and various moulding products.

Sweets
www.sweets.com
Database of building product information.

Thomas Register of American Manufacturers
www.thomasregister.com
Listing of 158,000 U.S. and Canadian manufacturers. Free online prod-
    uct information including DXF CAD product drawings.

Vintage Woodworks
Highway 34 South
P.O. Box 39
Quinlan, TX 75474
(903) 356-2158
www.vintagewoodworks.com
Victorian style wood details.

Walt Disney Studios Moulding Shop
500 South Buena Vista Street
Burbank, CA 91521-5220
Wood mouldings, flex resin molds, wood turnings, doors, windows, and sash.

Index